THE COMPLETE FOOD SAFARI

COMPLETE FOOD SAFARI

Delicious adventures through 44 cuisines

MAEVE O'MEARA

hardie grant books

MELBOURNE · LONDON

contents

To my lovely Toufic and my family –
Conor, Kitty and Scarlett, my mum
Maev and my late father John, brother
Matt and family – who have all made
the journey so much fun and who
have (almost) always revelled in my
delicious new finds.

PREFACE

Welcome to the culinary United Nations ...

This beautiful book aims to lead you by the hand through some of the most delicious and intriguing foods around the world. With its help you can become the food-savvy companion others turn to and ask, 'How much za'atar should I buy at one time?', 'What sort of chilli do I need for my Thai red curry?' and 'What the hell do I do with okra?!'

In these pages lie some of the secrets behind forty-four different cuisines that are all represented in Australia's rich and diverse society.

They include mouth-watering descriptions of traditional herbs and spices, seasonal vegetables, favourite drinks and snacks as well as tips on key ingredients and cooking implements. The recipes are simple, delicious and will always work – and will impress your family and friends. They have been gathered from talented cooks and chefs who have grown up learning from their mothers and grandmothers – their kitchen wisdom brings each cuisine alive.

So how did this exciting food adventure start? Well, many years ago I realised that my culinary boundaries growing up in a meat-and-three veg Irish–Australian family were fairly limited. I was always keen to explore more exotic flavours so I've gradually discovered and been welcomed into a world full of big, boisterous families and tables groaning under amazing food. It has been an honour to be included at the table of so many warm and welcoming new friends and I've enjoyed a delicious adventure at the same time.

I hope you'll love all of these new tastes and flavours and I wish you many delicious adventures of your own.

Maeve O'Meara

Here is a people and a place I've been truly beguiled by. Hearing Afghans speak of the country they knew before the wars, a beautiful mountainous region with vast deserts, alpine meadows and cold clear streams, you picture a rugged paradise. I was inspired to read novels and poetry all echoing the thought that Afghanistan was precious to everyone who had a connection to it - a wild crossroads where the Middle East, Central Asia and India intersect, and on the path of the ancient Silk Road that brought explorers such as Marco Polo and traders carrying silk, tea and spices.

Over the centuries it's been invaded by so many - Alexander the Great; Genghis Khan; Nader Shah Afshar, known as the Napoleon of Persia; and by Britain, Russia and the US. Despite such troubled history, its culinary traditions and hospitality are intact. Hospitality is linked to honour and reputation - one is considered to be of good character through being generous and welcoming to guests.

The table in an Afghan home doesn't groan with food because it is usually served on a *disterkhan* or cloth spread out on the floor, with guests seated on large colourful cushions called *toshak*. Lids are lifted on korma, pulao and a range of side dishes, creating wafts of fragrant steam to make your knees go weak. Everything is placed on the *disterkhan* at once so a meal is a feast for the eyes. There are accompanying sauces of chilli or fresh herbs called 'chutneys' (*chatni*), platters of fruit, and mounds of fresh naan bread. Nothing is done by halves and guests are expected to have second helpings.

In my time in the Afghan world I joined a talented cook in her home to pick the greenest and freshest stalks of *gandana*, a slim variety of leek that is chopped and added to handmade dumplings called *ashak*. These are served on a creamy bed of yoghurt with a delicious spiced meat and split pea sauce over the top and a scattering of dried mint. The result is like an exotic ravioli, with that lovely cosy carbohydrate feeling of good pasta, but much more exciting. Afghan women gather to make *ashak* together, catching up with news and gossip as they deftly fill hundreds of dumplings.

There's also a lot of work in making the national dish *Kabuli pulao*, but the results are absolutely worth it. In Afghanistan as in neighbouring Iran and Pakistan, long grains of aged basmati rice are so prized that they are treated as the centre of a dish and any meat or vegetables as the accompaniment. In *Kabuli pulao* the rice is soaked and boiled briefly, then drained and gently cooked again with tender meat, stock, spices and caramelised carrots and sultanas. It is served in a mound topped with a pretty mix of slivered pistachios and almonds.

Kebabs of so many types are a must-eat speciality. Lamb is the main meat used - it could be tender, lean backstraps flavoured with garlic and salt, threaded with red onion onto flat metal skewers that are called *seekh*, or minced lamb with spices. Other kebabs rely on fat in the meat sizzling onto the charcoal and encouraging flames to add a delicious smoky flavour - the smell of these cooking makes you immediately hungry. *Chopan* kebabs were traditionally made by *chopan*, or shepherds, with chunks of meat such as lamb shoulder and just salt to help the meat caramelise. Naan bread and a coriander, green chilli and garlic *chatni* are the best accompaniments.

Meals usually finish with tea, and taking Afghan tea is another ceremony where time stops and traditions take over. While the tea is sometimes green tea or on special occasions a milk tea called *sheer chai* served with clotted cream called *kaymagh*, black tea is the most common. It can be flavoured with cardamom pods and served with a sugar cube, which devotees hold between their teeth as they sip. It's said that the first cup of tea is offered to a stranger, the second to a friend, and the third to a family member - such is the power of tea in bringing people together.

ESSENTIAL FLAVOURS

AGED BASMATI RICE
The most expensive rice grains can be up to 2 centimetres long when cooked, and are chosen for classic dishes such as *Kabuli pulao*. Aging the rice for at least 12 months deepens its flavour.

BREAD
Bread is eaten with almost every meal. The large oval-shaped naan loaves are sprinkled with sesame and nigella seeds and cooked directly on the clay sides of the *tanur* oven. The breads are usually made with a mixture of white and wholemeal flour, and are especially enjoyed with kebabs and saucy kormas.

CARDAMOM
This is one of the most-loved spices of Afghan cooking – used in tea, sweets, to flavour stocks and to scent pulao.

DRIED FRUITS
Dried yellow plums add a sweet and sour flavour to dishes such as korma, while sultanas or raisins appear in *Kabuli pulao* like juicy jewels. Along with nuts, dried fruits are a common snack.

DRIED MINT
The aromatic aroma and flavour of dried mint is used to finish many Afghan dishes just before they're served. Dried mint over a hot dish such as steaming *ashak* adds an extra exotic element; and sprinkled over yoghurt and cucumber accompaniments, dips and vegetable dishes, it is an essential.

YOGHURT
Essential in dips and sauces, marinades and dishes such as korma. It's also drained and dried in balls as *quoroot*, a type of cheese. In summer a yoghurt drink called *dough* is made with yoghurt, cucumber, mint, salt and water.

Rice is the star of this dish - a fragrant pyramid of perfectly cooked, spiced basmati rice decorated with carrots, sultanas and nuts. Buried inside are tender chunks of lamb. Served on a show-off big plate and brought steaming to the table, this will delight your family and friends. Haseeb uses sella basmati rice, which is a parboiled rice that many people favour for biryanis and pulaos as the grains fluff up and separate beautifully. For the best results, soak the rice 4 hours ahead, or overnight if time permits.

'Kabuli pulao is always at the centre of the disterkhan - it's always a special occasion when this dish appears.'

KABULI PULAO

from Haseeb Miazad

Heat 2½ tablespoons of the oil in a large saucepan over medium heat and add the onion. Sauté for 5-6 minutes until golden brown. Add the lamb, garlic and half the salt and cook, stirring, until the lamb is browned all over. Add the water and bring to the boil, then reduce the heat to a simmer. Cook, skimming the surface occasionally, for 1½ hours or until the lamb is tender. Remove the lamb to a bowl and set aside. Reserve the stock.

Heat another tablespoon of the oil in a frying pan over medium-high heat. Add the carrot and half the sugar and stir for 5 minutes, until lightly caramelised and glossy. Add the sultanas and cook for another minute. Remove from the heat and stir in a pinch of cardamom. Transfer to a bowl and set aside.

Drain the soaked rice and put it in a pot. Cover with plenty of water and bring to the boil. Cook for 5 minutes, or until almost soft. Drain well, then return it to the pot.

While the rice is cooking, heat a small saucepan over medium heat and add the remaining sugar. Cook without stirring but gently shaking the pan until the sugar turns to caramel (around 5 minutes). Carefully add 250 ml (8½ fl oz/1 cup) of the lamb stock. Stir to combine, then add the remaining salt, 1 teaspoon of garam masala and another pinch of cardamom. Bring to the boil, then remove from the heat.

Pour the caramel mixture over the rice and stir well. Sprinkle the top of the rice with another pinch of garam masala and cardamom.

Heat the remaining 130 ml of oil in the frying pan used for the carrots. When smoking, remove it from the heat and drizzle evenly over the surface of the rice, and particularly over the spices, which should become aromatic. Don't stir the rice, but use the end of a spoon to poke holes all through the rice to allow the oil and steam to pass through.

Top the rice with the carrots and sultanas and the chunks of lamb. Cover the pot with a folded tea towel to absorb steam, then cover with a lid. Place over high heat (fold the ends of the tea towel up over the lid to make sure it is away from the flames) and cook for 5 minutes or until you hear a ticking sound, which is the rice starting to stick on the bottom of the pot. Reduce the heat to low and cook for another 10 minutes. Leave to stand off the heat for another 10 minutes before you remove the lid.

Remove the lamb and carrots to separate bowls (don't worry if some rice sticks to the pot). Stir the rice well.

Cover a large platter with some of the rice. Spoon over the lamb and cover with the remaining rice. Top with the carrots. Sprinkle with the almonds and pistachios.

SERVES 8

200 ml (7 fl oz) vegetable oil	75 g (2¾ oz/⅓ cup) sugar
1 onion, chopped	75 g (2¾ oz) sultanas
800 g (1 lb 12 oz) lamb leg or	(golden raisins)
shoulder, cut into large	freshly ground cardamom
chunks (the meat can remain	garam masala
on the bone, but if so you will	1 kg (2 lb 3 oz) sella basmati
need to get a butcher to cut	rice, soaked for 4 hours or
it for you)	overnight
1 tablespoon crushed garlic	35 g (1½ oz) slivered almonds
2 tablespoons salt	35 g (1½ oz) slivered pistachios
2 litres (68 fl oz/8 cups) water	
250 g (9 oz) carrots, cut into	
thin batons	

This is one of my favourite dishes from our latest television series. The little *ashak* dumplings with their leek filling are served on a bed of garlic yoghurt, with a meat and split pea sauce and a sprinkling of dried mint - like an exotic pasta with so much flavour. A thin Afghan leek called *gandana* is normally used, but regular leeks are a good substitute. Breshna makes her *ashak* in the style of tortellini (the way it's done in her province), but you can simply make them like ravioli with the pasta folded over the filling and the edges well sealed.

ASHAK

from Breshna Keshtiar

Rinse the dal and put it in a saucepan. Cover with water and bring to the boil, then reduce the heat to a simmer. Cooked until tender, then drain.

While the dal is cooking, heat the oil in a large saucepan over medium-high heat. Add the onion and fry for 5-6 minutes, until golden. Remove the onion from the pan, leaving behind as much oil as possible. Add the beef to the pan and cook, stirring, for 10 minutes, or until lightly browned and dry. Return the onion to the beef and add the garlic, chilli, capsicum, tomato, turmeric and salt. Mix well and cook for another 2 minutes, then add 125 ml (4 fl oz/½ cup) of water. Cover and simmer over low heat for 30 minutes, topping up with extra water if needed. Stir in the dal before removing from the heat.

To make the dough, put the flour, salt and oil in a large bowl. Gradually add water, mixing with your hands, to make a firm dough (you may not need all the water, or you may need a little more). Turn the dough out onto a lightly floured surface and knead for 10 minutes, until smooth and elastic. Return to the bowl, cover in plastic wrap and refrigerate for 30 minutes to 1 hour.

Combine all the ingredients for the filling in a bowl, mixing well. Set aside.

To make the garlic yoghurt, pound the garlic and salt to a smooth paste in a mortar. Scoop the yoghurt into a bowl and stir in the garlic paste, followed by the water. Whisk until smooth and refrigerate until ready to serve.

Lightly flour a large work surface. Divide the dough into quarters. Take one quarter, leaving the rest in the bowl

covered with plastic wrap, and roll it into a ball in your hands. Use a rolling pin to roll the ball out to a 20 cm (8 in) circle. Cut the circle in half. Begin rolling one half of the circle through a pasta machine on its widest setting. Then reduce the setting and roll the dough through again. Keep reducing the setting and rolling the dough, lightly dusting with flour when needed, until the dough is 2 mm thick. Lay the sheet out on the floured surface while you roll out the other half of the circle.

Cut the 2 sheets into 5 cm (2 in) squares. Place a teaspoon of the filling in the centre of each square. Moisten the edges of the square with a little water and fold the edges together to make a rectangle, pressing around the filling to seal. You can leave the dumpling as is, or otherwise bend the short edges around to meet each other and press them together, which should flip up the long edge of the dumpling like tortellini. Place on a tea towel-lined tray and repeat with the remaining squares. Cover the *ashak* with another tea towel, then proceed to roll out and make *ashak* with the remaining dough quarters.

Bring a large pot of water to the boil and cook the *ashak* in batches for 3-4 minutes, or until they float to the surface and start to roll over in the water. Scoop out the *ashak* and leave to drain while you continue cooking the remaining batches.

While the *ashak* are cooking, reheat the meat sauce, and spread the garlic yoghurt across a large serving platter (or you may like to do this directly onto individual plates or wide bowls). Place the *ashak* on top, then spoon over the meat sauce. Sprinkle generously with dried mint.

SERVES 6

SAUCE
- ½ cup *chana* dal (split chickpeas), soaked overnight
- 125 ml (4 fl oz/½ cup) vegetable oil
- 1 large onion, finely chopped
- 500 g (1 lb 2 oz) minced (ground) beef
- 2 garlic cloves, finely chopped
- 1 medium red chilli, finely chopped
- ½ red capsicum (bell peppers), finely chopped
- 200 g (7 oz) tinned diced tomatoes (or fresh tomato)
- 2 teaspoons turmeric
- 2 teaspoons salt

DOUGH
- 500 g (1 lb 2 oz/3⅓ cups) plain (all-purpose) flour
- 1 tablespoon salt

- ½ tablespoon vegetable oil
- about 250 ml (8½ fl oz/1 cup) water

FILLING
- 500 g (1 lb 2 oz) *gandana* or trimmed leeks, finely chopped
- 2 teaspoons freshly ground black pepper
- 2 teaspoons salt
- 1 tablespoon butter, softened
- ½ bunch coriander (cilantro), finely chopped

GARLIC YOGHURT
- 1 garlic clove
- ½ teaspoon salt
- 500 g (1 lb 2 oz) natural yoghurt
- 125 ml (4 fl oz/½ cup) water

dried mint to serve

The simplicity of this dish makes it a perfect weeknight meal, but the flavours have enough excitement to see it as part of a dinner party. Seek out dried plums from Afghan or Middle Eastern emporiums. The korma looks pretty with its garnish of red onion rings, coriander leaves and wedges of lime served with a big bowl of naan bread.

CHICKEN KORMA

from Farida Ayubi

Heat the oil in a pot over medium-high heat. Add the chicken pieces and fry, turning, until golden all over. Remove the chicken pieces from the pot and set aside.

Add the ginger and garlic to the oil and fry, stirring, for 1-2 minutes. Add the onion and fry until golden. Reduce the heat to low and add the yoghurt, turmeric and salt. Stir well and bring to a gentle boil. Return the chicken to the pot along with the dal. Cover and simmer for 5-6 minutes, adding a little water if necessary. Add the tomatoes, chillies and dried plums. Continue to cook, covered, for 10 minutes, or until the dal is soft. Turn the heat down and remove the lid to allow the sauce to thicken a little. The oil should rise to the surface when the korma is ready.

Garnish with red onion rings, coriander and lime wedges. Serve with naan bread.

SERVES 4-6

125 ml (4 fl oz/½ cup) vegetable oil
1 medium chicken (about 1.5 kg/3 lb 4 oz), cut into 8 pieces
1 tablespoon finely chopped ginger
1 tablespoon finely chopped garlic
1 medium onion, finely chopped
250 ml (8½ fl oz/1 cup) natural yoghurt
2 teaspoons turmeric
1 teaspoon salt
⅓ cup *chana* dal (split chickpeas), soaked for 3-4 hours or overnight

2 medium tomatoes, diced
4 medium green chillies, finely sliced
3 medium red chillies, finely sliced
10 dried plums, soaked for 1 hour

TO SERVE

red onion, sliced into rings
coriander (cilantro) leaves
lime wedges
naan bread

This milk fudge with walnuts, cardamom and rosewater is one of the fastest desserts I've seen come together. Simply make a sugar syrup, pour it over the dry ingredients, stir, and then pour the mixture into a shallow dish to set. *Sheer pira* is perfect with coffee or tea to end a banquet, or can be served with nuts and dried fruits for afternoon tea.

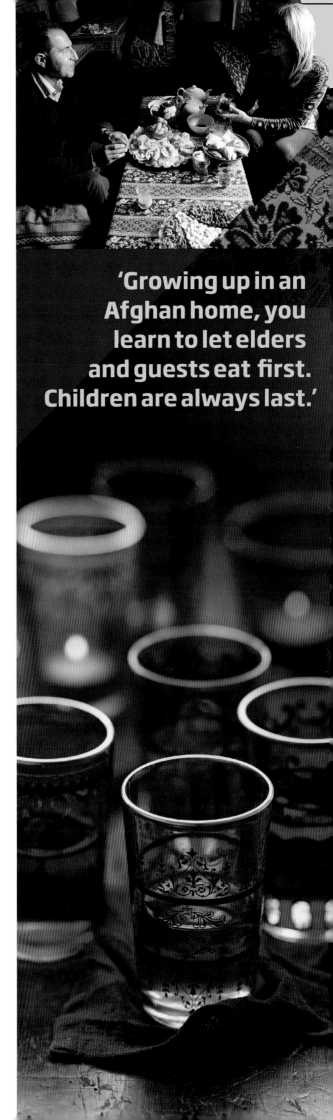

'Growing up in an Afghan home, you learn to let elders and guests eat first. Children are always last.'

SHEER PIRA

from Nouria Salehi

Combine the sugar and water in a medium saucepan and place over low heat. Stir until the sugar dissolves. Increase the heat to medium and boil without stirring for 12–15 minutes or until thickened but not coloured. It is ready when you drizzle a little down the side of a bowl and it almost holds without running.

Meanwhile, combine the milk powder, cardamom, rosewater and walnuts in a large bowl. Pour over the hot syrup and quickly mix together until well combined. Pour into a shallow dish and sprinkle the top with the ground pistachios.

Set aside for 1 hour to cool and set before cutting into diamonds or squares.

SERVES 10

- 440 g (15½ oz/2 cups) sugar
- 500 ml (17 fl oz/2 cups) water
- 440 g (15½ oz/4 cups) full-cream milk powder
- 1 tablespoon ground cardamom
- 1 tablespoon rosewater
- 100 g (3½ oz/1 cup) walnuts, chopped
- 1 tablespoon pistachios, ground

What an incredible mix of cooking styles, unusual ingredients and delicious surprises are found in this vast continent. Having travelled in the north and south of Africa, I have a keen interest in African food and have been lucky enough to have taken part in preparing it many times. Yet I was still blown away by the discoveries I've recently made closer to home. The marvellous spice mixes, deeply satisfying dishes, unusual serving arrangements and the sheer warmth and generosity of the African people I've met have been overwhelming – where one dish was enough, a whole feast would appear just because I showed an interest. Such generosity from people who come from a continent so often beset with natural and man-made disasters … It says something about the human spirit that dishes that have evolved in Africa are not just sustaining but truly magnificent.

THE WEST

West Africans love chilli and spices and will use these to add a little heat and extra flavour to many of their dishes. Ghanaians have developed a hot chilli and smoked fish accompaniment called *shitto* (yes, really!). It is an intensely smelly, wonderfully hot and salty paste that they use readily, even enjoying it simply with plain rice.

Red palm-fruit oil is the oil of choice in West Africa, and when it's heated, magic happens. The oil melts to the most wonderful, deep-ruby colour and it adds a golden crispiness to anything cooked in it. One of my great finds has been disks of plantain (green banana) fried in palm-fruit oil, like chunky potato chips – divine! This oil is often confused with its infamous, trans-fatty cousin made from the kernels of the palm oil tree. Palm-fruit oil comes from the fruit, which is pressed with the same technique used to make virgin olive oil, without any heat or solvents. As a result, the palm-fruit oil is high in betacarotene and antioxidants and is actually good for you.

THE HORN

Ethiopia, Eritrea and Somalia are home to *injera,* a wonderfully spongy, fermented bread that is a cross between a crumpet and a pancake and the size of a wide circular tray. It's baked on a large, flat griddle and almost every meal is served on it, the round flatbread working as an edible plate – the diner breaks off pieces of the bread to scoop up meat or vegetable stews.

One of the dishes I love is an Ethiopian slow-cooked stew called a *wat*. It starts with many kilograms of diced onions (chopping these is a tearjerker!) that are slowly cooked in a heavy-based pot for more than an hour.

No oil or fat is used to start the cooking process and what you end up with is a sweet, dark base of onion to which lots of the popular *berbere* spice is added, as well as other spices and meat or vegetables. The resulting stew is spicy and delicious, especially served with *injera.*

Another great Ethiopian tradition is the coffee ceremony, which is a crucial part of social and cultural life there – this is fitting, perhaps, as coffee was first discovered growing wild in Ethiopia centuries ago. Surprisingly, the green coffee beans are only roasted just before they're used. Enough beans for each pot are poured into a small

ESSENTIAL FLAVOURS

AFRICAN BASIL
A herb with a warm, sweet, camphorlike scent and a gentle taste with a hint of clove. This is used in many recipes from the Horn of Africa. The dried leaves and seeds are ground for use in spice mixes.

AFRICAN MINT (*EFIRI*)
Found in some plant nurseries and easy to cultivate, this has a distinctive fresh flavour.

BERBERE
A hot chilli and spice mix used widely in stews and sprinkled on top of many dishes for garnish and extra kick. Brick-red in colour, the mix usually includes red chillies, *timiz* (long peppers), cardamom, cumin, fenugreek, ginger, cloves, nutmeg, coriander (cilantro), allspice, rue berries and ajowan (a spice known as bishop's weed). Freshly ground then sun dried, *berbere* is best stored in an airtight container and used within six weeks. For Ethiopians and Eritreans, this is red gold! It is sold in African grocery stores and specialty spice shops.

BROWN CARDAMOM
Larger and more fibrous than green cardamom, these pods have a camphor-like aroma and smoky flavour. They are used in stews and spice mixes in the Horn of Africa.

NIGELLA SEEDS
When crushed these little black seeds smell a little like oregano. Their slight bitterness and fragrant aroma is useful in stews.

NITER KIBBEH
Spiced clarified butter that is usually made in large quantities and kept for daily use. Ingredients include cardamom, fenugreek and nigella seeds. Some recipes also add garlic, ginger, finely chopped onion, turmeric, nutmeg, cloves, cinnamon sticks, fennel seeds and *korseret* (a herb native to Ethiopia with a minty thyme flavour). While often homemade, *niter kibbeh* can be purchased from African grocery stores.

RED PALM-FRUIT OIL
Oil extracted from the fruit of the African oil palm. Not to be confused with palm-kernel oil. Native to Africa, red palm-fruit oil has long been appreciated as an excellent base for cooking.

metal pannier and roasted over a flame, then the beans are ground and water is added. The resulting brew has a deliciously soft flavour, which is sometimes intensified by the addition of spices, including kibbled ginger. The coffee ceremony involves the serving of three rounds of coffee accompanied by the burning of frankincense. It's a heady feast for the senses and takes at least an hour - very different from the Italian espresso you gulp while standing up in a coffee bar! No coffee ceremony is complete without popcorn, and sometimes dates and a sweet, soft bread called *himbasha* are also served.

THE EAST

Along the Swahili Coast of Kenya and Tanzania you find a wonderful culinary fusion of African, Indian, Arabic and British flavours, a legacy of spice trading in the area. Local produce such as fish, bananas and coconuts feature prominently and these are mixed with the more exotic tastes of curries, pickles, saffron, nutmeg and pomegranate. The Portuguese also had an impact on the cuisine of the region, as seen in the marinating and barbecuing techniques used there.

Further inland, cattle-breeding tribes like the Maasai live on a meat and milk-based diet, although maize meal, rice, potatoes and cabbage are becoming popular. In Uganda staple foods are steamed plantains called *matoke*, cassava, sweet potatoes, peanuts and beans. Simple and delicious food.

Making Fufu

In Africa, no meal is complete without a starchy porridge called fufu (also known as ugali, pap, iwisa, sadza or mealie meal). This is made from yams and sometimes plantains, cassava or maize and African people say they don't feel full unless they've had their fufu.

Making fufu to the required consistency takes some energy. Dried, pounded meal is mixed with water in a saucepan, which is placed over a fire or gas flame. As the fufu heats and thickens, the cook uses a large wooden spoon to stir it vigourously in a circular motion. It takes a good ten minutes to get the fufu just right - thick and smooth. When cooked it is scooped by the cupful into a bowl and, with a few spoonfuls of warm water added, is shaken back and forth until it forms a ball. It's then served with a little meat or some vegetables in a rich sauce on the side.

It takes practice to eat fufu with your hands. You pinch off a ball with your right hand, making an indentation with your thumb and at the same time not letting it touch the palm of your hand. You then deftly scoop up a small amount of the accompanying stew and eat. Let's say it's a delightful, tactile learning experience!

This is a typical dish of the Swahili Coast, with its Arabic and Indian influences, and it makes a delicious meal when served with lamb *suqaar* and the cardamom-spiced bread *mahamri*. *Suqaar* is a traditional Somalian stir-fry, which can use beef, chicken or lamb. *Mahamri* are known as 'Swahili buns' and are eaten plain for breakfast or used to slurp up sauce at dinnertime – you vary the amount of sugar in the recipe depending on what you're going to serve them with.

MAHINDI YA NAZ

Corn in Coconut Sauce

from Shukri Abdi

To make the *mahamri*, mix the flour, coconut milk powder, sugar, cardamom and yeast in a large bowl. Add the milk and combine well to form a dough. Cover the bowl and set aside in a warm place until the dough rises.

To make the coconut corn, put the corn pieces in a large saucepan. Mix the remaining ingredients together and pour over the corn. Cook over low heat for 10–15 minutes.

Once the *mahamri* dough has risen, form the dough into balls (about the size of tennis balls), roll out to ½ cm (¼ in) thick and cut into quarters.

Heat the oil for the *mahamri* in a deep, heavy-based frying pan. When the oil is hot, add the pieces of dough carefully, a few at a time, and fry until they puff up and turn golden. Remove with a slotted spoon and drain on paper towel.

Heat the olive oil for the *suqaar* in a frying pan over medium heat. Add the remaining ingredients and stir-fry for a few minutes until the meat is cooked. Remove from the heat and serve alongside the *mahamri* and coconut corn.

SERVES 6-8

MAHAMRI

450 g (1 lb/3 cups) plain (all-purpose) flour
1 cup coconut milk powder
55-110 g (3¾-4 oz) sugar
1 teaspoon ground cardamom
1 tablespoon dried yeast
250 ml (8½ fl oz/1 cup) milk
oil for deep-frying

COCONUT CORN

6 corn cobs, cut into 10 cm (4 in) pieces
1 cup coconut milk powder

500 ml (17 fl oz/2 cups) water
1 large onion, diced
3 tablespoons tomato puree
1 teaspoon turmeric
salt

SUQAAR

1 tablespoon olive oil
500 g (1 lb 2 oz) lamb, finely diced
1 onion, diced
½ red capsicum (bell pepper), finely diced
2 tablespoons tomato puree
pinch of salt

A *wat* is a stew that uses the marvellous red *berbere* spice mix and a rich base of onion. A vast quantity of onions is used so it is a good idea to finely dice these in a food processor. If six tablespoons of *berbere* sounds like a lot (it contains plenty of chilli powder), reduce the amount when you first cook this recipe - you can always make it hotter next time! For a healthier alternative you can replace the *niter kibbeh* with more olive oil. If you can't find African basil, simply leave it out. This dish is traditionally served on top of *injera* bread.

'The way to a Ghanaian man's heart is with a jar of *shitto*.'

DORO WAT

Ethiopian Red Chicken Stew

from Karim Degal

Place the onion in a large, heavy-based pot, cover with a lid and cook over low-medium heat, stirring occasionally. Do not add any oil or liquid. Cook for about 1 hour, until the onion has reduced.

While the onion is cooking, remove the skin from the chicken and cut into portions, trimming off any fat. (In Ethiopia, they cut it into 21 portions.) Mix the vinegar and lemon juice together and sit the chicken pieces in the liquid for 10-15 minutes, then drain.

Combine the ingredients for the mixed spices in a mortar and grind to a powder.

When the onion has reduced add the olive oil, *niter kibbeh* and *berbere* and stir well. Add the chicken. Bring the mixture to the boil, then reduce the heat to a simmer. Stir the spices into the stew and add extra salt if needed. Simmer until the chicken is cooked through, making sure the onion does not stick to the bottom of the pot. Spoon out some of the excess oil that settles on top.

Cut vertical grooves into the hard-boiled eggs to ensure the flavour seeps in. When the stew is cooked, add the eggs and turn off the heat. The *doro wat* can be served immediately with *injera* but is even better the following day when the spices have worked their magic.

SERVES 8

3 kg (6 lb 10 oz) onions, finely diced
1 large chicken, preferably free-range
100 ml (3½ fl oz) white vinegar
juice of 1 lemon
100 ml (3½ fl oz) olive oil
3 tablespoons *niter kibbeh* (see recipe on page 18)
6 tablespoons *berbere*
12 eggs, hard-boiled

MIXED SPICES

2 tablespoons cardamom seeds
2 tablespoons nigella seeds
2 tablespoons ajowan or fennel seeds
1 tablespoon dried African basil (optional)
2 teaspoons black peppercorns
2 tablespoons salt

Jollof rice, or *ceebu jen* as it's known in Senegal, is perhaps the best known West African dish because it's delicious, colourful and easy to prepare. It is a little like an African paella made from parboiled long-grain rice, vegetables and meat but without any butter or wine added. It is delicious served hot with fried plantain slices. The recipe calls for African mint (*efiri*), which you can buy in some plant nurseries – if you can't get it, simply leave it out of the recipe. If you prefer a milder dish, remove some of the seeds from the chillies.

JOLLOF RICE

from Kunle Adesua

To make the *obe ata*, use a hand-held blender to process the chopped tomato in a bowl. Blend the capsicum and chilli in a separate bowl.

Heat the oil in a saucepan and add the onion, shallots, spring onion, celery, African mint and salt and sauté, stirring well, until the onions are translucent. Add the tomato and the capsicum and chilli and cook over moderate heat for 10 minutes.

To make the fish and rice, sprinkle the fish cubes with the chilli flakes and salt and set aside.

Heat the oil in a large saucepan and add the carrot, capsicum, tomato and zucchini and salt. Cook over moderate heat for 10 minutes until softened a little. Add the fish, water and rice and the *obe ata* sauce. Gently mix together and bring to the boil. Cover the saucepan and simmer for approximately 45 minutes, until the rice and vegetables are cooked.

SERVES 10

OBE ATA SAUCE

5 tomatoes, chopped
3 red capsicums (bell peppers), chopped
6 small red chillies
100 ml (3½ fl oz) red palm-fruit oil
1 onion, finely chopped
3 shallots, finely chopped
3 spring onions (scallions), finely chopped
1 celery stalk, chopped
handful of African mint (optional)
pinch of salt

FISH AND RICE

1 kg (2 lb 3 oz) firm fish fillets such as marlin, cut into large cubes
25 g (1 oz) chilli flakes mixed with 1 teaspoon salt
2½ tablespoons red palm-fruit oil
2 medium carrots, chopped
1 red capsicum (bell pepper), chopped
1 green capsicum (bell pepper), chopped
2 tomatoes, chopped
2 zucchini (courgettes) (or 2 celery stalks with leaves), chopped
pinch of salt
250 ml (8½ fl oz/1 cup) water
2 cups parboiled long-grain rice

'The heart that does not eat chilli is a feeble one.'

'Do not eat alone – you will enjoy your food more when you share it with people.'

Fast, fresh, simple and delicious, *kulwha* is an Eritrean stir-fry that uses the spiced clarified butter called *niter kibbeh*. This recipe makes more *niter kibbeh* than you need, but it can be refrigerated for up to three months and used in other recipes. For a healthier alternative you can replace the *niter kibbeh* with more olive oil.

KULWHA

Eritrean Stir-fry

from Rahel Ogbaghiorghis

To make the *niter kibbeh*, heat the butter in a small saucepan over low–medium heat until it has begun to simmer gently. Simmer for about 30 minutes, skimming the foam off the surface, until the top layer of butter is completely clear. Strain the butter through a fine sieve over a bowl, leaving the milk solids in the bottom of the pan. Stir in the spices. Allow to cool then transfer to an airtight container, reserving 1 tablespoon for the *kulwha*.

To make the *kulwha*, put the *niter kibbeh*, oil, onion, chilli, half the tomato, the lamb and salt into a large frying pan and place over high heat. Stir-fry until the meat is cooked through (about 3 minutes) then add the *berbere* and the remaining tomato. Serve with *injera* or rice.

SERVES 4

NITER KIBBEH	KULWHA
500 g (1 lb 2 oz) unsalted butter	**1 tablespoon *niter kibbeh***
½ teaspoon ground cardamom	**1 tablespoon olive oil**
½ teaspoon ground fenugreek	**1 onion, sliced**
½ teaspoon nigella seeds, ground	**1 long green chilli, chopped**
	2 tomatoes, diced
	500 g (1 lb 2 oz) lamb fillet, diced into small cubes
	pinch of salt
	1 tablespoon *berbere*

Black-eyed beans are a popular ingredient throughout Africa and *akara*, or black-eyed bean fritters, are the national snack food of Senegal and Nigeria. These fritters are great for vegetarians and vegans and are especially delicious with the *kosayi* dipping sauce. A good red *kosayi* shouldn't be too hot – you should just be able to feel the heat. The sauce will keep for about six months in the refrigerator and the older it gets the better it tastes. Make the sauce at least two days before you want to use it.

AKARA WITH RED KOSAYI

Black-eyed Bean Fritters with Dipping Sauce
from Bathie Dia

To make the *kosayi*, place the whole capsicums and chillies in a large saucepan of cold water and bring to the boil. Simmer for 25 minutes or until the capsicums are soft. Remove from the heat, cover with a lid and set aside until cool.

When cooled, dry the capsicums and chillies and remove the seeds. Peel the capsicums. Place the capsicums and chillies in a food processor and blend to a paste. Press the mixture through a fine sieve to remove any remaining skin.

Add the oil, sugar, vinegar and salt and mix together well. Pour the mixture into a sterilised jar with a thin layer of olive oil on top and leave in the refrigerator for at least 2 days to mature.

To make the *akara*, bring a large saucepan of water to the boil, add the beans and boil for 2 minutes. Drain the beans and spread them out on a clean tea towel. Cover with a second tea towel and roll the beans back and forth between the towels using the palms of your hands. After a few minutes the beans will have shed their skins. Remove any skins that remain attached to individual beans by rubbing the bean between your thumb and forefinger. To separate the beans from the skins, tip them back into the saucepan, add lots of water and swirl around in a circular motion until the skins have risen to the top. Scoop out the skins and leave the beans to soak for 2 hours.

In a food processor blend the beans to a very fine paste. Knead the paste for 2–3 minutes, until the starch is released, then divide in half.

Place one half in a bowl over a saucepan of simmering water and stir continuously with a rubber spatula or wooden spoon until the mixture comes together like a dough. Take great care that the mixture does not cook or curdle. If necessary, briefly lift the bowl away from the heat from time to time. Then mix in the remaining paste and continue stirring over the simmering water for about 1 minute, so the dough comes together. Take the bowl off the heat and continue to stir until the dough has cooled to room temperature.

Season the bean dough and add herbs if using. Add the baking powder if you want a lighter texture. Shape into fritters roughly the size of eggs and shallow-fry in oil. (You can deep-fry the fritters if you prefer or wrap them in banana leaves and steam them.) Serve the fritters warm or cold with a dipping bowl of *kosayi*.

MAKES ABOUT 25 FRITTERS

RED *KOSAYI*

9 small red capsicums (bell peppers)
3 long red chillies
7 small red chillies
2 tablespoons vegetable oil
75 g (2¾ oz/⅓ cup) sugar
75 ml (2½ fl oz) white vinegar
1 teaspoon salt
olive oil

AKARA

500 g (1 lb 2 oz) black-eyed beans
salt and pepper
handful of fresh herbs such as flat-leaf (Italian) parsley or coriander (cilantro), chopped (optional)
1 teaspoon baking powder (optional)
oil for frying

Much soul-searching goes on in Australia to determine what constitutes our national cuisine. After many years travelling around our incredible country, tasting and learning – sitting around campfires and in family kitchens, dining in top restaurants and at laminex tables – I believe we certainly have our own cuisine.

We have a boldness, a willingness to try new things, to break the rules set half a world away; there's a freshness and confidence that goes with our food. Plus we have some of the best produce on earth – such an abundance of seafood, meat, vegetables and fruits, and our lesser-known bush foods that have existed for tens of thousands of years. The result is simply sensational seasonal food that makes your tastebuds come alive.

We are blessed to have had so many great cooks, chefs and artisans come to Australia, as well as those who have been raised here. Hardworking bakers, cheese makers, butchers, providores and spice merchants have helped ignite our passion for great flavours and authentic recipes.

In some parts of the country factors such as history, climate and isolation have led to the development of distinct regional cuisines. In our latest television series we travelled to Broome and Darwin, visiting family homes and open-air markets and discovering unique dishes that are truly worth celebrating.

BROOME

There's nowhere else on earth quite like Broome. For a start, it's incredibly beautiful with white sandy beaches, red rocks that turn purple in the setting sun, turquoise water and a relaxed lifestyle. It's one of the most remote settlements in the world but it's Broome's isolation that has contributed to its magic and the development of a distinct Australian creole cuisine.

The people who came to work in the pearling industry over a hundred years ago came from diverse backgrounds, and they shared recipes. Coupled with the limited ingredients available, this led to the creation of a number of unique dishes that have become part of everyday life for Broome families.

From the late nineteenth century Broome became a boom town because of its large, lustrous South Sea pearls. In the early days pearl shells were strewn on beaches and gathering pearls was relatively easy. It was not just the pearls that grew to be in demand in Europe, but also the shells used for inlay in furniture and small items like buttons, buckles and cutlery. Pearling in Broome became more intensive and dangerous as companies needed to hire divers to work in deeper waters. Aboriginal people were used at first, but experienced divers from Japan were soon the most sought after. It was exceptionally hard work and fatalities were common. By 1910 there were nearly 400 boats or luggers working the waters around Broome and 3500 people employed in the pearling industry. Broome was the largest pearling centre in the world at the time.

ESSENTIAL FLAVOURS

CLIVE OF INDIA CURRY POWDER

This was the one curry powder available in Broome for many decades, and the yellow tin was found in every household to flavour curries and satays.

COCONUT CREAM

Tinned coconut cream is used in curries and satay sauce ... Some Broome friends love it straight from the tin!

RICE

Rice is the staple in Broome and the Top End, even in indigenous communities. Jasmine rice is the most popular variety and is the first thing many kids learn to cook. Fish soup and rice is a classic Broome dish to feed a large family.

SALTED PLUMS

The snack food of choice for Broome kids (and Darwin ones as well). These small sweet-and-sour plums seasoned with salt are part of the region's Chinese heritage, and devotees say they're perfect for keeping thirst at bay on a hot day.

SHRIMP PASTE

Both Malaysian- and Thai-style shrimp pastes get a work out in the Top End. Malaysian shrimp paste called *belachan* comes as a compressed block and is featured in a sambal that is a delicious sauce for local seafood.

SOY SAUCE

Broome was devoted to a Singaporean brand of soy sauce called Young's, and the town went into mourning when it ceased to be made (some locals now use their own special mix of soy sauces to approximate the flavour of Young's). Soy sauce is added to satays, curries, Broome's version of Filipino *adobo*, susame and even pasta sauces.

THAI VEGETABLES

There is a big range of Thai and Asian vegetables available in Darwin, from the feathery leaves of *cha om*, which come from an acacia bush, to pea and apple eggplants, banana flowers and baby okra.

Other races came to help in the pearl and associated industries - Chinese, Malaysian, Filipino, Indonesian, Timorese and South Sea islanders all lived side by side. Many of the new settlers brought cooking styles and ingredients that became part of everyday life. For a good one hundred years Broome was the most multicultural place in Australia.

Over many visits I have been lucky enough to meet people who cook this cuisine that's a mix of Chinese, Japanese, Malaysian, Indonesian and Filipino, using local ingredients with a heavy reliance on fish and seafood. These are not dishes you find in restaurants. One of the favourite local dishes is 'susame' - the name comes from sashimi, and it is slices of the freshest raw fish cured with vinegar and soy sauce. It's usually eaten within an hour of the fish coming out of the ocean.

Another is fish soup and rice, fragrant with lemongrass and ginger. The Pigram Brothers celebrated this simple but marvellous dish in their song 'Going Back Home', dedicated to their mother Anges' cooking and to the ripe mangos and blooming frangipanis of Broome. The brothers are the town's most famous band and their distinct sound and music are known throughout Australia and the world.

When Broome people get together everyone has a special dish they make, and for Erica Pigram it's vermicelli chicken, another beloved dish of the area and one that is also found in Darwin. Cauline Masuda knows an invite means her classic mango cheesecake; Alan Pigram makes susame; and his brother-in-law TinSun makes his special Broome fried rice in the outdoor kitchen on the family's wide verandah. The McKenna sisters Raelene and Vicki get their daughters and granddaughters to help with a tray of satay skewers and a flavoursome peanut sauce. Raelene describes Broome food as 'heaven on earth'.

Roma lives up the red dirt road from Broome at a beautiful unspoiled place called Chilli Creek, an area of long white beaches, shady mangroves and a coastal camp. She has both Aboriginal and Filipino heritage, and calls the land that has been passed down through her family her supermarket and her pharmacy. She caught the largest crabs for us when she prepared this dish, which would be in the running for my last meal on earth. Fresh crab, delicious sauce - mmmm.

In the glory days of pearling in Broome, workers on the pearl luggers would often recharge with wontons when they came ashore. Local businesswoman Cori Fong remembers competitions when she was a young girl to see how many would be eaten in one sitting accompanied by cold beer. The record stood at ten dozen! This recipe is delicious and surprisingly easy to make, although Cori does suggest making the filling the day before.

BROOME CHILLI CRAB

from Roma Puertollano

Put the crabs to sleep by freezing them for 1-2 hours. Pull off their top shells and remove the grey gills. Use a sharp knife to cut the crabs in half through the middle. Clean the halves. Cut each half in two. Crack the claws in a few places with the back of a knife.

Heat the vegetable oil in a wok over high heat and deep-fry the crab pieces until the shells turn orange. Set aside.

Drain the oil from the wok, leaving about 2 tablespoons. Place over medium heat and add the onion, chilli, garlic and ginger. Toss for 2-3 minutes until the onion is soft. Stir in the remaining ingredients (apart from the crab) and simmer for 5 minutes.

Stir the crab pieces into the sauce. Simmer for another 2 minutes, then serve.

SERVES 4

2 medium mud crabs	400 g (14 oz) tin diced tomatoes
500-750 ml (25½ fl oz/3 cups) vegetable oil	1-2 tablespoons tomato sauce
1 onion, finely diced	2 tablespoons sweet chilli sauce
2 long red chillies, seeded and chopped	½ tablespoon fish sauce, or more to taste
2 garlic cloves, crushed	½ tablespoon mushroom soy sauce
2 teaspoons grated ginger	juice of 1 lemon
1 tomato, diced	

WONTONS

from Cori Fong

For the filling, combine all the ingredients in a bowl (other than the wrappers) and mix well with your hands. While you can use the mixture straight away, it is better to cover and refrigerate it overnight to let the flavours develop.

Take a wrapper in one hand and put a teaspoon of filling in the centre. Moisten the edges of the wrapper with water, then fold into a triangle and press the points together. Fold the two side corners up to meet at the same points so the wonton now resembles a money bag. Press together to seal. Repeat with the remaining wrappers and filling.

Bring a pot of water to the boil and cook the wontons in batches. After a short while they should rise to the surface. Cook for another 2-3 minutes from this point. Scoop out the cooked wontons and continue cooking the remaining wontons.

Serve the hot wontons in bowls with blanched greens and hot chicken broth poured over the top. Alternatively, serve with small bowls of soy sauce and chilli sauce for dipping.

MAKES 80 WONTONS

1 kg (2 lb 3 oz) finely minced (ground) pork	½ cup finely chopped bamboo shoots (optional)
2 tablespoons light soy sauce	1 heaped teaspoon grated orange zest (optional)
2 tablespoons sesame oil	splash of rice wine (optional)
2 tablespoons finely chopped ginger	2 × 270 g (10 oz) packets Shanghai (square white) wonton wrappers
2 tablespoons finely chopped garlic	
½ cup finely chopped water chestnuts	TO SERVE
white pepper	blanched Chinese greens and hot chicken broth
6 shiitake mushrooms, soaked in hot water for 30 minutes, drained, stalks removed, finely chopped (optional)	or soy sauce and chilli sauce

Pearl meat has long been prized in Broome – both because it can fetch a good price in Asia and southern Australia, and also because of its eating. It's the adductor muscle of the large *pinctada maxima* pearl oyster that works hard to open and close. After tenderising, it works beautifully sashimi-style mixed with soy or lime dressing (Neville gives two recipes here, so you can choose which one you like best). Abalone or scallops can be used in place of pearl meat.

This dish of the freshest fish, thinly sliced and quickly marinated, is best with a Broome sunset. The word 'susame' is the Broome version of 'sashimi' – a style of eating raw fish that came to Broome with the Japanese pearl divers. Alan likes to use Broome's very own variety of chilli in the marinade – the 'Broome chilli', which is medium-sized with a characteristically snubbed nose and good heat, but other chillies will do.

PEARL-MEAT APPETISERS

from Neville Poelina

Tenderise the pearl meat by placing each piece on a chopping board and whacking with a mallet or rolling pin about 10 times. Cut the pearl meat into thin strips.

Combine the chosen dressing ingredients in a bowl. Add the pearl meat and toss to coat, then serve. Or if preferred, you can chill the mixture in the refrigerator for a few hours before serving.

SERVES 6 AS AN ENTREE

meat from 4-5 pearl oysters

SOY DRESSING

80 ml (2½ fl oz/⅓ cup) dark soy sauce
1 tablespoon raw (demerara) sugar
2 teaspoons finely chopped garlic
2 teaspoons finely chopped ginger
1 long red chilli, seeded and finely chopped
1 long green chilli, seeded and finely chopped

LIME DRESSING

juice of 2 limes
1 teaspoon salt
2 teaspoons finely chopped garlic
2 teaspoons finely chopped ginger
1 long red chilli, seeded and finely chopped
1 long green chilli, seeded and finely chopped

SUSAME

from Alan Pigram

Place all the ingredients in a bowl and toss to coat the fish. Stand for 10 minutes or until the fish begins to turn opaque, then serve.

SERVES 8-10

800 g (1 lb 12 oz) very fresh fish fillets (kingfish, queenfish or threadfin salmon work well), skin and bones removed, finely sliced
½ lemon, finely sliced
½ onion, finely sliced
1 Broome chilli or any long green chilli, seeded and finely sliced
1 long red chilli, seeded and finely sliced
250 ml (8½ fl oz/1 cup) brown vinegar
1 tablespoon light soy sauce
1 tablespoon dark soy sauce

This chicken and vegetable stew with tomatoes, potatoes and shiitake mushrooms, and cellophane noodles stirred in at the end, makes a great family meal - satisfying and full of flavour.

Cauline is the daughter of one of Broome's Japanese pearl divers and her speciality is sweets. Mangos are everywhere in Broome and she uses them in this luscious cheesecake, which is the set-in-the-refrigerator variety, perfect for the tropics.

VERMICELLI CHICKEN

from Erica Pigram

Heat the oil in a pot over medium heat. Add the ginger and whole garlic and fry for 30 seconds, then add the chicken pieces and cook for 7-8 minutes, turning, until lightly browned all over. Add the remaining ingredients other than the noodles and stir well, breaking up the tinned tomatoes with your spoon. Bring to a simmer, then cover with a lid and cook over low heat for 30 minutes or until the chicken is just cooked through.

Five minutes before the chicken is ready, put the noodles in a bowl and add just enough boiling water to cover them. When the chicken is cooked, stir the noodles and their soaking water into the stew, then serve.

SERVES 6

2 tablespoons oil	2-3 potatoes, peeled and
8-10 cm (3-4 in) piece of ginger,	quartered
sliced	1 cup dried shiitake
4 garlic cloves, peeled	mushrooms, soaked in
1 chicken, cut into medium-	warm water for 30 minutes,
sized pieces	drained and finely sliced
1 tablespoon brown vinegar	1 tablespoon light soy sauce
1 celery stalk, sliced	1 teaspoon salt
1 large carrot, chopped	1 teaspoon freshly ground
2 tomatoes, chopped	black pepper
400 g (14 oz) tin peeled	250 g (9 oz) cellophane
tomatoes	(bean thread) noodles

MANGO CHEESECAKE

from Cauline Masuda

Butter a 24 cm (9½ in) springform cake tin. Put the biscuits in a plastic bag and crush them by rolling with a rolling pin. Alternatively, pulse to crumbs in a food processor. Empty into a bowl and add the walnuts and melted butter. Mix well. Press the crumbs into the base of the tin and refrigerate for about 1 hour, until firm.

To make the filling, pour the hot water into a bowl. It should be hotter than lukewarm, but not as hot as boiling water. Sprinkle the gelatine over the top, then stir until dissolved.

Whip the cream to soft peaks.

Beat the cream cheese on medium–high speed until smooth. Beat in the sugar, then reduce the speed to slow and gradually add the mango puree, followed by the gelatine water. Use a large metal spoon to fold in the whipped cream.

Pour the filling over the biscuit base. To decorate the top of the cheesecake, take a few of the smallest slices of mango and stand them up in a ring in the centre of the cake. Surround them with another ring of slightly bigger slices. Continue working in rings, making the pattern of a rose. As the slices get bigger lay them flatter on the cheesecake, opening out the rose. Refrigerate the cheesecake for 3-4 hours, until the filling is set.

SERVES 8-10

120 g (4¼ oz) Granita biscuits or	500 ml (17 fl oz/2 cups) cream
other plain sweet biscuits	500 g (1 lb 2 oz) cream cheese,
120 g (4¼ oz) walnuts, finely	softened
chopped	220 g (7½ oz/1 cup) caster
50 g (1¾ oz) unsalted butter,	sugar
melted	4 very ripe mangos, flesh
80 ml (2½ fl oz/⅓ cup) hot	roughly pureed, plus
water	2 firm-ripe mangos,
1½ tablespoons gelatine	thinly sliced
powder	

Darwin is a city of surprises - a vibrant paradise set on the Timor Sea, surrounded by farmland growing tropical fruits and Asian herbs and vegetables. It has its own laws and even some of its own language. Things are very different in the Top End.

There are some great food haunts in Darwin - the produce markets in Parap, Rapid Creek and Nightcliff are full of the aromas and fresh flavours of cities in Asia. Asian herbs especially need to be picked with the dew still on them, and to be at market by 5 am ready for the early shoppers.

You hear languages around you that span the range of Darwin's population - Vietnamese mixes with Khmer, Timorese dialects mingle with Chinese; there are broad Australian accents mixed with Greek. This is multicultural heaven in the warm air.

The night markets at Mindil Beach have become a pumping tourist attraction but locals still flock to make a circle with their folding chairs and order freshly cooked Asian food from the many stalls, then watch the sunset over the water. It's pretty magic, with the aromas of lemongrass and lime, a good rendang and some wok-tossed noodles mingling with souvlaki cooking and pita bread toasting.

Like Broome, Darwin adores its locally caught mud crab and fresh fish. The barramundi wrapped in paperbark and cooked on coals buried in the sand is one of the most delicious fresh flavours - served Territory style, with chopsticks fashioned from a nearby bush, and flavoured with soy sauce, which is regarded as an indispensable ingredient by my friend Roque Lee, who is of Chinese and Aboriginal heritage and is a pretty fabulous fisherman and bush cook.

It's interesting how pervasive Asian flavours have become in Darwin - many families grow their own chillies and lemongrass and always have a couple of chilli sauces and shrimp paste on hand in the pantry. Indigenous communities adore Malaysian sambals and Thai expats can find all the produce they need to create authentic dishes from home.

ESSENTIAL FLAVOURS

CHA OM

Cha om is a feathery bush from the *acacia* family that grows in the tropics, and its young shoots are used as a herb. Look out for it at Asian markets, particularly in spring. It resembles dill, although on closer inspection the leaves are small fern-like fronds. It has a strong smell and a flavour that is nutty and a little bitter - terrific mixed with eggs.

Robert Mills is an elder of the Larrakia people of Darwin and runs a local tourism venture called Batji Tours. He's also quite a cook and shared this family recipe on a warm afternoon under big trees in his backyard. The sambal, which is Malaysian in origin, is an all-purpose sauce that is hugely popular among the local Aboriginal community. It can be eaten with plain rice, but Robert's favourite way of serving it is tossing it through cooked seafood such as prawns and mussels. Balmain bugs and scallops on the shell work really well too.

This is *real* Thai food. *Cha om* is a feathery bush from the acacia family that grows in the tropics, and its young shoots are used as a herb. Look out for it at Asian markets, particularly in spring. It resembles dill, although on closer inspection the leaves are small fern-like fronds. It has a strong smell and a flavour that is nutty and a little bitter - terrific mixed with eggs and served with this hot and pungent shrimp-paste sauce.

BELACHAN SAMBAL

from Robert Mills

Heat the oil in a wok over medium-high heat. Add the onion, garlic, ginger and chilli and toss until the onion becomes translucent.

Add the tomatoes and cook for 3-4 minutes, then add the sauces. Add the shrimp paste, mashing it into the tomato mixture with a fork. Do the same for the tamarind pulp. Simmer for another 2-3 minutes, then add the palm sugar and lime juice to taste.

Serve with cooked prawns and mussels. Garnish with coriander leaves.

SERVES 4-6

3 tablespoons peanut oil	½ tablespoon soy sauce
2 onions, finely chopped	1 teaspoon fish sauce
4 garlic cloves, finely chopped	1 tablespoon Malaysian shrimp
2 teaspoons finely chopped	paste (*belachan*)
ginger	½ tablespoon tamarind pulp,
6-10 long red chillies, seeded	any seeds removed
and finely chopped	2 tablespoons grated palm
3 tomatoes, chopped	sugar
1 tablespoon oyster sauce	juice of 1-2 limes
	Cooked prawns (shrimp) and
	mussels to serve 4-6 people
	coriander (cilantro) leaves

CHA OM OMELETTE

from Saramat Ruchkaew

To make the sauce, combine the garlic and chillies in a mortar and pound to a paste. (The finer you pound the chillies, the hotter the paste becomes, so you may not wish to pound them completely.)

Add the pea eggplants and shrimp paste and continue to pound, lightly bruising the eggplants. Add the sugar and juice of half a lime and taste the sauce, adding more lime if desired.

To make the omelette, chop the *cha om* and put it in a mixing bowl. Add the eggs and beat with a fork, combining them with the *cha om*. Stir in the fish sauce and sugar.

Heat the oil in a frying pan over medium heat. When hot, pour in the egg mixture. As it cooks, put a spatula under the omelette and gently lift it up a few centimetres, allowing the uncooked egg to run from the top of the omelette to the bottom. Lower the omelette back down and continue to cook until the base is lightly golden. Flip the omelette (don't worry if it breaks a little) and cook briefly on the other side. Serve the omelette in pieces on a platter with the dipping sauce.

SERVES 4

SAUCE	OMELETTE
6 garlic cloves	1-2 handfuls *cha om* leaves and
handful of small red chillies,	tender upper stems
with a few green ones	6 eggs
included for colour	2 teaspoons fish sauce
large handful of pea eggplants	2 teaspoons sugar
(aubergines)	125 ml (4 fl oz/½ cup) oil
1-2 tablespoons shrimp paste	
2 tablespoons sugar	
juice of ½-1 lime	

Just-caught mud crab in the skilled hands of legendary Darwin chef Jimmy Shu – what could be better! This is a clever and delicious way of serving one of the Top End's great delicacies and it opened my eyes to young ginger as a beautiful fresh ingredient. Egg whites add a silken texture and restaurant-like finish.

STEAMED MUD CRAB WITH EGG WHITE, YOUNG GINGER AND RICE WINE

from Jimmy Shu

Put the crabs to sleep by freezing them for 1–2 hours. Pull off their top shells and remove the grey gills. Use a sharp knife to cut the crabs in half through the middle. Clean the halves. Cut each half in two. Crack the claws in a few places with the back of a knife.

Place the crab pieces in a bowl that will fit inside your steamer. Sprinkle the crab with the ginger and drizzle with the rice wine and soy sauce. Place the bowl inside the steamer, cover with the lid and steam for 10 minutes.

Drizzle the egg whites over the crabs and continue to steam for another 5 minutes. By this time, the crabs should be cooked through with their flesh opaque, but if not, you can steam for a few more minutes.

While the crab is steaming, mix some black vinegar in a bowl with extra ginger as a dipping sauce.

To serve, add another splash of rice wine and soy sauce to the crab and garnish with coriander and whole chillies. Serve with the vinegar and ginger.

Drongo – someone who 'has roos in the top paddock'. *Munjung* – a bit of a drongo, but a nice sort of a drongo.

SERVES 4

2 mud crabs
4 cm (1½ in) piece of young ginger, finely julienned, plus extra to serve
1 tablespoon rice wine, plus extra to serve

1 teaspoon soy sauce, plus extra to serve
2 egg whites
Chinese black vinegar
coriander (cilantro) leaves
red chillies

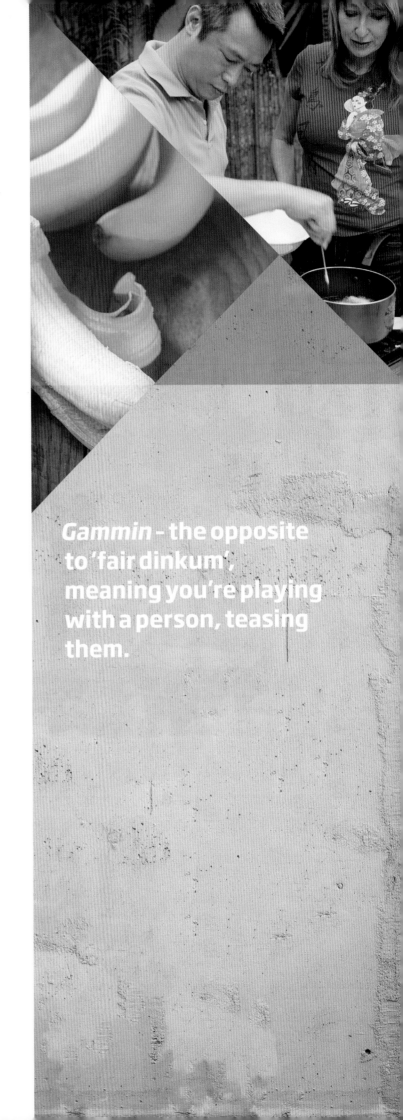

Darwin-based Danny Yeum is one of the fastest wok chefs I've ever seen, a true professional capturing the power of the roaring gas to create magic in minutes. Here he gives us his recipe for toffee bananas, which look so good they could be a magic trick.

TOFFEE BANANAS

from Danny Yeum

Combine the flours in a bowl and add the water and oil, whisking to a smooth batter.

Peel the bananas and cut each diagonally into 4 pieces. Dust the pieces in cornflour.

Put the sugar in a small saucepan and set aside without turning on the heat.

Heat the oil in a wok or saucepan until very hot. Roll the banana pieces in the batter and carefully add to the hot oil, frying until golden brown. Drain on paper towel.

Quickly place the sugar over medium heat. Cook without stirring, but shaking the saucepan if necessary, until the sugar melts and forms a caramel. While the sugar is cooking, get a small of bowl of water ready with ice cubes in it.

Roll a piece of fried banana in the toffee, then plunge it into the iced water for a few seconds to harden the toffee, then drain. Repeat with the remaining banana pieces.

Sprinkle the bananas with sesame seeds. Garnish with mint and serve with ice-cream.

SERVES 4

50 g (1¾ oz/⅓ cup) self-raising flour
25 g (1 oz) cornflour (cornstarch), plus extra for dusting
90 ml (3 floz) water

a few drops of vegetable oil, plus extra for deep-frying
2 bananas
120 g (4 oz) sugar
sesame seeds

TO SERVE

mint leaves
ice-cream

Gammin – the opposite to 'fair dinkum', meaning you're playing with a person, teasing them.

Brazilian food is an exuberant, colourful mix of Portuguese, African and native Amazonian flavours and in Australia we've embraced it wholeheartedly. We love the easy Brazilian lifestyle that mirrors our own, especially when it includes the *churrasco* barbecues, the fresh lime and sugarcane cocktails (*caipirinha*) and the tasty little cheese breads (*pão de queijo*) that are starting to be sold here.

Brazilians are people who like intensity and when they love a particular food, they eat it a lot – lots of salt, sugar, caffeine and chilli. The national dish is *feijoada*, a slow-cooked, dark mixture of black turtle beans, cured meats and *chouriço* (spicy sausage). It is so popular that Brazilians eat it twice a week – on Wednesdays and again on Saturdays. This dish originated with African slaves who were brought to Brazil to work on plantations developed by Portuguese settlers. Beans were cheap and the air-dried beef and pork off-cuts were the least attractive and most affordable parts of the animal. The resulting dish was simple but also rich, comforting and satisfying and has been treasured ever since.

The Africans also brought to Brazil red palm-fruit or *dende* oil, coconuts, plantains and okra. The Portuguese, who were able to sustain themselves on large voyages of discovery due to their salted cod, brought with them this useful fish as well as a love of cooking with onions and garlic and a passion for rich desserts made with many eggs and sugar. These elements were combined with the ancient foods of the native Indian inhabitants of Brazil, such as the Amazon forest berry called *açaí* (pronounced 'ah-sah-ee'), which contains loads of antioxidants and vitamins; guarana, another forest berry; hearts of palm, which are a terrible waste of a beautiful tree but very delicious; and cassava, a long tuber with pinkish-brown skin and milky white flesh that is now a staple of Brazilian cooking.

To add further to this mingling of cuisines, western European and Arab immigrants to coffee plantations in the southern part of Brazil brought with them the skills for cheese making and preserving meat. They also contributed to the diverse cuisine that is centred around the Minas Gerais region. Cheese became the basis for one of Brazil's most popular savoury snacks, the *pão de queijo*, which is a bite-sized cheese bread made with cassava flour. *Salgadinhos*, or snacks, in Brazil are always taken with strong, black coffee or the lime-based *caipirinha* cocktails.

One surprise is that the *caipirinha* can be served as early as mid-morning, as I've discovered at a number of Brazilian homes I've visited. And this alcohol is 45 per cent proof! The Brazilian sips cocktails at the same speed that ice melts – very slowly. Two or three cocktails will last them a whole evening.

ESSENTIAL FLAVOURS

CARNE SECA
Literally translates as 'dried meat' and describes varying cuts of beef that are salted, cured then rehydrated to make *feijoada*.

CORIANDER (CILANTRO)
In the northeastern region of Brazil, Bahia, fresh coriander leaves are a common garnish for seafood and poultry dishes.

DRIED SHRIMP
These tiny sun-dried shrimps add depth of flavour to Bahian dishes such as *xinxim de galinha*. They are finely blended to a powder and sometimes soaked first.

LIME
Regularly used in marinades for meat and fish or squeezed over seafood dishes. Lime is the key ingredient in the ubiquitous *caipirinha* cocktail.

MALAGUETA CHILLIES
An extremely hot chilli that is a popular addition to many Brazilian dishes. You can substitute with other hot chillies such as birdseye or jalapeño.

PLANTAIN
From the banana family, plantains are larger, firmer and lower in sugar content than regular bananas. They're used green (and therefore starchy) or ripe (and therefore sweet). When green they can be sliced diagonally and fried to make dense but delicious chips.

Another popular Brazilian export is the barbecue called *churrasco*. It originated in the south of Brazil where the *gauchos,* or cowboys, used a cut of meat from the top of the beef rump (in Brazil it's called the *picanha*), rolled it in rock salt and sometimes garlic, and cooked it rotisserie-style over charcoal on long skewers. The fat on the meat bastes it and keeps the meat moist and delicious. *Churrasco* restaurants are becoming increasingly popular, where long skewers of varied meats are ferried from charcoal barbecue grills straight to the table.

To finish meals, tropical fruit is abundant and eaten across Brazil but sweets are also very popular - and very sweet! Some are flavoured with fruits such as pineapple or with coconut - like *quindim*, which is a deliciously dense coconut custard.

An easy and delicious dish of chicken and prawns braised in coconut milk. Dried shrimp, garlic, ginger and crushed cashews add extra crunch and flavour. This is a great dish for a quick weeknight meal and also a fabulous main course. Seek out the red palm fruit oil that adds a beautiful colour as well as texture. As part of a Brazilian feast you could kick off with the adored *caipirinha* cocktails made with *cachaça* or sugar cane spirit, and finish with the luscious dessert *quindim* on page 43.

XINXIM DE GALINHA

from Regina Kyztia

Marinate the chicken in the lime juice, garlic, ginger and salt for 30 minutes.

Sauté the onion in the olive oil then stir in the marinated chicken. Add the tomato and palm-fruit oil and cook for about 10 minutes, then add the ground shrimp and coconut milk and simmer gently for another 10 minutes. Add the coriander, cashews or peanuts and prawns, cover with a lid and continue to simmer for another 5–10 minutes, until the prawns are cooked through. Stir in the chilli if using, add a little black pepper and taste for salt. Serve with rice and salad.

SERVES 4

1 kg (2 lb 3 oz) chicken thigh fillets, diced
juice of ½ lime
1 teaspoon crushed garlic
1 teaspoon grated ginger
salt
1 medium onion, finely chopped
1 tablespoon olive oil
200 g (7 oz) tinned diced tomatoes
1 tablespoon red palm-fruit oil

50 g (1¾ oz) dried shrimp, finely ground in a blender
125 ml (4 fl oz/½ cup) coconut milk
½ bunch coriander (cilantro), leaves picked
2 tablespoons crushed cashews or peanuts
200 g (7 oz) shelled green prawns (shrimp)
chopped chillies (optional)
black pepper

This national dish is made from various kinds of beef and pork, which are slow-cooked with black beans then served with crunchy *farofa*. The smoked and cured meats are available from Spanish, Portuguese and South American delis. When the *feijoada* is nearly ready, be careful not to use a fork or spoon (or in fact any metal utensil) in the dish. This is said to spoil the flavour and turn the dish sour.

FEIJOADA

from Edna Barzel

Place the beans, all the meat, chillies, bay leaves and half the garlic in a medium-sized pot (or pressure cooker) and season with salt. Add enough water to just cover. Bring to the boil then simmer, covered with a lid, for about 2 hours.

Sauté the onion and remaining garlic in olive oil in a separate frying pan. Once softened, add to the *feijoada*. Cook for another 15 minutes.

To make the *farofa*, melt the butter in a large frying pan and add the onion and bacon. Cook until the onion is soft, then add the cassava flour a little at a time until incorporated. Taste and season with salt and pepper. Transfer to a serving bowl and garnish with the parsley and spring onion.

Serve the *feijoada* with sliced orange or pineapple and the *farofa* on the side.

SERVES 4-6

500 g (1 lb 2 oz) black turtle beans, rinsed
500 g (1 lb 2 oz) *chouriço* sausage, diced
750 g (1 lb 11 oz) smoked beef ribs, divided into pieces thick piece of bacon or speck (about 250 g/9 oz), diced
400 g (14 oz) smoked pork loin, diced
500 g (1 lb 2 oz) *carne seca* (dried beef), diced and soaked in cold water for a few hours
small red chillies to taste
2 bay leaves
4 garlic cloves, finely chopped
salt

1 onion, finely chopped
olive oil
sliced orange or pineapple to serve

FAROFA

2 tablespoons butter
1 onion, diced
250 g (9 oz) bacon, diced
500 g (1 lb 2 oz) toasted cassava (manioc) flour
salt and pepper
3 flat-leaf (Italian) parsley sprigs, chopped
3 spring onions (scallions), chopped

'To compliment the chef say
"Que comida deliciosa!"
(What delicious food!)'

A marvellous seafood stew, with the fresh sexy flavour of lime and coriander and the mellow taste of red palm fruit oil, it is a Brazilian favourite. The aroma of this cooking at the little stalls along Brazil's famous beaches makes you hungry. You can use any fish or seafood for this quick-cook masterpiece.

This is luscious - dialled up to 11 - of course when you use 12 egg yolks you expect magic and this sweet, dense baked custard flavoured with coconut always delivers. Make it in advance for your Brazilian dinner party and watch your guests swoon.

MOQUECA DE PEIXE

from Patricia Nunes

Halve the fish fillets or cutlets and marinate in the lime juice with half the garlic for at least 30 minutes. If using prawns, marinate them whole.

In a large saucepan, sauté the remaining garlic, onion, ginger, chilli, capsicum and tomato in olive oil until a sauce is formed. Taste and add salt and pepper. Add the stock and fish and simmer gently until cooked. If using a combination of fish and prawns, add the prawns later as they cook in less time. Taste again for seasoning and stir through the chopped coriander. Place in a serving dish and squeeze over some extra lime juice. Sprinkle with the spring onions and extra coriander leaves and drizzle over the palm-fruit oil, if using. Serve with rice.

SERVES 4-6

1 kg (2 lb 3 oz) thick, firm, white fish fillets or cutlets or 1 kg (2 lb 3 oz) shelled green prawns (shrimp), or a mixture of both
juice of 2 limes, plus extra to serve
2 garlic cloves, chopped
1 onion, sliced
1 tablespoon grated ginger
5 long red chillies, chopped
1 red capsicum (bell pepper), sliced
5 tomatoes, chopped

olive oil
salt and pepper
250 ml (8½ fl oz/1 cup) fish or vegetable stock
1 bunch coriander (cilantro), chopped (reserve some leaves to garnish)
spring onions (scallions), finely sliced, to garnish
120 ml (4 fl oz) red palm-fruit oil (optional)

QUINDIM

from Doralice Silva

Preheat the oven to 180°C (350°F/Gas 4). Combine the ingredients other than the glucose syrup in a bowl and mix well.

Spread a thin layer of glucose syrup in the bottom of eight 250 ml (8½ fl oz/1 cup) individual baking moulds. Add the custard to three-quarters full. Bake the custards in a water bath for around 20 minutes.

Make sure they are cool before turning out. Serve cold.

SERVES 8

12 egg yolks
440 g (15½ oz/2 cups) sugar
250 ml (8½ fl oz/1 cup) water
100 g (3½ oz) shredded coconut

2 tablespoons butter, melted
1 teaspoon vanilla essence
glucose syrup

'Always cook with love and passion and everything will taste beautiful.'

Walk into a Chinese kitchen and you enter a realm of incredible skill. Each part of the kitchen is humming as pastry is made and rolled, dim sum stuffed, rice-flour sheets steamed and folded into *cheong fan*, vegetables chopped with cleavers at incredible speed and little golden pies baked. All around you deep-frying vats bubble, enormous bamboo steamers hiss and a steady stream of waiters and trolleys moves seamlessly in and out of the action. Amongst this the roaring flames under the row of woks sound like an express train. It's intense and fun and leaves you full of admiration for the chefs.

Chinese cuisine is, after all, one of the greatest in the world - complex, ancient and incredibly diverse. It varies throughout China's vast regions from exquisitely refined to deliciously simple and rustic.

As more people from all over China have moved to other countries, the Chinese restaurant scene in our major cities has really diversified, with eateries now specialising in the spicier Sichuan and Shanghai cuisines, the lighter flavoursome Chiu Chow and the robust hearty food of northern China. We're spoiled for choice with places to eat yum cha, the delicious series of steamed and fried snacks taken with tea. This tradition originated in the teahouses of Guangzhou and has spread throughout the world. There are numerous dim sum makers and dumpling houses, tea specialists and tofu makers. Major supermarkets now have most of the ingredients you need for a good stir-fry and many of us probably whip one up in our woks at least once a week.

We've also become familiar with the communal style of eating that is very popular throughout China. Although some remote communities in China still segregate men and women when eating, most Chinese enjoy a shared meal, especially a popular communal dish such as steamboat. With chopsticks and a little wire basket, diners add shaved meats (such as lamb), sliced vegetables and mushrooms, and seafood or poultry to a bubbling pot of stock, which cooks their choice of ingredients in front of them. The waft of fragrant steam as the lid of the steamboat is lifted at the table and the careful arrangement of the ingredients adds to the 'five senses experience', which is central to Chinese culture - eating with the eyes, smelling delicious aromas, and getting the taste buds ready for the tastes and textures to come.

To finish meals, many Chinese people will simply have tea. The hankering for sweets to round out a meal is very much a Western thing. In Shanghai, green tea finishes a meal; in the north it is jasmine tea; while in the south, oolong tea is preferred. Many older Chinese like the smoky taste of *bo lei* tea, which they believe helps to counter the fattiness of food and aids digestion.

KITCHEN TOOLS

BAMBOO STEAMER
Essential for steaming dim sum, vegetables and fish. Food is placed on a plate or large leaf in the steamer, which sits above a wok or saucepan of simmering water.

CHAN
A versatile tool used to flip and toss ingredients when stir-frying. It is also used to measure sauces and remove cooked food from the wok to a serving plate.

CLEAVER
Extremely useful for chopping through bones when cutting a chicken or duck into portions, and good for chopping vegetables. The flat side easily cracks open garlic cloves ready for mincing.

WOK
Used extensively for stir-fries, steaming and deep-frying. To season a new wok place it over a high heat and add a handful of salt, then scrub it with a brush and wash out the pan. Heat and repeat twice more, then add a teaspoon of oil, wipe the wok thoroughly and store.

ESSENTIAL FLAVOURS

FIVE-SPICE POWDER
A delightful, aromatic spice blend of star anise, Sichuan pepper, cinnamon, cloves and fennel seeds.

OYSTER SAUCE
A rich, thick, dark brown sauce with a pleasant saltiness that is added to marinades or to finish steamed green vegetables.

RICE WINE
Also known as Shaoxing cooking wine, this is like a medium-sweet sherry. It is made from fermenting steamed glutinous (sticky) rice and is fabulous for marinades and sauces.

SESAME OIL
With a rich, nutty flavour, this oil is extracted from toasted sesame seeds and is used in sauces, stir-fries and marinades.

SOY SAUCE
Made from soybeans that are fermented with roasted grain, water and salt. Light soy sauce is pleasantly salty and used in stir-fries, marinades and as a dipping sauce. Dark soy sauce has been left to ferment further, which develops the flavour and intensity but reduces the saltiness. It is used where a thicker sauce is needed, such as in braised dishes (especially with dark meats like beef) and heartier, spicy stir-fries. It also adds a rich caramel colour to food.

Here are the secrets to a tasty, healthy, tender beef stir-fry: buy good-quality beef, seek out vegies of many colours and have all the ingredients ready to cook before you fire up the wok. This is an easy and very popular recipe!

BEEF STIR-FRY

from Anthony Lui

Trim the beef and slice it thinly across the grain. Make a thin paste with the potato starch, 100 ml (3½ fl oz) of the water, ⅔ teaspoon of salt and the peanut oil. Add the beef, stir well to coat and set aside for 30 minutes.

Heat the remaining water in a wok until boiling. Add ½ teaspoon of salt and the baby corn and cook for 30 seconds. Add the mushrooms, snow peas and squash and cook for a further 30 seconds. Drain the blanched vegetables in a colander.

Heat the deep-frying oil in the wok until the surface is shimmering. Add the beef and fry until it just changes colour. Strain out the beef and empty the wok of oil, leaving 1 tablespoon.

Reheat the wok over a high flame and add the garlic, capsicum and beef. Stir-fry for 30 seconds then add the blanched vegetables, oyster sauce, sugar, ½ teaspoon of salt and the extra potato starch. Toss well. Finish with the rice wine and sesame oil for aroma and gloss. Serve immediately.

SERVES 2-4

400 g (14 oz) beef eye fillet	60 g (2 oz) snow peas, trimmed
1½ tablespoons potato starch, plus ½ teaspoon extra	4 yellow squash, sliced
750 ml (25½ fl oz/3 cups) water salt	1-1.25 litres oil (34-42 fl oz/ 4-5 cups) for deep-frying
1½ tablespoons peanut oil	1 garlic clove, chopped
6 fresh baby corn, halved diagonally	½ red capsicum (bell pepper), diced
4 fresh shiitake mushrooms, sliced	1 tablespoon oyster sauce
	1 teaspoon sugar
	1 tablespoon rice wine
	1 teaspoon sesame oil

'Toothpicks are frequently used between courses as it is believed that the tastes of one course should not be allowed to mar one's enjoyment of the next course.'

The secret to making this eggplant meltingly tender is to gradually add the water as the eggplant is cooking. The result is delicious and I now know why my friend Chris missed this dish so much when he first moved to Australia.

SHANGHAI-STYLE STIR-FRIED EGGPLANT

from Chris Yan

Cut or snap the eggplants into 5 cm (2 in) pieces. Heat the oil in a wok until shimmering. Add the chilli and garlic and cook for 20–30 seconds. Remove the chilli and reserve.

Add the eggplant and gently stir-fry. When the eggplant has soaked up all of the oil, add 1 tablespoon of the water. Keep adding water a tablespoon at a time until the eggplant is soft and you have used around half of the water.

Stir in the dark soy sauce and sugar then add the remaining water. Cover with a lid and cook for 1 minute. Remove the lid; the liquid should be absorbed. Return the chilli to the wok, toss for 30 seconds and serve.

SERVES 4 AS A SIDE DISH

500 g (1 lb 2 oz) Japanese eggplants (aubergines)
100 ml (3½ fl oz) oil
1 long red chilli, roughly cut into chunks

2 garlic cloves, bruised
200 ml (7 fl oz) water
3 tablespoons dark soy sauce
1 tablespoon sugar

I have wanted this recipe for so long that I was delighted when my friend Ying, a legendary restaurateur, graciously shared it. It makes more five-spice mix than you need but you can store the rest in an airtight container for another day.

'To thank someone for pouring you tea, tap your index and middle fingers twice on the table near the cup.'

SALT AND PEPPER SQUID

from Ying Tam

Combine the ingredients for the five-spice mix and set aside.

Clean the squid by pulling the tentacles from the body. Wash out the tube and remove the clear 'backbone'. Peel off the skin if desired. Cut the tentacles from the head and discard the head. Cut the tube into triangles, which helps the squid to curl during cooking.

In a bowl, mix the self-raising flour with 1 tablespoon of vegetable oil and a little water to make a paste. Add the squid pieces and tentacles and coat well. Sprinkle and toss with enough cornflour until the pieces are dry.

Heat enough vegetable oil in a wok for deep-frying. Add the squid in batches and cook until golden and crisp. Remove with a wire basket or slotted spoon. When all the squid is cooked, drain most of the oil from the wok.

Add the spring onions, garlic and chilli to the wok. Stir-fry for 30 seconds until aromatic. Return the squid to the wok, add 2–3 teaspoons of five-spice mix and toss well. Add the rice wine, toss and serve immediately.

SERVES 4

SQUID
500 g (1 lb 2 oz) fresh whole squid
2 tablespoons self-raising flour
vegetable oil
cornflour (cornstarch)
4 spring onions (scallions), chopped
2 garlic cloves, chopped
1 red chilli, chopped
½ tablespoon rice wine

FIVE-SPICE MIX
1 tablespoon ground ginger
1 tablespoon celery powder
1 tablespoon chicken stock powder
1 tablespoon salt
1 teaspoon five-spice powder

This is the lovely, sticky, red-coated pork you see in Chinese barbecue restaurants – it smells divine as it's cooking and is very easy and yummy. *Char siu* sauce is made from hoisin, rice wine, honey and sugar. It can be bought at most supermarkets or Asian grocery stores.

CHAR SIU PORK

from Jacky Mai

Combine the *char siu* sauce, spring onion, five-spice powder and oil in a large bowl. Add the pork fillets and marinate for at least 30 minutes or for up to 2 hours.

Preheat the oven to 200°C (400°F/Gas 6). Line the base of a baking dish with baking paper. Remove the pork fillets from the marinade and lay in the dish. Cook for about 40 minutes, basting occasionally and turning over halfway through the cooking time, until cooked through. Remove from the oven and brush with the honey while still warm. Cover with foil and rest for 5 minutes before slicing.

SERVES 2-4

⅓ cup *char siu* sauce
2 spring onions (scallions), chopped
1 teaspoon five-spice powder
1 tablespoon oil
450 g (1 lb) pork fillets, trimmed
1 tablespoon honey

'To praise a beautiful dish say "*Ho sek!*" ("Delicious!" in Cantonese).'

This is always on the menu at Frank Shek's restaurant China Doll, yet it is easy enough to make at home – and it's incredibly healthy! The recipe includes making a simple black-bean paste (briefly frying preserved black beans with garlic), although you may wish to use ready-made black-bean paste instead. Both preserved black beans and black-bean paste can be bought at Asian grocery stores or large supermarkets. Mushroom soy sauce is a type of dark soy flavoured with straw mushrooms.

WHOLE SNAPPER STEAMED WITH BLACK BEANS AND LEMON

from Frank Shek

Heat the oil in a wok or frying pan and fry the garlic for 2–3 minutes until it just begins to brown. Add the black beans and stir-fry for another 2 minutes. Remove from the heat and allow to cool. Reserve 1 heaped tablespoon of this black-bean paste for the fish, and store the rest in a sterilised jar in the refrigerator for up to 3 months. (You can also use the paste in stir-fries, marinades and braises.)

Rinse the fish and pat dry with paper towel. Lay on a chopping board and use a sharp knife to cut slashes in the flesh where it is thickest – cut them about 3 cm (1¼ in) apart crossways as well as lengthways. Turn the fish and do the same on the other side. Season inside and out with sea salt.

Place onto a large plate. Spread with the black-bean paste and arrange the lemon slices over the top. Place the plate into a large bamboo steamer over a wok of simmering water. Cover with a lid and steam for about 12 minutes.

Remove from the steamer and top with the chilli, spring onion and coriander. Drizzle with the mushroom soy sauce and a squeeze of lemon. Heat the peanut oil in a small frying pan until smoking and pour over the fish. This will sizzle the herbs, releasing their aroma. Serve with steamed jasmine rice.

SERVES 2

2½ tablespoons vegetable oil
50 g (1¾ oz) garlic cloves, finely chopped
100 g (3½ oz) Chinese preserved black beans, rinsed and drained
700 g (1 lb 9 oz) whole snapper (porgy), cleaned and scaled
sea salt
1 lemon, sliced, plus extra lemon to squeeze

1 long red chilli, sliced into strips
3 spring onions (scallions), thinly sliced on the diagonal
small handful of coriander (cilantro) leaves
1 tablespoon mushroom soy sauce
1 tablespoon peanut oil

This creamy mango pudding is so yummy that one is never enough. How do I know? When we filmed this recipe I managed to sample three and amazed my friend Rosetta. I'd always wondered how this yumcha trolley favourite was made and now whip them up at home. A great end to a Chinese banquet.

MANGO PUDDING

from Rosetta Lee

Stir the gelatine and sugar into the boiling water until thick and syrupy. Pour into a bowl. Stir in the ice-cream, evaporated milk, crushed ice and diced mango. Ladle into serving bowls or glasses and refrigerate for about 2 hours until set.

SERVES 6-8

1½ tablespoons powdered gelatine	1 litre (34 fl oz/4 cups) mango ice-cream, softened
165 g (6 oz/¾ cup) caster sugar	75 ml (2½ fl oz) evaporated milk
250 ml (8½ fl oz/1 cup) boiling water	1 cup crushed ice
	1 large mango, flesh diced

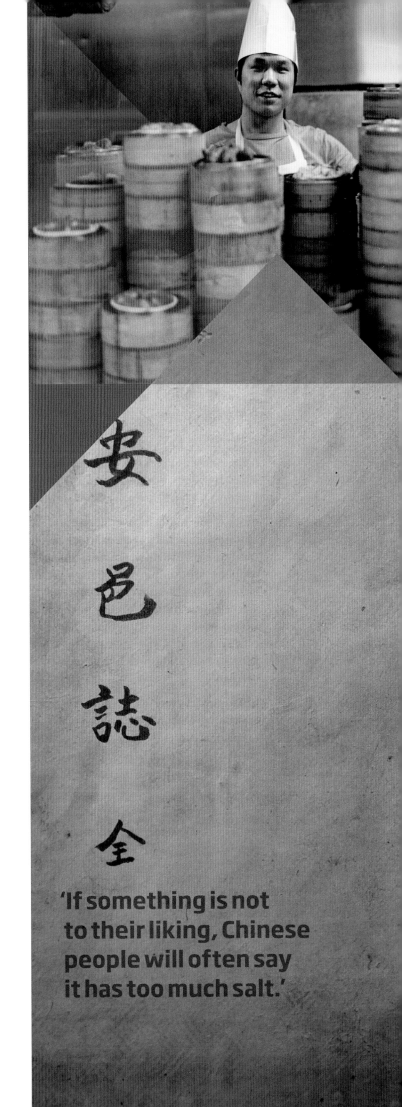

安邑誌全

'If something is not to their liking, Chinese people will often say it has too much salt.'

Ask Croatian people about the food they grew up with and their eyes grow moist remembering spit roasts and fish cooked perfectly over charcoal, intensely perfumed summer fruit and luscious cakes, and glorious wines and golden evenings. Their descriptions of this wonderful food make you want to go there ... But even in your own backyard you can summon up the aromas and flavours of Croatia.

The best addition to backyard Croatian cooking is a bell-shaped, metal cooking pot called a *peka*. It's like a barbecue but upside down. The food is placed in a large metal dish with the *peka* placed over the top. Red-hot coals are then heaped onto the *peka* so the food steams slowly in its own juices. Anything on the bone – like pork or turkey – tastes absolutely wonderful, especially when cooked with lashings of garlic and paprika, two of the favourite flavourings of Croatia.

Garlic and paprika star in the beloved smallgoods, which are the start to many Croatian meals. They also make the *sarma* (cabbage rolls) of central Croatia come alive and add flavour to lovely rich sauces and many stews.

It's no wonder the food is good when you see where Croatia lies on a map – right in the centre of Europe and spread along the beautiful Dalmatian Coast. Dotted near the coast are many islands, where the food is heavily influenced by the Mediterranean and dishes like risotto and polenta have been adapted to suit Croatian palates. For instance an Italian-inspired seafood stew called a *brodet* is traditionally served over soft polenta; and a rich, black risotto is made using squid ink. Almost every Croatian we met who had grown up by the sea told us they started fishing almost before they could walk, which is impressive. How they cook their catch is even more so. Seafood is basically a way of life there and even when simply grilled the fish is incredibly delicious.

It's rare to eat by yourself in Croatia – everything is shared. In the spring, whole lambs or pigs are cooked on the spit and everyone gathers for the feast. The smell of roasting meat, often stuffed with garlic and fresh herbs like rosemary, creates a mouth-watering aroma. Then there are the sweets – all throughout Croatia these are luscious, bountiful and beautiful.

My friend Mira makes a whole range of Croatian sweets and would never think of baking just one type of biscuit at a time. Her cakes, dumplings and tortes are filled with seasonal fruits like plums, apricots and apples and her biscuits are bursting with poppy seeds and walnuts. She'll often whip up *palacinke* pancakes too – just in case you have a little more room ... As one inventive Croatian friend put it, you have your stomach and then you have your 'sweets stomach' – that one can always try just one more delicious thing!

SMALLGOODS ESSENTIAL FLAVOURS

Croatians love smallgoods and have created many of their own special varieties. These include *kulen*, a spicy pure pork and garlic sausage in a natural casing made from pig's appendix; *suha slanina*, a type of speck that is used in soups and cabbage rolls; *csabai*, a sausage that is also found in Hungary and is popular on its own or layered with potato to make the dish *rakott krumpli*; *suha koljenica*, smoked hock used in soups, with cabbages or cooked with dried beans; and *čevapčiči*, a skinless sausage cooked over charcoal.

AJVAR
A relish made from grilled red capsicum (bell pepper), eggplant (aubergine), garlic and olive oil. Available in hot and mild variations, it is often served with grilled and roasted meat and *čevapčiči*.

CABBAGE
Eaten raw and finely shredded dressed with a simple vinaigrette in the famous Croatian coleslaw which is a popular accompaniment to grilled meats. Also used as shredded preserved leaves with a distinct sour taste (sauerkraut) and as pickled whole leaves for making cabbage rolls.

GARLIC
Used liberally in many Croatian dishes, garlic adds flavour to everything from soups to homemade sausages. One passionate Croatian cook says it's hard to imagine a single household in all Croatia that doesn't have a large supply of garlic.

PAPRIKA
Available in sweet and hot versions and most commonly used in the inland part of Croatia, close to the Hungarian border.

PROVDL
A beautiful, smooth Croatian spread made from small native plums. *Provdl* is favoured for baking as it tends to keep its shape rather than spreading while cooking.

This is the classic, spectacular seafood stew from the Dalmatian Coast. I was amazed to see Ino preparing the eel by running his hand down the length of it to break any small bones. If you're buying eel for the first time, get your fishmonger to show you how this is done - if you can find one that stocks eel! For the recipe you need to use at least three different kinds of fish and some shellfish - white-fleshed reef and rock fish are good choices. Ideally one fish will be for flavour, one for its flesh and one to boost the thickness of the stew. Scampi are great for flavour or you can use Balmain bugs or crabs instead. Serve with soft polenta.

BRODET

Seafood Stew

from Ino Kuvacic

Marinate the fish in the oil, lemon juice, a couple of tablespoons of the minced garlic and most of the parsley (reserve a little for garnish) for a few hours.

Heat some more oil in a large, heavy-based saucepan or claypot and sauté the remaining garlic, adding the onion after a few seconds. When the onion is lightly coloured, add the chopped tomato and cook for 1 minute. Add the wine and cook for about 20 minutes, until it loses its acidity.

Season each piece of the marinated fish with salt and pepper, making sure you get each piece. Add to the pan and stir well, then add the fish stock or water to just cover the fish. Bring to the boil over high heat then continue cooking rapidly for 20 minutes. Don't stir but carefully shake the pan instead to avoid breaking up the fish. Add the mussels, scampi (or Balmain bugs or crabs) and cherry tomatoes in the last 5 minutes.

Serve the stew with soft polenta. Garnish with parsley.

SERVES 6

1.5 kg (3 lb 4 oz) fish such as eel, rockling, coral trout or rock flathead, cleaned and scaled, heads and tails removed, cut into cutlets	1 large onion, finely chopped
	½ cup finely chopped tomatoes
	100 ml (3½ fl oz) white wine
	salt and pepper
100 ml (3½ fl oz) extra-virgin olive oil, plus extra for frying	500 ml (17 fl oz) fish stock or water
juice of ½ lemon	12 mussels, cleaned and de-bearded
20 garlic cloves, minced	6 scampi, Balmain bugs or crabs
½ bunch flat-leaf (Italian) parsley, chopped	12 cherry tomatoes

'You'll never find a single home in Croatia without garlic – it's unthinkable!'

A delicious recipe that is bursting with flavour. It is best served in the traditional Croatian way with lashings of creamy mashed potato. You can prepare the meat stock in advance (dried pork ribs are available from European delis). Note that whole pickled cabbage leaves come in jars from European delis and some butchers, and to be really authentic seek out a tin of Vegeta seasoning to use instead of vegetable stock cubes.

SARMA

Cabbage Rolls

from Branka Roncevic

Place the stock ingredients in a large pot. Cover with water, bring to the boil and simmer for 1 hour. Strain and cool before using, skimming the fat from the surface if necessary.

To make the rolls, heat the oil in a frying pan and fry the shallots, garlic and speck for a few minutes, then stir in the paprika. Remove from the heat and leave to cool. Combine with the minced meat, stock cube, mustard powder and pepper. Stir in the rice, egg and parsley. Mix well with your hands.

Place the cabbage leaves on a board and add 3 tablespoons of the mixture to each one. Shape the stuffing into a sausage and roll up inside the leaves, tucking the ends of the leaves back into the rolls.

To cook the rolls, lay the sauerkraut over the base of a large pot. Add the rolls, tucking the speck pieces in between. There will be 2–3 layers in the pot. Pour over the cooled stock and gently bring to the boil. Simmer for 1½ hours.

Heat the vegetable oil in a frying pan and add the garlic, shallots, mustard powder, flour, stock cubes and paprika. Stir to a thick paste then add a small amount of stock from the simmering rolls to make a smooth sauce. Pour over the rolls and stir through. Simmer the rolls for a further 30 minutes.

Serve with mashed potato.

SERVES 8–10

STOCK

500 g (1 lb 2 oz) chicken wings
250 g (9 oz) beef oxtail
1 piece of dried pork rib
2 celery stalks, roughly chopped
2 carrots, chopped
1 vegetable stock cube
salt and pepper

ROLLS

125 ml (4 fl oz/½ cup) vegetable oil
8 shallots, diced
3 garlic cloves, crushed
250 g (9 oz) speck, finely chopped
2 tablespoons sweet paprika
500 g (1 lb 2 oz) minced (ground) beef topside
500 g (1 lb 2 oz) minced (ground) pork neck
1 vegetable stock cube, crumbled

1 teaspoon mustard powder
1 teaspoon freshly ground black pepper
250 g (9 oz) arborio rice
2 eggs, beaten
½ cup chopped flat-leaf (Italian) parsley
20 pickled cabbage leaves (large leaves can be cut in half to make 2 leaves)

TO COOK

200 g (7 oz) sauerkraut
500 g (1 lb 2 oz) speck, cut into 4 cm (2 in) pieces
3 tablespoons vegetable oil
2 garlic cloves, crushed
2 shallots, diced
2 teaspoons mustard powder
2 tablespoons plain (all-purpose) flour
1–2 vegetable stock cubes
1 tablespoon sweet paprika

A dish that celebrates this delicious vegetable, which is only available fresh for a limited time in spring each year. My friend Dennis is a masterful chef and this recipe is a true favourite. It works well either as a main dish or an accompaniment.

A lovely, simple way of cooking lamb on a spit-roast barbecue grill. Tonci's tip on ageing the meat first is brilliant - it gives a richer, more flavoursome result. Afterwards, take the meat out of the fridge half an hour before cooking so it doesn't suddenly leap from the cold of the fridge to the extreme heat of the barbie.

PUNJENI ARTICHOKE

Stuffed Artichokes

from Dennis Valcich

Remove any old and loose leaves from the artichokes. With a sharp knife, cut off the stalks, reserving them for later. Slice about 2 cm (¾ in) off the top of each artichoke. Remove the choke by scooping it out with a teaspoon.

Make the stuffing by mixing the breadcrumbs, garlic, parsley and pepper. Gently open the leaves of each artichoke with your thumbs and add stuffing between the leaves.

Place the artichokes upright in the centre of a large saucepan. Add the potatoes around the artichokes. Scatter the peas, broad beans and artichoke stalks on top and sprinkle with any remaining stuffing. Season with salt and pepper. Drizzle with the olive oil and add enough water to cover the artichokes. Bring to the boil then reduce the heat to low and cook uncovered for about 1 hour. Don't stir; just shake the pan occasionally.

Serve the artichokes warm with crusty bread.

SERVES 2 AS MAIN COURSE, 4-5 AS AN ACCOMPANIMENT

5 large, tender globe artichokes	100 g (3½ oz) freshly shelled peas
1 cup fresh breadcrumbs	
3 garlic cloves, finely chopped	100 g (3½ oz) freshly shelled broad beans
½ tablespoon chopped flat-leaf (Italian) parsley	
pepper	salt
500 g (1 lb 2 oz) baby new potatoes	250 ml (8½ fl oz/1 cup) olive oil

BARBECUED RACK OF LAMB

from Tonci Farac

Place the lamb on a wire rack and refrigerate uncovered for a couple of days to age the meat.

Make shallow cuts all over the outer layer of fat and stud with rosemary sprigs, leaving some of the leaves exposed. Rub liberally with sea salt.

Spit-roast over high heat to seal. Reduce the heat and continue to cook to your liking. Slice into cutlets and serve with roasted vegetables.

SERVES 3-4

1 lamb rack with outer layer of fat intact (be sure the butcher doesn't remove it)
rosemary sprigs, broken into short pieces
sea salt

Delicious melting biscuits from the queen of sweets, my friend Mira. Make sure you find *provdl*, which is favoured for baking as it tends to keep its shape rather than spreading while cooking - it comes in jars and is found in European delis and some supermarkets.

PLUM JAM BISCUITS

from Mira Valcich

Mix the butter, cream, vanilla sugar and baking powder. Slowly add the flour to make a soft, stretchy dough. Knead for 5 minutes. Roll the dough out thinly and cut into 15 cm (6 in) triangles with a pizza cutter or sharp knife. Place a triangle in front of you with a wide edge facing you. Add 1 teaspoon of jam at the wide edge and roll the triangle up over the jam. Form the roll into a U shape. Repeat with the rest of the triangles.

Bake the biscuits at 200°C (400°F/Gas 6) until golden. Roll in caster sugar while still warm.

MAKES 24 BISCUITS

250 g (9 oz) unsalted butter, softened	1½ teaspoons baking powder
300 ml (10 fl oz) cream	400 g (14 oz/2⅔ cups) plain (all-purpose) flour
2 tablespoons vanilla sugar	*provdl* plum jam
	caster sugar

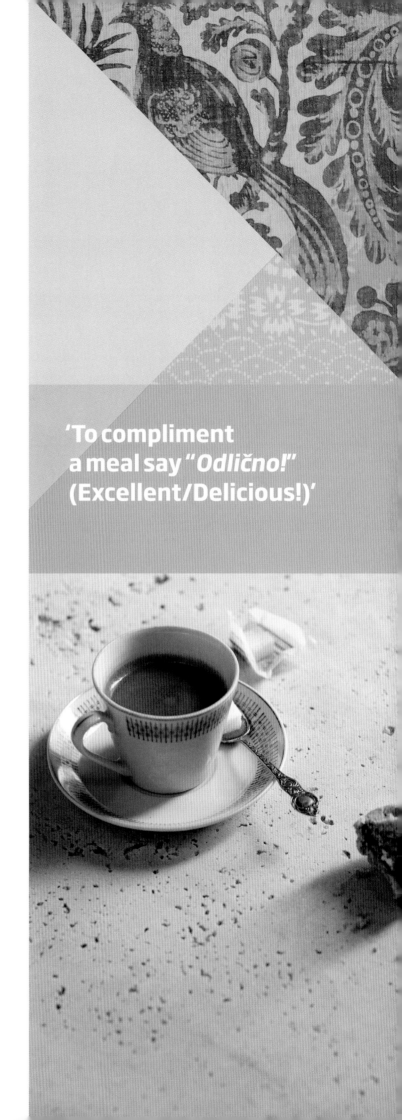

'To compliment a meal say "*Odlično!*" (Excellent/Delicious!)'

Cyprus is one of the world's most unusual islands. On it live people from Greek and Turkish backgrounds divided along a horizontal line that cuts the island in two – the top half Turkish, the bottom half Greek. Politics has kept each side separate and interestingly, both sides also feel they are separate and different from their mainland relations. The Greek Cypriots don't really identify with larger Greece – they see themselves as unique. As one friend was at pains to point out: 'We stand alone; our language has more in common with ancient Greek and we see ourselves as different.' In food, each side has recipes in common with their mainland, but some are different, given a special twist.

Across Cyprus there is actually a lot in common – both Greek and Turkish Cypriots love to cook food over a charcoal grill, and love using ingredients such as garlic and olive oil, cinnamon, caraway and coriander, as well as fresh seasonal vegetables. Another common factor is warm hospitality and sharing food with guests.

The food is fabulous. For many, Cyprus is summed up in the heady aroma of *sheftalia* on the grill. These are sausages of coarse minced pork flavoured with onion and fresh herbs, wrapped in caul fat and cooked over coals. 'There's nothing like it,' says one expatriate. 'The first thing I do off the plane ... I don't even want to get my luggage ... All I want to have is *sheftalia*.'

Another favourite taste on the island is haloumi cheese, cooked hot on a griddle so it's melting inside and browned on the outside, ready for a good squeeze of lemon. In fact, everything from *sheftalia* to haloumi, *loukaniko* (sausages made with pork, garlic, red wine and a spice called *shino*) and *bastouma* (sausages popular on the Turkish side of the island, made with beef, garlic, chilli and fenugreek) are all 'smashed with the lemon'.

Haloumi also appears in cubes and baked in bread, stirred into soup, or grated into *flaounes* – the traditional Easter cheese pastries of Greek Cypriots with a filling of mint, sultanas and loads of cheese. Families love to continue the tradition of baking *flaounes*, which links them with past generations and gives such mouth-watering results.

A dish that Cyprus and Greece have in common are rolls made of vine leaves – called dolmades in Greece, but *koupepia* in Cyprus. The rice and minced meat filling is scented with cumin, coriander and cinnamon, which add a heavenly taste and an irresistible smell as they cook.

When it comes to sweets, the Cypriots have a cake they love so much they call it the 'good thing' – *kalo prama*. It's a semolina cake drenched in syrup that is the perfect afternoon pick-me-up. Another treat is *soutzouko* – an unusual sweet that sees nuts such as almonds or walnuts threaded on a string dipped repeatedly into grape juice that has been cooked to a thick syrup. Gradually the fruity coating around the row of nuts grows until the sweet resembles a lumpy sausage. The treat traditionally helped sustain Cypriots through the winter months when fruit was scarce, and is often enjoyed with *zivania*, the strong white spirit of the island. Just like Cyprus, *soutzouko* is deliciously different.

ESSENTIAL FLAVOURS

BULGUR
Bulgur, also called burghul, resembles cracked wheat, but because it is precooked before being dried and ground to various sizes, it cooks quickly. It's essential in the shell of bulgur *kofte* or *koupes*, and is used in *pilafi*, which is like a no-stir wheat risotto.

HALOUMI
This is the cherished cheese of Cyprus, originating on the island. It's quite salty, has a squeaky texture when you bite it, and needs heat to be magic - it's great on the barbecue, baked in bread and pastries, and stirred into soup.

LOUKANIKO, BASTURMA, LOUNTZA
These smallgoods can be found at specialist Cypriot butchers. *Loukaniko* is a sausage made with pork, red wine and a berry-like spice called *shino*; *basturma* is another sausage made with beef, garlic and paprika; and *lountza* is the Cypriot version of ham - pork fillet cured with red wine and coriander seed.

TARO
Taro might seem an odd fit in Cypriot cuisine, but it is a relic since Roman times. *Kolokasi* is a deliciously comforting stew of the root cooked with pork and tomato.

TRAHANA
This is both the name of a soup, and the ingredient used to make the soup. Cracked wheat cooked with soured milk, yoghurt and lemon juice is dried in the sun and sold in packets - it resembles a grain or cereal. It is cooked with stock to make a healthy and sustaining soup.

It is said in Cyprus that you don't marry a woman who can't roll these little balls, which are also known as *koupes*. They are a popular street food in Cyprus - a deliciously textured wheat crust wrapped around a minced meat filling. While they can be a little painstaking to make, once you get the knack it's a joy. The trick is to work the bulgur to a dough-like consistency so it can be easily shaped and filled.

BULGUR KOFTE

from Ismail Tosun

Combine the bulgur, salt, pepper and paprika in a large bowl. Pour over 700 ml (23 ½ fl oz) of the boiling water and stir to combine. Cover with plastic wrap and set aside for at least 2 hours. The grains will completely absorb the water.

Meanwhile, make the filling. Heat the oil in a large saucepan over medium-high heat. Add the lamb and as it starts cooking, use a wooden spoon to break up the lumps to a fine crumble. Add a little salt to the meat, which helps draw out the moisture. Cook for around 10-15 minutes, or until all the moisture has evaporated and the lamb has started to fry and colour.

Add the onion, put a lid on the pan, reduce the heat to low and cook for a further 10 minutes, or until the onion is translucent. Stir regularly to stop the mixture sticking to the bottom of the pan.

Add the pine nuts, currants and parsley, and extra salt as well as pepper to taste. Stir well, then remove from the heat and set aside to cool.

Use your fingers to break the bulgur up until it resembles fluffy couscous. Pour over another 250 ml (8½ fl oz/1 cup) of the boiling water and mix into the bulgur with your fingers, being careful not to burn yourself. Start kneading the bulgur in the bowl while gradually adding the remaining 250 ml (8½ fl oz/1 cup) of boiling water (you may not need all the water). You need to work the bulgur for about 20 minutes – the extra water and the kneading action will stick the grains together to make a dough-like mass. But don't add so much water that the bulgur becomes soggy.

When you think the dough is ready, wet your hands and roll a golf ball-sized piece of dough into a smooth ball. Slowly push one finger through the centre to stretch the ball out to a short sausage shape, taking care not to push your finger through the other end. With the hollow sausage in one hand and a finger in the middle, push your finger down while slowly turning the sausage around to make the cavity a little wider and to press the casing out to an even thickness. Use a teaspoon to fill the hollow with the lamb mixture to three-quarters full. Moisten your hands and press the opening shut. Shape the sausage into points at each end to make a torpedo shape.

Continue making *kofte* with the remaining bulgur and lamb.

Heat enough oil for deep-frying in a large saucepan until very hot. Add the *kofte* in batches and fry until golden and crisp. Drain on paper towel. Serve with lemon wedges.

MAKES ABOUT 40 *KOFTE*

DOUGH

1 kg (2 lb 3 oz) fine bulgur
2 tablespoons salt
pinch of pepper
pinch of sweet paprika
1.2 litres (41 fl oz) boiling water

FILLING

80 ml (2½ fl oz/⅓ cup) olive oil
1 kg (2 lb 3 oz) lean minced (ground) lamb
salt

2 large onions, finely diced
2-3 tablespoons pine nuts, toasted
3 tablespoons currants, soaked in warm water for 20 minutes
1 cup chopped flat-leaf (Italian) parsley
pepper
sunflower oil for deep-frying

lemon wedges to serve

These pastries have a wonderful cheese and mint filling, with the sweet addition of sultanas making them unique. Yeast is also included in the filling, and the mixture must be mixed the day before and refrigerated overnight. It makes the texture light and fluffy. The pastry recipe includes two signature spices of the Mediterranean - mahlab (or mahlepi) and mastic, which together make the pastries smell so delicious as they cook. Mahlab is the inner kernel of a wild cherry and has a flavour that is between bitter almond and cherry, while mastic is the resin of a tree and has a refreshing taste.

FLAOUNES

Easter Cheese Pastries

from Mary Theodosi

To make the filling, combine the yeast, sugar and milk in a large bowl and dissolve the yeast into the milk. Add the cheeses, semolina, flour and eggs and mix well. Cover and refrigerate overnight.

To make the pastry, combine the yeast, sugar and 125 ml (4 fl oz/½ cup) of the milk in a bowl and dissolve the yeast into the milk. Put the flour, mastic, mahlab, salt and butter in a large bowl. Add the yeast mixture as well as the remaining 625 ml (21 fl oz/2 ½ cups) of milk and knead to form a dough, gradually adding extra milk (or flour) if needed. The pastry should be soft but not sticky. Cover with a tea towel and set aside for 1 hour to rise a little.

Stir the mint and sultanas into the cheese filling.

Put the sesame seeds in a fine sieve and rinse with water, then drain and spread out over a tea towel.

Take a quarter of the dough and roll out on a lightly floured surface to about 3 mm thick. Use a saucer about 15 cm (6 in) wide as a template to cut out rounds of pastry.

Place a round of pastry on top of the sesame seeds and press down firmly to stick the seeds to the bottom of the pastry. Add 2 tablespoons of cheese filling to the centre of the pastry. Fold in 3 sides of the circle, leaving the filling exposed in the centre. This should make a triangular-shaped pastry. Place on a tray lined with baking paper. Preheat the oven to 180°C (350°F/Gas 4) while you continue making pastries.

Brush the exposed fillings and some of the surrounding pastry with beaten egg yolk. Bake the pastries for 30 minutes or until golden.

MAKES ABOUT 30 PASTRIES

FILLING

50 g (1¾ oz) fresh yeast
    (or 25 g/1 oz) dried yeast)
½ teaspoon sugar
125 ml (4 fl oz/½ cup) milk,
    warmed
1 kg (2 lb 3 oz) kefalotyri or
    pecorino romano cheese,
    grated
250 g (9 oz) haloumi, grated
180 g (6½ oz/1 cup) fine
    semolina
150 g (5½ oz/1 cup) plain
    (all-purpose) flour
7 eggs
1 bunch mint, chopped
170 g (6¼ oz) sultanas
    (golden raisins)

PASTRY

40 g (1 ½ oz) fresh yeast
    (or 20 g/¾ oz) dried yeast)
½ teaspoon sugar
750 ml (25½ fl oz/3 cups) milk,
    warmed
1 kg (2 lb 3 oz) plain (all-purpose)
    flour
5 g (⅛ oz) mastic, ground to a
    powder
10 g (1¼ oz) mahlab (mahlepi),
    ground to a powder
pinch of salt
125 g (5 oz) unsalted butter,
    softened

250 g (9 oz) sesame seeds
2 egg yolks, lightly beaten

'On Easter Saturday we would be starving as we fasted ... We could smell the *flaounes* in the oven and we'd all want one so bad, but had to wait until midnight after church - that's when we were allowed to eat them.'

This is the classic falling-off-the-bone lamb that we all dream about. The name comes from days when Cyprus was a wilder place; when lambs and goats were sometimes stolen by *kleftis*, or robbers. The men would make ovens in the ground and seal them up with mud to cook their meat, and there would be no smoke on the horizon to give them away. Nick's pride and joy is his *fourno*, or wood-fired oven, which he uses to cook his lamb, although this can also be cooked in a conventional oven. Serve with a Greek salad.

This very simple soup has been comfort food for Cypriots for hundreds of years. It is based on trahana, which is cracked wheat cooked with soured milk, yoghurt and lemon juice. The mixture is left to dry in the sun, traditionally as a food for winter. Look out for it in Greek stores where it is sold in packets and resembles a grain or cereal (it can also be brought frozen). This recipe has egg stirred through the soup but cubes of haloumi are another option.

KLEFTIKO

Robber's Lamb

from Nick Kastrappi

If using a wood-fired oven, light it 2–3 hours earlier so the coals burn down to embers and the heat is radiant. The temperature should be around 350°C (660°F) at the start and will slowly decrease.

If using a conventional oven, preheat it to 150°C (300°F/Gas 2).

Place the lamb pieces on a large, deep tray with the potatoes and unpeeled garlic cloves. Season generously with salt and pepper, drizzle with the olive oil and lemon juice, and sprinkle with the rosemary and oregano. Toss with your hands. Add a cup of water to the tray, then cover tightly with foil. Cook for 4 hours in a wood-fired oven, or 5 hours in a conventional oven.

SERVES 6–8

2.25 kg lamb shoulder, cut through the bone into 12 or more chunks by your butcher	salt and freshly ground black pepper
1.5 kg (3 lb 4 oz) potatoes, peeled, cut in half if large	125 ml (4 fl oz/½ cup) olive oil
8–10 garlic cloves	juice of 2 lemons
	handful of rosemary leaves
	handful of oregano leaves

TRAHANA SOUP

from Jenny Nicodemou

Put the trahana in a bowl and add the water. Soak for 4–5 hours.

Pour the stock into a large saucepan and bring to the boil over medium heat. Add the trahana and its water and return to the boil, stirring constantly so the trahana doesn't clump together. Once boiling, you can stop stirring. Reduce the heat to a simmer and cook for a few minutes or until thickened. Season with salt to taste. Add the eggs and stir gently to form strands, then remove from the heat. Add cubed haloumi to the soup a few minutes before serving.

SERVES 6

350 g (14 oz) Cypriot or Greek trahana	salt
750 ml (25½ fl oz/3 cups) water	2 eggs, lightly beaten
2 litres (68 fl oz/8 cups) chicken or beef stock	200 g (7 oz) haloumi, cut into small cubes

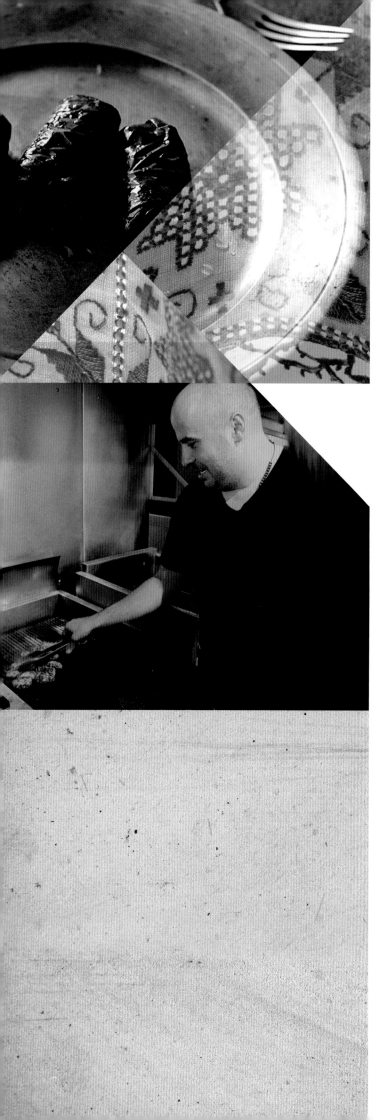

It's worth mastering these homemade sausages wrapped in caul fat – an exotic thing to serve at your next barbecue or as part of a *mezedes* spread. The caul fat cooks to a crisp coating and the meat stays beautifully tender. Chrys likes to serve his sausages with fresh pita bread that's been oiled and grilled, with extra parsley, red onion and a squeeze of lemon.

SHEFTALIA

Cypriot Sausages

from Chrys Xipolitas

The caul fat should already be washed by your butcher, but it's worth washing it again. Then, soak it in a bowl of cold water with a little vinegar added until ready to use.

Combine the pork, onion, parsley, salt and pepper in a large bowl. Use your hands to mix well.

Lay out a piece of caul fat on a work surface and scoop 1–2 tablespoons of sausage mixture towards the bottom of the fat. Fold up the bottom edge of the fat, tuck in the sides, and roll up. Trim excess fat with a sharp knife, then use this piece of fat for wrapping the next sausage. Continue making sausages until you have used all the mixture.

Heat the grill of a barbecue to medium. Place the sausages on the grill and sprinkle with a little extra salt. Turn the sausages as they brown, but don't turn them too early as the fat may stick to the grill. Remove from the grill when browned all over and serve immediately.

MAKES ABOUT 50 SAUSAGES

400 g (14 oz) caul fat	2–3 bunches flat-leaf (Italian) parsley, chopped
white vinegar	
1 kg (2 lb 3 oz) minced (ground) pork leg or neck	1 tablespoon salt, plus extra for sprinkling
2–3 red onions, finely chopped	1 tablespoon freshly ground black pepper

For this recipe Ifigenia uses fresh grape-vine leaves - and if she has pumpkin flowers in the garden, she uses the same filling to stuff those too, placing them on top of the *koupepia* to cook at the same time. If you don't have access to fresh vine leaves, then you can use leaves in brine. The recipe is fun to make with a couple of friends and is incredibly more-ish served with bread to mop up the juices.

'If I go somewhere
I don't give chocolate.
I give haloumi because
it's homemade ...
Everybody loves things
that are homemade.'

KOUPEPIA

Stuffed Fresh Vine Leaves

from Ifigenia Michael

If you are using fresh leaves, bring a pot of water to the boil. While you are waiting for it to boil, trim the stems from the leaves, wash, and stack up in a pile. When the water is boiling, turn off the heat. Drop a quarter of the leaves into the water and allow them to wilt, then lift them out of the water into a colander. Repeat with the remaining leaves.

Heat 3 tablespoons of the oil in a large saucepan over medium heat. Add the onion and cook, stirring, for 3–4 minutes or until soft. Remove from the heat.

Combine the pork, beef, fresh tomato and tomato puree, herbs, salt, spices and rice in a large bowl. Add the fried onion and mix well.

Lay a vine leaf on a work surface and place about 1 tablespoon of mixture in the centre (or more or less, depending on the size of each leaf). Fold the bottom of the leaf over the filling, then fold in the sides and roll up. Place in the bottom of a heavy-based pot. Continue making rolls and adding them to the pot in a neat layer. Once you have completed the layer, start building more layers on top.

Pour water over the rolls to almost cover them, then drizzle over the remaining 125 ml (4 fl oz/½ cup) of oil and the lemon juice. Weight the rolls down with a small plate. Cover with a lid and cook over low heat for 30–45 minutes.

Serve with an extra squeeze of lemon.

MAKES ABOUT 50 ROLLS

500 g (1 lb 2 oz) fresh unsprayed grape-vine leaves (about 50 leaves), or 500 g (1 lb 2 oz) vine leaves in brine, rinsed thoroughly
185 ml olive oil
2 onions, finely chopped
500 g (1 lb 2 oz) minced (ground) pork
500 g (1 lb 2 oz) minced (ground) beef
1–2 ripe tomatoes, finely chopped
250 ml (8½ fl oz/1 cup) tomato puree

1 bunch flat-leaf (Italian) parsley, chopped
2 tablespoons chopped mint
large pinch of salt
¼ teaspoon cinnamon
¼ teaspoon ground cumin
¼ teaspoon ground coriander
200 g (7 oz) parboiled long-grain rice, rinsed
juice of 1 lemon, plus extra to serve

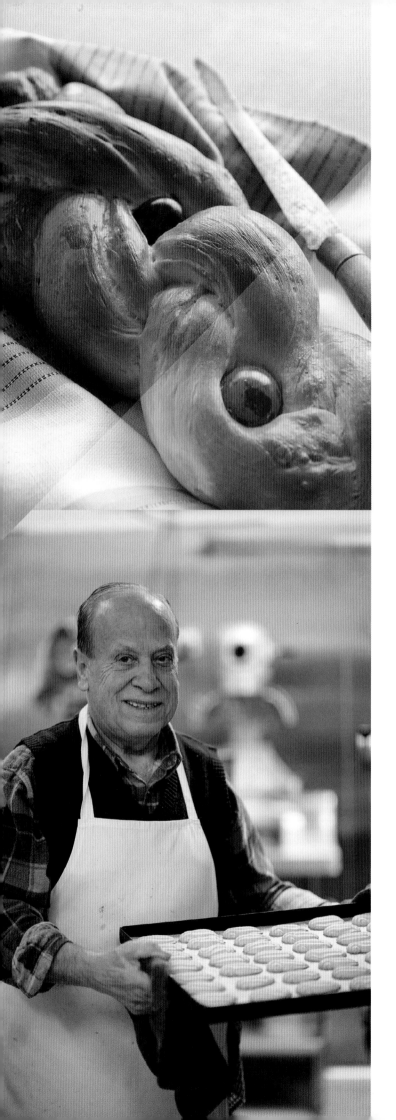

The name translates as 'good thing', so it's not surprising that this cake is adored by Cypriots. It is very sweet but perfect with coffee made Greek- or Turkish-style, and it keeps well. Baking in Cypress goes back hundreds of years with people traditionally using the village oven. Now people make cakes like this one at home at least once every couple of weeks to have something delicious for dessert or to welcome guests. It's part of Cypriot hospitality to always have something sweet to serve.

KALO PRAMA

Semolina Syrup Cake

from Kyriakos Panayi

Preheat the oven to 180°C (350°F/Gas 4) and butter a loaf tin (around 22 × 11 cm/8½ × 4½ in).

Place all the ingredients for the cake except the eggs and almonds in the bowl of an electric mixer and beat for 2 minutes on medium speed. Add the eggs and beat at high speed for 5 minutes. Scrape the mixture into the tin. Use a knife to cut a faint line down the centre of the cake lengthwise, and then crosswise as if cutting thick slices. Put an almond in the centre of each slice, which should be roughly square. (The marks will disappear in the oven but they help you put the almonds in the right places.) Bake the cake for 30 minutes, or until a skewer comes out clean.

Meanwhile, combine the syrup ingredients in a saucepan and stir over medium heat until the sugar dissolves. Bring to the boil, then remove from the heat.

When the cake is cooked, recut the slices, going through to the bottom this time. Pour the hot syrup over the cake (if it doesn't all fit in the tin, simply wait for some to be absorbed before pouring the rest on).

Serve the cake warm or at room temperature.

SERVES 12

CAKE

200 g (7 oz) fine semolina
100 g (3½ oz) caster sugar
100 g (3½ oz/⅔ cup) self-
    raising flour
100 g (3½ oz) unsalted butter,
    softened
pinch of vanilla sugar
¼ teaspoon baking powder
small pinch of mastic, ground
    to a powder

3 eggs
blanched almonds

SYRUP

400 g (14 oz) sugar
200 ml (7 fl oz) water
pinch of vanilla sugar
juice of ½ lemon

The Danes are a stylish race ... Just look at the clean, simple lines of their furniture and interiors and you get a sense of order and cleverness. It's not surprising that the same principles guide their delicious cuisine. The flavours are based on the seasons: the long cold winter and the delightfully slow summer, with its days that stretch well into the evening. Summer's growing season seems to make all produce taste delicious.

'Everything grows slowly and our soil is so rich that the taste of root vegetables is amazing,' explains chef Jesper Hansen. 'The carrots are super crispy and a deep orange colour, with a bit of sweetness and so much flavour. The celeriac, potatoes, leeks and onions are the same. I took my partner into our fields and showed him the soil and he thought I had mixed loads of rich potting mix in ... but this is how it is. His family are on the land in Dubbo and their soil is rock hard!'

Danish friends talk about the intense berry sweetness of the dessert they like to tease foreigners to try and pronounce - *rødgrød med fløde*. It's one of the beautiful taste memories of Kristine Lindbjerg, who shared her recipe with us. She spent her holidays with her grandparents in South Jutland where there is a strong cake and dessert tradition. Her summers were punctuated by picking berries with her grandmother and enjoying feasts laid out on picnic rugs. 'Nothing was processed; even breakfast was like a treat, but pure - toasted oats with brown sugar and butter,' she remembers. 'We'd start baking in November for Christmas ... so we would have at least seven types of biscuits on hand.'

To my surprise, Danish homes are often decorated in the national colours of white and red. It just shows the respect for tradition and history.

Even in sparkling modern cafes and restaurants, the past is never far away - treasured recipes that date back to the days of the Vikings are still enjoyed. *Gravet laks* or 'grave salmon' is hugely popular, getting its name from times when the fish was buried in the cold ground to cure. It was ready to eat in under a week, or could be left to ferment for longer as a food for winter when the icy waters made fishing difficult. *Gravet laks* is cured with salt, sugar, dill and fennel seeds and still stars on lunch tables and on top of the beloved *smørrebrød*.

Denmark's cold winters led to the wonderful tradition of long lunches, which see families and friends gather at noon to enjoy a series of courses. It usually starts with seafood and fish - anything from the ubiquitous herring to prawns, smoked eel and trout, salmon or fried fish. Afterwards comes a meat dish of some kind - often pork - served with a range of side dishes. Then, dessert. Heaven!

I learnt a new favourite word in the Danish world - *hyggelig*. I may be doing grave injustice to a great language, but it seems to be pronounced 'hoogley', and it means getting cosy, snuggling in, gathering people around you, and usually eating. It's charming and is *exactly* what you want to do in cold weather. 'We love lighting candles and having friends in to enjoy comfort food like slow-cooked pork or salted fish and a good red wine,' says Jesper Hansen. 'We love getting together in winter time.'

One of my realisations through spending time in Danish kitchens is that sugar is an important part of the cooking, but it's always in balance. It's in side dishes such as sugar potatoes; in *gravet laks*; and in the ever-present cucumber salad, or pickled cucumbers. Perhaps it's because the Danes grow a lot of sugar beets, so have grown accustomed to having sugar close to hand.

The words 'Nordic terroir' are very much in vogue with the rise of new young chefs who celebrate Danish produce and the traditions of the past with techniques such as drying, pickling, fermenting and smoking, plus add their own new ways of preparing food that has purity, simplicity and freshness.

ESSENTIAL FLAVOURS

BUTTER
Danish butter is renowned for its mellow flavour and soft texture that makes it perfect for spreading on bread or cooking in a range of savoury and sweet dishes. It's the absolute heart of the pastries we know as 'danishes'.

CAPERS
Capers are a classic partner for any type of fish – cured, smoked, pickled or fresh. They are also stirred into creamy sauces.

DILL
This feathery herb with its gentle aniseed flavour is used to garnish beautiful *smørrebrød* creations, and is added by the handful when curing *gravet laks*.

HERRING
This small oily fish from the cold waters of Scandinavia is a beloved ingredient, whether fried, smoked or pickled; and served with a range of sauces, in salads or on top of *smørrebrød*. It is one of the stars of the Danish *koldt bord* (cold table). Pickled or marinated herrings are available in jars.

VINEGAR
Pickling with salt or vinegar is one of the great traditions used to preserve fish and vegetables to go through winter. Vinegar is also essential in side dishes and salads such as cucumber salad.

Smørrebrød

The culinary masterpieces called *smørrebrød* are a delicious combination of Denmark's beloved dense rye bread – *rugbrød* – and a series of toppings. Served as a kind of open-faced sandwich, *smørrebrød* is always eaten with a knife and fork. The combinations of toppings are endless but could be *gravet laks*, curried herrings or roast pork or beef, along with a pretty arrangement of pickled or fresh vegetables, and a dollop of some kind of sauce such as mustard sauce.

The bread is first spread with a good layer of butter or spiced pork lard. 'We spread it so you can see the teeth marks,' says Bente Grysbaeck.

'*Smørrebrød* is all about colour and presentation,' describes baker Michael Klausen. 'The *smørrebrød* in restaurants can cost a great deal. It's a beautiful, important dish and in some places is like artwork.'

Pickled herrings are adored across Scandinavia and Jesper says this dish is a perfect introduction to the delicious fish: 'Everyone loves them - they're crunchy with a good fresh flavour.' He mixes them with crisp apple and salty capers, which are a nice contrast to the creamy mayonnaise and sour cream. Topped with chopped egg and a delicate scattering of dill, this dish is also very pretty.

Serve this as a side dish to meatballs or roast pork or duck, or as a topping on *smørrebrød*. This really is a combination of food groups - the cabbage, the sharp fresh flavour of lingonberry or cranberry juice, the white wine vinegar, and the rich duck fat. It all looks very pretty too.

CURRY-PICKLED HERRINGS

from Jesper Hansen

Heat the oil in a small frying pan over medium heat. Add the onion and a pinch of salt and sauté for 3-4 minutes, until just soft. Add the curry powder and continue to cook, stirring, for another minute. Remove from the heat and leave to cool.

Combine the herrings, mayonnaise, sour cream or crème fraîche, capers, apple and dill in a bowl. Add the onion mixture and stir to combine. Season with extra salt to taste. Serve on slices of rye bread that have been cut into quarters. Top each with a little chopped egg and extra dill.

SERVES 6-8

1 tablespoon olive oil
1 small onion, finely chopped
salt
1 tablespoon mild yellow curry powder
500 g (1 lb 2 oz) jar marinated herrings, drained, patted dry and cut into bite-sized pieces
100 ml (3½ fl oz) thick mayonnaise

100 ml (3½ fl oz) sour cream or crème fraîche
3 tablespoons capers, rinsed and finely chopped
1 small green apple, peeled, cored and finely diced
3 tablespoons finely chopped dill, plus extra to serve
1 egg, soft-boiled and chopped
sliced rye bread to serve

RØDKÅL

Sweet and Sour Red Cabbage

from Jesper Hansen

Blanch the cabbage in salted boiling water, then drain.

Combine the cabbage, lingonberry juice, vinegar and duck fat (if using) in a large saucepan. Bring to the boil, then reduce the heat and simmer for 30-40 minutes, until the cabbage is soft.

Tip the cabbage into a colander set over a bowl to catch the liquid. Once all the liquid has drained from the cabbage, return the liquid to the saucepan and cook until reduced by half. Stir in the cabbage, heating it through. Season to taste.

SERVES 6-8

1 kg (2 lb 3 oz) red cabbage, finely sliced
300 ml (10 fl oz) lingonberry juice (or cranberry juice)
300 ml (10 fl oz) white-wine vinegar
1 tablespoon duck fat (optional)
salt

'"*Hyggelig*"is often translated as "cosy", but in my family it means "what do you want to eat?"'

Every Danish mother has her secret recipe for meatballs. This one is from our friend Jesper's mum. Softened with milk and flavoured with a reduction of chicken stock and red wine, they are truly great meatballs. Serve with cucumber salad.

Cucumber salad (or pickled cucumbers) is one of the essentials of Danish cuisine - an accompaniment to roast pork, meatballs and many other dishes, and sometimes appearing on the open-faced sandwiches called smørrebrød (see page 76). Bente likes to make her salad with thin ribbons of cucumber, but you can cut the cucumber into traditional round slices if you prefer.

FRIKADELLER

Meatballs

from Jesper Hansen

Combine the stock and wine in a saucepan and bring to the boil. Cook until reduced to ½ cup, by which time the liquid should look like a rich glaze. Leave to cool.

Combine the minced meat and salt in a large bowl and knead together with your hands. Add the onion, flour and breadcrumbs and season with pepper. Knead until well combined, then add the eggs and reduced stock and wine and knead again. Gradually add the milk, kneading until it has all has been incorporated. Refrigerate the mixture for at least 1 hour.

Heat a tablespoon of oil and plenty of butter in a large frying pan over medium heat. When the butter is foamy, start adding meatballs to the pan in spoonfuls, or quenelles if preferred. (To make a quenelle, use 2 dessertspoons. Take a generous scoop of mixture on the first spoon, and use the second spoon to scoop the mixture from the first spoon onto the edge of the second spoon, shaping the mixture into a neat torpedo shape. Carefully drop the quenelle into the pan.)

Cook the meatballs until golden on one side, then flip and cook them on the other side. Spoon the oil and butter over the meatballs as they cook. Remove to a plate and keep warm while you continue cooking the meatballs in batches with more oil and butter as needed.

Serve with cucumber salad.

SERVES 8

500 ml (17 fl oz/2 cups) low-salt chicken stock	50 g (1¾ oz/⅓ cup) plain (all-purpose) flour
100 ml (3½ fl oz) red wine	100 g (3½ oz) dried breadcrumbs
1 kg (2 lb 3 oz) minced (ground) pork and veal	freshly ground black pepper
20 g (¾ oz) salt	3 eggs
1 onion, finely chopped	500 ml (17 fl oz/2 cups) milk
	olive oil
	butter

AGURKESALAT

Cucumber Salad

from Bente Grysbaeck

Slice the cucumbers into long thin ribbons using a mandolin, a peeler or a sharp knife. Place in a bowl, add the salt and mix well. Set aside for 1 hour.

Combine the remaining ingredients in a small saucepan. Heat, stirring, until the sugar has dissolved. Set aside to cool.

Rinse the cucumber and drain well. Return to the bowl and stir through the cooled dressing. Leave to stand for 1 hour before serving (or refrigerate if making in advance).

SERVES 4-6

4 Lebanese cucumbers	1 teaspoon yellow mustard seeds
1½ tablespoons salt	
100 ml (3½ fl oz) white vinegar	½ teaspoon black peppercorns
100 g (3½ oz) sugar	1-2 bay leaves

'*Frikadeller* [meatballs] are a Danish invention - not Swedish!'

This is what you want to make every time guests come over. It's so simple and delicious and friends will be amazed you've made it yourself. Just serve it with fresh rye bread. Note: your work is done in under 10 minutes, but the salmon needs 3 days to cure.

GRAVET LAKS

Cured Salmon

from Jesper Hansen

Trim off any fat from the salmon. Place the fillet skin-side down on a tray lined with baking paper. Sprinkle with the salt, then the sugar, then the ground fennel, and finally the dill. Cover with another piece of baking paper, then wrap the tray tightly in plastic wrap and place another tray on top as a gentle weight on the salmon. Refrigerate for 3–5 days, depending on how deeply coloured and intense-tasting you like your salmon.

To make the dressing, combine the ingredients in a bowl and stir until the sugar has dissolved.

To serve, scrape the curing mixture from the fish and sprinkle the fish with finely chopped dill. Use a sharp knife to thinly slice the fish, leaving the skin behind. Spread a spoonful of dressing on rye bread and top with salmon.

SERVES 12 AS AN ENTREE

1 side of salmon with the skin on, weighing approximately 1.5 kg (3 lb 4 oz), pin-boned
60 g (2 oz) salt
60 g (2 oz) sugar
80 g (2¾ oz) fennel seeds, toasted and ground
3 bunches dill, roughly chopped

DILL AND MUSTARD DRESSING

5 tablespoons dijon mustard
100 g (3½ oz / ½ cup) brown sugar
½ bunch dill, finely chopped

sliced rye bread to serve
finely chopped dill to serve

Pork is one of the heroes of the Danish table; in fact, the Danes are some of the biggest consumers of pork in the world. This classic roast rack of pork with crunchy crackling is easy to make and is really impressive when you bring it to the table. The potatoes are coated in a caramel sauce, which seems rather wicked but only requires a little sugar. Other perfect accompaniments to this meal are sweet and sour red cabbage (page 77) and cucumber salad (page 78).

FLÆSKESTEG OG BRUNEDE KARTOFLER

Roast Pork and Sugar Potatoes

from Lasse Hansen

Boil the potatoes whole until just cooked, then drain. When cool enough to touch, peel away their skins. Refrigerate the potatoes until completely cooled.

Preheat the oven to 180°C (350°F/Gas 4) for at least 20 minutes. Use a sharp knife to score the skin of the pork in close parallel lines from bottom to top. Place the pork in a deep roasting tray and splash a little water over it. Add some coarse salt and rub it over the meat, particularly into the skin. Slide the bay leaves into a few of the scored lines. Add water to the tray to a depth of 3 cm (1 in).

Roast the pork in the oven for 1 hour and 45 minutes, opening the oven door every 20 minutes. Do this to quickly let out steam and help the skin to crackle. Add more water to the tray if it is getting low.

Remove the pork from the oven and let it rest for 20 minutes while you finish the potatoes and make a gravy. (If you are not satisfied with your crackling, you can also cut it off the roast now and return it to a very hot oven – around 250°C ([480°F/Gas 8]) – until crisp. Alternatively crisp it under a grill, watching carefully to make sure it doesn't burn.)

To finish the potatoes, put the sugar in a frying pan and place over low heat. Cook slowly, without stirring but occasionally shaking the pan, until the sugar melts and becomes a golden caramel.

While the sugar is melting, make the gravy. Melt the butter in a saucepan over medium heat. Add the flour and stir to form a paste, then cook, stirring, for 1–2 minutes. Strain the juices from the roasting tray into the pan and continue cooking and stirring until you have thick gravy. Colour with a few drops of Parisian browning essence if desired, and season to taste.

When the sugar for the potatoes has formed a caramel, add the butter and shake the pan to mix it into the caramel. Add the potatoes, continuing to shake the pan to coat them. The caramel may become a bit lumpy when you first add the potatoes, but should start to spread over the surface of the potatoes. You may need to add a little water to soften the caramel and help spread it evenly. (If shaking the pan doesn't seem effective, use tongs to turn the potatoes once or twice.) Cook for 5–10 minutes, or until the potatoes are nicely golden and hot through. Season with salt to taste.

Carve the rested pork between the rib bones and serve immediately with the hot potatoes and gravy.

SERVES 6

SUGAR POTATOES	ROAST PORK AND GRAVY
700 g (1 lb 9 oz) kipfler potatoes or other small potatoes	**rack of pork with 6 rib bones (ask your butcher to remove the chine or back bone and french the rib bones)**
50 g (1¾ oz) sugar	**coarse salt**
50 g (1¾ oz) butter	**3-4 bay leaves**
salt	**1 tablespoon butter**
	2 tablespoons plain (all-purpose) flour
	Parisian browning essence for colour (optional)

This chicken is pot-roasted with handfuls of fresh parsley and served with a pretty rhubarb compote, crushed potatoes and *mormor salat* – 'granny's salad', which is soft lettuce leaves in a traditional sweet cream and lemon dressing. Together with cucumber salad (page 78), this is what Bente served the young Danish royals when engaged as their chef on one of their visits to Australia.

POT-ROASTED CHICKEN WITH RHUBARB COMPOTE, CRUSHED POTATOES AND MORMOR SALAT

from Bente Grysbaeck

To make the rhubarb compote, preheat the oven to 180°C (350°F/Gas 4). Put the rhubarb in a small baking dish with the red-currant jelly and icing sugar (or white sugar if preferred). Cover with foil and bake for 25–30 minutes, or until soft. Remove the foil and strain off some liquid if the rhubarb seems too juicy. Lightly mash the rhubarb with a fork and leave to cool.

Reset the oven to 170°C (340°F/Gas 4). Heat the butter in an ovenproof pot over high heat. Add the chicken pieces and cook for 3–4 minutes on each side, until browned. Add the parsley and stock and bring to the boil. Cover with a lid and transfer to the oven to roast for 35–40 minutes, or until the juices run clear when the thickest sections of chicken are pierced with a skewer.

Remove the chicken pieces from the pot and place the pot on the stovetop over medium heat. Boil the stock until reduced to about a third.

While the stock is reducing, boil the potatoes until soft (15–20 minutes).

Crisp up the lettuce leaves by soaking them in a bowl of iced water for 10 minutes, then drain and spin dry or wrap in a tea towel to absorb excess water. Combine the cream, lemon juice and icing sugar in a bowl and whisk until slightly thickened.

Add the cornflour mixture to the reduced chicken stock, stirring until thickened. Season to taste and return the chicken to the pot to heat through.

Drain the cooked potatoes and leave to steam for 1 minute, then place in a bowl, add the butter and crush with a fork until you have a nice chunky consistency. Season with salt.

Toss the lettuce with the cream dressing. Divide the potatoes between four serving plates and add a piece of chicken to each. Pour over the reduced sauce. Serve with the rhubarb compote and salad.

SERVES 4

RHUBARB COMPOTE

1 bunch rhubarb, cut into chunks
1 tablespoon red-currant jelly
1 tablespoon icing sugar
(2–3 tablespoons white sugar can be used instead of the red-currant jelly and icing sugar if desired)

CHICKEN

50 g (1¾ oz) butter
1 large chicken (about 1.8 kg/3 lb 14 oz), cut into quarters
1 bunch flat-leaf (Italian) parsley, chopped
1 litre (34 fl oz/4 cups) chicken stock
1 tablespoon cornflour (cornstarch), mixed to a paste with a splash of water

CRUSHED POTATOES

1 kg (2 lb 3 oz) dutch cream potatoes (or another waxy variety), peeled and cut into large chunks
150 g (5½ oz) butter, diced
sea salt

MORMOR SALAT (GRANNY'S SALAD)

inner leaves of 2 butter lettuces
100 ml (3½ fl oz) cream
juice of 2 lemons
1–2 tablespoons icing sugar

"'Smørrebrød" was originally "smør og brød", which translates as "butter and bread"'.

The long, slow ripening season of summer in Denmark means some exceptional berries full of flavour. This simple but perfect dessert is a mixture of cooked berries set with a little potato flour, covered with cream. The result is the colours of the Danish flag.

RØDGRØD MED FLØDE

Red Berry Pudding with Cream
from Kristine Lindbjerg

Combine the strawberries in a medium saucepan with the sugar and water. Bring to the boil, then reduce the heat to a simmer and cook for 2–3 minutes.

Remove from the heat and stir in the potato flour paste, followed by the raspberries and blueberries.

Pour the mixture into a large serving bowl, or into individual serving glasses or bowls. Sprinkle the surface with a little sugar, which helps to stop a skin from forming. Chill in the refrigerator for at least 2–3 hours.

Pour a layer of cream over the pudding to serve.

SERVES 4-6

500 g (1 lb 2 oz) strawberries,
   hulled and cut in half if large
110 g (4 oz/½ cup) sugar, plus
   extra for sprinkling
250 ml (8½ fl oz/1 cup) water
1 tablespoon potato flour,
   mixed to a paste with a
   splash of water

100 g (3½ oz) raspberries
100 g (3½ oz) blueberries
250 ml (8½ fl oz/1 cup) cream

The amazing thing about Egyptian food is that dishes that were popular in the days of the pharaohs are still being enjoyed today. Some crops have been cultivated on the Nile River's fertile flood plain for thousands of years and are still being prepared and eaten in much the same way. As one of the world's most ancient civilisations, Egypt certainly got its recipes right from the very start!

Then, as now, pulses and beans are the centre of the Egyptian diet for both rich and poor. They're used extensively and creatively – as a source of protein and fibre and for comfort. *Ful medames* (slow-cooked fava beans with lentils) makes a great breakfast and is described as a 'stone in the stomach', capable of sustaining a worker all day. Egyptian expatriates say the *ful medames* sold on the streets of Cairo is unsurpassed – there's a flavour imparted from cooking such large quantities that apparently can't be equalled at home. An ingenious system of pulleys and baskets allows apartment dwellers high above the streets to lower a basket and get their '*ful* fix', a cumin-scented bowl of warm *ful medames* to eat with bread and fresh herbs. I've only eaten this in Sydney, without the vibrancy of Cairo around me, but it was still delicious … and sustaining.

The other national dish revered above all others is *molokhia* soup. This tall, leafy vegetable has been cultivated for centuries. It has the highest amount of protein and folic acid of any green leafy vegetable and is also rich in betacarotene, iron, calcium and vitamin C. When cooked, *molokhia* develops a wonderfully mucilaginous quality loved by Egyptians – who also believe it has aphrodisiac powers.

While *molokhia* is still an Egyptian secret, another Egyptian mainstay has been readily embraced. This food is dukkah, a fragrant mix of whole spices toasted and mixed with nuts and seeds.

The traditional bread of Egypt is a flatbread called *eish baladi* – *eish* means 'life' or 'survival'. It's dipped into oil then dukkah and eaten. And, as in the Middle East, the flatbread is used as plate, cutlery and napkin and is an essential part of every meal.

Meat is still a luxury for many in Egypt and many dishes make a little go a long way. You can smell meat cooking on the streets – tantalising aromas from juicy marinated skewers cooking over hot charcoal or tagines of lamb slowly cooking with spices and vegetables.

Fresh fruit is the healthy conclusion to most Egyptian meals, along with strong coffee, black tea or the delicious, refreshing red tea called *karkade*, made from dried hibiscus flowers and said to reduce high blood pressure.

ESSENTIAL FLAVOURS

BAHARAT
Arabic for 'spice mix'. This all-purpose blend is popular for enhancing the flavour of fish, chicken, beef, vegetables - particularly *bamya* (okra) - tomato sauces and soups. To make Egyptian *baharat* mix equal quantities of ground white pepper and cinnamon with half quantities of black pepper, nutmeg and cloves.

CORIANDER (CILANTRO)
Coriander leaves and coriander seeds feature prominently in Egyptian cooking. The seeds (whole or ground) are used to make dukkah and are also a key ingredient in one of the national dishes of Egypt, *molokhia* soup.

CUMIN
This is the most popular spice in Egypt. It is bought weekly and used liberally in *ful* (beans), seafood dishes, marinades and dukkah.

FAVA BEANS
Dried fava beans, or broad beans, are hugely popular in Egypt. This ancient staple is eaten for breakfast as *ful medames* and split fava beans are used in Egypt's version of falafel called *tameya*.

MOLOKHIA
Molokhia is a leafy green vegetable with a slippery consistency much like okra, and it is available fresh for just a few weeks at the height of summer. The taste of the famous *molokhia* soup varies according to the method of cooking and the stock that is used. It can be made from fresh, frozen, dried or preserved leaves, which are sold in most Middle Eastern emporiums.

PREPARING A NEW TAGINE

Tagine (pronounced 'tar-gen' in Egypt) are shallow terracotta plates with conical lids that are used for slow-cooking. To prepare a new tagine before cooking, first soak it overnight in water. The next day fill it with fresh water, add some salt and a few bay leaves and cardamom pods. Heat over a low gas flame until boiling to infuse the herbs into the porous terracotta. If your tagine is used regularly this won't need to be redone. Tagines can be used on the barbecue (grill), charcoal or low gas flame but are not recommended for electric cook tops or in the oven. The ceramic finished tagines are better for serving while the hard-wearing terracotta versions are best for cooking.

This thick stew of tender lamb and baby okra is a common dish in Egypt - okra is the edible fruit pod of a plant related to the hibiscus and is used in many dishes for its thickening properties. Lamb backstrap or fillet is lean and quick and easy to use, although other cuts of lamb would work - the meat from the leg or shoulder is lovely too. The secret to this dish is the long, slow simmering that brings the flavours gently together.

This national dish is cooked very slowly, traditionally overnight in a copper pot so it is ready for a hearty breakfast. It is typically eaten with Egyptian bread as a tasty and filling start to the day, particularly during Ramadan when Muslims fast during daylight hours. It goes beautifully with many spicy, crunchy treats such as the bright-pink pickled turnips (coloured with beetroot) and crunchy pickled cucumbers that are sold in Middle Eastern food stores.

BAMYA (OKRA) WITH LAMB

from Nadia Fawzi

Melt the ghee in a saucepan and sauté the onion until soft, then add the garlic. Fry for a couple of minutes then add the lamb and toss until sealed and lightly browned.

Add the tomato puree and paste and season to taste with salt and pepper. If you think more liquid is needed, add the stock or water. Cover and simmer for 30–35 minutes.

Add the okra and cook for another 5–10 minutes. Add the lemon juice and remove from the heat. Serve with rice.

SERVES 4-6

1 tablespoon clarified butter (ghee)	1 tablespoon tomato paste (concentrated puree)
1 medium onion, diced	salt and pepper
2 garlic cloves, finely chopped	250 ml (8½ fl oz/1 cup) stock or water (optional)
500 g (1 lb 2 oz) lamb backstrap, cut into thick pieces	500 g (1 lb 2 oz) baby okra, topped and tailed
2 × 400 g (14 oz) tins pureed tomatoes	juice of 1 lemon

FUL MEDAMES

Slow-cooked Fava Beans with Lentils

from Alice Ibrahim

Drain the soaked beans and lentils and rinse again. Place them in a large saucepan and cover with 750 ml of water. Boil over high heat until frothy. Skim the froth as it accumulates then cover the saucepan and simmer on the lowest heat for up to 5 hours or until the beans are very soft and the liquid has reduced. The *ful* thickens as it cools, so be careful not to reduce the liquid too much.

Add salt, pepper, a generous amount of cumin and lemon juice to taste. Drizzle a liberal amount of olive oil over the top.

For a sandwich-style snack, serve the *ful* in a pocket of flat bread with fresh salad, tahini, pickles and banana chillies. Or simply scoop the warm *ful* up with bread.

SERVES 6

2 cups dried fava beans (broad beans), rinsed and soaked overnight	salt and pepper
	ground cumin
	lemon juice
1 cup red lentils, rinsed and soaked overnight	olive oil

'If you share bread and salt, you're a friend for life.'

Kushari is a delicious dish made from green lentils, macaroni and rice mixed together with caramelised onions. It is served with a tomato-based sauce and finished with a crispy onion garnish and is best accompanied by a garden salad.

KUSHARI

from Therese Shehata

Prepare the crispy onion by heating sufficient oil in a saucepan, adding the onions and deep-frying until dark brown. Remove from the oil and drain on paper towel. Leave to cool.

To make the sauce, place a saucepan over moderate heat and add the oil and onion. Cook until the onion is soft. Add the garlic and fry to pale brown. Stir in the tomato paste and *baharat* and add salt, pepper and chilli flakes (if using) to taste. Add the water and simmer for 15–20 minutes or until the sauce has reduced by half. Remove from the heat.

Heat 2 tablespoons of olive oil in a separate saucepan over moderate heat. Add the rice and 1 teaspoon of salt and fry for 2 minutes, then add 500 ml (17 fl oz) of water. Stir well and bring to the boil. Once boiling, lower the heat, cover and simmer for 15 minutes until the rice is cooked.

Meanwhile, place the lentils in another saucepan with 500 ml (17 fl oz) of water and simmer until tender then drain. In another saucepan boil the macaroni with a little salt until al dente then drain. Heat 80 ml (2½ fl oz/⅓ cup) of olive oil in a frying pan and cook the onions until soft and caramelised.

To serve, reheat the tomato sauce. Place the hot macaroni in a large serving dish and coat with a little extra olive oil. Add the hot rice, lentils and caramelised onions and mix through.

Sprinkle with the *baharat* and pour over the desired amount of tomato sauce. Garnish with the crispy onions.

SERVES 4-6

CRISPY ONIONS

oil for deep-frying
2 onions, finely sliced

SAUCE

2 tablespoons olive oil
1 small onion, finely diced
2 garlic cloves, crushed
250 g (9 oz) tomato paste
 (concentrated puree)
1 teaspoon *baharat* (spice mix)
salt and pepper
chilli flakes (optional)
250 ml (8½ fl oz/1 cup) water

RICE, MACARONI
AND LENTILS

olive oil
1 cup medium-grain rice
salt
1 cup green lentils, rinsed
 until the water runs clear
2 cups small macaroni
2 large onions, finely sliced
1 teaspoon *baharat*

'In Egypt the worst thing you can do as a host is to eat with your guests – you must make sure they have the best of everything!'

The Egyptian tagine is much like the better-known Moroccan tajine – the conical-topped clay cooking pot that cooks spicy stews to perfection. This recipe uses barramundi instead of the traditional Nile perch, but the squid and prawns are authentic, being fruits of Egypt's Mediterranean coastline and its famous river.

If you are using frozen *molokhia*, add it to the soup without thawing it, don't over-stir it and make sure it never reaches boiling point otherwise it can split from the stock. *Molokhia* can also be made with duck, beef or rabbit. With rabbit it is said to be the meal of the pharaohs as only the wealthy could indulge in it.

FISH TAGINE

from Ramy Megalaa

Place the barramundi, squid and prawns in a mixing bowl and add the remaining marinade ingredients. Mix well and marinate for 4 hours.

To make the sauce, use a hand-held blender or food processor to blend the capsicum (including its seeds) with the tomato, celery and cumin.

Heat the olive oil in a large frying pan over high heat and fry the red onion until soft. Add the blended sauce and bring to a high simmer. Stir in the tomato paste, coriander and salt and pepper to taste.

Preheat the oven to 180°C (350°F/Gas 4). Cover the base of the tagine with some of the sauce, add the seafood, then cover with the remaining sauce. Place the tagine on the stove over medium heat for a few minutes to start the cooking process. Transfer to the oven and cook for 40–45 minutes.

Serve with fresh bread, couscous or rice.

SERVES 3

MARINATED FISH	SAUCE
1 barramundi fillet, cut into 2 cm (¾ in) pieces	1 red capsicum (bell pepper), roasted and peeled
1 squid tube, sliced	3 tomatoes, chopped
250 g (9 oz) green prawns (shrimp), shelled and de-veined	1 cup chopped celery
	1 teaspoon ground cumin
½ tablespoon olive oil	2 tablespoons olive oil
1 tablespoon crushed garlic	1 red onion, sliced
juice of ½ lime (or lemon)	1 tablespoon tomato paste (concentrated puree)
1 teaspoon ground cumin	small handful of coriander (cilantro) leaves
½ cup roughly chopped coriander (cilantro)	salt and pepper
salt and pepper	

MOLOKHIA AND CHICKEN SOUP

from Ramy Megalaa

Place the chicken in a pot and add the onion, whole garlic, bay leaves and salt and pepper. Cover with boiling water and bring to a simmer. Cook until the chicken is tender. Remove the chicken and strain the stock.

Cut the chicken into pieces and fry them in ghee or butter.

Meanwhile, bring 1 litre (34 fl oz/4 cups) of the stock back to the boil, reduce the heat and add the *molokhia*. Simmer uncovered for 10 minutes. The soup should be thick and sticky; if it seems too thick, add more stock.

The next stage is known as preparing the *tasha*. Heat a frying pan and fry the chopped garlic in a little ghee or butter until light brown. Add the coriander then stir the mixture into the hot soup. Leave the soup to sit for 2 minutes, then serve with the fried chicken and with steamed rice.

SERVES 4

1 large chicken, preferably free-range	salt and pepper
1 large onion, halved	clarified butter (ghee) or butter
5 garlic cloves, 2 left whole, 3 finely chopped	500 g (1 lb 2 oz) fresh *molohkia* leaves, very finely sliced
3 bay leaves	1 tablespoon ground coriander

This sweet semolina cake topped with a rosewater and lemon syrup is incredibly easy to make. The addition of yoghurt makes this lovely and rich. With its fragrant syrup, these little diamond-shaped slices not only taste delicious but keep for a long time - perfect with a short black coffee or scented tea.

BASBOUSA

from Amira Georgy

Preheat the oven to 190°C (375°F/Gas 5). Mix the semolina, coconut, sugar, flour, yoghurt, melted butter and vanilla in a bowl. If the mixture seems too thick, add a little milk - but it should still be fairly stiff. Spread the mixture with your hands in a buttered 30 × 25 × 5 cm (12 × 10 × 2 in) baking tray. Cut it into diamond shapes, pressing hard. Place an almond in the centre of each diamond. Bake for 35-40 minutes until golden brown.

Meanwhile, make the syrup. Place the sugar and water in a saucepan and bring to the boil, stirring until the sugar dissolves. Simmer for 5 minutes without stirring. Stir in the lemon juice and rosewater and remove from the heat. Leave to cool.

Pour the syrup over the cake while the cake is still hot. Cool to serve.

MAKES 25-30 PIECES

2½ cups coarse semolina
1 cup desiccated coconut
220 g (1 cup) caster sugar
75 g (2¾ oz/½ cup)
   self-raising flour
200 g (7 oz) thick yoghurt
200 g (7 oz) unsalted butter,
   melted
1 teaspoon vanilla extract

milk if needed
25-30 blanched almonds

SYRUP

330 g (1½ cups) sugar
250 ml (8½ fl oz/1 cup) water
1 teaspoon lemon juice
1 teaspoon rosewater

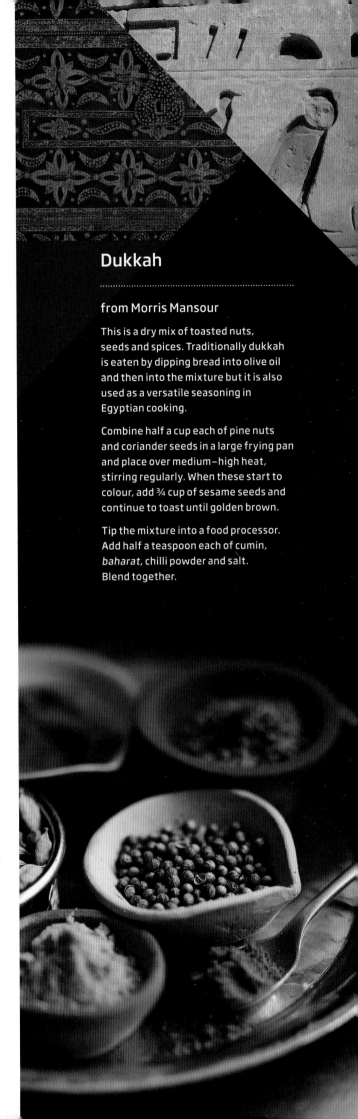

Dukkah

from Morris Mansour

This is a dry mix of toasted nuts, seeds and spices. Traditionally dukkah is eaten by dipping bread into olive oil and then into the mixture but it is also used as a versatile seasoning in Egyptian cooking.

Combine half a cup each of pine nuts and coriander seeds in a large frying pan and place over medium–high heat, stirring regularly. When these start to colour, add ¾ cup of sesame seeds and continue to toast until golden brown.

Tip the mixture into a food processor. Add half a teaspoon each of cumin, *baharat*, chilli powder and salt. Blend together.

ENGLAND

The author W. Somerset Maugham once remarked that the only way to eat well in England was to have breakfast three times a day! Another wit decided that the British zeal for colonising the world was motivated by their longing for a decent meal. That said, English food is popular and can rise above its reputation – often thought of as simple comfort food, there is still much pleasure in it and much to learn.

The ingenuity of English food interests me – using up stale bread, clever ways with secondary cuts of meat, turning unwanted fish into something so yummy it is now popular throughout the world ... The story of fish and chips goes like this: When the English fishermen in the North Sea adopted the use of long-haul nets in the nineteenth century, they found they were landing a huge by-catch as well as the prized fish they were after. So as not to waste good food, the poorer-quality fish was sent along the newly built rail networks to every town and village throughout the country. The fish was filleted, fried in batter and served with another cheap staple, potatoes, which were sliced into chips and also fried. The chippie or chipper was born and the tradition is still going strong in the English-speaking world – as are many other age-old English recipes and ingredients.

Much Anglo Australian food has English roots – the Sunday roast with gravy, roast vegetables and all the trimmings dates from the Middle Ages; while bangers and mash, which is comfort food in Australia, is also quintessentially English and made with distinct sausages in each region. Our pasties and meat pies can be traced back to English baking – lovely crescent-shaped Cornish pasties, steak pies, and deep pork pies, which are part of many a good pub lunch served cold with pickles or chutney.

No English meal is complete without dessert such as a steamed pudding or the all-time classic that is bread and butter pudding. It's a delicious winter warmer with the added virtue of being cheap to make – a handy use of stale bread in this culture of 'waste not, want not'.

We must mention sandwiches too – named after the Earl of Sandwich, who came up with the idea of meat tucked between two slices of bread in the eighteenth century. English sandwiches featuring combinations such as cured meats and lovely yellow English mustard, cheese and pickles, or egg and mayonnaise are staples throughout the world, especially in the British colonies.

English-style afternoon tea is another tradition that has travelled the globe. When asked what time afternoon tea is generally served, our dear friend Daphne Guinness replied in surprise: 'Four o'clock of course. Everyone knows that!'

ESSENTIAL FLAVOURS

CHEESE

While there are many cheap, commercial versions of traditional English cheeses around, there are still a number of farmhouse dairies that make the old favourites the original way. Cheddar and cheshire are the heart of a ploughman's lunch. Stilton is the classic English blue-vein cheese.

HADDOCK

A member of the cod family, generally fished in the North Atlantic. Smoked haddock is the most common fish used to make kedgeree, a breakfast dish that was popular among British colonials in India and later found favour in England. Haddock is also frequently the fish of choice for fish and chips.

MALT VINEGAR

Made by malting barley, and traditionally light brown in colour. It is served with fish and chips at the traditional 'chippie'. A cheaper synthetic alternative, labelled as a 'non-brewed condiment', is popular in northern England.

MEAT AND OFFAL

British beef is a traditional favourite however English cooking also uses many cheaper, tougher cuts of meat for slow cooking like ears, tongues and cheeks. Kidneys and lamb's fry, or liver, are breakfast staples. Kidneys are celebrated in steak and kidney pie.

The making of smallgoods is an art form and there are numerous local sausages that differ from region to region, as well as cured cuts of pork, gammon, and the famous black pudding or blood sausage.

PICKLES

Pickling fish or vegetables is a tasty way of preserving fresh produce to eat throughout the year. Rollmops are pickled fish fillets that are often wrapped around a pickled cucumber or onion. Pickled onions are common in a ploughman's lunch and served with strong cheddar cheese. Branston Pickle is a popular commercial relish of pickled cooked vegetables in a dark, tangy chutney.

'Always wait till Wednesday to make scouse.' (Scouse is a Liverpool dish made up from leftovers of Sunday's lamb roast dinner – the flavours would be stronger and the meat more tender later in the week.)

Traditionally a rollmop is a pickled herring that is rolled around a pickled cucumber or onion, secured with a toothpick and eaten as an appetiser or as part of a light meal. This recipe is light and delicious and with the beetroot and watercress it looks great too.

WHITING ROLLMOPS WITH BEETROOT COMPOTE

from Jeremy Strode

To make the pickled fish, place the water, vinegar, sugar, seeds and herbs in a large saucepan and bring to the boil. Remove from the heat and leave to cool (to speed the cooling process you could pour the liquid into a large bowl).

To prepare the fish, trim the edges if needed so the fillets are more or less an even width. Place the fish skin-side down and roll up from the tail end. Pierce each roll with a sturdy toothpick to hold it in place and add to the cool pickling liquid. Leave the fish to pickle in the refrigerator for 1–2 days.

To make the dressing, whisk the egg yolks, mustard and vinegar in a bowl and gradually whisk in the oils as if making a mayonnaise. Thin out with a little pickling liquid if necessary.

Finally whisk in the cream and season to taste.

To make the beetroot compote, sweat the onions and garlic in a little olive oil, seasoning well. When very soft and starting to colour, add the beetroot, vinegar and mustard seeds. Cook until the beetroot is al dente. Use more oil as required to prevent sticking. Leave to cool.

Serve the rollmops with the beetroot compote, dressing and fresh watercress.

SERVES 6

PICKLED FISH

1 litre (34 fl oz/4 cups) water
1 litre (34 fl oz/4 cups) white-wine vinegar
1 kg (2 lb 3 oz) sugar
2 tablespoons fennel seeds
2 tablespoons mustard seeds
6 thyme sprigs
6 bay leaves
12 small king george whiting fillets

DRESSING

2 egg yolks
2 teaspoons grain mustard
1 teaspoon white-wine vinegar
200 ml (7 fl oz) extra-virgin olive oil
200 ml (7 fl oz) olive oil
2½ tablespoons cream
salt and pepper

BEETROOT COMPOTE

4 onions, finely diced
4 garlic cloves, finely chopped
olive oil
salt and pepper
6 medium beetroots, peeled and cut into small cubes
200 ml (7 fl oz) white-wine vinegar
2 tablespoons mustard seeds

watercress sprigs to serve

'Never make pastry after the sun comes up.'

This is a nice crispy batter that helps to steam the fish – make sure you buy firm, thick, white fillets such as flathead. The secret of the best chips is in the double cooking! It is also a good idea to use a variety of potato that has a low water content.

CLASSIC ENGLISH FISH AND CHIPS

from Sue Pearson

Place the flour in a large mixing bowl. Make a well in the centre and pour the beer into it. Start whisking the flour with the beer and, if necessary, adding water into the mix little by little to avoid lumps forming. Keep whisking until all the flour is incorporated and the batter is smooth.

Whisk in the yeast and salt to taste. Leave the batter in a warm place for 1–1½ hours. Just before using add the olive oil, which adds gloss to the batter.

Peel and slice the potatoes, pat dry and cut into chips 1.5 cm (½ in) wide. Heat sufficient oil in a deep saucepan and fry the chips for 5 minutes. Remove from the oil with a slotted spoon and leave to cool and drain on a wire rack for 10 minutes.

Reheat the oil and cook the chips again for 7–10 minutes until golden with a crunchy outer layer. Season with salt.

Dust the fish in flour and lightly coat in batter. Add to the hot oil and cook for up to 3 minutes, turning regularly. Drain on paper towel, season with salt and serve with the chips.

SERVES 4

300 g (10½ oz/2 cups) plain (all-purpose) flour, plus extra for dusting
375–500 ml (12½–17 fl oz) dark beer
1 tablespoon dried yeast
salt
1 teaspoon olive oil
6–8 potatoes such as Dutch cream
canola oil for deep-frying
8 flathead fillets

Sean's recipe for this classic dish is just lovely – the meat becomes tender and full of flavour and the puddings act as little cups for the gravy, which is made with a good pinot. Yorkshire puddings were traditionally served as a filler before the main roast but they make an excellent accompaniment. The secret of the puddings is to make sure the fat in the muffin tins is smoking before pouring in the batter. If you don't have any dripping on hand, speak to your butcher who could give you some beef fat to render down.

'Always use the beef dripping from last week's roast for next week's Yorkshire pudding.'

ROAST BEEF AND YORKSHIRE PUDDINGS

from Sean Connolly

Combine the flour, mustard powder and pepper and dust over the surface of the meat. Stud the meat with rosemary. Do not season with salt as it has a tendency to draw the moisture out.

Preheat the oven to 180°C (350°F/Gas 4). Heat some of the oil in a frying pan and seal the beef on all sides, allowing it to caramelise a little. In a large roasting tray add the remaining oil and the onion, carrot and garlic and place the beef on top.

Sprinkle with thyme and salt and roast for 1½ hours until medium–rare.

Meanwhile, prepare the puddings. Sift the flour into a bowl and stir in the salt. Beat the eggs and milk together in a separate bowl. Make a well in the centre of the flour and add the egg and milk mixture one-third at a time, whisking vigorously to incorporate. Once the batter is smooth, rest it in the refrigerator. Warm a muffin tray in the oven during the last 15 minutes of cooking the beef.

Transfer the beef to a warm plate and rest covered in foil for 30 minutes. The meat juices will pool on the plate to be used in the gravy.

Remove the vegetables from the tray and keep warm (or you can pop them back in the oven for 10 minutes prior to serving). Keep the roasting tray aside for the gravy.

Turn the oven up to 200°C (430°F/Gas 7). Melt the dripping or fat in a saucepan and pour 1 cm (½ in) into the base of each mould in the warm muffin tray. Place in the oven until the fat is smoking. Pour the batter into each mould to three-quarters full. Bake in the oven for 15–20 minutes until crisp and golden brown.

Meanwhile, make the gravy. Heat the beef stock in a saucepan. Warm the roasting tray gently over low heat loosening the sediment at the bottom with a wooden spoon. Pour in the pinot and boil until reduced by half. Add the juices from the beef plate and the hot stock and reduce once more. If you prefer your gravy on the thick side, you can make a cold paste of 2 teaspoons of butter with 2 teaspoons of plain (all-purpose) flour and whisk this into the gravy, simmering over low heat for 8–10 minutes.

Slice the beef and serve with the vegetables and puddings. Pour on the gravy.

SERVES 8-10

2 teaspoons plain (all-purpose) flour
2 teaspoons mustard powder
freshly ground black pepper
2 kg (4 lb 6 oz) wagyu rump or scotch fillet
rosemary sprigs
2-3 tablespoons olive oil
4 red onions, halved
4 large carrots, halved
8 garlic cloves, unpeeled
thyme sprigs
sea salt

1 litre (34 fl oz/4 cups) beef stock
½ bottle good pinot noir

YORKSHIRE PUDDINGS

200 g (7 oz/1⅓ cups) plain (all-purpose) flour
10 g (¼ oz) salt
4 eggs
450 ml (15 fl oz) full-cream milk
beef dripping or duck or goose fat

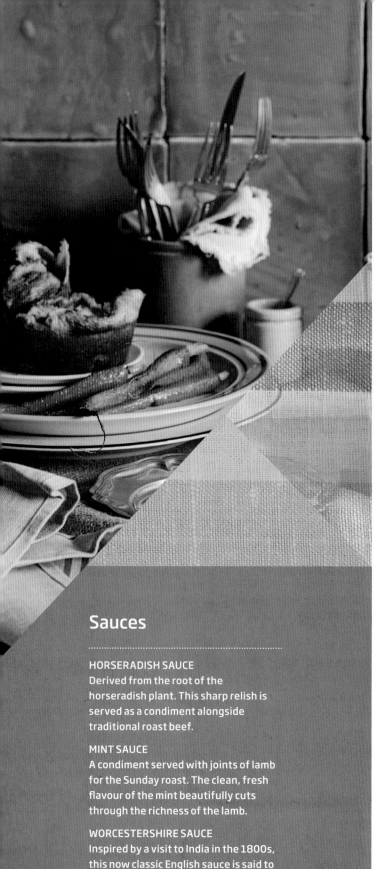

This dish is a wonderful way of using up leftover meat. Alice's version has a few additions to add extra flavour, like a dash of soy sauce for saltiness, cider for a little sweetness and lemon zest for a slight tang. As well as leftover meat, Alice says you can add other leftovers from the fridge such as peas, gravy and leeks. Topped with creamy mashed potato that forms a crispy crust when baked, this dish is delicious at any time of the day.

SHEPHERD'S PIE

from Alice Parsons

Mince the lamb in an old-fashioned mincer or in a food processor. Put the potatoes in a large pot of water and boil until soft.

Meanwhile heat the olive oil in a large frying pan and add the onion and celery. Fry until the onion is translucent then add the carrot. Cook over medium heat for 3–5 minutes, stirring occasionally. Season with salt and pepper.

Stir in the lamb, then add the flour and mustard powder along with the stock for moisture. Stir well. Add the soy sauce, Worcestershire, mace, lemon zest and apple cider – the mixture should be gooey but not sloppy. Add the bay leaves and parsley and take off the heat. Once the potatoes are soft, drain and mash with the butter and warm milk. Season to taste and stir in the egg.

Butter a large baking dish and add the meat mixture. Top with a thick layer of mashed potato. Sprinkle with grated cheese if you wish. Glaze the mash with some extra melted butter. Bake in a moderate oven for 20 minutes or until the potato is golden on top.

SERVES 8-10

500 g (1 lb 2 oz) cooked lamb (or whatever meat you have left over)	dash of soy sauce
	generous splash of Worcestershire sauce
8-10 medium potatoes such as desiree	3 pinches of ground mace
	grated zest of 1 lemon
2 tablespoons olive oil	125 ml (4 fl oz/½ cup) apple cider
1 onion, finely chopped	
2-3 celery stalks, diced	2 bay leaves
2 carrots, finely diced	½ bunch flat-leaf (Italian) parsley, chopped
salt and freshly ground black pepper	
	1 tablespoon butter, plus extra for glazing
2-3 teaspoons plain (all-purpose) flour	
	warm milk
2 teaspoons mustard powder	1 egg, lightly beaten
about 125 ml (4 fl oz/½ cup) stock (chicken, beef or vegetable)	grated cheese (optional)

Sauces

HORSERADISH SAUCE
Derived from the root of the horseradish plant. This sharp relish is served as a condiment alongside traditional roast beef.

MINT SAUCE
A condiment served with joints of lamb for the Sunday roast. The clean, fresh flavour of the mint beautifully cuts through the richness of the lamb.

WORCESTERSHIRE SAUCE
Inspired by a visit to India in the 1800s, this now classic English sauce is said to have tamarind as its secret ingredient.

BREAD SAUCE
Dating from medieval times, this sauce accompanies chicken or turkey. It is made with milk, and butter or cream, flavoured with onion, cloves, mace, bay leaves, salt and pepper and the fat from the roasting pan, then thickened with stale bread.

This traditional English pudding is a favourite - it is easy, uses up stale bread and makes the most of the bright colours and tangy flavours of fresh summer berries. Matthew's recipe is so simple and perfect for right through the berry season when the fruit is at its best. It's just the thing to finish a beautiful dinner. Ramekins are a great investment for this recipe, and for the Brazilian dessert *quindim*, French cheese soufflés and Portuguese flans.

SUMMER PUDDING

from Matthew Kemp

To make the coulis, boil the water and sugar together in a saucepan for 5 minutes. Transfer to a bowl and return 125 ml (4 fl oz/½ cup) of the syrup to the pan and add the berries and mint (refrigerate the remaining syrup for another use). Cook until the fruit is soft. Discard the mint then puree the coulis in a food processor or rub through a sieve.

Cut the bread into circles (leaving the crusts behind) to fit inside 8 large ramekins - you will need 3 circles per ramekin. Dip the bread circles into the coulis and lay out on a tray. Set aside.

Reheat the remaining coulis in a medium saucepan and bring to the boil over moderate heat. Add the strawberries, blackberries (or mulberries) and blueberries. Bring back to

the boil then immediately remove from the heat. Drain off one-third of the coulis and reserve, and transfer the remaining fruit and coulis to a bowl to cool.

Place a soaked bread circle in the bottom of each ramekin followed by 1 tablespoon of the fruit, another circle of bread and more fruit. Top with a final circle of bread and a small amount of coulis. Press down firmly. Chill and set in the refrigerator for 4 hours or more.

Run a knife around the inside of the ramekins and turn the puddings out onto serving plates. Garnish with the raspberries or mixed berries and drizzle with reserved coulis. Serve with luscious thick cream if desired.

SERVES 6-8

BLACKCURRANT COULIS	PUDDING
250 ml (8½ fl oz/1 cup) water	**1 day-old loaf of sliced white bread**
250 g (9 oz/1 cup) sugar	**200 g (7 oz) small strawberries, hulled and quartered**
250 g (9 oz) blackcurrants (or mixed berries)	**100 g (3½ oz) blackberries or mulberries**
1 mint sprig	**100 g (3½ oz) blueberries**
	100 g (3½ oz) raspberries or mixed berries for garnish

From all the different cuisines that I've sampled, I'd have to say that the dishes I went up a dress size after were the French ones! France is simply gastronomic heaven. There the people love food and really focus on it - there are few places on earth where so much attention is paid to what people are going to eat and how they then eat it. Those of you who have experienced the pure joy of a freshly baked baguette with its warm, golden crust, or a small wedge of one of the thousands of French cheeses, or a spoonful of something as simple and rustic as French onion soup will know what I mean.

It has been so interesting visiting both restaurants and homes to see how this exquisite food comes together and what French people simply will not compromise on in the kitchen - good butter, fresh seasonal vegetables and fruits, the best oil and vinegar to dress salads, and good quality meat, cheese and wine.

This refined cuisine is the result of many years of evolution. It was fostered at the royal court centuries ago and gradually spread once the subsequent revolution removed many class barriers and people became more prosperous. In professional kitchens there was a strict hierarchy and a rigorous chef's apprentice system which rewarded excellence. Add to this local farmers and suppliers who are proud of the quality of their ingredients and an adoring, food-obsessed audience and you have the right climate for flavours and dishes to really become perfected.

This focus on food has elevated French chefs to almost godlike status, as has the coveted Michelin star system that rates top chefs and restaurants. In 1900, the Michelin tyre company first sponsored the now-famous *Michelin Guide* in an effort to encourage people to explore France by road. For more than a century, this guide has awarded stars to a select number of European restaurants of outstanding quality - these stars are recognised and renowned worldwide.

The recognition of quality is also behind the French movement to certify regional products - from cheese and butter to salt and wine - with the label AOC (Appellation d'Origine Contrôlée). Across France, the origin of produce is of critical importance and this labelling guarantees authenticity and quality - French shoppers will always seek out the best. With an abundance of local produce markets, they are spoiled for choice and many people shop every day to source the freshest food. Some even visit the baker twice a day to get baguettes that are just out of the oven and most bakers continue baking through the day to satisfy their exacting customers.

ESSENTIAL FLAVOURS

BUTTER
A churned cream that is washed to remove leftover buttermilk, which improves the texture and flavour.

The addition of salt improves the shelf life. French butter is often slightly fermented for an extra depth of flavour.

It is essential to many traditional sauces, for sautéing, for baking, for making pastry and of course to spread on crusty French bread.

CHARCUTERIE
A collective term meaning 'cooked meat', including *rillettes* and pâtés, terrines, confit and various types of *saucisson* (sausage).

DIJON MUSTARD
Pale yellow in colour with a creamy, smooth consistency and mild flavour, dijon mustard is used in sauces, rubbed on roasts and whisked in the classic vinaigrette dressing.

HERBS
Herbs are to French cooking as spices are to Asian cuisine and a large range is used including basil, chervil, mint, marjoram, parsley, rosemary, tarragon, thyme, sage and savory.

SHALLOTS
These small bulbs are a type of onion but have a sweeter, more delicate and less pungent flavour. They are very typical in French cooking.

TRUFFLES
A finely veined tuber formed in a magical underground exchange by the bonding of its filaments with the roots of certain types of trees, most traditionally oak. Season, climate, soil conditions and an element of great mystery surround the cultivation process, making the truffle a highly prized and expensive ingredient.

TURNIP
Believed to have first been cultivated in 2000 BC, turnips are picked young at the beginning of summer when they are small and sweet. The French love them pureed, pan-fried, steamed or paired with duck in the classic *canard aux navets* or in lamb navarin.

Everything you'd want from a good soufflé - it's light and full of lovely creaminess. Serve straight away! Seek out the best gruyère, use top quality eggs at room temperature and grate your own nutmeg.

It's the simplicity of this traditional fish dish from the city of Grenoble in the French Alps that is so seductive - it takes less than 15 minutes to cook and looks and tastes sensational.

SOUFFLÉ AU FROMAGE

Cheese Soufflé
from Marie Helene Clauson

SNAPPER GRENOBLOISE

from Meyjitte Bourgenhout

Preheat the oven to 200°C (400°F/Gas 6). Butter a large soufflé dish.

To make a roux, melt the butter in a heavy-based saucepan over low heat and add the flour, stirring with a wooden spoon until the mixture foams. Add the milk in small amounts and heat, stirring, until smooth and thick. Add the cheese and season to taste with salt, pepper and nutmeg. Remove from the heat and stir in the egg yolks.

In a large bowl, beat the egg whites with a pinch of salt to stiff peaks - they should be firm but not dry. With a large metal spoon gently fold a little cheese mixture into the egg whites.

Once incorporated, pour in the remaining cheese mixture and mix gently.

Pour into the soufflé dish and smooth the top. Bake in the centre of the oven for 10 minutes. Turn the oven down to 180°C (350°F/Gas 4) and cook for another 25–30 minutes until well risen and golden brown. Serve immediately.

Score the snapper fillets with a couple of shallow cuts on the flesh side and season the flesh with salt and pepper.

Bring the fish stock to a simmer and add the potatoes, cinnamon and star anise. Cover and cook until just soft then set aside.

Heat 1 tablespoon of the olive oil in a frying pan and fry the snapper skin-side down until crispy, for approximately 3–4 minutes. Turn the fish over, turn the heat down to low and cook for another 5 minutes. Remove from the pan.

Add the remaining oil to the pan and quickly wilt the spinach, adding salt and a dash of fish stock from the potatoes. Remove from the pan.

Add the butter to the pan along with the remaining ingredients and 1 tablespoon of the fish stock. Warm briefly, seasoning to taste.

Place slices of potato in the middle of each plate followed by the spinach and then the fish. Top with the ingredients from the frying pan.

SERVES 4-6

60 g (2 oz) butter	salt and pepper
60 g (2 oz) plain (all-purpose) flour	grated nutmeg
	6 eggs, separated
500 ml (17 fl oz) milk	
200 g (7 oz) good-quality gruyère cheese, grated	

SERVES 4

4 ×150 g (5½ oz) thick snapper (porgy) fillets, skin on	1 tablespoon butter
sea salt and pepper	3 tablespoons croutons made from sourdough
250 ml (8½ fl oz/1 cup) fish stock	2 tablespoons slivered almonds
2 large potatoes, peeled and cut into thick slices	2 teaspoons capers
1 cinnamon stick	2 tablespoons chopped flat-leaf (Italian) parsley
1 star anise	2 tablespoons semi-dried tomatoes
2 tablespoons olive oil	
2 bunches young spinach, trimmed	

A lovely dish with tender beef cooked to perfection. The speck adds a delicious smoky pork flavour and the carrot puree stirred through towards the end adds colour and sweetness. Serve with fresh sourdough.

BEEF BOURGUIGNON

from Guillaume Brahimi

Heat the oil in a large heavy-based saucepan over medium-high heat. Brown the beef in batches. Remove the final batch of beef from the pan, leaving the oil, and add the carrot, celery, leek, onion and shallots. Sauté for 5-8 minutes.

Place the beef and vegetables in a large casserole pot. Stir in the thyme, bay leaves and speck. Pour over the red wine, season with salt and pepper and cover with a lid. Bring to the boil then reduce the heat to very low and cook for 40 minutes.

Meanwhile, prepare the carrot puree by boiling the carrots with salt until just soft. Puree. To make the mashed potatoes, boil them whole with salt until soft. Peel, return them to the saucepan and mash finely. Stir the mash over medium heat for 3-5 minutes to remove excess water (this will also add air to the potatoes, making them light and fluffy). Warm the milk in a separate saucepan and gradually add to the mash. Stir in the butter. Cover the mash with a lid or plastic wrap and keep warm.

Add the mushrooms and carrot puree to the bourguignon and cook for a further 10 minutes. Sprinkle with the parsley.

Serve the bourguignon with the mashed potatoes and with sourdough.

SERVES 6-8

125 ml (4 fl oz/½ cup) extra-virgin olive oil
1 kg (2 lb 3 oz) beef (preferably wagyu but any braising beef such as rump, topside or chuck steak is fine), cut into large chunks
2 carrots, halved lengthwise and sliced
2 celery stalks with leaves, halved lengthwise and sliced
1 leek, halved lengthwise and sliced
1 onion, chopped
5 shallots, halved
10 thyme sprigs
7 bay leaves
300 g (10½ oz) speck, diced

500 ml (17 fl oz) red wine, boiled briefly to reduce acidity
salt and pepper
300 g (10½ oz) button mushrooms
1 bunch flat-leaf (Italian) parsley, chopped

CARROT PUREE

5 carrots, chopped
salt

MASHED POTATOES

6 large desiree potatoes
salt
200 ml (7 fl oz) milk
100 g (3½ oz) butter

'French food rule number one – only buy what is season.'

Cheese

Legendary French chef Joël Robuchon believes cheese is more than a food - it reflects nature and history. 'A concentrate of that life-giving liquid, namely milk, it allows us to conserve its many qualities. The extent of our range of cheeses ... mirrors the diversity of our land as well as the art of dairymen and women and of social and economic developments over the ages.' France, of course, produces the greatest number of cheese in the world. Here are some of the main types.

FRESH CHEESE
Fresh, rindless cheese that is shaped and kneaded and eaten within a day or two - fromage frais

SOFT BLOOMY RIND CHEESE
Uncooked, unpressed, soft cheese with white mould - camembert, brillat-savarin, brie de meaux

SOFT WASHED RIND
Uncooked, unpressed soft cheese with a washed rind - munster, vacherin, livarot
Uncooked, unpressed soft cheese with a natural mould sometimes covered in ashes -chèvre, fleur du maquis

BLUE CHEESE
Uncooked, unpressed soft cheese with veins of blue mould - roquefort, fourme d'ambert

PRESSED / UNCOOKED
Uncooked, pressed semi-hard cheese sometimes with a natural mould - ossau iraty, morbier, cantal

COOKED / PRESSED
Cooked, pressed hard cheese - beaufort, comté, abundance

The secret of this classic dish is to buy the best onions - they should be really fresh with papery skins - and the best gruyère and a fresh, crusty baguette. I am amazed at the depth of flavour of this simple, lovely soup.

SOUPE À L'OIGNON

French Onion Soup

from France Vidal

Melt the butter in a heavy saucepan and add the onion. Sauté for 25 minutes, stirring from time to time, until deep golden brown and beginning to caramelise.

Add the flour and stir for 2 minutes then add the water and wine and season with salt and pepper. Stir in the cubes of cheese and bring to the boil, then reduce the heat, cover and simmer for 20–25 minutes. Check the seasoning.

Slice the baguette and sprinkle the slices with the grated cheese. Grill until the cheese melts.

Ladle the soup into bowls and serve with slices of cheese baguette on top.

SERVES 6

60 g (2 oz) unsalted butter	salt and pepper
4-5 onions, finely sliced	100 g (3½ oz) good-quality
50 g (1¾ oz/⅓ cup) plain	gruyère, ½ cut into cubes
(all-purpose) flour	and ½ grated
2 litres (68 fl oz/8 cups) water	1 baguette
200 ml (7 fl oz) white wine	

This delicate dessert, made with a fresh soft cheese called *fromage blanc* (smooth quark), is a speciality of Gabriel's native region of Anjou in France. The *coeur* or 'heart' is moulded in a special heart-shaped porcelain dish that is perforated with holes to drain off the excess moisture of the cheese. A colander can be used as an alternative (although you won't end up with the same heart shape). Here it is served with fresh raspberries.

COEUR À LA CRÈME D'ANJOU

Cream Heart from Anjou

from Gabriel Gaté

Beat the egg whites and cream of tartar until stiff peaks form. Add one-third of the sugar and continue beating until smooth.

Beat the cream in a separate bowl until it just starts to stiffen.

Beat the quark in a separate bowl with another third of the sugar and one-third of the lemon juice. Fold in the whipped cream then gently fold in the beaten egg whites.

Place the heart-shaped mould on a tray. Line the mould with damp muslin (cheesecloth) cloth then fill it with the cream mixture. Cover with the cloth and drain in the refrigerator for at least 4–5 hours or overnight.

Puree half the raspberries with the remaining sugar, lemon juice and orange juice. Pass through a sieve to remove the seeds. Refrigerate until 10 minutes before serving.

Carefully turn the heart out onto a serving plate. Top with the remaining whole raspberries and dust with icing sugar. Serve with the raspberry sauce.

SERVES 6-8

2 egg whites	juice of 1½ lemons
pinch of cream of tartar	600 g (1 lb 5 oz) raspberries
110 g (4 oz/½ cup) caster sugar	juice of 1 orange
200 ml (7 fl oz) whipping cream	icing (confectioners') sugar
250 g (9 oz) smooth quark	

Crepes are a delightful way to start the day - as many French families do every Sunday. As the French do - buy the best crepe pan you can and look after it. The suzette butter is so aromatic and alcoholic that this also makes an incredible dessert and the flambéing is pure fun and theatre. It's not that hard to master and the citrus butter becomes lovely and caramelised.

CREPES SUZETTE

from Laurent Branover

Combine the flour, sugar and salt in a large bowl and make a well in the centre. Add the eggs and start whisking with the flour. Slowly add the milk and whisk until smooth. Add the liqueur and leave the batter to rest for 1 hour.

To make the suzette butter, combine the butter, caster sugar and orange zest in a bowl and mix well. Rub the sugar cubes against the skin of the lemon to absorb its flavour. Place the cubes in a separate bowl and add the juice of half an orange. Crush the sugar cubes with a fork, mixing them into the juice. Stir the juice into the butter along with the cognac and liqueur. Segment the remaining oranges and warm them in a shallow pan.

Heat a crepe pan and add a small knob of butter. Add a ladleful of crepe batter, tilting the pan to spread it out to a thin crepe. Cook until golden at the edges, then flip and cook the other side. Continue cooking crepes until you have used all the batter.

Add a knob of suzette butter to the pan and when it melts (without colouring), place a crepe in the pan and coat it in the butter. Flip the crepe to coat the other side in butter, then fold the crepe in half, and in half again to a triangle. Keep the crepe warm and repeat with the rest of the crepes.

To flame the crepes, return all the folded crepes to the pan and pour on the cognac and liqueur. Carefully flame by tilting the pan towards the stove flame or by setting a match to it. Sprinkle the sugar on the flame and prepare to serve. (You can also flame each serve individually if you prefer.) Serve with warm orange segments.

MAKES 10-16 CREPES

250 g (9 oz/1⅔ cups) plain (all-purpose) flour
50 g (1¾ oz/¼ cup) caster sugar
pinch of salt
3 eggs
500 ml (17 fl oz) milk
2 tablespoons citrus-flavoured liqueur such as Cointreau, Grand Marnier or curaçao butter

SUZETTE BUTTER

150 g (5½ oz) butter, softened
180 g (6 oz) caster sugar
2 oranges, one orange zested to give fine shreds
3 sugar cubes
1 lemon
2 tablespoons cognac
2 tablespoons citrus-flavoured liqueur

TO FLAME

2 tablespoons cognac
2 tablespoons citrus-flavoured liqueur
1 tablespoon caster sugar

'A lunch that does not finish with cheese is like a beautiful woman with only one eye.'

Here's a country that's serious about its food. Germans do nothing by halves – their love of food and their cold climate mean that they delight in big, hearty servings of well-cooked dishes. Think of pork knuckle with crunchy, golden crackling served with potatoes, sauerkraut and apple sauce ... They also enjoy many varieties of delicious sausages, hams and cheeses; dense, seed-rich breads; and pretzels dusted with salt. These foods are all delicious but the culinary tradition I love most is that the whole country stops at 4 pm for coffee and cake – and serious cake at that, with liqueur-laced layers, rich toppings and cream ... And they do this every day!

One fond memory I have of travelling to Germany is of the groaning breakfast buffets, full of sliced hams and *wursts* (sausages), different types of cheese including the beloved quark, six different sorts of bread, rollmops and pickles and still more tables laden with yoghurts, cake and muesli. Breakfast is a real showcase of the best this rich farming country has to offer.

And how many sausages come from this one country! There are hundreds of variations on three main types: sausages similar to frankfurters come under the heading *brühwurst,* which means a parboiled sausage made from finely chopped meat; then there's *rohwurst,* which is a raw sausage made from cured meat; and also *leberwurst,* which is a fully cooked sausage. Sausages make great snack food between meals and are sold at street stalls in a bun with lashings of mustard.

As in most European countries, local wines and artisan beers are always accompanied by food. In Bavaria, bar food might consist of a salty pretzel, elsewhere you might get a smoked sausage or a selection of cold cuts, known as *aufschnitt.* German beer is dear to many hearts and the 1200 breweries around the country have firmly supported local purity laws, which stipulate that only hops, barley, yeast and water can be used to make their beer.

Back to those cakes – one of the most popular recipes included here is my friend Martin's show-stopping black forest cake, known in Germany as *schwarzwälder kirschtorte.* This cake was originally created in the late sixteenth century in the Black Forest region of Baden-Württemberg, known for its sour cherries and *kirschwasser* (or kirsch, a double-distilled, clear brandy made from the sour morello cherry). Cherries combined with layers of chocolate cake and cream, topped with little shavings of chocolate to represent the bark of trees ... this is a seriously good cake. I'd stop every day at 4 pm for a slice of this!

ESSENTIAL FLAVOURS

CABBAGE

Both white and red cabbage are used extensively in German cooking. Sauerkraut is the most popular dish, where the cabbage is finely shredded and pickled. Red cabbage is slightly sweeter and sometimes cooked with apple.

JUNIPER BERRIES

Naturally occurring in the evergreen forests of Germany, juniper berries are commonly used to flavour game dishes such as rabbit, goose and duck. They have a clean, sharp flavour that is a bit spicy or savoury. They are considered an essential ingredient in sauerkraut.

MUSTARD

The mustard plant is native to Europe and is therefore a very cheap spice, widely used in European cooking. The seeds of the mustard plant are ground into a paste, which in Germany is a distinctive dark colour and is used as an essential accompaniment to *wursts* (sausages).

QUARK

A fresh curd cheese made from skim milk. With its neutral flavour, quark accounts for approximately half of all the cheese consumed in Germany. It can be used in sweet and savoury dishes.

Smoked pork belly or hock is the basis of the stock used to make this hearty soup. Celery, carrot and parsnip are also used, although any other good stock vegetables can be included. Traditionally eaten during the autumn harvest in the wine region of Germany, this soup recipe can be stretched depending on how many people you're feeding – this version feeds six people. You can happily make more than you need as the soup keeps well and gets better with time - simply freeze or store in the refrigerator for up to five days.

LENTIL SOUP

from Michael Vieh

Place the belly or hock, celery, carrot and parsnip in a large pot and cover with the water.

Add 2 teaspoons salt (or less if the pork is very salty) and bring to the boil. Simmer gently for a couple of hours.

Remove the pork and strain the stock, discarding the vegetables. Bring the stock back to a simmer and add the lentils. Cook for 10 minutes.

Cut the pork into rough smallish chunks and add back to the pot. Simmer for a few more minutes then add the potato. Cook for another 15-20 minutes.

Melt the lard in a frying pan and add the flour and brown lightly. Add to the soup being careful not to let it splash and burn; as the flour cooks it will thicken the soup.

SERVES 6

1 smoked pork belly or hock	4 cups green lentils, soaked for 2 hours
2 celery stalks, roughly chopped	3 large, waxy potatoes, cut into cubes
2 carrots, roughly chopped	1 tablespoon lard
1 parsnip, roughly chopped	1 tablespoon plain (all-purpose) flour
2-3 litres water	
salt	

'If you don't sweat in the kitchen while you cook, the food will taste only half as good!'

Sauerbraten (sour roast) is said to be Germany's national dish. It's a long-marinated meat dish that uses some of the great flavours of German cooking - juniper berries, allspice and red wine. Detlef likes to use star anise and the red-currant jelly, sour cream and sultanas are added for a slightly sweet finish. This recipe is very yummy and the bread dumplings are worth the work!

SAUERBRATEN WITH NAPKIN DUMPLINGS AND SAUTÉED CABBAGE

from Detlef Haupt

Bring the red wine, vinegar and water to the boil. Add the spices and bay leaves and allow to cool. Place the beef, vegetables and parsley in a deep bowl and pour over the red-wine marinade. Marinate in a cool place (or in the refrigerator) for a minimum of 2 days, turning the beef frequently.

Take the beef out of the marinade and pat dry with paper towel. Rub the beef generously with salt and pepper. Heat some olive oil and a knob of butter in a heavy-based oven-proof pot and quickly seal the meat, browning well all over. Add the vegetables from the marinade and sauté with the beef.

Pour over the marinade liquid and add the gingerbread if using. Bring almost to the boil then reduce the heat, cover and braise the beef over low heat for 1½–2 hours or until the meat is tender. Add more water if necessary to keep the beef covered while it cooks.

Meanwhile, make the dumplings. Place the bread pieces in a bowl. Heat the milk and pour it over the bread. Sauté the onion and speck in a little duck fat or lard until the onion is glossy and the speck is cooked and add to the bread. Add 4 eggs, one at a time, mixing well with a wooden spoon. Add the parsley and nutmeg and season well with salt and pepper. If the mixture seems too dry you may need to add another egg or two. If it appears too wet, add a handful of breadcrumbs. Turn the mixture onto a piece of muslin (cheesecloth) and shape into a large sausage. Roll up inside the cloth and tie the ends tightly with butcher's string.

Carefully slide the dumpling into a saucepan of boiling salted water and cook for about 40 minutes. Remove from the water and let it cool a little before unwrapping and cutting into slices 2 fingers thick. You can serve the dumplings like this, or pan-fry the slices in butter to add a bit of extra flavour and crunchiness.

When the beef is cooked, remove it and keep warm. Strain the liquid, discarding the vegetables, and return it to the pot to reduce a little and form a sauce. Whisk in the sour cream and red-currant jelly and season well. Rinse the sultanas or raisins under warm water and add to the sauce. Keep simmering at very low heat.

To make the cabbage, sauté the onion and speck in the duck fat or lard until the onion is glossy and the speck is cooked. Add the cabbage and sauté for 2–3 minutes. Add the caraway seeds and a little salt.

Slice the beef and arrange on a warm plate. Dress with the sauce and serve with the hot dumplings and cabbage.

SERVES 8

200 ml (7 fl oz) red wine
200 ml (7 fl oz) red-wine vinegar
500 ml (17 fl oz/2 cups) water
6 juniper berries (or more to taste)
a few star anise or whole allspice berries
a few peppercorns
2 bay leaves
1 kg (2 lb 3 oz) piece of beef brisket or rump
2 carrots, roughly chopped
2 celery stalks, roughly chopped
1 onion, roughly chopped
1 leek, roughly chopped
a few flat-leaf (Italian) parsley stalks
salt and pepper
olive oil
butter
60 g (2 oz) gingerbread from last Christmas, crumbled (optional)
2 tablespoons sour cream
100 g (3½ oz) red-currant jelly

150 g (5½ oz) sultanas (golden raisins) or raisins

DUMPLINGS

1 large good-quality, day-old vienna loaf, crusts discarded and cut into chunky cubes
150 ml (5 fl oz) milk
1 onion, diced
100 g (3½ oz) speck, diced
duck fat or lard
4-6 eggs
½ bunch flat-leaf (Italian) parsley, finely chopped
a little freshly grated nutmeg
salt and pepper
fresh breadcrumbs if needed
butter (optional)

CABBAGE

1 onion, diced
100 g (3½ oz) speck, diced
1 tablespoon duck fat or lard
½ cabbage, finely sliced
1 teaspoon caraway seeds
salt

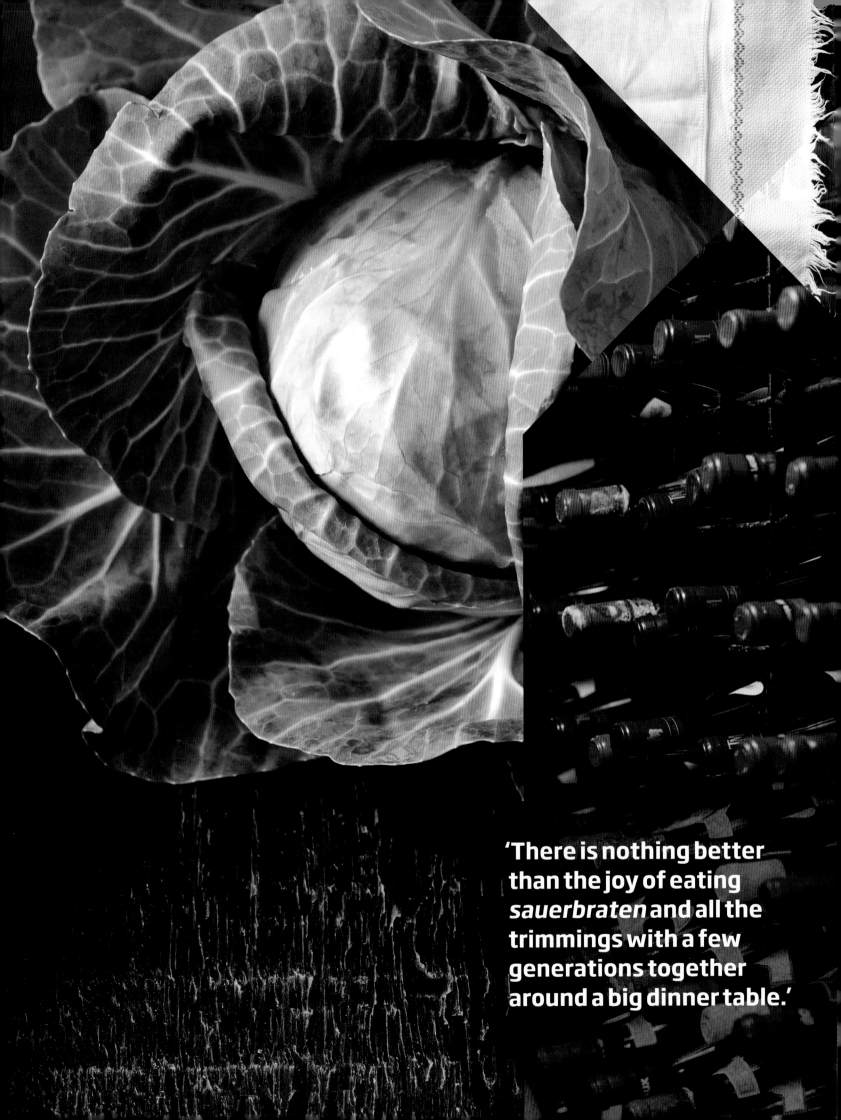

'There is nothing better than the joy of eating *sauerbraten* and all the trimmings with a few generations together around a big dinner table.'

A favourite all over Germany, these pork knuckles (otherwise known as hocks) are the perfect mix of crunchy crackling and tender meat – and they're so easy to cook. Here they're infused with garlic and caraway and served with delicious potato dumplings and slow-cooked red cabbage. For a really deluxe meal, add some fried onion rings and apple sauce. Start the dumplings and cabbage the day before. A perfect dish to prepare on lazy winter days.

PORK KNUCKLE WITH POTATO DUMPLINGS AND BRAISED RED CABBAGE

from Max Dietz

The day before, boil the potatoes for the dumplings in their skins until soft. Leave to cool. For the red cabbage, combine the cabbage, apple, half the onion, the spices, bay leaves, sugar, salt, pepper and wine and leave to marinate overnight.

The next day, preheat the oven to 180°C (350°F/Gas 4). Rub the skin of the pork hocks with generous amounts of salt, garlic and oil. Sprinkle with the caraway seeds. Place in a baking dish with 2 cm (¾ in) of water and roast for 2 hours.

To make the potato dumplings, peel the cooked potatoes and mash them. Incorporate with the flour, egg, chives, salt, pepper and nutmeg. Roll into a long sausage and cut into pieces about the size of golf balls. Roll into balls.

To cook the red cabbage, fry the remaining onion and bacon in the butter. Add a splash of red wine, then add the marinated cabbage mixture.

Cover and braise for 20 minutes over low heat until soft. Season to taste. Cook the dumplings in salted boiling water until they float (around 2 minutes) then drain.

Arrange the roast pork with the dumplings and red cabbage on a serving plate and carve at the table.

SERVES 4-6

POTATO DUMPLINGS

500 g (1 lb 2 oz) potatoes
100 g (3½ oz/⅔ cup)
    plain (all-purpose) flour
1 egg
1 bunch chives, finely chopped
salt and pepper
freshly grated nutmeg

RED CABBAGE

2 red cabbages, finely sliced
2 apples, peeled, cored and
    finely sliced
1 onion, finely sliced
2 juniper berries
2 cloves
2 bay leaves
2 tablespoons sugar
salt and pepper
250 ml (8½ fl oz/1 cup) red
    wine, plus a splash extra
2 bacon rashers, finely sliced
1 tablespoon butter

PORK KNUCKLE

1 kg (2 lb 3 oz) pork hocks
2 tablespoons salt
finely chopped garlic
olive oil
caraway seeds

I'm ordering this for every birthday – Martin's version of the classic cake makes your knees go weak. He uses a chocolate mousse recipe from Heston Blumenthal's book *In Search of Perfection* (but any basic mousse recipe is fine) and likes to garnish the cake with fresh cherries that have been marinated in kirsch for one week.

BLACK FOREST CAKE

from Martin Boetz

To make the butter cake, preheat the oven to 180°C (350°F/ Gas 4) and butter a cake tin. Cream the butter and sugar. Beat in the eggs one at a time then fold in the flour and baking powder. Pour into the tin and bake for 55 minutes. Leave to cool.

Butter another cake tin of the same size for the chocolate cake. Melt the chocolate and butter together in a bowl set over a saucepan of simmering water then leave to cool. Beat the eggs and sugar together. Fold in the melted chocolate then the flour. Pour into the tin and bake for 1 hour. Leave to cool.

To make the chocolate mousse, beat the egg yolks with the sugar for 5 minutes or until stiff. Gently warm the milk in a saucepan then remove from the heat. Stir in the egg yolks and return to medium heat. Cook for 2–3 minutes, stirring frequently. Use a digital probe to monitor when the temperature of the mixture reaches 80°C (176°F) and remove from the heat.

Place the chocolate in a mixing bowl and pour over the warm milk and egg mixture, stirring until the chocolate has melted. Add the salt and leave to cool.

Whip the cream until soft peaks form then fold into the cooled chocolate mixture. Spoon into a piping bag and refrigerate to stiffen. (*Continued over*)

SERVES 16

BUTTER CAKE

300 g (10½ oz) butter
300 g (10½ oz) caster sugar
6 eggs
300 g (10½ oz/2 cups) plain
** (all-purpose) flour**
1½ teaspoons baking powder

CHOCOLATE CAKE

250 g (9 oz) chocolate, chopped
180 g (6 oz) butter
6 eggs
250 g (9 oz) caster sugar
225 g (1½ cups) plain
** (all-purpose) flour**

CHOCOLATE MOUSSE

4 egg yolks (combined weight
** of 80 g [2¾ oz])**
200 g (7 oz) caster sugar
100 ml (3½ fl oz) full-cream
** milk**
150 g (5½ oz) top-quality dark
** chocolate, chopped**
generous pinch of salt
200 ml (7 fl oz) whipping cream

CHOCOLATE GANACHE

95 ml (3¼ fl oz) whipping cream
1 teaspoon glucose syrup
pinch of salt
95 g (3¼ oz) top-quality dark
** chocolate, chopped**
20 g (¾ oz) unsalted butter

CHERRIES

680 g (1½ lb) jar sour (morello)
** cherries**
1 vanilla bean, split
1 tablespoon sugar

TO ASSEMBLE

kirsch
whipped cream
shards of dark or milk chocolate
10 whole fresh cherries
** (preferably soaked in kirsch**
** for 1 week)**

To make the chocolate ganache, gently heat the cream, glucose syrup and salt. Place the chocolate in a bowl and add the warm cream, stirring until the chocolate melts. Add the butter and stir until it melts.

Strain the cherry juice into a saucepan. Add the vanilla bean and sugar and simmer until reduced to a syrup.

Carefully cut each cake into three slices. Place a layer of butter cake on a flat plate and splash with a little kirsch. Pipe a rim of mousse around the top of the cake to form a wall to keep in the cherries. Fill with some cherries then top with a layer of chocolate cake. Spread with whipped cream. Repeat the layers but instead of topping the cake with cream, spread with ganache. Allow it to run down the sides of the cake or if preferred, use a spatula to smooth the ganache around the sides of the cake. Sprinkle with chocolate shards (to resemble the bark of trees in a forest) and garnish with whole cherries. Leave the cake to set for 3–6 hours – in the refrigerator if necessary but take it out at least 1 hour before serving.

Thank God they came! When the Greeks began emigrating in large numbers in the 1950s and '60s, our culinary landscape started to change for the better. Greek households transplanted their native flavours and grew much of what they needed in their own gardens – a pot of basil at the back door to ward off the evil eye, and healthy rows of herbs and vegetables as well as fruit trees in the backyard. Often there was an extra kitchen installed in a big double garage or cellar where some of the 'heavy duty' cooking was done, such as the preserving of sweets in heavy syrup. Called 'spoon sweets', these intense little treats are served on a glass saucer with a small teaspoon and a glass of icy-cold water as soon as a visitor is two steps inside the house.

Since their arrival we've embraced the Greeks and their approach to food whole-heartedly: fetta, a wide range of olive varieties, olive oil. Taramasalata is a word most people recognise and vine leaves are used in dishes around the country. We also readily cook with filo pastry and add oregano and garlic to our lamb roasts.

And we love the fact that Greek food is so damned good for us. Much of what is preached as ideal eating in the food pages of magazines is integral to Greek cuisine – simplicity, seasonality and freshness. Bunches of spinach and silverbeet so fresh they almost squeak, ripe tomatoes that really do taste like tomatoes, very fresh cucumber with its sweetness and crunch, thick creamy Greek yoghurt and olive oil ... (Although the oil isn't used quite as liberally as one would in Greece. My friend George laughs that his grandmother would hold a whole conversation as she upended the olive oil in whatever dish she was making!)

The key to Greek cuisine is the power of the *yia yia* (usually the grandmother and sometimes extended to include the aunties). She is the keeper of recipes and traditions, the one who knows whether moussaka has the right amount of salt just from smelling it, who knows exactly how hot the oil should be for *loukoumades*, and whose oven never quite cools down in the huge baking frenzy that happens in the run-up to Greek Easter.

My friend Peter, a great chef, says the focus on food is unwavering: 'Greek women chase you round with a spoon from the minute you open your eyes in the morning. It's all about the food!' There was a time not long ago when no self-respecting Greek would be seen in a Greek restaurant.

Firstly, Greek cooking is generally so good at home that you'd never go out and eat an inferior version of what your mum could make, and then there's the public humiliation – 'Our mothers would kill us if they thought we were eating Greek food away from home. What if someone saw? Everyone would think Mum couldn't cook!'

ESSENTIAL FLAVOURS

CHEESE

Fetta: Traditionally made from sheep's or goat's milk, it is salted and cured in a brine solution. It is traditionally used for baking or in the classic Greek salad. *Piperati* is a barrel-aged, highquality, piquant fetta with a creamy texture that is used in Greek salads.

Haloumi: A Cypriot cheese that is usually fried until molten - it must be eaten immediately.

Kasseri: A mild, soft sheep's milk cheese that's similar to cheddar and is usually eaten on its own.

Graviera: A hard cheese with a mild taste that resembles gruyère in texture, it is served with meals or used grated over pasta or other dishes.

Kefalograviera: A hard, salty cheese that is like a cross between *graviera* and *kefalotyri*, it is used as a grating cheese and also fried for saganaki recipes.

Kefalotyri: A sheep's or goat's milk cheese that is grated and added to dishes as they cook or fried in olive oil for saganaki.

DRIED OREGANO (*RIGANI*)

This is the main herb in Greek cooking and the flower buds are used more commonly than the leaves. It is used in many dishes, from *pastitsio* (baked pasta) to moussaka, or sprinkled over Greek salads. You can buy bunches of *rigani* at any Greek or Mediterranean food store. Simply crush the buds over your dish to get a shower of this fragrant dried herb.

MASTIC

A gum resin from trees that grow only on the Greek island of Chios. It is used in the making of ice cream, sweets, chewing gum and liqueur and also has medicinal and pharmaceutical properties. It has an earthy, musky, vanilla-like flavour.

MEZEDES

In Greece you rarely drink without eating and a whole tradition of small snacks (*mezedes*) surround what you take as an aperitif. *Mezedes* (plural for 'meze') include anchovy fillets, salted fish, *pastourma* (dried and spiced meat - originally camel but now commonly beef), yellow cheese, dips such as taramasalata, *melitzanosalata* (eggplant dip) and tzatziki, as well as *kafteri* (spicy fetta), calamari (squid), octopus (either grilled or braised in various ways), *tiropita* (cheese pastries), zucchini (courgettes) patties, *keftedes* (meatballs), fried haloumi and *loukanika* (spicy Greek sausages), and let's not forget olives and pickled peppers.

OLIVES

Kalamata: These strong, salty olives range in size from small, mammoth and colossal to super colossal.

Throumbes: From the island of Thasos, these sun-dried olives have a raisin-like flavour.

Skordalia is a sauce or dip usually made from potato and flavoured with garlic, olive oil, lemon juice and parsley. This white bean version is fast and delicious. Once you have this in the fridge you'll find a way to slather it on toasted sourdough, add to roasted meats, and use as a dip with sliced fresh vegetables. And it's a one minute recipe!

Such a fabulous combination of flavours - spinach, dill and spring onions with a creamy mix of cheeses. My daughter is always cooking this at home. The spinach can be prepared a day ahead - it must be as dry as possible to ensure the spanakopita doesn't become soggy.

BEAN SKORDALIA

from George Calombaris

Puree the cannellini beans with the lemon juice, garlic and olive oil until smooth.

MAKES 2 CUPS

400 g (14 oz) tin cannellini (lima) beans, drained	2 garlic cloves, roughly chopped
juice of 1 lemon	3 tablespoons olive oil

'The ultimate compliment
for a Greek cook is
"*Yia sta heria!*"
(I kiss your hands!)'

SPANAKOPITA

from Dimitra Alfred

Trim the roots from the spinach or if using silver beet, cut out the stems. Wash leaves and drain well. Coarsely shred and set aside.

Place the fetta in a large bowl and roughly mash with a fork. Add the ricotta, hard cheese, eggs, breadcrumbs, nutmeg, pepper, oil, dill and spring onions. Mix with the fork to combine.

Preheat the oven to 180°C (350°F/Gas 4). Lightly oil or butter a 20 × 30 × 5 cm (8 × 12 × 2 in) baking dish. Lay the filo out on a work surface. Line the dish with a sheet of filo and brush it with butter. Top with another sheet of filo brushed with butter and continue until about half the filo is used. When not using the filo, cover it with a dry tea towel and then a damp one to keep it from drying out.

Add the spinach or silverbeet to the fetta mixture and mix well, using a large spoon or your hands, until thoroughly combined. Tip into the filo base and spread out evenly. Layer with the remaining sheets of filo brushed with butter, ensuring the final sheet is well buttered. Trim off any over-hanging pastry and tuck in the sides.

Use a sharp knife to score the pastry into diamonds. Pierce the pastry once or twice to allow air to escape during baking. Sprinkle lightly with water and bake in the oven for 45–60 minutes or until well browned. Gently shake the baking dish; the spanakopita should slide easily when it is cooked. Cover with foil if it is over-browning.

Cool on a rack for 15 minutes before cutting to serve.

SERVES 8-10

1 bunch spinach or silverbeet	½ teaspoon freshly ground black pepper
300 g (10½ oz) fetta	3 tablespoons olive oil
100 g (3½ oz) ricotta	2 dill sprigs, chopped
40 g (1½ oz/½ cup) finely grated hard cheese such as *kefalograviera*, parmesan or pecorino	4 spring onions (scallions), chopped
5 eggs	375 g (13 oz) fresh (not frozen) filo pastry
2 tablespoons dry breadcrumbs	125 g (4½ oz) butter, melted
¼ teaspoon ground nutmeg	

This is a change from the usual leg of lamb recipe - it uses lamb neck which is incredibly cheap and here it cooks until very tender, especially after its baked in yoghurt and honey - who else but George would have added the classic Greek breakfast favourite to lamb and made such a delicious dish. It's finished on the barbecue to add a rich caramelised flavour that marries beautifully with the crunch of thinly sliced fennel and fresh parsley.

GREEK LAMB WITH FENNEL AND PARSLEY

from George Calombaris

Preheat the oven to 160°C (320°F/Gas 3). Season the lamb with salt. Place 100 ml (3½ fl oz) of olive oil in a deep ovenproof pot and seal the lamb until golden brown on all sides. Add the onion, shallots, garlic, lemon zest, *rigani* and white wine to the pot. Cover the lamb with the yoghurt and drizzle with honey. Cover and bake for 1½ hours.

Remove the lamb from the pot and leave to cool. Refrigerate for at least 1 hour.

Strain the vegetables from the pot and place in a bowl. Add the fennel and parsley. Season to taste and drizzle with oil.

Slice the lamb into thin strips. Place the strips on a barbecue and cook on both sides. Serve with the fennel salad.

SERVES 4

500 g (1 lb 2 oz) boneless lamb neck	1 tablespoon *rigani* (dried Greek oregano)
sea salt	250 ml (8½ fl oz/1 cup) white wine
olive oil	
1 onion, roughly chopped	200 g (7 oz) natural yoghurt
6 shallots, roughly chopped	1 tablespoon honey
2 garlic cloves, sliced	1 fennel bulb, finely sliced
grated zest of 1 lemon	6 flat-leaf (Italian) parsley sprigs, leaves picked

When cucumbers and tomatoes are at their summer best, there is nothing to match this fresh-tasting salad. Seek out the best fetta you can find. In this beautiful fresh salad - even the dressing left in the bottom of the salad bowl is delicious - grab some crusty bread to mop up the salad dressing - flavoured with the juice of the fresh vegetables.

There is an art to getting the foamy crema, or *kaimaki*, on top just right when you brew coffee in a *briki* (a Greek coffee pot that is like a small jug meets saucepan). If you perfect it, then you're deemed to be marriageable!

GREEK SALAD

from George Calombaris

Break the bread into rough pieces and bake in the oven until golden brown. Set aside to cool.

Combine the cucumber, tomato, olives, shallots, *rigani*, fetta and dill in a bowl. Drizzle over the oil and vinegar and season with salt. Add the bread and toss. Serve immediately.

SERVES 4

½ ciabatta loaf, crusts discarded	1 teaspoon *rigani* (dried Greek oregano)
2 Lebanese cucumbers, peeled, quartered lengthwise, diced	100 g (3½ oz) fetta, crumbled
2 vine-ripened tomatoes, diced	5 dill sprigs, leaves picked
handful of kalamata olives	100 ml (3½ fl oz) olive oil
3 shallots, finely sliced	2½ tablespoons brown vinegar
	salt

GREEK COFFEE

from Liz Kaydos

Measure an espresso cup of water per person into the *briki*. Add 1 heaped tablespoon of coffee per person and 1 teaspoon of sugar if desired and stir briefly. Place over high heat. When the coffee just comes to the boil and there is a thick layer of foam (*kaimaki*) on top, remove from the heat and let stand for about 15 seconds for the foam to settle. Pour or spoon some foam into each cup, then carefully pour in the coffee keeping the foam on the surface.

water
pulverised Greek coffee
sugar

'To raise a toast say 'Stini yamas!' (To your health!)'

Pastries and Biscuits

Greek pastries and biscuits are wickedly addictive – from the first satisfying crunch of baklava filled with crushed nuts and bathed in syrup to a large forkful of a creamy, custardy wonder still warm from the oven ... you'll be enchanted for life.

Amigdalota: Almond swirl biscuits that are chewy inside and crunchy outside.

Baklava: A symphony of filo pastry, ground nuts (usually almond or cashew) and syrup traditionally cut into a diamond shape.

Galaktoboureko: Thick custard between crunchy filo pastry served warm with syrup – an experience that will make your eyelids flutter.

Kataifi: A shredded pastry that replaces filo to make pastries filled with nuts and drenched in sugar syrup. It is extra crunchy and looks amazing too.

Kourambiedes: The most heavenly, melting shortbread crescents made with toasted almonds and smothered in icing (confectioners') sugar.

Melamakarona: Honey and orange biscuits shaped in a lozenge, topped with crushed walnuts and with a wonderful cinnamon aroma.

Is there anything sexier than a fresh fig – ripe, heavy in its skin, luscious and honeyed inside? This recipe combines the classic *loukoumades* (fried doughnuts) with gorgeous figs. Simply divine!

FIG LOUKOUMADES WITH RASPBERRY SYRUP

from Peter Conistis

To make the batter, place the dry ingredients in a bowl and whisk in enough water to make a smooth batter with the consistency of thick pouring cream. Set aside for 15 minutes.

To make the syrup, place the sugar, water and lemon juice in a saucepan and bring to the boil, stirring until the sugar dissolves. Turn the heat back to a simmer and add the raspberries and rosewater, stirring to loosen the raspberries. Bring back to a simmer then remove from the heat.

Heat the oil in a saucepan. Dust the figs in flour then skewer each one with a fork to dip them into the batter, rolling them around to coat them evenly. Drop the figs into the hot oil and cook until golden brown. Drain on paper towel then arrange on a serving platter. Spoon over the raspberry syrup.

SERVES 4-6

BATTER

150 g (5½ oz/1 cup) plain (all-purpose) flour
2 teaspoons dried yeast
pinch of sea salt
2 tablespoons sugar
water

SYRUP

440 g (15½ oz/2 cups) sugar
500 ml (17 fl oz) water
juice of 1 lemon
1 cup raspberries (fresh or frozen)
1 teaspoon rosewater

oil for deep-frying
12 green figs
2 tablespoons plain (all-purpose) flour for dusting

I'm always intrigued by the beloved family cooking pots and pans that make the long journey to their new homes from far away. For my Hungarian friend Stephen (Istvan), it was a heavy witch's cauldron called a *bogrács* that could not be left behind. In this he makes the superb dish that's synonymous with Hungary - *gulyas* (goulash). A stew of tender chunks of meat in a rich paprika-laced sauce, *gulyas* has been made since the nomadic tribes rode the Great Plain (although paprika came to be included later). The name *gulyas* actually means 'herdsmen'. Over centuries *gulyas* came to be eaten by all Hungarians and rose to the heights of a national symbol when Hungary took a stand to protect its distinctive language, culture and gastronomy. That was 200 years ago. *Gulyas* and its variations - *paprikas*, *tokany* and *porkolt* - are still adored and cooked all the time.

During the summer months groups of Hungarian men and sometimes women hold cook-off competitions in central Hungary, gathering in the countryside to vie for the title of best *bogrács gulyas* (kettle goulash). This title is treasured and respected - recipes are carefully guarded and getting everything right is paramount.

The key ingredient in *gulyas* and many other Hungarian dishes is paprika. Paprika was introduced by the Bulgarians and Turks in the sixteenth and seventeenth centuries and is used in Hungary in its powdered form as well as in pastes. Stephen says that when the oil, onion and paprika are starting to cook for *gulyas*, the heart and soul of the dish is born. Each Hungarian dish calls for different types of paprika, ranging from 'exquisitely delicate' through to hot. The paprika pastes are held so dear to people's hearts that they actually have nicknames - *edes anna* ('Gentle Anna') is mild while *eros pista* ('Strong Stephen') is hot and fiery. This is truly a fascinating spice!

Also fascinating and a world unto themselves are Hungarian sweets. These were elevated to an art form in the days of the Austro-Hungarian Empire when many delectable confections were created and celebrated - strudels filled with apple, sour or sweet cherries, cream cheese, poppy seeds and walnuts; elaborate layered cakes like the magnificent *dobostorta*, with its mahogany toffee topping; the light, yeasty *kugelhoph* cake; the sweet, festive *beigli* pastries and many more delights. I fell completely under the spell of these Hungarian cakes and - true confession here - I polished off an entire *kugelhoph* by myself over a day or two. How could I resist this delicious yeast cake with its seam of pure chocolate ... It was exceptional!

ESSENTIAL FLAVOURS

CARAWAY SEEDS
Thought to be one of the oldest spices in Europe, they have an anise-like flavour and aroma and are a key ingredient in *liptauer* (a spicy cheese spread), some meat stews such as *gulyas*, soups and breads.

MORELLO CHERRIES
A variety of griotte or dark sour cherry. They are grown extensively in Hungary and used in both sweet and savoury dishes, including *hideg meggyleves* (sour cherry soup) and strudels.

PAPRIKA
Paprika comes in seven categories including special, mild, delicate, sweet, semi-sweet, rose and hot. For fiery-hot, look for paprika that is labelled 'eros'. Any paprika labelled 'sweet' or 'edesnemes' is more mild than hot. It is usually available in dried or paste form.

POPPY SEEDS
Blue-grey in colour and slightly nutty in flavour, poppy seeds are sprinkled over pasta and used extensively in Hungarian baking - in strudels, tortes and the festive *beigli*.

SAUERKRAUT
A fermented cabbage. Sauerkraut is an excellent source of vitamin C and is commonly eaten with Hungarian *kolbas*, salami or *csabai* sausages. Sauerkraut is generally consumed as part of a traditional dish such as stuffed cabbage or *székely gulyas*.

SOUR CREAM
Traditionally made by leaving cream to sour naturally, it's now made by pasteurising and homogenising single cream and adding a pure form of bacteria that grows until the desired tartness and consistency is reached. Sour cream is used liberally in Hungarian cooking, in both savoury and sweet dishes.

Porkolt is a beautiful casserole of tender veal cooked with paprika and garlic. Beef can be used instead (cuts such as chuck steak or gravy beef), as can pork (neck or leg). Traditionally this is served with *nokedli* – quick homemade pasta served with lashings of butter.

PORKOLT WITH NOKEDLI AND CUCUMBER SALAD

from Stephen (Istvan) Orosvari

To make the cucumber salad, mix the ingredients other than the paprika in a bowl and refrigerate for a couple of hours for the flavours to develop. Sprinkle with paprika before serving, if using; it will not change the taste but will make the dish more attractive.

To make the *porkolt*, sauté the onion in the oil until golden. Remove from the heat and add the paprika (removing from the heat ensures the colour and flavour is released without burning). Stir for a minute then add the stock or water and return to the heat. Simmer until slightly reduced. Add the meat, salt, garlic and paprika paste and stir well. Simmer until the meat is halfway tender (30–60 minutes depending on the meat). Add the banana chilli and tomato and continue to cook until the meat is tender. Taste for seasoning.

While the *porkolt* is cooking, make the *nokedli*. Bring a large pot (5 litres/169 fl oz) of water to the boil and add 20 g (¾ oz) of salt. Meanwhile, beat the eggs with the water. Sift the flour and a pinch of salt into a bowl and lightly mix in the egg and water. (Be careful not to over-mix, which will make the dough unworkable.) Push the dough through a *nokedli* maker or *spatzle* press into the boiling water. Cook until the *nokedli* rise to the surface then remove with a slotted spoon. Toss in butter or oil.

Serve the *porkolt* on the *nokedli* alongside the cucumber salad.

SERVES 8

CUCUMBER SALAD
- 1.5 kg (3 lb 4 oz) long cucumbers, peeled and finely sliced
- 2½ tablespoons white vinegar
- 80 g (2¾ oz) sugar
- pinch of salt and pepper
- 1 garlic clove, crushed
- paprika (optional)
- 5 g salt
- 3 garlic cloves, crushed
- 1 teaspoon hot paprika paste (*eros pista*)
- 3 banana chillies (mild Hungarian capsicums), roughly chopped
- 1 large tomato, roughly chopped

PORKOLT
- 1 large onion, finely chopped
- 100 ml (3½ fl oz) oil
- 20 g sweet paprika
- 200 ml (7 fl oz) stock or water
- 1.4 kg (3 lb 1 oz) veal leg or shoulder, diced into 2 cm (¾ in) cubes

NOKEDLI
- salt
- 4 eggs
- 650 ml (22 fl oz) water
- 800 g (1 lb 12 oz) plain (all-purpose) flour
- butter or oil

This recipe creates tender chicken with a lovely golden coating and it is delicious with mashed, boiled or fried potatoes. We make it at home at least every couple of weeks and love the simple recipe.

CHICKEN SCHNITZEL

from Csaba Cserfalvi

Place the chicken breasts on a chopping board and use a sharp knife to slice horizontally through the breasts to create 2 or 3 (depending on the thickness) thin, even slices per breast.

Flatten the slices with a meat mallet.

Lay out 3 wide bowls. Put the flour in one and season it with salt and pepper. In another, beat the egg with the water. Place the breadcrumbs in the other.

Using one hand, lightly coat each piece of chicken in the flour, shaking off the excess. Dip into the egg then coat with breadcrumbs.

Heat a deep frying pan with the oil and fry the schnitzels one or two at a time, cooking until golden brown on each side. When cooked, stand upright in a deep bowl lined with paper towel to drain. Cook the remaining schnitzels.

Serve with mashed, boiled or fried potatoes.

SERVES 4-6

2 large chicken breasts
150 g (5½ oz/1 cup) plain
   (all-purpose) flour
salt and pepper

1 egg
1 tablespoon water
2 cups dry breadcrumbs
500 ml (17 fl oz/2 cups)
   vegetable oil

'"Jo etvagyat, barataim!"
(Enjoy your meals, my friends!)'

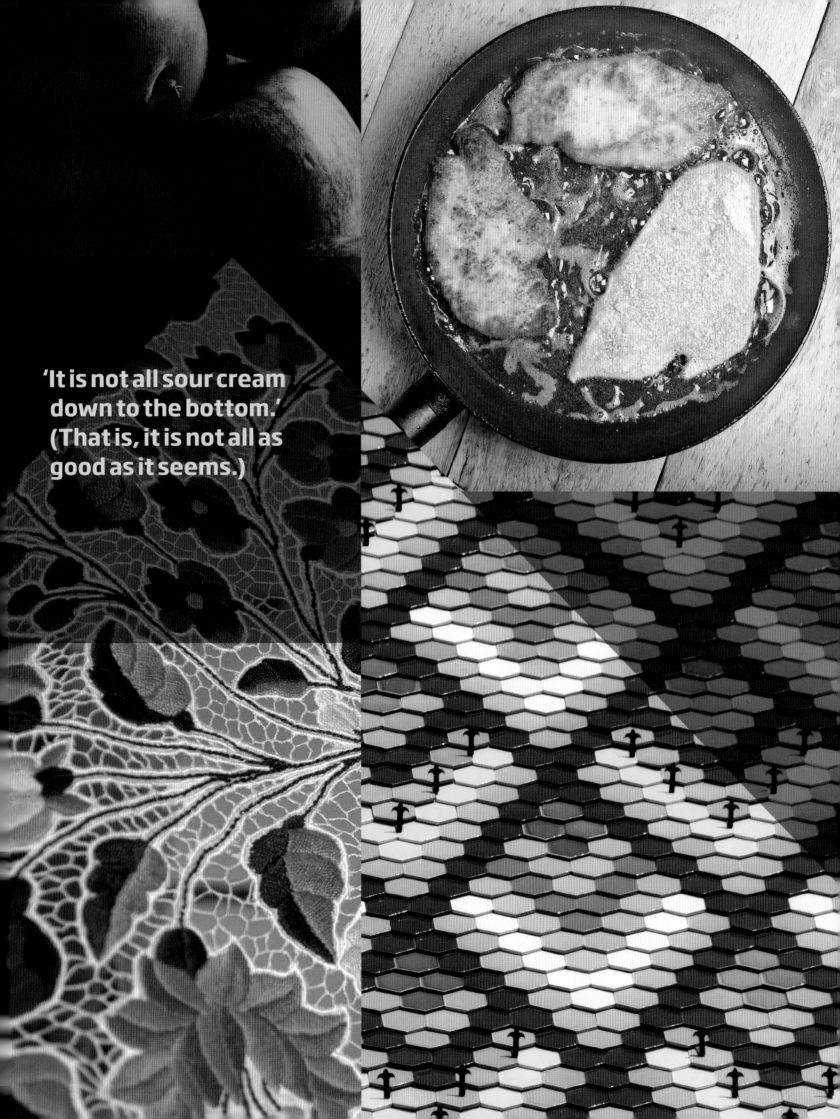

'It is not all sour cream down to the bottom.'
(That is, it is not all as good as it seems.)

A luscious mixture of cherries and cheese encased in golden flaky pastry from a great cook, my friend Janelle, who learned the art of baking from her beloved Hungarian grandmother. If time allows, drain the ricotta in the fridge for 1–2 hours before making the filling.

NAN'S CHERRY AND CREAM CHEESE STRUDEL

from Janelle Bloom

Preheat the oven to 200°C (400°F/Gas 6) and line a baking tray with baking paper.

Combine the ricotta, cream cheese, sugar and vanilla and beat until smooth and creamy.

Add the egg and beat well.

Lay a sheet of filo on a work surface and brush with melted clarified butter. Top with another sheet brushed with butter. Repeat until you have used all the sheets (there should be some butter remaining).

Sprinkle the breadcrumbs evenly over the pastry. Spoon the cheese mixture along one long edge, leaving a small border. Top with the cherries and sprinkle with the almonds. Fold in the ends of the pastry and roll up, enclosing the filling.

Brush the edge with butter to stick it down.

Place on the tray and brush the top with the remaining butter.

Bake for 15 minutes then reduce the oven temperature to 180°C (350°F/Gas 4) and bake for a further 5 minutes, until the pastry is crisp and deep golden. Allow to cool for 30 minutes before dusting heavily with icing sugar, slicing and serving.

SERVES 8-10

125 g (4½ oz) full-cream ricotta, drained for 1-2 hours
125 g (4½ oz) cream cheese, softened
3 tablespoons caster sugar
1 teaspoon vanilla extract
1 egg
5 filo pastry sheets

80 g (2¾ oz) clarified butter (ghee), melted
2 tablespoons dry breadcrumbs
680 g (1½ lb) jar sour (morello) cherries, drained
1 tablespoon flaked almonds, toasted
icing (confectioners') sugar

INDIA

In a country of extremes – of intense colour, of incredible architecture, of rich and poor – you know that the food is never going to be dull. And given this country stretches from the tropics almost to the world's highest mountain, it is not surprising that there's an amazing range of cooking styles and ingredients used.

When investigating Indian cuisine I was struck by the enormous difference between an Indian kitchen and one you'd find in the 'white-bread' suburbs. An Indian home has a lovely aroma of spice in the air as if these magic ingredients have a life of their own, even when they're not being used for cooking. The other big difference is that the cooking essentials are all within reach. Whether in a kitchen of gleaming, uncluttered bench tops or that of a more compact apartment, every Indian cook has the same glass-topped pannier of spices kept by the stove. Like an artist's palate, this array of six or seven key spices is used to colour and flavour all of their dishes. There is no fiddling with spice canisters in cupboards; instead they're to hand and spooned in with confidence. After years of intense training Indian cooks know how a dish should look and smell so there is no checking of recipes.

And what wonderful spices they are. Some are used whole and toasted in a dry pan then ground, others are pre-ground, others are fresh … Each recipe calls for a variety and it's this clever blending of spices that creates the depth of flavour in great Indian dishes. Devotees of Indian food can easily pick the difference between regional dishes, particularly those of the north and south – the north favours richer food with lots of ghee, meat and wheat; the south is full of intense tropical flavours, coconut milk and rice.

In just over a generation, we have become a nation that knows its korma from its tandoori – in the UK, where Indian cuisine reigns supreme, vindaloo is almost the national dish. Indian cuisine certainly deserves to be studied and enjoyed as it has made our multicultural tapestry even richer and more fabulous.

KITCHEN TOOLS

KADHAI
A round-bottomed cooking pan similar to a wok. Because of its shape it uses less oil and is especially good for cooking ingredients in their own juices. It's a versatile pan used for everything from deep-frying, stir-frying, steaming and of course making curries.

SPICE GRINDER
Another handy gadget is a spice grinder (you can use a coffee-bean grinder if you reserve it specifically for this purpose). Spices always taste better when freshly ground, and you don't need to double up on both whole and ground varieties.

SPICE TRAY OR BOX
There are many different spices used in Indian cooking so most Indian cooks keep a tray of spices in small bowls or a special glass-topped pannier near the stove ready for use. A spice box with compartments for a variety of spices was once a part of a young girl's dowry.

ESSENTIAL FLAVOURS

BLACK MUSTARD SEEDS
These add a nice pungent heat to dhal and a tangy pop when cooked in hot oil at the start of many dishes.

CORIANDER SEEDS
Essential in all masala mixes. The lighter coloured seeds have a lemony aroma and taste while the green Indian seeds taste more like the fresh herb.

CUMIN
Used in many dishes including curries, rice dishes, breads and chutney for its warm, earthy flavour.

DAL
Whole or split beans, peas and lentils are referred to as 'dal' and become 'dhal' when cooked. They are a staple of Indian cooking and are high in both protein and fibre. There are many varieties of dal including *urid, mung, toor* and *masoor* to name just a few.

GARAM MASALA
Meaning 'spice blend', this always includes green cardamom, cloves and cassia, among other spices. It is widely used as part of the harmony of spices that makes up many Indian dishes, and also as a natural medicine due to its antiseptic properties. It can be bought at Indian food stores or made at home by grinding toasted whole spices in a mortar or spice grinder.

TURMERIC
Used widely in many curries to give them their distinctive warm, yellow colour.

I was delighted to learn the secret of this beautiful green dish - and how to keep it green as well (by blanching the spinach, pureeing it and then cooking it only briefly in the finished dish). Instead of pureeing the spinach, you can chop it to achieve a more textured dish typically served in Indian homes. You can also substitute frozen spinach for fresh - and that's already chopped! *Paneer* (firm Indian cottage cheese) is now available in supermarkets.

For potato lovers who like a hint of spice, this is the best thing in the world. The snap, crackle and pop as you fry the spices is part of the joy. Think about taking these fragrant wonders along to your next barbecue and watch people enjoy an exotic and clever take on a staple.

PALAK PANEER

Firm Cottage Cheese in Spinach Puree

from Daisy Rajan

Blanch the spinach in boiling water for 3-4 minutes then refresh in cold water, drain and squeeze out the excess water. Puree until smooth.

Heat the oil in a heavy-based saucepan. Add the cumin seeds, ginger, garlic and onion and fry until golden brown. Add the tomatoes and cook until they become a soft paste. Stir in the spinach puree and season with salt. Add the *paneer* and heat through. To finish, add the dried fenugreek leaves, garam masala and cream.

SERVES 4

2 bunches spinach, leaves picked	200 g (7 oz) chopped tomatoes (fresh or tinned)
2 tablespoons vegetable oil	salt
1 teaspoon cumin seeds	225 g (8 oz) *paneer*, cubed
2 cm (¾ in) piece of ginger, crushed	1 teaspoon dried fenugreek leaves
6 garlic cloves, crushed	pinch of garam masala
1 medium onion, finely chopped	1 tablespoon thickened cream

GUJARATI POTATOES

from Daisy Rajan

Boil the potatoes until soft, then cut into cubes.

Place the potato, ground cumin, coriander, turmeric and chilli in a bowl and season with salt. Toss to coat the potatoes evenly.

In a heavy-based pan or *kadhai*, heat the oil and add the mustard, cumin and fenugreek seeds and cook until sizzling (this is called tempering the spices). Add the potato and stir gently to coat in the oil. Stir in the coconut, sesame seeds and chopped coriander and serve with Indian bread.

SERVES 4

400 g (14 oz) pontiac or other waxy potatoes, peeled	1 teaspoon black mustard seeds
1 teaspoon ground cumin	1 teaspoon cumin seeds
1 teaspoon ground coriander	5-6 fenugreek seeds
1 teaspoon turmeric	1 tablespoon desiccated coconut
½ teaspoon chilli powder	2 teaspoons sesame seeds
salt	3-4 coriander (cilantro) sprigs, chopped
2 tablespoons vegetable oil	

'Always add a pinch of salt when cooking your onions. It will prevent them from burning.'

Kumar's recipe for this famous Kashmiri dish is a winner. The lamb becomes meltingly tender and the spices smell enticing as you're cooking them. The choice of saucepan is very important - the ingredients should fill no more than a quarter of its depth, so you need quite a deep pan with a heavy base to retain an even temperature.

Is there anything better than tender spiced chicken? My friend Ajoy has an unusual technique for cooking this dish, which involves covering the saucepan with a bowl with a little water inside it instead of a lid. As the chicken cooks in its own juices, it creates steam that holds the bowl in place, sealing in all the delicious flavours. The result is amazingly tender - as if the chicken has been steamed. Ajoy is also a master at blending spices.

ROGAN JOSH

from Kumar Mahadevan

Heat the oil in a large, heavy-based saucepan until almost smoking. Add the bay leaves, cloves, brown and green cardamom pods, cassia, fennel seeds and dried chillies and cook until sizzling (the brown cardamom is the most fun - it always explodes and all its flavours go into the oil). Add the onion and ½ teaspoon of salt and fry until the onion is brown and sweet.

Stir in the crushed ginger and garlic and then the turmeric, chilli powder and ground coriander.

Stir in the crushed fresh chilli and add a little water to stop the spices from burning. Add the tomato, tomato puree and a good pinch of salt and stir well to combine. Turn the heat up to high and add the meat, searing all over and coating in the flavours. Add a little more water.

Cover with a lid and cook for 35-40 minutes.

Remove from the heat and add the chopped coriander.

SERVES 4-6

3 tablespoons vegetable oil	½ tablespoon crushed garlic
3 bay leaves	1 teaspoon turmeric
2 teaspoons cloves	1 teaspoon chilli powder
3 brown cardamom pods	3 teaspoons ground coriander
1 tablespoon green cardamom pods	1 tablespoon crushed fresh chilli
piece of cassia bark	2 tomatoes, chopped
1 teaspoon fennel seeds	1 tablespoon tomato puree
4 small dried chillies	1 kg (2 lb 3 oz) cubed lamb
1 kg (2 lb 3 oz) red onions, sliced	(from a leg or shoulder)
salt	2 tablespoons chopped coriander (cilantro) leaves
½ tablespoon crushed ginger	

HYDERABADI CHICKEN

from Ajoy Joshi

Cut the chicken into large cubes without trimming off the fat, as this keeps it moist.

Toast the sesame seeds and peanuts in a dry frying pan then grind to a paste. Mix the paste with a little milk. This paste will thicken and bind the sauce for the chicken.

Heat the oil in a heavy-based saucepan and add the onion and 2 pinches of salt. Cook over medium–high heat until caramelised and golden brown (about 5 minutes). Remove from the heat.

Place the peanut paste, ginger, garlic, chilli, turmeric, yoghurt, garam masala, cumin seeds and a pinch of salt in a large bowl and mix together. Stir in the fried onion and then the chicken. Leave to marinate for 10 minutes (the acidity of the yoghurt will help to tenderise the chicken, but if left for longer, too much moisture will be drawn out of the meat).

Put the chicken and marinade in the saucepan used for the onions and set a large stainless steel bowl over the top so that it seals around the rim. Add ¼ cup of water to the bowl. The heat of the saucepan will cause suction and hold the bowl in place, creating steam and improvising a pressure cooker. Cook the chicken over medium heat for 30-40 minutes - when the water in the bowl has evaporated you'll know the chicken is cooked. Just before serving add the lemon juice.

SERVES 4-6

1 kg (2 lb 3 oz) chicken thigh fillets	1 tablespoon crushed ginger
1 heaped tablespoon sesame seeds	1 tablespoon crushed garlic
	1½ tablespoons crushed green chilli
50 g (1¾ oz) peanuts	pinch of turmeric
milk	1½ cups natural yoghurt
80 ml (2½ fl oz/⅓ cup) oil	1 teaspoon garam masala
1 onion, sliced	¼ teaspoon black cumin seeds
salt	1 tablespoon lemon juice

Dhal is a simple meal of cooked, spiced beans, peas or lentils. It is high in protein and fibre. This version uses *toor* dal, or yellow split peas, but other varieties include *urid*, *mung* and *masoor* to name just a few. To me this recipe redefines dhal - it is so yummy that you can have it for dinner on its own, although it is perfect served with steamed rice or Indian bread. The fresh tomatoes and coriander give it real fresh ness and the asafoetida is worth seeking out to counter the gassy effects of the split peas - it is available from most Indian food stores.

TOOR DAL TADKA

from Daisy Rajan

Put the *toor* dal, turmeric and water into a heavy-based saucepan and boil for 45–60 minutes, until the peas are soft when pressed between the thumb and index finger.

Meanwhile, pound the garlic, ginger and a good pinch of salt to a paste in a mortar. Heat the oil in a small frying pan over low heat. Add the mustard seeds and allow them to pop. Add the cumin seeds, dried chillies, curry leaves, chilli powder, asafoetida and ginger and garlic paste and fry until fragrant. Stir into the dhal.

Add the chopped tomatoes and simmer for another 10 minutes. Season to taste with salt and garnish with coriander leaves.

SERVES 4-6

250 g (9 oz) *toor* dal (yellow split peas), washed and drained
1 teaspoon turmeric
1 litre (34 fl oz/4 cups) water
6 garlic cloves
1 cm (½ in) piece of ginger
salt
2 tablespoons vegetable oil

1 teaspoon black mustard seeds
2 teaspoons cumin seeds
2-3 dried chillies
8-10 curry leaves
1-2 teaspoons chilli powder
pinch of asafoetida powder
200 g (7 oz) chopped tomatoes

coriander (cilantro) leaves

A simple and quick cheat's version of the reduced-milk sweet *burfi*. This is a lovely end to an Indian feast and is often served at special occasions. Try these with tea or even better a lovely spiced chai. I have to say – worth every calorie!

COCONUT CARDAMOM BURFI

from Raini Singh

Mix 200 g (7 oz) of the coconut and the remaining ingredients in a bowl.

Heat a non-stick frying pan over low heat and add the mixture to the pan. Stir until the mixture starts to dry and rolls easily into a ball. Remove from the heat and leave for 5-10 minutes until cool enough to handle.

Place the remaining coconut on a plate. Using damp hands, roll the *burfi* mixture into balls and then roll in coconut. The balls can be stored in the refrigerator for up to 1 week.

MAKES 15-20 *BURFI*

250 g (9 oz) desiccated coconut
395 g (14 oz) tin sweetened condensed milk
10 cardamom pods, husks discarded, seeds ground to a powder

handful of pistachios, roughly crushed

'Food is cooked with hands, but the taste comes from the heart.'

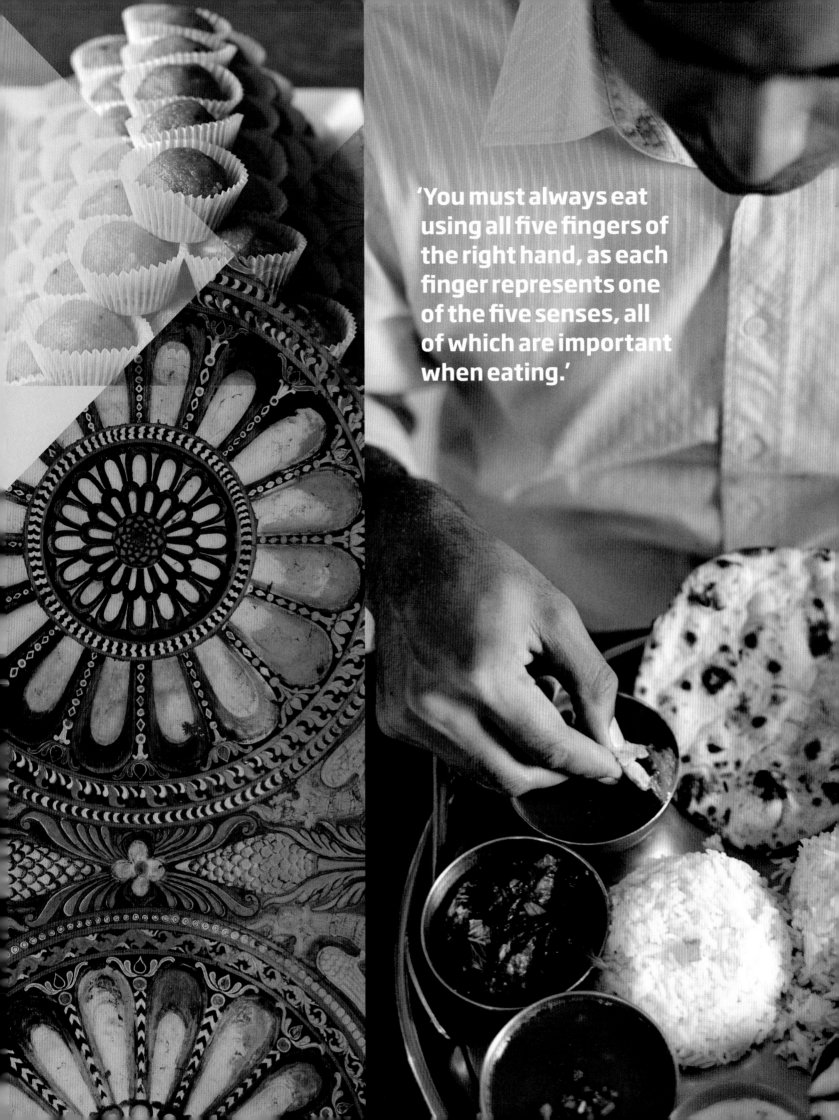

'You must always eat
using all five fingers of
the right hand, as each
finger represents one
of the five senses, all
of which are important
when eating.'

There's nothing meek and mild about Indonesian food – it's one of the most vibrant cuisines in the world, full of intense, hot flavours and varied textures, and its devotees wouldn't have it any other way. In fact, some say they can't live without chilli at every meal – in hot climates without chilli to kick-start the taste buds 'you simply don't have an appetite,' says my friend Rohanna from North Sumatra. In the exotic Indonesian tropics, chilli is used in spice pastes, in sambals (spicy side dishes), in stir-fries and even children eat it from a young age.

Indonesian kitchens often have just one or two gas burners yet great recipes come together there – woks sizzle and smoke from fresh ingredients that are tossed together with spices and the beloved sweet, thick soy sauce called kecap manis. It's a kind of theatre and is often breathtaking to watch as feasts materialise in a tiny amount of time.

Most cooking starts with the pounding of garlic, onion, chilli, lemongrass and fresh turmeric, which is the basis for many Indonesian spice pastes. These pastes are then cooked in oil, followed by dry spices, meat or fish and vegetables. It's noisy and sometimes smelly, especially when trassi (shrimp paste) is toasted over a flame to release its deep magic. When mixed into pastes and sambals, the intensely salty and fishy trassi adds a new depth of flavour.

Rice is always being cooked and eaten and is the central part of every Indonesian meal. Polished long-grain rice is most commonly used, particularly in dishes such as nasi goreng. Along with rice they serve sambals based on chilli and garlic to kick-start the palate, pickles for a sour crunch and small portions of meat, seafood or vegetables often in curry form.

The variations on this theme are endless across the 6000 islands that make up Indonesia. Rice is also used as a foundation for sweet desserts such as bubur ketan hitam, a sticky black rice pudding made with coconut milk.

Two foods other than chilli that are adored by Indonesians are tempeh (fermented soybeans made into blocks, which are high in protein and fibre and quite delicious) and krupuk (thin, deep-fried crackers made from wheat, rice, potato or cassava flour that are flavoured with prawn, seafood or vegetables; they are eaten at the start of a meal, often with kecap manis as a dipping sauce).

I love the old name for Indonesia – the Spice Islands. It's very romantic-sounding and fitting for a place that grows nutmeg, mace, pepper and cloves, which Indonesians cook with all the time along with other local favourites like coriander seeds, cardamom pods, cinnamon quills and cumin seeds. All of these spices are used in various ways by the melting pot of nationalities that have added their touch to Indonesian food – the Indians, Chinese, Arabs, Portuguese, Spanish, English and Dutch.

As many Indonesians are Muslim, the Islamic code of generosity to the guest means newcomers are welcomed and a banquet prepared. Whether it's a traditional nasi lemak, some lemper (rice rolls with spicy filling), or a range of fragrant curries, satays or stir-fries, your senses will be working overtime – and loving it!

ESSENTIAL FLAVOURS

CANDLENUTS
Similar to macadamia nuts, these have a high oil content and are loved for their creamy texture in sauces. Inedible in their raw state, the candlenut is a common thickener in curry pastes. They are available from most Asian food stores.

FRESH TURMERIC
A finger-shaped rhizome prized for its vivid yellow colour and fragrance, fresh turmeric is often used in Indonesian curry pastes.

KECAP MANIS
A dark, sweet soy sauce made with palm sugar (jaggery) – it is much sweeter and thicker than its Chinese or Japanese counterparts. 'Manis' means sweet in Indonesian.

LEMONGRASS
A tall, bulbous grass with a fragrant, creamy centre that has a tangy lemony taste. The outer leaves are peeled off and the interior is finely ground for spice pastes. Alternatively the entire grass is bruised or tied in a knot and added to curries and soups for extra flavour.

PALM SUGAR (JAGGERY)
Made from the sap of the palm tree, which is boiled down to a concentrated, moist sugar. It can range from a light honey-coloured shade to a dense dark brown, which is richer and more caramel in flavour. Usually bought as a hard block, it is best grated for easy use.

PETAI
Affectionately known as 'smelly beans', petai are seeds from a vine native to Malaysia and Indonesia. Bright green in colour, the seeds are slightly bitter in flavour and used in stir-fries, curries and sambals. In Australia they are available frozen in packets from Asian food stores.

SHRIMP PASTE
Made from fermented, dried shrimp, which is compressed and cut into blocks. Called trassi (known as belachan in Malay), shrimp paste is a key ingredient in many types of sambal. A small block is commonly wrapped in foil and briefly roasted in the oven or toasted over a flame, then crumbled into dishes to add an intense fishy flavour and smell.

TAMARIND
An acidic fruit, the sour pulp of which is used to balance the salty, sweet and hot flavours in Indonesian dishes. It's used in everything from salads to sauces and is the key flavour note in assam fish. It can be used in liquid or block form – soak the block in warm water and remove the seeds before cooking.

TEMPEH
A thin, nutty cake made from fermented soybeans, tempeh originates from Indonesia. It is a highly nutritious and versatile ingredient and its firm texture allows it to be cooked in many different ways - marinated, deepfried, boiled or steamed.

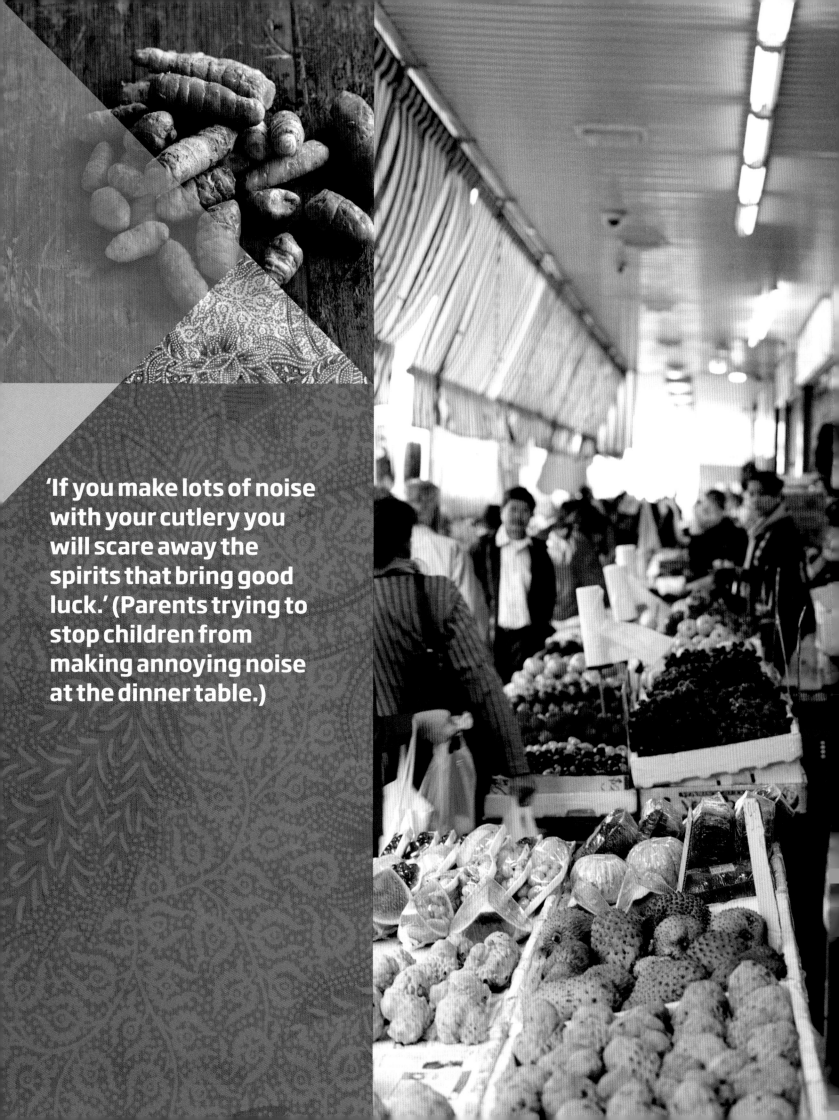

'If you make lots of noise with your cutlery you will scare away the spirits that bring good luck.' (Parents trying to stop children from making annoying noise at the dinner table.)

Belado is a magic sauce as it tastes different depending on what you match it with. Its chilli flavour is warm and delicious and makes you feel wonderful. I'll echo its creator and say 'I LOVE the *belado*!' Instead of prawns, you can use other seafood and meat such as squid, fish or chicken, and also vegetables such as eggplant or potatoes, and tempeh, eggs or tofu. If using eggs or tofu, spread the sauce over the top just before serving. All this dish needs is a simple accompaniment such as sliced cucumber.

'When you're halfway through eating a whole fish, never overturn it to get to the meat under the bones. Remove the bones first, otherwise it'll bring bad luck if you travel by boat or ship.'

UDANG BELADO

Prawns in Belado Sauce

from Rohanna Halim

Blend the shallots and tomato for 5 seconds in a blender then add the chilli. Continue blending briefly to a coarse paste.

Heat a wok over medium heat and add the oil, chilli paste, sugar and salt. Lower the heat and fry, stirring occasionally, for 10–15 minutes. The chilli will become fragrant, the mixture will thicken a little and the colour will change to deep red. Add lime juice to taste and the *petai*, if using, and remove from the heat.

Heat the oil in a saucepan and briefly deep-fry the prawns then drain on paper towel. Reheat the *belado* and stir-fry the prawns in the sauce. Serve with sliced cucumber.

SERVES 4

5-6 shallots, chopped	3 tablespoons sugar
1 medium tomato, chopped	2 tablespoons salt
300 g (10½ oz) red chillies, roughly chopped (long and small chillies can be mixed according to desired heat)	juice of 1 lime
	handful of *petai* ('smelly beans'), optional
	oil for deep-frying
3 tablespoons vegetable oil	1 kg (2 lb 3 oz) shelled green prawns (shrimp)

Creamy with ground candlenuts and coconut milk, fragrant with lemongrass, ginger and spices and vibrant yellow from fresh turmeric, this chicken curry is just as easy to cook for a week night as it is to really impress your friends at a dinner party. As with most curries, it's even better the next day and even freezes well if you have some left over.

KARI AYAM

Chicken Curry

from Alina Lucas

Blend the chilli, shallots, garlic, candlenuts, turmeric, ginger and 2 tablespoons of oil to a smooth paste.

Heat a little more oil in a frying pan and fry the paste until it darkens in colour. Add the remaining ingredients other than the chicken, potatoes and fried shallots and bring to the boil. Add the chicken and potatoes and simmer gently until the chicken is tender and the potatoes are soft. If the sauce is too thick, thin out with a little water.

Sprinkle with fried shallots and serve.

SERVES 8

- 100 g (3½ oz) medium-hot red chillies, seeded
- 100 g (3½ oz) shallots, roughly chopped
- 25 g (1 oz) garlic cloves
- 5 candlenuts
- 40 g (1½ oz) fresh turmeric, sliced
- 15 g (½ oz) ginger, sliced
- vegetable oil
- 2 lemongrass stalks, bruised
- 25 g (1 oz) galangal, roughly chopped
- 1 litre (34 fl oz/4 cups) coconut milk
- 2 teaspoons ground cumin
- 2 teaspoons ground coriander
- 1 teaspoon fennel seeds, toasted and ground
- 1 cinnamon stick
- 1 teaspoon grated nutmeg
- 5 cloves
- 15 g (½ oz) shrimp paste, roasted and crushed
- 1 tablespoon salt
- 75 g (2¾ oz/⅓ cup) sugar
- 1.5 kg (3 lb 4 oz) chicken thigh fillets, cut into bite-sized pieces
- 500 g (1 lb 2 oz) potatoes, peeled and quartered
- fried shallots

'If you leave uneaten rice on your plate, your future wife or husband will have lots of pimples.' (Parents trying to get stubborn children to eat.)

This is the perfect satay recipe from a man who has mastered the art of the barbecue and who loves the flavours he grew up with. Paul has modified his mum's recipe and created meat that is beautifully spiced, incredibly tender and becomes a little caramelised from the sugars in his marinade. His peanut sauce (*katjang*) is also full of flavour. Try this for your next outdoor feast!

SATAY SAPI

Beef Satay

from Paul Rast

Combine the ingredients for the skewers, mixing the beef in well. Marinate in the refrigerator for 3-4 hours.

Soak some bamboo skewers in cold water for 1 hour.

To make the sauce, blend the peanuts and hot water to a smooth paste. Heat a wok over medium heat and add a splash of oil. Briefly fry the chopped candlenuts and coriander, then add the onion, garlic and chilli and cook for 2-3 minutes until the onion softens. Add the peanut paste, coconut milk and *kecap manis*, stirring well until the sauce starts to simmer. Add the lime juice and season with salt and palm sugar to taste.

Thread the beef onto skewers and barbecue (grill) over medium heat. Spoon over the warm peanut sauce.

SERVES 6

SKEWERS

1 kg (2 lb 3 oz) rump steak, cut into bite-sized chunks
1 medium onion, finely chopped
4 large garlic cloves, finely chopped
100 ml (3½ fl oz) *kecap manis*
2 tablespoons peanut oil
½ teaspoon sea salt
½ tablespoon grated palm sugar (jaggery)
1 teaspoon ground coriander

PEANUT SAUCE

225 g (8 oz) roasted peanuts
200 ml (7 fl oz) hot water
peanut oil
1 candlenut, finely chopped
1 teaspoon ground coriander
1 medium onion, finely chopped
3 large garlic cloves, finely chopped
2-3 small red chillies, finely chopped
200 ml (7 fl oz) coconut milk
1 tablespoon *kecap manis*
juice of ½ lime
salt
grated palm sugar (jaggery)

'If you don't cry or your eyes don't water when you're chopping onions, you're an unemotional and stubborn person.'

A classic Balinese ceremonial dish that's easy enough to cook in your barbecue. It's full of flavour and incredibly moist. My thanks to Tjok Gde, a prince of the Balinese royal family, for the recipe. Serve with rice, steamed snake beans or Chinese greens, and a hot sambal.

BEBEK BETUTU

Balinese Barbecued Duck
from Tjok Gde Kerthyasa

Preheat a barbecue with a hood (a Weber is ideal). Alternatively preheat the oven to 160°C (320°F/Gas 3). Wash the duck inside and out in a bowl of water infused with the turmeric.

Place the seasoning paste ingredients in a blender and blend to a chunky paste.

Combine half of the paste with the spinach leaves and set aside. Rub the remaining paste over the duck inside and out. Stuff the cavity of the duck with the spinach mixture and the cinnamon stick or cassia bark. Wrap the duck well in banana leaves or foil. Whether using leaves or foil, wrap the parcel in a final layer of foil. Place the parcel on an oven tray.

Cook the duck in the barbecue for 4 hours. Alternatively cook it in the oven for 2 hours, then turn down the temperature to 120°C (250°F/Gas 1) and cook for a further 2 hours.

Remove from the barbecue or oven and drain the juices into a saucepan. Simmer until reduced slightly and combine with a little stuffing from the duck. Serve in a bowl alongside the duck.

SERVES 8

1 duck (preferably free-range and organic, just like Balinese ducks!)
1 cm (½ in) piece of fresh turmeric, sliced
200 g (7 oz) spinach leaves, blanched and roughly shredded
1 cinnamon stick or piece of cassia bark
1 roll of banana leaves (optional)

SEASONING PASTE

10 shallots or 2 medium onions, chopped
cloves from 1 head of garlic
4 candlenuts, crushed
2 teaspoons shrimp paste, roasted
1 cm (½ in) piece of galangal
1 cm (½ in) piece of ginger
1 cm (½ in) piece of fresh turmeric
3 red chillies, roughly chopped (optional)
1 lemongrass stalk, outer leaves discarded, chopped
1 tablespoon grated palm sugar (jaggery)
1 teaspoon black peppercorns, crushed
2 teaspoons coriander seeds, crushed
3 tablespoons lime juice
3 kaffir lime leaves, finely sliced
2 tablespoons peanut oil
2 tablespoons water
3 teaspoons salt

Pronounced 'ess-chen-doll', this is a dessert or aperitif consisting of highly textural 'green worm' noodles called *cendol* that are made of mung bean flour and coloured with pandan essence. (If you can't find mung bean flour then rice flour will suffice but the *cendol* will be mildly different in flavour, more like the Malaysian version than the traditional Indonesian one.) The noodles are accompanied by a selection of fruit that you can vary as you please (this recipe includes tinned toddy palm seeds and jackfruit) and topped with coconut milk, shaved ice and palm sugar (jaggery) syrup. Yum! If you have something of the child in you and a bit of sweet tooth, this wild confection is just right – and it's so much fun to shave the ice. (Or you can bang ice cubes together in a tea towel until they're crushed ... although an ice shaver can be found in Asian emporiums for very little).

ES CENDOL

from Benjamin Moechtar

Pour some water into a large bowl and add plenty of ice.

Pour another 100 ml (3½ fl oz) of water into a saucepan and bring to a simmer. Slowly add the mung bean flour, stirring constantly. Once the mixture is thick and paste-like, stir in the pandan essence and remove from the heat. Push the paste through the holes of a colander directly into the ice bath to form short noodles. The noodles will harden in the water and can remain there for a while, but if you are making them in advance, they can be scooped out and stored in a container with some coconut milk in the refrigerator.

Finely shave some palm sugar and stir it into a small amount of hot water to make a dark syrup. Shave or crush some more ice.

To serve, layer the ingredients in a tall glass, starting with the *cendol* noodles, then the toddy palm seeds and jackfruit. Top with coconut milk and lots of shaved ice and drizzle with a little palm sugar syrup. Serve with a long spoon and straw.

SERVES 6

ice
225 g mung bean flour
a few drops of pandan essence
palm sugar (jaggery)
1 tin toddy palm seeds in syrup, drained and cut into small bite-sized pieces
1 tin jackfruit in syrup, drained and cut into small bite-sized pieces
coconut milk

Where would we be as a nation without the culinary input from the many Italians who have come to our shores. They have taught us how to appreciate good coffee, good olive oil and the silky joy of fresh pasta. We have discovered that the colours of the Italian flag can be absolutely delicious – the ripe red of tomatoes for pasta sauce and salads; the zingy greens of rocket, rape, zucchini and fragrant basil; and the milky whites of fresh Italian cheeses – ricotta, buffalo mozzarella and bocconcini. (Thankfully we have managed to evolve from a country that believed all cheese was yellow!) Such has been the influence of Italian cuisine that spaghetti bolognaise is almost our adopted national dish.

To enter the Italian realm is to experience generosity, abundance and seasonal food prepared simply and well. The spirit of sharing is one of the things I adore about Italians – from the baskets of home-grown zucchini that would appear on my front doorstep when I lived in an Italian suburb, to Italian shopkeepers wanting you to try something new they thought you'd like, to the kisses on both cheeks and endless stream of food when you spend any time in an Italian home.

One of the things I've learned is that in Italy food is respected. The salami, *coppa* and prosciutto for antipasti are not pre-packaged but are sliced for you onto waxed paper at the deli. The bread is eaten still warm from the bakery and any leftover bread is used to make delicious salads such as *panzanella* or for breadcrumbs and stuffings. The freshest seasonal vegetables and herbs are used for salads, often straight from the garden – a tomato and bocconcini salad is served with basil picked from big pots just outside the back door and tomatoes plucked from the veggie patch.

Pasta is adored. Some families make their own fresh pasta from flour and eggs, which takes little time to cook and is soft and delicate. Of the dried pastas, the best is made from durum wheat, with the surface dusted with a hint of flour. This should be cooked to al dente (see page 158).

For the *primi* (first) and *secondi* (main) courses, dishes vary across regions – *fegato alla veneziana, ministrone alla milanese, minestra di trippa alla piemontese, gnocchi alla romana, calamaretti alla napoletana* and so on down the country. And each family has its own recipes that have been perfected for generations. Seafood and meat are used cleverly. Sometimes the secondary catch or what would be considered secondary cuts of meat are transformed into masterpieces such as stuffed calamari, braised octopus, delicious fish stews, osso buco, *cima alla genovese* (shoulder of veal stuffed with vegetables, eggs and cheese) and *involtini* (flattened pieces of meat rolled up with delicious fillings such as herbs, minced meat, cheese, breadcrumbs and spices). Other times the best-quality meat is stretched to serve many people – *porchetta abruzzese* is a whole roast pig that is usually served with many accompaniments so everyone feels satisfied. Servings of all dishes are usually generous and communal – the worst thing, the unthinkable thing, would be to not have enough food for one's guests.

The selection of *dolci* (sweets) is vast and beguiling and has been a vehicle of creativity for many Italian cooks. At home, women bake several types of biscuits and cakes at one time – a single choice is never enough! Out of the home and in the *pasticcerie* (bakeries), most of the bakers are men and in Australia many of the best *dolci* masters are from Sicily, where sweets are renowned – *cassata, cannoli,* gelato …! Whenever sweets are served, as with everything Italian, there are always plenty and they are all delicious.

ACQUEDOTTO
COMUNE
CASTELLINA
DI CHIANTI

ESSENTIAL FLAVOURS

BALSAMIC VINEGAR

A dark, thick, syrupy vinegar with a complex, sweet taste, which originated in Modena in the north of Italy.

It is much more expensive than common vinegars – check the label to ensure it is authentic balsamic (*aceto balsamico*) and check if it has a star rating (eight stars is top of the range).

BASIL

A leafy Herb used to flavour sauces and salads or added to pizza after cooking. It is a central ingredient in the symbolic red, white and green of the *caprese* salad as well as the classic pesto, originally from Liguria – a magic combination of basil, pine nuts, parmesan and olive oil. Basil should be torn not sliced for optimum flavour.

EXTRA-VIRGIN OLIVE OIL

Common to many Mediterranean countries, olive oil is indispensable to Italian cuisine. It is used for dipping bread into, drizzling over salads and other dishes, and for cooking with. Each region has its own olive oil with its own distinctive flavour, ranging from the light Ligurian olive oils to the deep rich greens of some Sicilian oils. Look for cold-pressed extra-virgin olive oil for optimum flavour.

PARMESAN

Known as the 'the king of cheeses', there are two types of parmesan: Parmigiano reggiano: is matured for 4 years and has crystals throughout the cheese that melt in your mouth, releasing their flavour. It's best served after a meal with fruit and wine. Grana padano: has been matured for only 18 months. It is freshly grated and sprinkled over pasta to lift the flavour – my friend John describes it as essential to pasta as tomato sauce is to a meat pie.

TOMATOES

Although they came from South America, Italy adopted the tomato as it own, calling it *pomodoro*, which translates as 'golden apple'. The perfect combination of acidity and sweetness, it is celebrated fresh in salads, particularly the fleshy ox-heart variety or the sweet san marzano; the roma variety is popular for the classic tomato *sugo* (sauce) made at the end of summer and preserved in glass bottles.

The Golden Rules of Pasta

Pasta is used daily in Italian cooking and is very easy to make but here are a few simple tips to help you make yours even more delicious and in the true Italian style ...

1. Fill a large pot with plenty of water, add salt and bring to a rolling boil.

2. Drop the pasta into the water and stir. Fresh pasta is cooked when it rises to the surface - usually after 2-5 minutes; dried pasta should be cooked according to the packet instructions - generally it takes 7-14 minutes.

3. Don't rinse cooked pasta - if you do, the sauce won't cling to it. Drain but leave some of the cooking water still clinging to the pasta (you can also scoop a little pasta water into a cup before draining the pasta, in case you want to thin the sauce later).

4. Don't drown the pasta with sauce - it should be lightly coated, not swimming in it.

This dish is so simple, and even better if you know a few tricks – Maurizio shaves his garlic into very thin discs using a mandolin slicer, prefers shallots to onions for their sweetness, mashes up the best-quality Italian tinned tomatoes with his hands, and tears the basil, adding it last so it stays fresh and green. What a delight!

'If you don't feel like cooking, stay away from the kitchen. Cooking shouldn't be work but a passionate endeavour.'

FETTUCINE NAPOLETANA

from Maurizio Esposito

Heat 100 ml (3½ fl oz) of olive oil in a heavy-based saucepan and add the garlic and shallots. Fry briefly and in the meantime, empty the tomatoes into a bowl and crush them with your hands. Add to the pan and simmer for 10–15 minutes.

Cook the pasta in a large pot of salted boiling water according to the packet instructions, then drain and return to the pot. Pour half the sauce over the pasta and fold through, adding more sauce if needed, but be careful not to add too much. The sauce should just coat the pasta.

Tear the basil leaves into the pasta, season to taste, drizzle with a little more olive oil and lightly toss again.

SERVES 6

olive oil
2 garlic cloves, finely sliced
2 shallots, finely diced

800 g (1 lb 12 oz) tin Italian tomatoes
500 g (1 lb 2 oz) fettuccine
salt
6 large basil leaves

Nail this and you have the all-purpose recipe for lunch, dinner, and snacks. Maurizio says it's his snack after work, which is often after midnight. He advises buying the best pasta and good quality parmesan, the rest is in the tossing of the pan, where the pasta cooking water and oil emulsify to create a simply wonderful taste and texture.

SPAGHETTI ALIO, OLIO E PEPPERONCINO

Spaghetti with Garlic, Oil and Chilli

from Maurizio Esposito

Cook the pasta in a large pot of salted boiling water according to the packet instructions.

About 4 minutes before the pasta is ready, heat 100 ml (3½ fl oz) of olive oil in a large frying pan and sauté the garlic and chilli. When the garlic turns nut-brown, add ½ cup of hot pasta water to stop the garlic cooking any further. Remove from the heat while you drain the pasta.

Return the pan to high heat and add the pasta, parsley and a little more olive oil. Keep tossing the pasta – the pasta water and oil will emulsify, thickening and coating the spaghetti. Season to taste with salt and pepper and sprinkle with parmesan if you like.

SERVES 4

400 g (14 oz) spaghetti
salt
olive oil
2 garlic cloves, finely sliced
1 small red chilli, finely sliced

½ cup roughly chopped
    flat-leaf (Italian) parsley
pepper
freshly grated parmesan
    (optional)

'"*Butta la pasta*" is the kitchen cry for "the pasta is going into the water". If you arrive late the pasta will be overcooked, which will be your own fault.'

Saltimbocca translates as 'jump in the mouth' and it is indeed so delicious that your mouth sings! It is a wonderful veal dish of thin girello steaks that are traditionally pan-fried in butter and served with *gnocchi romano* (semolina gnocchi). Girello is a cut of veal from the back leg. You can buy this as a whole piece then trim off the sinew and cut into 1-cm thick slices. The veal trimmings can be used with vegetables to make a stock (*brodo*), which you can use in this dish instead of a store-bought one.

SALTIMBOCCA

from Guy Grossi

Beat the veal steaks with the flat side of a meat mallet to an even thickness. Place a sage leaf on each followed by a piece of prosciutto. Fold the steaks in half to enclose the sage and prosciutto and tap again with the mallet to keep them closed. Lightly dust the steaks with flour.

Heat the olive oil and butter in a heavy-based frying pan and add the veal steaks. Sauté quickly on one side until light golden – the heat should just kiss the meat. Sprinkle with salt, pepper, garlic and parsley before turning over and adding the stock and wine. Cook for another few minutes.

Transfer to serving plates and spoon over the foaming sauce.

SERVES 6

6 veal girello steaks	salt and pepper
6 sage leaves	1 garlic clove, chopped
3 prosciutto slices, cut in half	1 tablespoon chopped
50 g (1¾ oz/¼ cup) plain	flat-leaf (Italian) parsley
(all-purpose) flour	2 tablespoons stock
2 tablespoons olive oil	splash of dry white wine
20 g butter	

Nothing is wasted in an Italian kitchen. This salad uses stale bread, which soaks up the flavours of the dressing while retaining a slightly crunchy texture - it is incredibly yummy, especially if you use a good loaf of bread. Proper ciabatta should be crusty on the outside and not too doughy or airy inside.

Salads are not just for summer - some of the winter fruits and veggies make magical salads. This winter salad of fennel and blood orange looks as beautiful as it tastes.

PANZANELLA

Bread Salad

from Graziella Alessi

Bake the bread in a warm oven until golden brown and dry. Leave to cool.

Place the oil, vinegar and garlic in a bowl, add the bread and toss together. Add the tomato and onion and tear in the basil leaves. Toss again, season to taste and serve immediately.

SERVES 6

1 day-old ciabatta loaf, crusts cut off, cut into cubes	1 garlic clove, crushed
300 ml (10 fl oz) extra-virgin olive oil	5 ripe tomatoes, roughly chopped
100 ml (3½ fl oz) balsamic vinegar	1 small red onion, finely sliced
	½ bunch basil
	salt and pepper

BABY FENNEL AND BLOOD ORANGE SALAD

from Graziella Alessi

Use a small, sharp knife to cut the peel from the oranges, making sure to remove all the white pith. Holding the oranges over a bowl to catch any juice, cut on either side of each segment, removing wedges of flesh but leaving the membranes.

Place the wedges in a mixing bowl (use the juice for another purpose).

Add the fennel and chervil leaves to the orange. Drizzle with the oil and vinegar and season to taste with salt and pepper. Toss and serve immediately.

SERVES 6

2 blood oranges	120 ml (4 fl oz) extra-virgin olive oil
5 baby fennel bulbs, very finely sliced	2 tablespoons white-wine vinegar
6 chervil sprigs, leaves picked	salt and pepper

'The onion. The garlic.
The oil. The beginning.'
(Guy Grossi)

'*Tiramisu*' means 'pick-me-up' and this dessert is sure to do just that. When Vanessa first made this for me I thought it would be dense and luscious but instead it's wonderfully light after all that beating - dangerously so ... I ate an enormous bowl and could have eaten a second!

TIRAMISU

from Vanessa Martin

Beat the egg yolks with the sugar until thick and white (this will take at least 15 minutes). Add the mascarpone and beat until just combined but smooth.

Combine the coffee and liqueur (as little or as much as you like) in a bowl. Quickly dip the biscuits into the liquid and set aside on a plate.

Beat the egg whites until thick and stiff then gently fold into the mascarpone mixture.

Line a glass bowl with soaked biscuits, then layer mascarpone cream and soaked biscuits into the bowl. Finish with mascarpone cream. Refrigerate for at least 2-3 hours. Before serving, top with finely grated chocolate.

SERVES 6

6 eggs, separated
220 g (8 oz/1 cup) caster sugar
500 g (1 lb 2 oz) mascarpone
1 cup freshly made hot, strong, espresso coffee
liqueur (Vanessa loves a mixture of Tia Maria, Kahlua and amaretto)
400 g (14 oz) packet *pavesini* biscuits (a slim version of *savoiardi* - if unavailable, use *savoiardi*)
good quality chocolate, finely grated

'In an Italian home, never even think of saying you're not hungry - they won't understand you!'

To explore what makes Japanese cuisine so unique and delicious you must enter a world where food is much more than sustenance. Not only is most Japanese food incredibly refined and elegant, its preparation and presentation have been honed over the centuries and are part of the pleasure of eating – the food is like an edible artwork complete with pure, delicate flavours.

Those clean flavours are the perfect way to start the day according to my friend Tetsuya Wakuda, now a legendary, world-renowned chef. Tetsuya says a bowl of miso soup in the morning is essential. One of the unusual flavours in his world is *dashi* – a gentle stock made from seaweed (in the form of a dried kelp called *kombu*) and shavings of smoked, dried bonito fish. *Dashi* is the basis of miso soup and many other recipes and its flavour is described by Tetsuya as 'tastiness' – in Japanese this is '*umami*', the fifth taste after sweetness, saltiness, bitterness and sourness.

I can attest that you will feel wonderful to your bones after a miso soup made from scratch. You can feel the pure, fresh flavours of this golden broth doing you good. I love the way when you make the *dashi* the *kombu* starts as a bit of shrivelled black stuff, like very dried banana skin, but when soaked in hot water becomes a large piece of flavoursome green seaweed. A bit of a magic trick and one of the many wonders of this special cuisine.

Japanese food is generally not the sort one hoes into – these are dishes to be enjoyed first with the eyes, and the choice of bowl is as important as what is served on it. One of my Japanese friends told me her ten-year-old son was horrified at the thought of eating something she had prepared from an ordinary bowl – his enjoyment would be marred by the less than perfect presentation! No doubt, even at such a young age, he was able to appreciate the importance of attention to detail in a cuisine where the empty parts of a serving platter are seen to emphasise the exquisite beauty of the food.

I must say a Japanese women's cooking group collapsed into giggles as I attempted to eat and drink as carefully and delicately as they did. When I asked for an explanation I was told I held my teacup like a man – around the top like you'd hold a glass of water. Japanese women – wellbrought-up ones – hold their tea with two hands, one around the cup and the other lightly underneath. The care these women took with their teacups was also evident in the food they were making – exquisite autumn recipes in autumn colours, including the first persimmons of the season and red maple leaves to decorate the serving plates. The dishes were all true to the Japanese reverence for celebrating each new season's flavours, textures and colours.

The clean flavours and simplicity of Japanese food also means it's generally extremely healthy. It is low in fat and often uses ingredients that are very beneficial to one's health – fish, seaweed, buckwheat and soy products. So it's no wonder many of us have followed the 'Why Japanese Women Don't Get Fat' model and rejoiced in the results!

On weight loss, Tetsuya is very enthusiastic about a 'zero calorie' substance made from potato starch called *konnyaku* – it looks like a block of grey agar-agar jelly with tiny black dots through it. 'Wow,' I thought, 'What a find!' However its slight chewiness and lack of flavour made me realise this probably wasn't going to be the diet food of the future – at least not for me!

Another of Tetsuya's suggestions has proved wonderful, which is that rice-wine vinegar makes an amazing salad dressing. Instead of mixing a plain vinegar or wine vinegar with oil, the less acidic rice-wine vinegar gives a beautiful, mellow flavour. I'm often intrigued that ingredients suitable for one cuisine can, almost accidentally, be perfect in another.

ESSENTIAL FLAVOURS

BONITO

Steam-processed bonito fillets are dried to wood-like hardness and shaved into flakes, known as *katsuobushi*. It is one of the two essential ingredients of the basic soup stock, *dashi*. The bonito, a member of the mackerel family, has been an important part of the Japanese diet from perhaps as early as the eighth century. From about the fifteenth century, the fillets of this fish were dried and used as they are today.

DASHI

Often referred to as the defining ingredient of Japanese cuisine, this is a delicate golden stock made from a combination of *kombu* (dried giant kelp) and *katsuobushi* (flakes of dried bonito fish). It is used to make miso, blanch vegetables or added as an essential ingredient to many dishes. *Dashi* is also available as a ready-made liquid or instant powder.

KONNYAKU

Made from the root of the konjac plant (also known as devil's tongue), *konnyaku* is regarded as a health food especially good for intestinal function.

After processing it becomes dense with a slightly chewy texture and it's always parboiled before use. Most commonly used as a vegetable, it is a great absorber of surrounding flavours and is an essential ingredient in *sukiyaki*.

MIRIN

A pale amber-coloured cooking wine used for a hint of sweetness and as a glaze for grilled dishes.

MISO

A fermented paste made predominantly from soybeans, miso has been a fundamental part of Japanese cooking for centuries. It is extremely versatile and is used to make miso soup, to flavour pickles and grilled dishes, or it can be thinned and made into a dressing. As a general rule, the darker the colour, the stronger the flavour.

There are three main types:

Aka (red): This has the strongest flavour and is often used in eastern Japan for soup.

Shinshu (brown): The most commonly available and widely used miso, it originates from the central Honshu region of Japan.

Shiro (white): Also known as *saikyo* miso, this is the palest and sweetest miso and is used in Kyoto for soup. Also excellent in dressings.

SHIITAKE MUSHROOMS

Usually found in dried form and reconstituted in water ready for use in salads, soups, sushi and more. The liquid the mushrooms have soaked in can also be used to flavour dishes.

SHISO

A herb from the mint family, also called perilla, that has a fresh flavour comparable to mint or fennel.

SOY SAUCE (SHOYU)

These have a relatively fresh taste and aroma and are generally sweeter and less salty than Chinese sauces. Most commonly available are the light (*usukuchi*) and dark (*koikuchi*) varieties. Light *shoyu* contains a higher salt content and is paler in colour – it is often used with vegetables or clear soups. Dark *shoyu* is more mild and is used as a marinade or in simmered dishes. *Tamari* is another type of *shoyu* that is wheat free and slightly thicker – it is excellent with sashimi.

WASABI

Wasabi root is rarely seen in its fresh state in Australia and is most readily available as a powder or prepared paste. As a green paste it is traditionally served with sushi and sashimi to add a sharp edge to the fresh tastes of the fish.

Sea Vegetables

As a group of narrow islands, Japan has great access to the sea and makes good use of its bounty.

Kombu: The second most widely produced seaweed in Japan behind *wakame*. Usually sold in dried form, it is easily reconstituted by soaking in water and is used to make *dashi*.

Nori: Believed to be made from seaweed, *nori* is actually made from dried algae. It is primarily used to wrap sushi, to garnish and to flavour noodle soups. The darker its colour and greater its aroma, the higher its quality.

Wakame: A variety of seaweed that comes fresh or dried (and like *kombu*, can be easily reconstituted in water). An integral component of miso soup.

This recipe contains numerous tips for making these beautiful rolls. Take your time and you'll be rewarded with a sensational result. Masako gives four different filling ideas - the *kampyo* filling is deliciously unusual (*kampyo* is strips of dried gourd sold in packets at Japanese grocery stores).

NORIMAKI

Nori Rolls
from Masako Fukui

To make the sushi rice, wash the rice well in cold water and soak in fresh water for 30 minutes. Place the rice and 1 litre (34 fl oz/4 cups) of water in a saucepan and cover with a lid. Bring to the boil then reduce to a simmer and cook until all the water is absorbed (alternatively, steam the rice in a rice cooker). Remove the lid, cover with a damp cloth and leave to cool for 15 minutes.

Heat the rice vinegar, sugar and salt over low heat until the sugar and salt dissolve.

Place the rice in a mixing bowl and evenly pour over the vinegar mixture. Mix in well with a cutting action so as not to squash the rice.

Fan for a few minutes until the rice has cooled a little (it can still be warm when assembling).

To make the *kampyo* filling, rub the *kampyo* with salt then wash in cold water. Put in a saucepan of water and bring to the boil, then refresh in cold water and squeeze out the excess water.

Simmer with the remaining ingredients until tender.

To make the shiitake filling, remove the mushrooms from their soaking water and measure 2½ tablespoons of the water into a saucepan.

Thinly slice the mushrooms and remove their stalks if necessary, then add with the remaining ingredients to the pan and cook until all the liquid evaporates.

To make the carrot filling, cook the carrot in boiling water until just beginning to soften.

Drain, then simmer in the remaining ingredients until tender.

To make the omelette filling, place all the ingredients other than the egg in a saucepan and heat until the sugar dissolves. Mix into the egg without over-beating. Cook the omelette in a lightly oiled frying pan (ideally a Japanese square omelette pan). The omelette should be quite thick. Leave to cool and cut into thick strips.

To assemble the rolls, place a sheet of nori shiny-side down on a work surface (or ideally on a bamboo rolling mat). Wet your hands with rice vinegar and spread 230 g (8 oz) of rice over the nori, leaving a 1 cm (½ in) border on one long edge. Be careful not to squash the grains of rice as you spread it.

Place the filling ingredients in a line down the centre of the rice. Dip your index finger in rice vinegar and run along the exposed edge of nori to moisten it slightly. Roll the rice and filling up inside the nori to form a squarish cylinder.

You should apply firm but gentle pressure (the mat helps if you are using one). Slice the rolls into rounds.

MAKES 6 LARGE ROLLS

SUSHI RICE

4 cups *koshihikari* rice
120 ml (4 fl oz) rice vinegar
2½ tablespoons sugar
1 teaspoon salt

KAMPYO FILLING

50 g (1¾ oz) *kampyo* (dried gourd strips)
salt
200 ml (7 fl oz) *dashi* stock (see miso soup recipe on page 170, or use instant *dashi* powder or liquid)
3 tablespoons sugar
2½ tablespoons *shoyu* (Japanese soy sauce)
1 tablespoon cooking sake

SHIITAKE FILLING

10 dried shiitake mushrooms, soaked in a bowl of cold water until soft
3 tablespoons sugar
3 tablespoons *shoyu* (Japanese soy sauce)
1 tablespoon cooking sake

CARROT FILLING

1 large carrot, cut into long, thin strips
200 ml (7 fl oz) *dashi* stock (see page 170)
2 tablespoons sugar
1 teaspoon salt
1 tablespoon mirin

TAMAGOYAKI (OMELETTE) FILLING

2½ tablespoons *dashi* stock (see page 170)
2 tablespoons sugar
1½ tablespoons *shoyu* (Japanese soy sauce)
1 teaspoon mirin
6 eggs, beaten

TO ASSEMBLE

6 nori sheets
rice vinegar

If your experience of miso soup has only been of the instant kind, this recipe will be a revelation - it touches your soul. It is made with fresh tofu and *wakame* seaweed, but other classic combinations are daikon and fried tofu, potato and *wakame,* clams and spring onions, and pumpkin and spinach. If using ingredients that need to be cooked (unlike the tofu and *wakame,* which just need to be heated through), you can cook them in the *dashi* (stock) before adding the miso.

MISO SOUP

from Yuki Totsuka

To make the *dashi,* wipe the surface of the *kombu* with a dry or slightly damp cloth (don't wash under water as the surface holds flavour). Using scissors, make a few snips in the *kombu* to help release the flavours when soaking. Place in a saucepan with the water and leave to soak for at least 30 minutes.

Slowly bring the *kombu* and water to the boil. Just before it reaches boiling point, remove the *kombu* and discard. When the water comes to the boil, turn off the heat and stir in an extra ladleful of cold water followed by the *katsuobushi.*

Return the saucepan to the heat until the water comes back to the boil, then remove from the heat again and leave until the *katsuobushi* settles on the bottom of the pan.

Strain the *dashi* through a fine sieve. Don't squeeze out the flakes as this will make the stock too fishy.

To make the miso, soak the *wakame* in cold water for 10 minutes. Drain and squeeze out the excess water. Cut into bite-sized pieces.

Heat the *dashi.* While heating, remove a cup of the *dashi,* dissolve the miso in it and return to the pan. Don't let the soup boil after the miso is added.

Add the tofu and *wakame* and gently heat through. Serve garnished with spring onion.

SERVES 6

DASHI
10 cm (4 in) piece of *kombu*
750 ml (25½ fl oz/3 cups) water
15 g (½ oz) *katsuobushi*
   (bonito flakes)

5 g (¼ oz) dried *wakame*
2-3 tablespoons miso (to taste)
150 g (5½ oz) tofu, cut into
   1.5 cm (½ in) cubes
finely sliced spring onion
   (scallion)

'Be careful when washing rice –
if even one grain goes down
the drain, you'll go blind!'

This delicious tuna salad is what I'd happily eat every day, the flavours are so fresh and clean-tasting. The beautiful jewels of tuna with grated daikon and the finely sliced beetroot, ginger and spring onion make it such a healthy mix as well. Most Asian groceries have daikon and fresh perilla leaves and its worth seeking out the Japanese citrus vinegar - once tasted you will make this again and again!

Hundreds of years old, this versatile marinade recipe can be used for fish, poultry or beef. I love that one of the world's greatest chefs has shared a recipe that he cooks all the time. *Saikyo* miso is sweet and pale and blends beautifully with the flavour of the fish. He suggests serving this with pickled ginger. Although garlic isn't popular in Japan, Tetsuya Wakuda says 'Add ginger if you like ginger, a little garlic if you like - after all, you are the one who is going to eat it!' You can buy a special ginger grater from most Asian food stores. Always grate ginger along the grain, not across.

ABURI MAGURO

Seared Tuna Salad
from Kimitaka Azuma

Season the tuna with salt and white pepper. Heat a small amount of oil in a heavy-based frying pan and sear the tuna for about 10 seconds on all sides, so the tuna is coloured on the outside but still raw inside. Leave to cool then cut into 1 cm (½ in) slices and lay in a wide serving bowl.

To make the dressing, mix the onion with two-thirds of the citrus vinegar. Combine the rest of the vinegar with the grape-seed oil, whisking just briefly. Whisk in the onion and vinegar mixture, sesame oil and pepper.

Pour ½ cup of the dressing over the tuna. Combine the daikon and onion and scatter over the top. Sprinkle with the spring onion, beetroot, ginger, garlic and baby celery and shiso leaves.

SERVES 6

2 pieces of sashimi tuna (approximately 4 ×2 × 20 cm [1 ½ × ¾ × 8 in] each)
salt and white pepper
vegetable oil
1 cup very finely grated daikon
⅓ cup very finely grated white onion
2 tablespoons finely sliced spring onions (scallions)
1 beetroot, finely julienned
2 tablespoons ginger, finely julienned
1 garlic clove, finely sliced and fried to golden

½ tablespoon shredded baby celery leaves
1½ tablespoon shredded shiso (perilla) leaves

PONZU DRESSING

¼ white onion, very finely grated
360 ml (10½ fl oz) Japanese citrus vinegar
200 ml (7 fl oz) grape-seed oil
½ tablespoon sesame oil
pinch of white pepper

SAIKYO YAKI

Fish Cooked with Saikyo Miso
from Tetsuya Wakuda

Combine the miso, sake and mirin in a bowl, stirring well. Stir in the ginger and garlic and then the grape-seed oil. Spread a little of the marinade in the base of a small rectangular dish. Add a piece of fish, flesh-side down, and cover with more marinade. Top with the remaining fish spread with marinade. Cover and refrigerate overnight.

Scrape off the excess marinade from the pieces of fish. Place on a tray skin-side up and cook under a griller until the skin is golden brown. Serve with pickled ginger.

SERVES 4

1 cup *saikyo* miso
1 tablespoon cooking sake
2 tablespoons mirin
1 tablespoon grated ginger

½ garlic clove, crushed
2 tablespoons grape-seed oil
4 sea-perch fillets, skin on

What a unique world this is. The orthodox Jewish kitchen is governed by ancient rules that are strictly adhered to. Many devout Jews I've visited have two kitchens and two sets of everything – sinks, plates, cooking pots and cutlery – to separate foods into 'milk' and 'meat', which must not be eaten together. The *kashrut* (kosher) laws are derived from the Torah, the five books written after God spoke directly to Moses, which sets out a blueprint for the Jewish way of life. 'Kosher' basically means 'proper' and these laws relate to what is to be eaten, how it is to be prepared, what it is to be combined with and, finally, how it is to be served.

While the cooking aromas in Jewish kitchens vary according to which part of the diaspora people come from, the basic laws are the same. The way meat is slaughtered and prepared for sale is dictated the *kashrut*. Indeed where food is concerned everything follows these ancient rules that 'go back to the desert', according to the head of one orthodox family.

It seems like a mad rush to have a whole feast ready for the moment on Friday evening when the stars first appear in the sky, marking the start of Shabbat (the Jewish day of rest). However I came to realise that Jewish families would be some of the best time and motion studies in the world!

Some foods are prepared in advance, some clever shortcuts are made and everything comes together as it should – and is of course delicious. A lot of the burden seems to fall on the women of the family, who are working around the prohibition of turning any electricity or gas on during Shabbat.

Clever Jewish housewives, who turn out vast quantities of food for big families after Temple, traditionally serve either hearty, slow-cooked dishes (like braised brisket or a stew called *cholent*) or dishes that can be served cold (like *gefilte* fish). In recent times a 'Shabbat' mode on ovens has meant that 'keeping it kosher' (and hot and delicious) is possible.

The payoff for the mad flurry at the start of Shabbat is that an entire day is then devoted to family being together and not having to work – something we often forget in this hyper-fast world. And the food! Over Shabbat I have eaten some of the best cakes of my life, including a custard chiffon cake that is like a sweet whisper (made by my friend Merelyn) and a dense orange and almond cake that I now make all the time. I've also tasted *cholent* that reminds me of my Irish heritage and the best chicken soup in the world. I have met women compiling a cookbook of Jewish recipes and learning how to do a six-plait *challah* (sweet egg bread) and I recently ate the first *gefilte* fish I've ever really liked – made by Melbourne food legend Rita Erlich.

KOSHER BUTCHERY

ESSENTIAL FLAVOURS

CARROTS

In Jewish cooking sweet, golden carrots are hugely symbolic. At Jewish New Year *tzimmes* (honey-baked carrots with prunes or sultanas) is a favourite dish, symbolising a sweet year ahead. In *gefilte* fish, each fish patty is traditionally topped with a round of carrot, which represents a gold coin.

CHICKPEAS

As a kosher source of protein, chickpeas are highly prized in Jewish cooking. Sephardic Jews have used chickpeas for hundreds of years. In Israel (as in other Middle Eastern countries), they are commonly used in hoummus and falafel. Ashkenazi (Eastern European) Jews add chickpeas to stews, soups and salads.

DILL PICKLES

Small pickled cucumbers that are particularly popular in Polish Jewish households for eating with chopped liver, herrings and egg and onion salad.

EGGS

Popular in all forms in Jewish cooking. They are mostly used for doughs, cakes, *lokshen* (noodles) and the quintessentially Jewish egg and onion salad. In kosher supermarkets only white eggs are available - these have been tested up to the light for blood spotting in strict adherence to kosher law. Otherwise, eggs need to be broken into a cup one by one to check for blood.

MATZO

Unleavened flatbread made from flour and water and baked quickly. It's a substitute for bread during the Jewish holiday of Passover, when eating bread and leavened products is forbidden. According to Jewish tradition, when the Israelite slaves were fleeing from Egypt, they did not have time to wait for their bread to rise - the result was this cracker-like matzo. In commemoration of the Exodus, Jews eat matzo every year during Passover.

After baking, matzo may be ground into fine crumbs, known as matzo meal. The coarse version of matzo meal is used to make matzo balls (or *knaidlach*) for chicken soup at Passover. It's added to other foods, such as *gefilte* fish, to hold the ingredients together instead of flour. Passover cakes and biscuits are also made with fine matzo meal - they are more dense than conventional flour versions.

This is a family recipe from Ramona's book *Jewish Cooking, Jewish Cooks*. It can be served either hot in winter or as a refreshing cold soup in summer. It is made with water, although you can use either water or chicken stock to cook the beetroots (to be kosher, if you're using stock don't serve the soup with sour cream or yoghurt).

Known as 'Jewish penicillin', chicken soup is regarded as a cure-all and is a mainstay of the Ashkenazi Shabbat table. Begin the soup and matzo balls a day in advance.

BORSCHT

from Ramona Koval

Place the beetroot in a large saucepan. Add half the lemon juice and the stock or water and bring to the boil over medium heat. Cook for 40 minutes, until the beetroot is soft when pierced with a knife.

Drain the beetroot and cut into small pieces. Return to the empty saucepan and add the potato, onion, dill (reserve a little for garnish), sugar, salt and remaining lemon juice. Season with pepper and add the water. Cover and bring to the boil then simmer for 20–30 minutes.

Puree the soup. Serve either steaming hot with a boiled potato added to each bowl, or chilled and icy cold. Top each serve with a spoonful of sour cream or yoghurt and a sprinkling of dill.

SERVES 6

1 kg (2 lb 3 oz) beetroots, topped, tailed and peeled	1 tablespoon sugar
juice of 1 lemon	2 teaspoons salt
2 litres (68 fl oz/8 cups) chicken stock or water	freshly ground black pepper
3 small potatoes, peeled and diced	extra 750–1000 ml (27–34 fl oz) water
1 large onion, roughly chopped	6 boiled potatoes if serving the soup hot
1 large bunch dill, roughly chopped	sour cream or yoghurt

CHICKEN SOUP WITH MATZO BALLS

from Shirley Hirsch

In a large pot, cover the chicken with cold water and bring to the boil. Simmer until the chicken is cooked through. Skim off any foam. Add the vegetables, cover and simmer for 2 hours. Strain the soup, discarding the solids, and refrigerate overnight.

To make the matzo balls, beat the eggs in a bowl. Add the remaining ingredients and mix well. Refrigerate overnight.

To cook the matzo balls, bring a large saucepan of salted water to a simmer. With damp hands, form golf ball–sized portions of the matzo mixture. Drop the balls into the pot. Cover and simmer for 20–25 minutes.

Remove any solidified fat from the soup before reheating. Place several matzo balls in each serving bowl and ladle over the hot soup.

SERVES 8–10

1 kg (2 lb 3 oz) meaty chicken bones	MATZO BALLS
1 onion, cut into chunks	2 eggs
3 carrots, cut into chunks	3 pinches of salt
1 leek, cut into chunks	½ teaspoon cinnamon
2 parsnips, cut into chunks	2 cups coarse matzo meal
	125 ml (4 fl oz/½ cup) light olive oil
	125 ml (4 fl oz/½ cup) water

'My mother always told me to never make chicken soup with anything but kosher chickens.'

A popular mainstay in Ashkenazi Jewish cooking, *gefilte* fish (literally 'stuffed fish') is traditionally made by carefully removing the skin of a fish (leaving it intact), mincing the flesh with ingredients such as egg, spices, onion and carrot, stuffing this back into the skin and baking the fish in the oven. This recipe is much easier as it is made from minced fish fillets formed into patties or balls, which are poached to a delicate shade of pale. Salmon or ocean trout give the *gefilte* fish a lovely rosy hue. It's delicious served with grated horseradish.

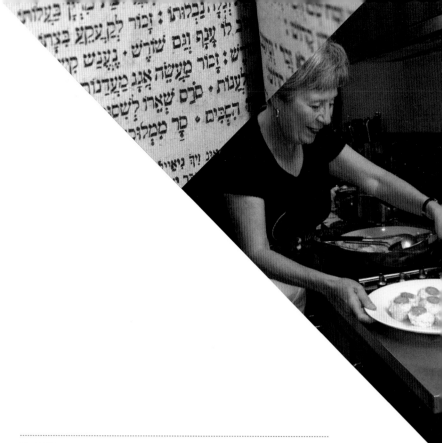

GEFILTE FISH

from Rita Erlich

To make the stock, place the ingredients in a saucepan and bring to the boil. Simmer for 40 minutes then strain, discarding the solids.

To make the fish patties, boil the quartered onion with 3 of the eggs for about 15 minutes. Allow to cool, then peel the eggs. Mince the boiled onion and egg in a food processor and place in a large mixing bowl.

Mince the fish in the food processor and add to the minced onion and egg, beating well with a wooden spoon to incorporate.

Add the almond meal and sugar and season with salt and pepper. Add the remaining raw eggs one at a time, beating well (the better the mixing, the lighter the patties; allow 10 minutes of beating in total). If you think the mixture needs softening, add some chilled water.

Refrigerate the mixture for 10 minutes to set a little. Form into medium-sized patties.

Lay the sliced onion in the base of a wide saucepan and add the ginger. Place the patties over the onions in a tight layer. Top each patty with a slice of carrot.

Carefully pour in enough stock to come half- to three-quarters of the way up the patties. Gently bring to a simmer and cook for 40 minutes. Leave the patties to cool in the pan, then lift them into a wide dish. Strain the liquid over the patties, discarding the onion.

Cover and chill in the refrigerator; the liquid should set into a light jelly.

Serve the carrot-topped patties and a little of their jelly with grated horseradish.

STOCK

skin and bones from the fish
   fillets (see patties)
1 carrot, sliced
1 onion, sliced
1 leek, sliced
slice of ginger
1–1.25 litres (34–42 fl oz/
   4–5 cups) water

FISH PATTIES

3 large onions, 2 quartered,
   1 sliced
6 eggs
1 kg (2 lb 3 oz) mixed fish fillets
   such as flathead, snapper
   (porgy), dory, salmon or
   ocean trout
60 g (2 oz) almond meal
2 teaspoons sugar
salt and white pepper
2 slices of ginger
1 carrot, sliced in thin rounds

'Never make anything ready-made if you can make it yourself.'

Every Jewish community around the world has its own version of *cholent*. A hearty mix of beef, marrow, beans and barley, this is the perfect slow-cooked meal to prepare before the start of Shabbat on Friday evenings. This *cholent* is cooked for four hours in a low-moderate oven, but for the ultimate slow-cooking, Merelyn says you can cook it overnight at 100°C (200°F/Gas ½). To stick to tradition, brown the meat in *schmaltz* instead of olive oil (*schmaltz* is rendered chicken fat that is sometimes flavoured with onions, apples and seasonings) and buy the ribs from a kosher butcher, where they only use the top half of a carcass (in a regular butcher these would be sold as *asado* cut). Merelyn serves leftover *cholent* as a base for barbecued lamb chops – heavy but delicious, and you don't need much!

CHOLENT

from Merelyn Frank

Preheat the oven to 160°C (320°F/Gas 2-3).

Heat the oil in a large ovenproof pot. Brown the meat on all sides then remove from the pot.

Add the onion and sauté until dark golden. Stir in the garlic and paprika and add the water, salt and pepper. Return the meat to the pot and add the drained beans and remaining ingredients.

Bring to a simmer. Cover the pot with foil then with a tight-fitting lid and bake in the oven for 4 hours.

Check the water levels during cooking to make sure the *cholent* isn't drying out. After 3 hours, the meat should rise to the top of the dish and look brown and crunchy. In 4 hours, the meat will be falling apart, melting into the beans, and the marrow should be falling out of the bones. Taste for seasoning before serving.

SERVES 10

3 tablespoons olive oil
700 g (1 lb 9 oz) beef top ribs, cut into pieces
700 g (1 lb 9 oz) beef shin (gravy beef), cut into pieces
2 large onions, chopped
3 garlic cloves, crushed
2 tablespoons sweet paprika
2 litres (68 fl oz/8 cups) water
1 tablespoon salt
1 teaspoon freshly ground black pepper
1 cup dried cannellini (lima) beans, washed and soaked overnight
1 cup dried borlotti beans, washed and soaked overnight
½ cup pearl barley
½ large marrow bone (ask the butcher to saw it into pieces)
3 desiree potatoes, quartered with the skin on
3 large carrots, cut into chunks

This recipe has caused an orange and almond cake revolution! A classic Passover dessert that draws on the Sephardic traditions of Morocco, the Mediterranean and the Middle East, this version has seduced the tastebuds of many - even people who normally never make cakes love its simplicity. The oranges boil for two hours and are then pureed, skin, pips and all.

ORANGE AND ALMOND CAKE

from Batia Slater

Wash the oranges and cook in boiling water for 2 hours. Drain and allow the oranges to cool before pureeing. This can be done ahead of time.

Preheat the oven to 190°C (375°F/Gas 5). Butter a 20 cm (8 in) springform cake tin and dust it with a little caster sugar. Place the eggs and 250 g (9 oz) of caster sugar in a mixing bowl and beat well. Stir in the orange puree followed by the almond meal and baking powder. Pour into the tin and dust the top with more caster sugar. Bake for 1-1½ hours, until the top is golden brown. Dust with icing sugar to serve.

SERVES 10-12

2 oranges
250 g (9 oz) caster sugar,
    plus extra for dusting
6 eggs

250 g (9 oz) almond meal
1 teaspoon baking powder
icing (confectioners') sugar

'You can never have enough time if you love preparing Jewish food - the sheer quantity and variety of delicious options will take every spare minute you have.'

ORANGE AND ALMOND CAKE

Years ago my friend Yang took me into his world – into emporiums stacked with heavy stone bowls and garlic sold by the sackful, into *kimchi* factories where mounds of wombok (Chinese cabbage) were chopped by cleaver near huge pots of chilli, into butchers where they were busy slicing frozen beef for *bulgogi,* and into restaurants and tiny cafes all packed with Korean people enjoying themselves ... It's such a different world and Korean cuisine and the etiquette that surrounds it are unlike anywhere else on earth.

Korean food is fascinating – not only is it beautifully presented, fresh-tasting and healthy, it's also a very tangible celebration of culture and tradition. Because Korean people view the preparation of food as a link with the past and their ancestors, many dishes have changed very little over the centuries. Whether in Korea or away from it, Korean people are devoted to their food and treat it with great reverence.

Kimchi is a great example. This is the fermented vegetable dish made from salted wombok and sometimes daikon, spring onion or cucumber, which are mixed with chilli powder, garlic and sometimes fish sauce.

Kimchi originally started as a means of preserving vegetables in salt through the very cold winter but when chilli was brought from the New World in the seventeenth century, the colour and flavour of *kimchi* changed dramatically.

Kimchi can form a simple meal with rice and it is an essential part of breakfast, lunch and dinner. In fact, a meal without *kimchi* is nearly unthinkable. Some Koreans say they actually feel 'weird' without *kimchi*; others speak of the longing and emptiness they feel if they go without it for more than a day. I was intrigued to meet one young man who carried an emergency pack of *kimchi* with him, just in case his mates suggested going out to pizza. 'I just don't feel right unless I eat *kimchi* with whatever I'm having for dinner – whether it's Korean food or pizza, it tastes great and helps digestion.' Now that's devotion!

Its digestion-aiding properties are renowned, making Korea one of the most health-conscious nations. Because of its pungency, many Koreans store their *kimchi* in special ceramic jars and some families invest in a *kimchi* refrigerator, which is about the size of a bar fridge and stores a whole winter's supply – only to be found in Korea!

Some families in Korea still gather to make their *kimchi* every year although most buy it ready-made. There is enough work involved in putting meals together already – Korean food is very labour intensive. As well as the main fare of meat or fish, noodles or rice, most meals are served with at least five different side dishes (*panchan*). These could be pickled bean sprouts; sliced potato with a sprinkling of chilli; spinach; stuffed cucumber; whole radish *kimchi*; cabbage *kimchi* ... and that's just the side dishes! While traditions are treasured, all this preparation takes time and as more women enter the workforce in Korea some of the more elaborate meals are being scaled down. Now three side dishes, even bought readymade, are acceptable!

ESSENTIAL FLAVOURS

DOENJANG

A fermented soybean paste made from boiled, ground soybeans which are dried and fermented in blocks then brined. It is a salty condiment used to make rich, thick stocks and stews with vegetables and tofu. It's also used on its own as a condiment with *bulgogi*.

GARLIC

Korean food couldn't exist without garlic. It is used abundantly, either crushed or slivered, and is adored in its raw state as well as used in cooking. Slivers of raw garlic are often served as an accompaniment to *bulgogi*.

GOCHUJANG

A chilli paste made from dried chillies, salt, fermented soybeans and rice powder to produce a dark-red, spicy paste. It is mixed into soups, stews and marinades and dolloped onto dishes like *bibimbap* (seasoned vegetables and rice) and *bulgogi*.

NASHI PEAR

Grated nashi pear (*bae*) is often used in marinades, especially for beef – as well as tenderising the meat it adds a natural sweetness. Nashi are equally loved as a cleansing, crisp finish to a meal.

SESAME SEEDS AND OIL

With its cultivation dating back thousands of years, sesame has long been harvested for its seeds, which appear after the pods ripen and split. Tiny hulled sesame seeds are used in abundance in Korean cuisine. Often toasted and used whole or ground to a paste, their nutty taste is loved across the country. Sesame oil can be cold-pressed from raw seeds or, more commonly, hot-pressed from toasted, hulled seeds, which creates a dark colour and nutty flavour. It is often used as a marinade or to drizzle on dishes after cooking.

WOMBOK

A long, barrel-shaped cabbage with tightly packed, crinkled, green–yellow leaves, commonly known as 'Chinese cabbage'. Wombok is used for making Korean *kimchi*.

Etiquette

This is a cuisine with many rules and traditions, where Westerners can blunder in and cause offence without knowing it!

Table settings are very important and food is as much about 'eating with the eyes' as the mouth. Korean people like a sense of order and many different colours and textures on the table, as well as many beautifully presented side dishes, or *panchan*. They recognise that the number of side dishes denotes the importance of the meal.

Koreans always use flat, metal chopsticks for side dishes and meat but a spoon for rice and soup. You shouldn't use chopsticks and a spoon at the same time. And once the meal is finished, all utensils should be arranged neatly as they were originally set at the table.

You should never hold a bowl in your hands as you eat.

When eating *bulgogi* (barbecued lean beef wrapped in a lettuce leaf with condiments) the parcel should be eaten in one bite.

When eating *kimchi* one Korean friend recommends you have some chewing gum and brush your teeth afterwards as the garlic will scare people away! Another friend adds: 'We do not talk much directly after eating kimchi.' This same man told me most Koreans consume seven heads of garlic a week!

Japchae is a dish of deliciously chewy cellophane noodles made from sweet potato starch. The noodles are tossed with julienned vegetables and sometimes meat (this recipe includes marinated beef), and each component is separately stir-fried. It's a popular Korean dish for parties and can be served hot or cold. Vary the vegetables as you please - others to consider are green beans and spinach, or make a mushroom *japchae* with a selection of Asian mushrooms.

JAPCHAE

from Youngkyu Kwon

Combine the beef with the marinade ingredients and set aside.

Soak the noodles in cold water for a few minutes, then cook in plenty of boiling water for 5 minutes. Rinse in cold water and drain well.

Cut the noodles into 10–15 cm (4–6 in) lengths approximately.

Mix with the soy sauce, sugar and sesame oil.

Stir-fry the onion in a little oil with a pinch of salt. Scoop onto a plate and repeat with the carrot, then the capsicum, then the shiitake mushrooms.

Beat the egg yolk and white separately and fry as two thin omelettes. Cut into strips and place in a bowl.

Stir-fry the beef and add to the plate of vegetables. Stir-fry the noodles for a couple of minutes and put into a large mixing bowl. Toss with the meat and vegetables. Add more soy sauce, sugar or sesame oil to taste. Serve garnished with the sliced omelettes.

SERVES 4

MARINATED BEEF
100 g (3½ oz) lean beef, cut into thin strips
1 tablespoon soy sauce
½ tablespoon sesame oil
2 teaspoons sugar
pepper

200 g (7 oz) *japchae* sweet potato noodles
80 ml (2½ fl oz/⅓ cup) soy sauce

2 tablespoons sugar
2 tablespoons sesame oil
1 onion, finely sliced
vegetable oil
salt
1 carrot, julienned
1 green capsicum (bell pepper), julienned
6 dried shiitake mushrooms, soaked until soft, finely sliced
1 egg, separated

'Never pour drinks using one hand – using both hands is a sign of respect for the person you're serving.'

This is a tasty dish of marinated beef, tenderised and flavoured with a blend of nashi pear and onion then cooked on a hot plate. Koreans love to eat *bulgogi* wrapped in lettuce leaves, sometimes with a small amount of steamed rice in the lettuce too, and with condiments such as *kimchi*, *gochujang* (chilli paste) or *doenjang* (soybean paste), which are all available from Korean food stores.

BULGOGI

Marinated Beef

from Chung Jae Lee

Combine the beef with the soy sauce, water, garlic, sugar, salt and pepper. Puree the pear and chopped onion and stir into the beef. Leave to marinate for approximately 30 minutes. Just before cooking, stir through the sesame oil.

Heat a heavy-based frying pan and add a little oil. Grill the beef (in batches if necessary) for around 3 minutes, adding some of the marinade towards the end so the beef doesn't dry out.

Add the sliced onion and spring onion and cook for another minute.

Garnish the beef with sesame seeds, pine nuts and chilli. Serve immediately with lettuce leaves and condiments.

SERVES 4

600 g (1 lb 5 oz) beef scotch fillet, sliced as thinly as possible
185 ml (6 fl oz) soy sauce
3 tablespoons water
1 tablespoon crushed garlic
40 g (1½ oz) sugar
pinch of salt and pepper
1 nashi pear, peeled, cored and roughly chopped
1½ onions, 1 roughly chopped and ½ finely sliced
1 tablespoon sesame oil
grape-seed or olive oil
3 spring onions (scallions), finely sliced

GARNISHES AND ACCOMPANIMENTS

sesame seeds
pine nuts
red chilli, very finely julienned
lettuce leaves
kimchi, gochujang (chilli paste) or *doenjang* (soybean paste)

'*Kimchi* tastes best when made by hand.'

This is the most delicious mix of rice, beef and vegetables cooked with garlic and sesame oil, topped with an egg yolk and *gochujang* (chilli paste). The ingredients are cooked individually then beautifully arranged in a stone bowl called a *dolsot*, which is heated until the rice turns golden and crispy on the bottom. You mix everything together when you eat it. You will need four *dolsot* bowls, available from Korean grocery stores. The amount of garlic used might seem high but remember that this is a culture in which most people eat seven heads of garlic a week! You can use less garlic if you like but once cooked it is delicious and not overpowering.

DOLSOT BIBIMBAP

Stone-bowl Bibimbap

from Suzanna Kim

Rinse the rice in cold water and drain, then repeat twice to make sure the grains are thoroughly washed. Put the rice in a saucepan and place a hand flat over the top. Fill with cold water to the top of your hand. Cover with a lid and simmer until the water is absorbed (approximately 20 minutes).

Combine the beef with 1 tablespoon of the soy sauce, a little sesame oil, 3 teaspoons of the garlic, the sugar and a pinch of pepper. Stir-fry until the beef is golden brown and set aside.

Mix the mushrooms with the remaining soy sauce, a little sesame oil, 2 teaspoons of the garlic and pepper and set aside.

Stir-fry the carrot in a little sesame oil with 2 teaspoons of the garlic and a pinch of salt and pepper. Scoop onto a plate and repeat with the daikon and zucchini.

Bring a saucepan of water to the boil and blanch the spinach leaves for 15 seconds, then scoop out, drain, place in a bowl and toss with some sesame oil, a little garlic, and salt and pepper. Repeat with the bean sprouts.

Put a teaspoon of sesame oil in the base of each stone bowl. Put some rice in the bowls and arrange small mounds of beef and vegetables over the top. Gently place an egg yolk in the middle and a teaspoon (or more to taste) of *gochujang* to the side. Pour another tablespoon of sesame oil around the edge of each bowl.

Place the stone bowls over high heat on the stove for approximately 5 minutes, or until you can hear the rice popping and crackling.

Carefully remove the hot bowls from the heat and serve.

SERVES 4

- 2 cups short-grain rice
- 400 g (14 oz) beef scotch fillet, finely sliced into strips 5 cm (2 in) long
- 1½ tablespoons soy sauce
- 150 ml (9 fl oz) sesame oil
- 3 tablespoons crushed garlic
- pinch of sugar
- pepper
- 1 cup dried shiitake mushrooms, soaked until soft, finely sliced
- 2 small carrots, cut into matchsticks
- 1 small daikon, cut into matchsticks
- 2 small zucchini (courgettes), cut into matchsticks
- 1 bunch spinach, leaves picked
- 1 generous cup bean sprouts
- 4 egg yolks
- *gochujang* (chilli paste)

Here is one of the healthiest cuisines in the world – based on vegetables, grilled or steamed meat, and mountains of herbs. Many ingredients are foraged from the wild, whether it be bamboo shoots or mushrooms, frogs, river weed or fish from the country's large rivers such as the Mekong. There is nothing processed, and the flavours are a balance of sweet, sour, salty, bitter and spicy.

Lao people love their chillies and use them liberally – in *jeow*, which are fresh pounded relishes; in salads and soups; and even in drinking games according to our friend and chef Tony Inthavong. He describes a game where green papaya salad is made with a number of chillies to match the person's age. Plenty of drinks are required to wash the burning salad down …

Sticky rice is found just about all across the country (an exception is the Hmong communities who actually prefer regular rice). Walk through any village and you'll see big silver bowls of the rice soaking, ready for steaming the next day. Lao people even refer to themselves as '*luk khao niaow*' – 'children of sticky rice'.

'We eat sticky rice with everything,' explains Tony. 'This is like a staple to us, just like pasta is to Italians.' The rice is used in sausages, sweets, and ground to a paste to thicken soups. The raw grains are also tossed in a wok until deeply golden, sometimes with kaffir lime leaves and lemongrass, then ground to a powder and added to the beloved *larb* meat salad for a toasty flavour and texture.

Sticky rice is traditionally cooked in a special bamboo steaming basket that looks like a pointy hat. It sits pointy-end down over a rounded pot that contains boiling water. These two items are the first gifts a newly married Lao couple receives. The next essential thing is the small bamboo baskets with lids that slide up and down for serving the rice. They're so tightly woven they keep the rice warm for a long time, making them the perfect takeaway containers for farmers to take to the field each day.

It's worth mastering the Lao style of eating sticky rice – you tamp a bite-sized ball of rice in your fingers and pick up some meat or vegetables alongside it, or dip it into a *jeow*. The grains of glossy, translucent, slightly chewy rice stick to each other, but not to your fingers, so eating with your fingers isn't messy.

Sharing food is all-important – it's the glue that brings families and communities together. As Lao people say before they eat: 'Food eaten together always tastes good; eaten alone, it tastes bad!'

ESSENTIAL FLAVOURS

CHILLI

Small fiery bird's eye chillies called 'rat poo' chillies (*mak phet khi nu*) are used in abundance in Lao cooking. While one or two chillies in a green papaya salad might be enough for most Westerners, Lao people regularly make theirs with ten or more.

HERBS

The range of herbs used by the handful in Lao cooking includes mint, coriander, sawtooth herb, lemon basil, dill, kaffir lime leaves and lemongrass.

PADEK

This fermented fish sauce is 'the secret to the taste of all Lao food'. Pieces of river fish are tossed with salt and rice bran and left for up to a year, sometimes more. The resulting muddy juices add deep savoury flavour to soups, salads and many other dishes (*padek* is used in combination with shrimp paste in green papaya salad for one almighty flavour kick). Many Lao people living abroad make their own *padek*, but for the rest of us, anchovy sauce is a good substitute.

COOKING STICKY RICE

STICKY RICE

Otherwise known as glutinous rice, this rice is opaque when raw, translucent when cooked - the opposite of regular rice. It is soaked for 8 hours or more before being steamed, giving glossy, slightly chewy grains of rice that stick together in a mass. The rice accompanies almost every Lao meal, as well as being used to thicken soups or dry-roasted and ground to add texture and flavour to salads.

Soak the desired amount of sticky (glutinous) rice in cold water overnight - as a guide, 3 cups of rice should be enough for 4-6 people. The next day, drain and rinse the rice and tip it into a Lao conical steaming basket, or another steamer lined with thin cloth if necessary so the rice doesn't fall through the gaps. Steam for 15 minutes, then flip the rice over in a mass and continue to cook for another 8 minutes. At the end the rice should be glossy and tender.

Tip the cooked rice onto a work surface and use a wooden spoon to fold and turn it a few times, driving off some steam and getting rid of any lumps, then transfer to serving baskets or to a bowl covered with cloth until ready to serve.

This salad is such a wonderful mixture of textures and flavours. Rice balls flavoured with a fresh red curry paste are deep-fried until crisp, then broken into pieces and mixed with peanuts, herbs, fish sauce, lime juice and the sour pork. The dish is fabulous eaten on its own as a big salad, or in lettuce cups or betel leaves in the style of san choy bao, which is how Mini likes to serve it. The sour pork - *som moo* - can be purchased at some Asian grocers and butchers, but Mini likes to make her own. It's the Lao answer to ham, she says, and is delicious. Minced pork is mixed with sticky rice, garlic and shredded pork skin and left to cure or ferment for four days. Make sure you buy freshly minced pork that is as lean as possible (fat gives an unpleasant taste) and also finely ground (minced twice is ideal).

NAM KHAO JIN KUP SOM MOO

Crispy Rice Ball Salad with Sour Pork

from Mini Loh

To make the sour pork, put the cooked rice in a medium bowl and cover with warm water. Leave for a few minutes, then squeeze the rice with your hands. The aim is to open up some of the grains. Do this for a minute or so, then drain the rice. The rice will no longer be sticky. This process aids in the fermentation of the pork.

Combine the rice and remaining ingredients in a large bowl and knead in the bowl for 15 minutes until you have a sticky and very well amalgamated mixture that resembles a dough. Pack down into a container that fits the mixture tightly, and cover the surface with plastic wrap before putting the lid on. Leave to stand at room temperature for 1 day. The following day, put the container into the refrigerator and leave to cure for another 3 days. The pork is now ready to be used, or you can continue to store it in the refrigerator for a further few days until ready to make the salad.

Make the red curry paste by combining all the ingredients in a mortar and pounding to a paste.

Put the coconut for the rice balls in a small bowl and add enough warm water to cover. Leave to soak while you prepare the rice.

Put the hot rice in a large bowl and stir in the salt. Set aside to cool for 15 minutes.

Squeeze out the shredded coconut, reserving the water. Add the shredded coconut to the rice along with the curry paste, crabmeat, fish sauce, sugar and one of the eggs. Gently combine, then roll the mixture into golf balls.

Mix the cornflour with the reserved coconut water in a small bowl. In a separate bowl, beat the remaining eggs.

Heat enough oil for deep-frying in a large saucepan or wok until very hot. Dip the rice balls into the cornflour (cornstarch) mixture and then into the beaten egg, and carefully add to the oil. Deep-fry the balls in batches until golden (around 4 minutes). Drain on paper towel and leave to cool. If desired, keep the oil hot once you have finished frying the balls and fry a few extra dried chillies for 10 seconds or until crisp, to serve with the salad.

Once the rice balls have cooled for 15 minutes or so, you can assemble the salad. Crumble all the pork into a large bowl. Add the fish sauce, lime juice, lime leaves, sugar and salt and toss well. Break the rice balls into rough pieces and add to the pork along with the crushed peanuts, spring onions and coriander. Mix well. Scatter the salad with the whole peanuts and garnish with the fried chillies if using. Serve wrapped in lettuce or betel leaves if desired.

SERVES 10 AS AN ENTREE OR 4-6 AS A MAIN DISH

SOUR PORK

½ cup cooked sticky rice
500 g (1 lb 2 oz) finely minced (ground) lean pork
150 g (5½ oz) pork skin, boiled for 45 minutes until soft, then cooled, scraped of fat and finely shredded
5 garlic cloves, crushed
2 teaspoons sugar
2 teaspoons salt

RED CURRY PASTE

6 dried long red chillies, softened in warm water for 10 minutes, seeded and sliced
grated zest of 1 kaffir lime (or 6 kaffir lime leaves, very finely sliced)
10 shallots, sliced
4-5 cm (1½-2 in) piece of galangal, sliced
2 lemongrass stalks, white part only, sliced
1 tablespoon shrimp paste

RICE BALLS

1 cup shredded fresh coconut
4 cups hot cooked jasmine rice
pinch of salt
175 g (6¼ oz) cooked crabmeat, flaked
2 tablespoons fish sauce
2 teaspoons sugar
3 eggs
2 tablespoons cornflour (cornstarch)
vegetable oil for deep-frying

2 tablespoons fish sauce
juice of 1 lime
4 kaffir lime leaves, very finely sliced
1 teaspoon sugar
pinch of salt
½ cup crushed roasted peanuts
3 spring onions (scallions), finely sliced
½ cup coriander (cilantro) leaves

TO SERVE

½ cup whole roasted peanuts
extra dried long red chillies (optional)
butter lettuce leaves or betel leaves (optional)

In Laos, even people who claim they can't cook can whip together a *jeow*. These relishes or dipping sauces, which often have a wonderful smoky flavour due to chargrilling the ingredients before they are pounded, can turn something as simple as sticky rice into a delicious meal. A *jeow* is also the perfect accompaniment to grilled meat or fish, or steamed vegetables. Another bonus is that a *jeow* keeps well for a good few days in the fridge.

JEOW MAK LEN

Spicy Tomato Relish

from Stephanie Souvanavong

Preheat the grill of a barbecue. Thread the unpeeled garlic, shallots and chillies separately onto bamboo skewers. Place the skewers together with the tomatoes on the grill and cook, turning, until charred. (The skewers are for ease of turning, and to stop the small ingredients from falling through the grill.)

Peel the skins from the garlic, shallots, chillies and tomatoes.

Put the garlic, shallots and chillies in a mortar with the coriander and sugar and pound to a fairly smooth paste. Add the tomatoes and continue to pound to a chunky paste. Add the sauces and mix well.

Serve scattered with chopped coriander.

MAKES 1½ CUPS

4 large garlic cloves
6 shallots
2 small red chillies
2 green banana chillies
4 tomatoes
small handful of coriander
   (cilantro), roughly chopped,
   plus extra to serve

½ teaspoon sugar
1 tablespoon fish sauce
1 tablespoon *padek* or
   anchovy sauce

Making this classic Lao (and Thai) salad with its power-punch of flavour begins with shredding a green papaya. The traditional way is to hold the peeled papaya in your hand and chop into it many times with a cleaver, then shave off the chopped section to give rough shards, slowing working your way around the papaya until you have reached the core.

(Another option is to use a papaya scraper, which looks like a vegetable peeler with a crinkly blade, or a mandolin.) The salad needs to be served straight away, however if you are preparing it for guests, you can shred the papaya in advance but pound the salad just before serving, ideally using the traditional deep mortar and pestle.

TAM MAK HOONG

Green Papaya Salad
from Sourina Simmalavong

Peel the green papaya and shred it either by hand with a cleaver as described above, or with a papaya scraper or mandolin.

Combine the chillies, garlic (if using), salt and sugar in a mortar and pound to a paste. Pound in the shrimp paste, then add the remaining ingredients, including the papaya. Pound the mixture for a few minutes, using a spoon to turn the mixture in the mortar while you pound. The aim is to bruise the ingredients to release their juices.

Taste the salad for a balance of hot, sweet, sour and salty flavours, adjusting if necessary.

Serve with cabbage wedges and sprigs of water spinach on the side, along with a separate plate of pork crackers.

SERVES 4

1 green papaya
4-6 small red chillies (or to taste)
1 garlic clove (optional)
½ teaspoon salt
1 tablespoon sugar
2 teaspoons shrimp paste
125 g (5 oz) cherry tomatoes, halved
3 snake beans, cut into 3 cm (1 in) pieces, or 3 apple eggplants (aubergines), cut into thin wedges (optional)

juice of 1–2 limes or lemons (plus 1 lime cut into thin slivers, if desired)
1–2 tablespoons *padek* or anchovy sauce
1 teaspoon fish sauce

TO SERVE

wedges of cabbage
young sprigs of water spinach
pork crackers (deep-fried pork skin)

'When Lao people cook bamboo everybody is happy – we cook it in a big pot and share it, so we extend friendship to everyone.'

Every Lao celebration from *Songkran* (New Year) to christenings features plates piled high with these delicious treats wrapped in banana leaves. This recipe has beans mixed through the coconut-flavoured rice, with the option of banana or taro inside. Ketty also shares her technique for making coconut milk from scratch.

'When I grate coconut it helps me to remember the old things.'

KHAO TOM

Sweet Sticky Rice Parcels
from Ketty Inthavong

Drain the soaked rice and give it a rinse, then drain it again. Steam the rice for 25 minutes or until soft. (The Lao style is with a conical steaming basket, but you can use any steamer you have. If the holes in the bottom of the steamer are large, line it with a thin cloth so the rice doesn't fall through.)

While the rice is steaming, place the grated coconut (if using) in a bowl with the salt and 250 ml (8½ fl oz/1 cup) of warm water. Use your hands to work the coconut into the water, squeezing it together. Once well combined, take a large handful of coconut and squeeze it out over a clean bowl, pressing out as much coconut milk as you can. Continue until you have squeezed all the coconut. Discard the grated coconut. Strain the milk to remove any grated coconut that fell in.

Measure out 250 ml (8½ fl oz/1 cup) of coconut milk (or use tinned coconut cream) and tip it into a saucepan. Add the sugar and heat, stirring, until dissolved. Stir the kidney beans into the hot milk and remove from the heat.

Tip the hot cooked rice into a large bowl and pour over the coconut milk and beans, stirring well.

Soften the banana leaf squares by steaming them for 5 minutes.

Place 3–4 tablespoons of the rice mixture on each banana leaf and spread slightly to form a rectangle in the middle of the leaf. Add some banana or taro in a line down the centre. Roll the banana leaf into a cylinder, causing the rice to encase the banana or taro. Fold over the ends of the parcel and place in a steamer while you make the remaining parcels.

Steam the parcels for 35 minutes.

MAKES 12 PARCELS

500 g (1 lb 2 oz) sticky rice, soaked overnight	banana leaves cut into 12 pieces of roughly 22 × 20 cm (8½ × 8 in)
2 cups grated fresh coconut (or use 250 ml [8½ fl oz/1 cup] tinned coconut cream)	4 lady finger bananas, halved lengthwise then sliced diagonally, or 200 g (7 oz) taro, peeled and cut into sticks and boiled for 2 minutes, then drained
pinch of salt (if using fresh coconut)	
200 g (7 oz) sugar	
200 g (7 oz) cooked kidney beans	

This is the soul of Lao food - grilled meat, chillies, loads of fresh herbs, fish sauce, lemon juice, nutty toasted rice powder. It's simple, balanced and incredibly delicious. *Larb* is traditionally made with minced meat, but Manivone likes to use beef fillet chargrilled to medium-rare and finely sliced, along with slices of cooked tripe. *Larb* is always served with sticky rice rolled into small balls in the hand, to be eaten with scoops of the spicy meat.

BEEF LARB

from Manivone Phimiphisane

Place the beef fillet in a bowl and add the fish sauce and chicken stock powder (if using). Toss the fillet until evenly coated. Cover and marinate in the refrigerator for 30 minutes.

Put the sticky rice in a wok and toast over medium heat, stirring, until dark golden. Grind to a fine powder in a mortar.

Add the galangal, lemon juice, *padek* or anchovy sauce and salt to the beef and mix well.

Preheat the grill of a barbecue (a charcoal one if possible) and cook the beef to medium-rare (around 4 minutes on each side, but depending on the thickness of the beef). Remove and rest the meat for 5 minutes before thinly slicing.

Place the beef in a large bowl. Add the toasted rice powder, tripe, fresh and dried chilli, kaffir lime leaves, spring onion and herbs. Toss well and add extra *padek* or anchovy sauce, fish sauce and lemon juice to taste.

SERVES 4-6

250 g (9 oz) beef fillet
2 tablespoons fish sauce, plus extra to taste
1 tablespoon chicken stock powder (optional)
½ cup raw sticky rice
1 tablespoon finely grated galangal
2 tablespoons lemon juice, plus extra to taste
1 tablespoon *padek* or anchovy sauce, plus extra to taste
2 teaspoons salt
250 g (9 oz) cooked tripe, finely sliced

2 teaspoons finely sliced small red chillies
2 teaspoons dried chilli flakes
4 kaffir lime leaves, very finely sliced
3 spring onions (scallions), finely sliced
1 cup mint leaves, roughly chopped
½ cup coriander (cilantro) leaves, roughly chopped
1-2 tablespoons Vietnamese mint leaves, shredded

'The real Lao taste is not from a can. We love quite natural food - not modified too much, with many herbs and ingredients that are good for our health.'

It's amazing what a day's marinating can do to a rather confronting-looking ox tongue. Green papaya is included in the marinade as it has enzymes that tenderise the meat. The result when cooked is 'better than fillet steak' says Tony, who loves cooking this in big quantities on the barbecue for his friends. He serves it with *jeow som* – a fiery, punchy dipping sauce with plenty of lime juice ('*som*' means sour) – as well as steamed or sticky rice.

BARBECUED OX TONGUE WITH JEOW SOM

from Tony Inthavong

Cut the ox tongue in half lengthwise and place the halves in a bowl. Add the remaining ingredients and mix well, ensuring the tongue is well coated. Cover and refrigerate overnight.

To make the *jeow som*, combine the garlic, chilli and sugar in a mortar. Pound to a fine paste. Mix in the remaining ingredients and taste for a good balance of sweet, sour and salty flavours, adjusting if needed.

Preheat the grill of a barbecue (a charcoal one if possible). Scrape the excess marinade from the pieces of tongue and cook for 3–5 minutes on each side, until nicely coloured.

Finely slice the tongue and serve immediately, dipping into the *jeow som*.

SERVES 4

1 ox tongue, skin removed by your butcher
1 cup shredded green papaya
¼ onion, finely chopped
1 garlic clove, crushed
½ teaspoon salt
2 tablespoons sugar
2 teaspoons freshly ground white pepper
2 teaspoons freshly ground black pepper
1 tablespoon oyster sauce
3 teaspoons fish sauce
3 teaspoons light soy sauce

JEOW SOM

3 garlic cloves
2–4 small red chillies
1 tablespoon sugar
1 shallot, finely sliced
¼ bunch coriander (cilantro), roots and stems included (roots scraped and cleaned), finely chopped
juice of 2–3 limes
2 tablespoons fish sauce

Making this soup starts with getting your hands on the star ingredient - fresh bamboo shoots. They can be tracked down at the best Asian markets in spring. The difference between fresh and tinned bamboo is immense - the flavour is cleaner and the texture firmer. Try it and you'll see what we mean.

The soup also features yanang leaves, from the climbing yanang vine native to Laos and Thailand. Many Lao families living abroad grow the vine on their back fence. The leaves are rubbed together in water to produce a dark green, nutrient-rich liquid that colours the soup and gives it a bright chlorophyll-like flavour. In lieu of fresh leaves, tinned yanang juice from an Asian grocer can be used instead. This soup also features fresh and dried mushrooms, pumpkin and gourd - and pork can be added too, or you can keep it vegetarian.

KAENG NOR MAI

Bamboo and Yanang Soup

from Keo Vanthanavong

To make a quick pork stock if using pork, put the pork belly in a saucepan and cover with around 650 ml (22 fl oz) of cold water. Bring to the boil, then reduce the heat to a simmer and cook for about 20 minutes. Use a slotted spoon to scoop the meat into a bowl, reserving the stock.

If using fresh yanang leaves, put them in a large bowl and add 750 ml (25½ fl oz/3 cups) of cold water. Take the leaves in your hands and roughly scrub them against each other until the water begins to turn green. Keep working the leaves until no more colour is leaching into the water. Squeeze out the leaves and discard, and reserve the liquid.

Pour two-thirds of the yanang extract into a large saucepan. Add the cooked bamboo shoots, padek or anchovy sauce, fish sauce and pork stock (or otherwise use 500 ml (17 fl oz/2 cups) of water) and bring to the boil without stirring, or stirring only gently. (Stirring dishes that use padek is said to bring out an unpleasant flavour.)

Once boiling, add the pork belly (if using), lemongrass, pumpkin and drained black fungus and simmer for another 5-10 minutes, or until the pumpkin is just tender. Add the gourd, oyster mushrooms and chillies and simmer for another 2 minutes.

Add the remaining yanang extract, sugar, salt, basil or rice paddy herb and the sticky rice paste. Cook, stirring gently, until the rice paste has slightly thickened the soup, then remove from the heat. Serve with the extra basil or rice paddy herb as well as extra chilli if desired.

SERVES 4-6

300 g (10½ oz) pork belly, diced (optional)
2 handfuls yanang leaves or 750 ml (25½ fl oz/3 cups) tinned yanang extract or juice
1 fresh bamboo shoot trimmed down to its tender core, finely sliced and boiled for 10 minutes
1½ tablespoons *padek* or anchovy sauce
1½ tablespoons fish sauce
1 lemongrass stalk, white part only, bruised
1 cup peeled and diced pumpkin
¼ cup dried black fungus (wood-ear mushrooms), soaked in water until soft
1 angled gourd (also called ridged gourd or luffa), ridges peeled off, thickly sliced, and then the slices cut into quarters
1 cup oyster mushrooms
5 small chillies, bruised, plus extra to serve if desired
2 teaspoons sugar
small pinch of salt
1 cup lemon basil leaves or rice paddy herb, plus extra to serve
¼ cup raw sticky rice, soaked for a few hours, drained and ground to a fine paste with a splash of water

Here's a delicious salad of steamed cabbage, spinach, beans and mushrooms mixed with a paste of chargrilled onion, garlic, ginger and chilli, topped with a generous sprinkling of crushed toasted sesame seeds. It's perfect with sticky rice.

SOOP PAK

Steamed Vegetable and Sesame Salad

from Manivone Phimiphisane

Toast the sesame seeds in a dry frying pan or wok until golden and fragrant, then grind in a mortar until mostly crushed.

Preheat the grill of a barbecue. Thread the onion pieces, unpeeled garlic and ginger, and chillies onto bamboo skewers and grill, turning, until charred all over. Peel the onion, garlic and ginger when cool enough to touch and place in a mortar with the chillies. Pound to a paste.

Pile the cabbage, water spinach, beans and mushrooms in a large steamer and steam for 3–4 minutes or until tender. Transfer to a large bowl and add the bamboo shoots.

While the vegetables are still warm, add the chilli paste, fish sauce, *padek* or anchovy sauce, salt, sugar, stock powder (if using) and lemon juice. Toss until well combined.

Scatter the salad with the ground sesame seeds, spring onion and coriander.

SERVES 4-6

⅓ cup sesame seeds
1 onion, quartered with the skin on
1 large garlic clove
4 cm (1½ in) piece of ginger
3 dried long red chillies
¼–½ cabbage, cut into chunks
1 bunch water spinach, cut into 5 cm (2 in) lengths
125 g (5 oz) green beans, halved
1 cup dried black fungus (wood-ear mushrooms), soaked in water until soft, finely sliced (or other mushrooms)

½ cup sliced bamboo shoots
1 tablespoon fish sauce
1 tablespoon *padek* or anchovy sauce
½ teaspoon salt
½ teaspoon sugar
½ teaspoon chicken stock powder (optional)
2 tablespoons lemon juice
4 spring onions (scallions), finely sliced
handful of coriander (cilantro) leaves

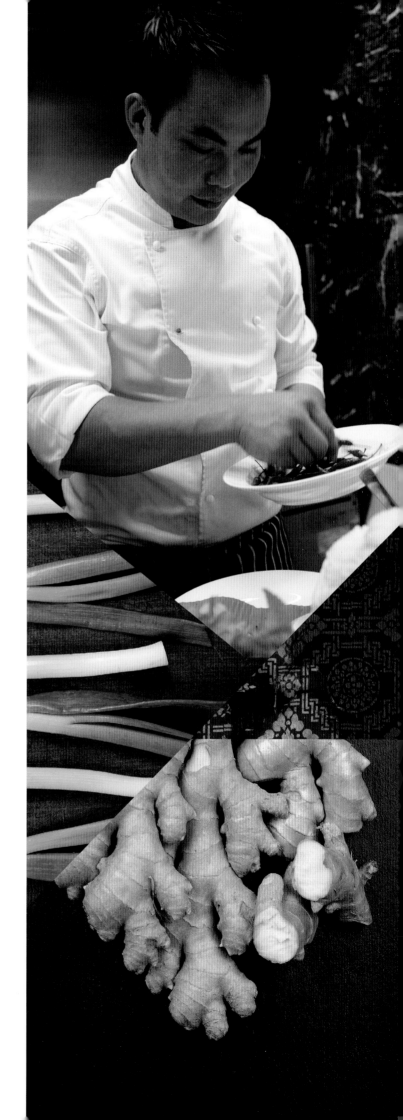

Wherever you go in the Lebanese world, there is a waft of fragrant spices and fresh herbs. The emporiums, bakeries and restaurants all have a beguiling aroma of cinnamon, cumin, coriander, parsley and mint that signals the delicious and exotic dishes awaiting you. If you're in a Lebanese home you'll be treated like royalty. Two steps through the door you'll be greeted by beautiful baking smells or the intense, fresh scent of parsley being carefully cut for tabbouleh – and it will be a miracle if you get any further without being offered food. The first of many delicious offerings is usually roasted nuts or salt-dusted roasted pumpkin seeds. The tradition of hospitality is something that runs deep and when combined with a cuisine that is effortlessly generous and abundant, you have a recipe for pure culinary magic.

'*Sahteyn*' is a word you'll often hear in Lebanese homes - loosely translated it means 'twice your health' and is a form of welcome to join a family and share delicious food. In a Lebanese household, food is life and sharing it is one of the great joys of being alive. Even for simple dinners at home, there will be a variety of dishes on the table. The meal will start with small dishes known as mezze, which centre around dips and salads. The salads are all presented snap-fresh and dressed with olive oil and lemon juice. It's not unusual to have a number of salads and dips to start a meal - these are all fairly labour intensive but beautiful to look at and taste.

Needless to say, dinners can last some hours.

One of the things I've learned from hanging around Lebanese kitchens and cooks is that you must be exacting about ingredients. The parsley for tabbouleh, for example, must be young, soft and just picked - no hard supermarket bunches are allowed here; the same for the mint, and both herbs are bunched and sliced finely (almost shaved). Another hallmark of Lebanese cooking is that many dishes are mixed with the hands and people say it's the touch of the hands that elevates the food to the heavens. Certainly the salads are some of the best I've ever tasted.

I also love the way the food easily translates between cultures - my dear friend Fouad, a legendary chef, remarked that Lebanese *kafta* (minced lamb and beef that can be shaped as patties or wrapped around skewers) are perfect for a barbecue. And he's right!

Sweets are pure artwork and there are endless variations on a theme - for instance, *baklawa* comes in many shapes and with differing amounts of nuts and syrup. There are also wickedly creamy sweets filled with a clotted cream called *ashta* and melting shortbread that is sometimes filled with a date paste or nuts - and much more. Lebanese sweets are generally served in between meals with black coffee or tea and are an essential part of any celebration. *Sahteyn*!

ESSENTIAL FLAVOURS

ASHTA
A form of clotted cream made by skimming boiling milk. It is used in many Lebanese sweets, especially *nuraset* or ladies' arms and Damascus rose (filo rounds topped with *ashta*, syrup and pistachios).

BAHARAT
Used throughout the Middle East, each region has its own distinctive blend of spices. In Lebanon the blend includes paprika, pepper, cumin, cassia, cloves, coriander seed, cardamom and nutmeg.

BASTURMA
Air-dried beef, similar to pastrami, that is coated with spices and usually sliced finely.

LABNEH
A type of cheese that is made from yoghurt, which is hung in a fine cloth for a day and drained of moisture. It is rich and creamy with a nice tang and is used to spread on bread and as the basis of many dips.

SUMAC
A ground, dried berry with a peppery, lemony flavour and a reddish-purple colour. It is very common in Lebanese dishes such as *fattoush* (a fresh salad of tomato, cucumber, parsley, mint and toasted bread).

TAHINI
A popular paste made from hulled or unhulled sesame seeds. It is thick and creamy with a slightly nutty flavour and is used in many sauces and dips – it is a key ingredient in hoummus.

ZA'ATAR
A blend of thyme, toasted sesame seeds, sumac and salt. It is often mixed with a little olive oil to make a fragrant dip for Lebanese bread or spread with olive oil on *manoush* (a thin pizza that is served as a breakfast dish) and baked, then topped with tomato, mint, onion and black olives.

A classic dip that is made almost every day in most Lebanese homes. The secret is to cook the chickpeas until they're really soft. If you can, seek out the prized nine-millimetre chickpeas grown in the Ord River region of Western Australia - they're fabulous.

HOUMMUS

from Greg Malouf

The day before you wish to make the hoummus, place the chickpeas in a large saucepan and add enough cold water to cover by 10 cm (4 in) or more. Add the bicarbonate of soda and leave to soak overnight.

The next day, rinse the chickpeas, return them to the saucepan and cover with more water.

Bring to the boil then simmer for approximately 1-2 hours, until the chickpeas are soft and shedding their skins. Drain and allow to cool.

Place the chickpeas in a food processor and blend until soft and creamy. Add the tahini, lemon juice, garlic and salt and blend again until the mixture is smooth. Scoop into a serving bowl and make a well in the centre. Pour the oil into the well and sprinkle paprika and parsley on top.

MAKES 4 CUPS (APPROX)

500 g (1 lb 2 oz) dried chickpeas	2 teaspoons salt
2 tablespoons bicarbonate of soda	1 tablespoon extra-virgin olive oil
1½ tablespoons tahini	1 teaspoon sweet paprika
1 tablespoon lemon juice	finely chopped flat-leaf (Italian) parsley
1-2 garlic cloves	

'Respect the ingredients that you cook with - they are a gift and precious.'

It's quite nerve-wracking to just pop a whole eggplant directly on a gas flame, but without the smoky flavour you get as the eggplant sizzles, you wouldn't have a true baba ghanouj. This is a foolproof and creamy recipe for this beautiful dip.

This recipe is a revelation - make it and see how crisp and lovely this salad should really be. Tightly bunching the parsley in your hand ready for cutting is crucial, as is using a very sharp knife - both help you to shave the parsley as finely as possible. Tabbouleh can be prepared a couple of hours ahead, but add the salt, pepper and oil just before serving. Serve it alongside almost any Lebanese dish (try the *kafta* on the next page), or simply spoon onto baby cos (romaine) lettuce leaves, roll up and enjoy.

BABA GHANOUJ

from Katya Faraj

Grill the eggplants whole over a gas flame, turning with tongs until the skin is evenly blistered and the flesh is soft. Soak in cold water for 10 minutes to cool.

Peel the eggplants and leave to drain for 15–20 minutes.

Place the eggplants in a food processor with the tahini, lemon juice, garlic and salt and process until well combined and creamy. You may wish to add extra tahini, lemon juice or salt to taste.

Scoop into a serving bowl and make a well in the centre. Pour the oil into the well and sprinkle paprika, parsley and tomato on top.

MAKES 3 CUPS (APPROX)

3 medium eggplants (aubergines)	1 tablespoon extra-virgin olive oil
1½ tablespoons tahini	1 teaspoon sweet paprika
1 tablespoon lemon juice	finely chopped flat-leaf (Italian) parsley
1–2 garlic cloves	finely diced tomato
2 teaspoons salt	

TABBOULEH

from Samira Saab

Gather the parsley in a tight wad in your hand and finely shred the leaves with a very sharp knife, almost in a shaving action. Do the same with the mint. Tip the herbs into a colander. Wash the chopped herbs and drain well.

Squeeze the lemon juice over the burghul and leave to soften for 10 minutes.

Combine the parsley and mint, softened burghul, tomato and spring onion in a bowl. Season with salt and pepper, add olive oil and mix with your hands.

SERVES 4

1 bunch fresh, soft flat-leaf (Italian) parsley	3–4 medium tomatoes, diced
handful of mint leaves	4 spring onions (scallions), finely chopped
1–2 lemons	salt and pepper
2 tablespoons fine burghul	olive oil

These meat skewers are like the ultlmate handmade sausages and they're incredibly simple. Make sure you buy the best-quality minced lamb and beef – or even better, mince the meat yourself. If you don't have metal skewers you can simply shape the mixture into patties. Great on the barbie, great in a pan, great in the oven – just great!

'If you lick the saucepan, it will rain on your wedding day!'

KAFTA

from Fouad Sayed

Place all the ingredients in a large bowl and use your hands to combine and knead the mixture until smooth.

Dampen your hands with water and shape the mixture around metal skewers. Barbecue (grill) until golden brown and cooked through.

To serve, split open some flatbread and fill with tabbouleh. Top with a *kafta*, close the bread around it and hold firmly as you slide out the skewer. Use torn-off pieces of bread to pick up some of the *kafta* and tabbouleh.

SERVES 10-12

1 cup finely chopped flat-leaf (Italian) parsley
500 g (1 lb 2 oz) minced (ground) lamb
500 g (1 lb 2 oz) minced (ground) beef
1 large onion, very finely chopped

1 teaspoon salt
½ teaspoon freshly ground white pepper

TO SERVE

flatbread
tabbouleh

I was thrilled when my friend Judy shared this family recipe with me, and found it fun to hollow out the zucchini using a *manakra* (a tool like a long apple corer designed for this purpose; you can find them in Middle Eastern food stores). The best zucchini to use is the small, slightly bulbous, pale green variety often sold as Lebanese zucchini. To adapt this recipe for vegetarians, use chickpeas instead of minced beef.

KOUSA MAHSHI

Stuffed Zucchini

from Judy Saba

Thoroughly mix the stuffing ingredients together.

Cut off the zucchini stalks, then slice off the dried tips at the opposite ends without removing too much flesh. Carefully hollow out the zucchini from the stalk end by pushing and turning a *manakra* into the flesh. The tool will remove thin fingers of flesh at a time; keep hollowing until you have a generous cavity (reserve the zucchini flesh for another purpose such as an omelette).

Fill a bowl with water and add a teaspoon of salt. Wash the zucchini in the salted water (this helps to keep them firm when cooking), then drain.

Fill each zucchini with the stuffing, leaving 1 cm (½ in) free at the top to allow the filling to expand.

It's easiest to fill the zucchini by hand, tapping them on the bench every now and then to settle the stuffing down. If you have any leftover stuffing, form it into meatballs.

Fill a large saucepan with water and add 2 tablespoons of salt and the tomato paste. Add the stuffed zucchini and any meatballs and bring to the boil. Simmer over low heat for about 1 hour, allowing the sauce to reduce. Serve the stuffed zucchini with a little of the sauce and a dollop of yoghurt.

SERVES 4-6

STUFFING

1 cup long-grain rice, washed
250 g (9 oz) lean minced (ground) beef
1 medium tomato, finely diced
½ onion, finely diced
⅓ cup chopped flat-leaf (Italian) parsley
⅓ cup chopped mint
⅓ cup chopped coriander (cilantro)
¼ teaspoon chilli powder
1 teaspoon *baharat* or allspice
1 teaspoon ground cumin
½ teaspoon freshly ground black pepper
2 teaspoons salt
20 g (¾ oz) butter, softened
2 tablespoons olive oil

10 small Lebanese zucchini (courgettes), approximately 10 cm (4 in) long
salt
2 heaped tablespoons tomato paste (concentrated puree)
natural yoghurt

'Before you use any Lebanese food, you make the sign of the cross over it and say "*Bis mis Salib*" (In the name of the Cross).'

This is one of the best dishes I've eaten in my life and is now our show-off dinner party and Christmas lunch dish. The combination of perfectly cooked fish, a tahini and yoghurt dressing, freshly chopped herbs and walnuts, and a hint of chilli is fresh and delicious. The dish is served at room temperature, so you can cook the salmon up to four hours in advance.

'TARATOR-STYLE' BAKED SALMON

FROM GREG MALOUF

To make the dressing, place the garlic and salt in a mortar and crush well. Stir the garlic, yoghurt and tahini together until it becomes a thick paste. Thin slightly with lemon juice (it should be the consistency of pure cream). Taste for salt and refrigerate.

Preheat the oven to 150°C (300°F/Gas 2). Place the salmon on a large sheet of baking paper. Season all over with salt and pepper and drizzle with 2½ tablespoons of the oil. Wrap the salmon in the paper, place on a tray and bake in the centre of the oven for 25 minutes. Gently turn the salmon over and cook for a further 25 minutes, by which time it should be medium–rare. Remove from the oven and open the paper to stop the salmon cooking further. Leave to cool to room temperature.

Turn the oven up to 200°C (400°F/Gas 6) and roast the walnuts for 5 minutes. Remove from the oven and rub briskly in a clean tea towel to remove as much of their skin as possible. Chop finely and set aside.

Close to serving time, use a sharp knife to cut through the skin along the back of the salmon from head to tail. Peel away the skin from one side. Scrape away the thin layer of grey flesh (the blood line) to expose the pink flesh underneath.

Carefully transfer the salmon to a large serving plate. Brush ½ cup of the yoghurt dressing over the top of the salmon.

In a bowl, whisk the remaining oil with the lemon juice, salt and pepper. Add the onion and chilli and whisk lightly. Add the chopped walnuts, herbs and sumac. Spoon the salad over the salmon, covering it as neatly as possible.

Use a metal spoon to 'cut' portions of the salmon and salad. Serve with the remaining dressing.

SERVES 10-12

DRESSING
1 garlic clove
1 teaspoon sea salt
400 g (14 oz) natural yoghurt
100 ml (3½ fl oz) tahini
lemon juice

BAKED SALMON
1 Tasmanian salmon (4-4.5 kg)
sea salt and freshly ground
 white pepper
170 ml (5½ fl oz/⅔ cup)
 extra-virgin olive oil

150 g (5½ oz) walnuts
juice of 1-2 lemons
1 medium red onion,
 finely diced
3 long red chillies, seeded
 and finely diced
2 cups coriander (cilantro)
 leaves, chopped
½ cup mint leaves, shredded
20 g (¾ oz) sumac

If I could have my childhood over again, I'd grow up in Malaysia. Every expatriate I've spoken to sighs wistfully as they recall sumptuous banquets and simply prepared yet exquisite dishes. Like the story of the *kway teow man*, a mobile foodstall dedicated to a single great Malaysian offering – *char kway teow* noodles. This dish uses glossy, fat rice noodles mixed with plump, fresh prawns, thin discs of sweet-savoury Chinese *lup cheong* sausage, sometimes a little diced chicken, bean sprouts, garlic chives and a dash of soy sauce and chilli. It's all tossed together in a smoking-hot wok and the finishing touch is a beaten egg, which is whisked through to make a creamy sauce. The whole dish is made even more enticing by that special X-factor, the 'breath of the wok' – that's the '*char*' in the dish's name.

And to think that this wonder actually comes to your front doorstep – does it get better than that?

Char kway teow encapsulates the magic of Malaysian food – a layering of tastes and textures that is well thought-out, elegantly spiced, simply beautiful and a perfect blend of Indian, Malaysian, Chinese and Nyonya (Straits Chinese) flavours. Malaysia has a rich cultural mix and in a wider sense this dish allows a glimpse of the way the world could be, with many races existing harmoniously together.

Malaysian food is also the result of a whole nation of dedicated – no, obsessive – food lovers who focus on taste and texture to achieve culinary nirvana. This nirvana has been described to me by my chef friend Jess as 'making your tastebuds jump up and down!'.

I had a glimpse of this nirvana when I discovered a flavour secret in the cheat's laksa recipe that follows – not only does the base flavour of nutty sweetness come from the dried shrimp used, it's also from the prawn heads and shells, which are cooked briefly in hot oil. What a revelation to see the oil change colour and catch the delicious aroma of the scraps that most of us would throw in the bin! In all these recipes I also found that you can get fairly close to authentic restaurant or hawker stall flavours at home when you know how.

The sweets that finish Malaysian meals are marvellous concoctions of rice flour, coconut and palm sugar (jaggery). These take various forms, from the multicoloured steamed rice confections called *kueh*, to *sago gula melaka* in all its wonderfully sweet, dark stickiness. This is a great cuisine!

ESSENTIAL FLAVOURS

CHILLI
There are many sizes, shapes and colours available in Malaysia. As a general rule, the smaller the chilli, the hotter it will be. Red chillies are simply green chillies which have been left to ripen. Green chillies are more peppery and the red have a slightly sweeter heat. If you prefer a milder flavour, keep them whole and remove before serving or remove the seeds and membranes before chopping.

DRIED SHRIMP
Tiny dried prawns (shrimp) used in laksa pastes and sambals (spicy side dishes).

IKAN BILIS
Small dried anchovies that add a crunchy texture and salty taste to the national dish *nasi lemak*.

KECAP MANIS
A sweet, dark soy sauce used predominantly in Indonesian and Malaysian cooking. The sweetness comes from the addition of palm sugar (jaggery) and it is flavoured with star anise and sometimes garlic.

LEMONGRASS
A tall, thick-stemmed grass with a lemony aroma and flavour. It can be very woody so look for young, fresh stems and use the white part closest to the base of the stem.

LUP CHEONG
Dried sausages that are red in colour and usually made from pork meat and spices. They are sweet and slightly spicy. Slice very thinly and stir-fry, or steam whole then slice.

PALM SUGAR (JAGGERY)
A golden sugar with a rich caramel flavour and a hint of coconut. It can be grated or sliced. If not available, brown sugar may be substituted.

PANDAN LEAF
The Asian equivalent of vanilla bean. Its subtle aroma is released when bruised by tying one or two long leaves into a knot. The leaves can also be used to wrap chicken or fish before cooking. Pandan leaf is also available as an essence and a powder to flavour and colour cakes. It is often used when cooking curries, rice and desserts.

THICK CARAMEL SOY SAUCE
Even more viscous than dark soy sauce, this is used to add a depth of colour and flavour to many dishes. Surprisingly, despite its name, it is not sweet.

This is known fondly as Sunday night noodles in our house. It's everything a good dish should be – full of great flavour and texture with the silky noodles contrasting with the crunchy fresh sprouts and the creamy egg. Heat the wok well and have all the ingredients standing by in bowls ready to cook. The wok must be very hot as the secret to this dish is cooking quickly over high heat. A good tip is to heat the noodles first (if they are cold from the fridge), which is easily done in the microwave. And only cook enough for one person at a time to avoid the wok being too full and the ingredients 'stewing'.

CHAR KWAY TEOW

from Jess Ong

Use a quarter of the ingredients to cook for each person individually. Heat the wok over high heat. When thoroughly heated, add oil, sausage, fish balls, spring onion and garlic and stir-fry for a few minutes. Add the noodles and toss briefly, then add the soy sauces and toss through the noodles. Scrape everything to the side of the wok and add the prawns, cooking until they change colour. Move the prawns to the side and add the egg. Cook until the egg is nearly set, then gently fold it into the noodles. Add the bean sprouts and chives, toss, and serve immediately.

SERVES 4

80 ml (2½ floz/⅓ cup) oil	1 tablespoon dark soy sauce
2 *lup cheong* sausages, sliced	1 tablespoon light soy sauce
12 fish balls, sliced	24 shelled green prawns
8 spring onions (scallions), sliced	(shrimp)
8 garlic cloves, chopped	4 eggs, beaten
5 handfuls fresh rice noodles, warmed	4 handfuls bean sprouts
	⅓ cup chopped garlic chives

'In Malaysia, tastebuds are triggered by various sounds. A cow's bell ringing is the mobile hawker selling *pulut hitam* (sweet coconut black rice), a beep is for laksa, a bicycle bell for satay, a lady's bellowing for Nyonya *kueh* (rice-flour sweets) ...'

This is a recipe to treasure and make again and again - thanks to my friend Alvin for sharing it. Try to source all the ingredients (from Asian food stores) for the best authentic flavour, and remember that once you've found turmeric leaves they'll freeze well for next time. Like all great slow-cooked dishes, rendang calls for meat with a bit of fat through it - it will become succulent, soft and absolutely delicious.

BEEF RENDANG

from Alvin Tan

Place the chilli, onion, garlic, galangal, ginger and lemongrass in a blender or food processor and blend to a paste, adding some soaking water from the chillies as needed.

Heat a frying pan over low heat and toast the coconut to golden. Grind in a mortar, blender or food processor and set aside.

Heat the oil in a heavy-based saucepan and add the paste and the turmeric and lime leaves.

Fry for 3-4 minutes, until fragrant. Add the meat, then stir in the coconut milk and curry powder. Add the water and toasted coconut (which will thicken the rendang) and bring to a simmer. Cook for 1-1½ hours, until the meat is tender. Add extra water during cooking if the rendang is drying out. To finish, add the soy sauce and season to taste with salt.

SERVES 4-6

- 6 dried long chillies, torn in half (seeded if you want less heat), soaked in hot water until soft
- 150 g (5½ oz) red onions, chopped
- 5 garlic cloves, chopped
- 3 cm (1¼ in) piece of galangal, chopped
- 3 cm (1¼ in) piece of young ginger, chopped
- 1 lemongrass stalk, finely chopped
- 1 cup desiccated coconut
- 3 tablespoons vegetable oil
- ¾ turmeric leaf, rolled and finely chopped (optional)
- 6 kaffir lime leaves, rolled and sliced
- 1 kg (2 lb 3 oz) topside or chuck steak, cut into 3 cm (1¼ in) cubes
- 250 ml (8½ fl oz/1 cup) coconut milk
- 4 tablespoons Malaysian 'meat' curry powder
- 125 ml (4 fl oz/½ cup) water
- 1-2 tablespoons thick caramel soy sauce
- salt

This was first described to me as a ten-minute laksa but it takes a little bit longer to prepare – but not much! What I love is that you're adding delicious fresh ingredients to a commercial laksa paste (look for this in Asian food stores), so a lot of the work is already done for you. This is a great dish to serve for a group of friends if you've set the table already and have all the garnishing to hand. Make it up to the adding of the noodles and you'll be blessed as a culinary genius!

CHEAT'S LAKSA

from Aryan Mansour

Place the shallots, garlic, ginger, chilli, dried shrimp and water in a blender or food processor and blend to a smooth paste.

Shell the prawns. Heat the oil in a large saucepan and fry the shells for about 1 minute, until they turn red. Scoop out the shells leaving the coloured oil. Add the blended paste to the oil and fry for a minute before adding the laksa paste.

Fry until fragrant, then add the stock and bring to the boil. Add the coconut cream and turn the heat back to a simmer. Add the fish balls, tofu and sugar, along with fish sauce and salt to taste.

Add the lime juice.

Cook the rice noodles in a separate saucepan of boiling water, then scoop into a colander. Add the egg noodles to the water to heat through and remove to a separate colander. Poach the shelled prawns in the same water.

Put some noodles and prawns in each serving bowl. Ladle over the broth and top with chicken and bean sprouts. Scatter with spring onion, chilli, coriander and fried shallots. Add a wedge of lime to squeeze in before eating.

SERVES 4

4-5 shallots, chopped	fish balls
6-7 garlic cloves, chopped	fried tofu puffs, cut in half
thumb-sized piece of ginger, chopped	1 teaspoon sugar
	fish sauce
1 red chilli (more if you want extra kick)	salt
	juice of 1 lime, plus extra wedges to serve
1 heaped tablespoon dried shrimp	dried rice vermicelli
125 ml (4 fl oz/½ cup) water	fresh egg noodles
12 green prawns (shrimp)	shredded cooked chicken
80 ml (2½ fl oz/⅓ cup) vegetable oil	bean sprouts
	finely sliced spring onion (scallions)
4 tablespoons laksa paste	finely sliced red chilli
1 litre (34 fl oz/4 cups) chicken stock or water	coriander (cilantro) leaves
400 ml (13½ fl oz) coconut cream	fried shallots

Nasi Lemak is known as the national dish of Malaysia and is served with *ikan bilis*, roasted peanuts, hard-boiled eggs and spicy sambals. Delicious and fragrant, *Nasi Lemak* is a perfect accompaniment to beef rendang. I never cook plain old rice any more after learning this recipe! You can cook this in a rice cooker if you have one.

Pale little pearls – that's how the sago looks once cooked. Add the mellow caramel made from palm sugar (jaggery) and it's a match made in heaven. This pudding looks really impressive when it's set in a fluted ring mould.

NASI LEMAK

Coconut Rice

from Alvin Tan

Rinse the rice twice and drain. Put in a saucepan with the remaining ingredients, cover with a lid and bring to the boil. Simmer gently until the liquid is absorbed (about 15 minutes). Remove from the heat and leave covered for another 5 minutes before serving.

SERVES 6

3 cups long-grain rice	1 pandan leaf, split and
200 ml (7 fl oz) coconut milk	tied in a knot
200 ml (7 fl oz) water	¾ teaspoon salt
2 cm (¾ in) piece of ginger, bruised	

SAGO GULA MELAKA

Sago with Palm Sugar Syrup

from Suzanne Goh

Bring a large saucepan of water to the boil and add the sago. Stir as the water returns to the boil to stop the pearls sticking to each other. Cook until the sago floats to the surface and is transparent (approximately 15 minutes). Drain and rinse in cold water a couple of times to remove the starch.

Beat the egg white until soft peaks form. Stir in the sago. Pour into a jelly mould and chill for at least 1 hour to set.

Heat the palm sugar and water over medium heat, stirring to dissolve the sugar. Stir in the white sugar. When completely dissolved, strain through a fine sieve and leave to cool.

Turn the sago pudding onto a serving plate.

Cut into wedges and serve topped with a little coconut milk and syrup.

SERVES 6

300 g (10½ oz) sago	125 ml (4 fl oz/½ cup) water
1 egg white	75 g (2¾ oz/⅓ cup) white sugar
200 g (7 oz) palm sugar (jaggery), chopped	400 ml (13½ fl oz) coconut milk

When you hear the story of how Maltese people have survived and thrived for centuries on their rocky island in the centre of the Mediterranean (between Sicily and North Africa), you have to hand it to these tenacious people. Most of the land isn't suitable for grazing or cultivation and yet has given birth to some beautiful rustic recipes that sing of Mediterranean flavour and freshness.

That same spirit of getting on with it persists in the homes of Maltese immigrants. One inspiring woman called Polly missed the cheese she had grown up with so much that she decided to buy a couple of cows and learn to milk them so she could make the cheese herself. Impressive!

And after a morning spent cheesemaking – and this is energetic work – Polly then decided that she would whip up lunch for our crew of four and her family, in 30 minutes creating delicious *bragioli* (beef olives). A real Maltese favourite, this consists of a rolled escalope of beef filled with minced veal, herbs and cheese then cooked in a lovely fresh tomato sauce. She served the cooking sauce with some pasta then the meat was the main course - ingenious and delicious. The famous Maltese stews of rabbit (*stuffat tal-fenek*) and octopus (*stuffat tal-qarnit*) are served the same way.

Other simple but yummy things I tasted were a dip called *bigilla* made from dried fava beans (broad beans) that are cooked then mashed with some garlic, chilli and anchovies and eaten with crusty bread; and a Maltese open sandwich made from crusty bread called *hobz biz-zejt* (which translates as 'bread with oil'). To make *hobz biz-zejt*, thick slices of bread are spread with the beloved sweetish tomato paste called *kunserva* and topped with ingredients such as tuna, anchovies, capers, olives and garlic plus black pepper and a drizzle of olive oil. It is very Mediterranean and very tasty.

And how could I forget the most famous snack of Malta - the flaky, golden pastries traditionally filled with ricotta and mushy peas called *pastizzi*, which are sold on street corners and village bars and eaten hot with black tea or coffee.

Because of its close proximity to Italy, there are a lot of Italian influences in Maltese dishes like *timpana* (a deep pasta pie) and *ravjul* (ravioli stuffed with ricotta cheese) but the ravioli are generally larger than the Italian variety and Maltese pasta is usually cooked to a softer texture than al dente.

Maltese sweets also reveal the influence of other countries – Arabic culinary traditions are seen in *qaq tal-ghasel,* a pastry stuffed with a date and honey mixture; and the English bread and butter pudding has been transformed into *puddina*, a more solid chocolate version with dried fruit, which is eaten hot or cold and is also great with a cup of tea. Chilled fruit is always served as part of a dessert spread - stone fruits, figs, melons, pears, grapes, citrus fruits and pomegranates.

ESSENTIAL FLAVOURS

CAPERS
These small, salty buds grow wild in bushes along the roadside and are used in many dishes. They are essential to the ultimate Maltese open sandwich, *hobz biz-zejt*.

EXTRA-VIRGIN OLIVE OIL
Olive trees grow in abundance on the rocky island. Olive oil is used liberally in the Maltese cuisine in salad dressings and as cooking oil.

GBEJNIET
Gbejniet is the name for a type of cheese adored by the Maltese. This is generally made with cow's milk.

There is a soft fresh version like a silky cross between mozzarella and ricotta; a sun-dried version of the same, which hardens after a month into a little sweet, nutty round of cheese; and another version of hard cheese, which is rolled in a pepper powder and served with grapes or figs or as part of an antipasto selection.

KUNSERVA
This rather sweet tomato paste (concentrated puree) is used in pasta sauces and to boost any dish that contains tomatoes. It is a key ingredient in the favourite national snack, the *hobz biz-zejt* sandwich.

PULSES
Pulses in various guises are widely used in Maltese cooking. Green split peas are popular for soups and in the famous mushy pea and ricotta filling for *pastizzi* pastries. Broad beans are used fresh and dried in soups and in the beloved *bigilla* dip eaten with crusty bread.

A simple, delicious soup made from fresh vegetables including kohlrabi, peas and broad beans. It's healthy and low fat. If you can find soft *gbejniet* cheese (available from selected delis and cheese makers), pop it into the hot soup for a few minutes before serving and you'll enjoy the beautiful taste of molten cheese too.

Malta's number one snack food is an open sandwich slathered with *kunserva* (sweetish tomato paste) and topped with the best the Mediterranean has to offer. Shane especially likes to use white anchovies, which are pickled in vinegar rather than preserved in salt or oil and have a mild, sweet flavour.

SOPPA TAL-ARMLA

Widow's Soup
from Alex Vella

Heat the butter and oil in a large saucepan and add the onion, garlic and most of the parsley.

Sauté until soft. Add the vegetables, tomato paste and enough stock to cover. Stir well and season to taste with salt and pepper. Bring to the boil, cover and simmer for 15–20 minutes, until the vegetables are just cooked.

Add the *gbejniet* and press down lightly to submerge. Cover and cook for a couple of minutes to heat the cheese. Add the remaining parsley to the soup and stir through.

Ladle the soup into bowls, topping each with a round of *gbejniet*.

SERVES 6

1 tablespoon butter	1 cup podded peas (fresh or frozen)
1 tablespoon olive oil	½ large or 1 small cauliflower, cut into bite-sized pieces
1 onion, diced	
3-4 garlic cloves, crushed	
⅔ cup chopped flat-leaf (Italian) parsley	1½ tablespoons tomato paste (concentrated puree)
2 potatoes, peeled and chopped	chicken or vegetable stock
2 carrots, peeled and chopped	salt and pepper
1 kohlrabi, peeled and chopped	6 soft *gbejniet* (small Maltese cheeses)
2 celery stalks, sliced	
1 cup podded broad beans (fresh or frozen)	

HOBZ BIZ-ZEJT

Open Sandwich
from Shane Delia

Spread the bread with *kunserva*. Sprinkle capers over the top, then add anchovies or tuna. Season with salt and pepper, scatter with parsley and drizzle generously with oil. Enjoy!

slices of dense, crusty bread	sea salt and freshly ground black pepper
kunserva (Maltese tomato paste)	flat-leaf (Italian) parsley leaves
capers	extra-virgin olive oil
white anchovies or tinned tuna in oil, drained	

'Give bread only to people who know how to eat it (Get an expert if you want a job done properly).'

Timpana is the ultimate pasta pie. Macaroni or penne is cooked and added to a rich bolognaise-style sauce, often enhanced by chicken livers. With the addition of cheese and eggs, the pasta and sauce is spooned into a pastry case and cooked until golden.

TIMPANA

from Louis Bigeni

Heat the butter in a saucepan and add the onion and garlic. Sauté for 5 minutes. Add the bacon and pork, stirring well to separate, then add the beef and continue cooking for 10 minutes, stirring every so often. Add the chicken livers if using and cook for 5 minutes. Add the stock, stir well and bring to the boil. Simmer for 20 minutes. Add the tomato paste and puree, simmer briefly and remove from the heat.

Meanwhile, cook the pasta in a large pot of salted boiling water until just undercooked.

Drain, then mix through the sauce. Stir in the cheeses and egg and season with salt and pepper.

Preheat the oven to 180°C (350°F/Gas 4). Line a buttered baking dish with the pastry, extending it up the sides. Spoon in the pasta and cover with another layer of pastry. Prick the *timpana* all over with a knife to let steam escape. Beat the egg and milk for the glaze and paint it over the *timpana*. Bake for 1–1¼ hours.

SERVES 6-8

75 g (2¾ oz) butter
250 g (9 oz) onions, finely diced
2 garlic cloves, crushed
150 g (5½ oz) bacon, finely diced
150 g (5½ oz) minced (ground) pork
150 g (5½ oz) minced (ground) beef
150 g (5½ oz) chicken livers, diced (optional)
250 ml (8½ fl oz/1 cup) chicken or beef stock
100 g (3½ oz) tomato paste (concentrated purree)

125 ml (4 fl oz/½ cup) tomato puree
250 g (9 oz) macaroni or penne
75 g (2¾ oz) parmesan, grated
75 g (2¾ oz) tasty cheese, grated
4 eggs, beaten
salt and pepper
250 g (9 oz) puff pastry sheets

GLAZE

1 egg
2½ tablespoons milk

'A donkey does not appreciate cake
(sometimes people don't realise
when they are onto a good thing).'

The joy of this recipe is that you don't need the best cuts of meat to make a delicious meal. Thin slices of tenderised beef are stuffed with minced veal, herbs and flavourings and gently cooked in a tomato-based sauce. This can also be served as two meals in the traditional Maltese way with the cooking sauce paired with pasta as a first course.

This is a marvellous slow-cooked dish that's full of flavour, with meat so tender it falls off the bone. Paul says his family always has this dish two ways - the rich red sauce (and there's a lot of liquid in this dish) is used for an entrée of pasta and then the main event is the rabbit served with potatoes. Rabbit is the most popular meat in Malta and many Maltese homes in Australia still raise rabbits for the table.

BRAGIOLI

Beef Olives
from Polly Vella

To make the sauce, heat the oil in a large saucepan and add the onion and garlic. Fry until softened.

Add the remaining ingredients and leave to simmer while you prepare the *bragioli*.

Flatten the beef slices with a mallet and set aside. Mix the remaining ingredients together well, seasoning with salt and pepper. Place a generous tablespoon of mixture on each slice of beef, spreading out well. Roll up and secure with toothpicks or tie with butcher's string. Place the rolls in the sauce and simmer for 1½ hours over low heat.

SERVES 6

SAUCE	BEEF
3 tablespoons olive oil	6 thin slices of topside or
2 large onions, diced	round steak
5 garlic cloves, crushed	400 g (14 oz) minced
400 g (14 oz) tin tomatoes	(ground) veal
1 cup flat-leaf (Italian) parsley	2 bacon rashers, diced
leaves	2 garlic cloves, crushed
½ cup basil leaves	½ cup finely chopped
2 bay leaves	flat-leaf (Italian) parsley
250 ml (8½ fl oz/1 cup) red wine	1 tablespoon finely chopped
500 ml (17 fl oz/2 cups) water	oregano
salt and pepper	1 spring onion (scallion),
	finely sliced
	½ cup grated *gbejniet*
	(Maltese cheese)
	2 eggs, beaten
	salt and pepper

STUFFAT TAL-FENEK

Rabbit Stew
from Paul Camilleri

Remove the rabbit kidneys and liver and set aside. Chop the rabbit into pieces: remove the front and back legs and cut each in half, and chop the body or saddle into 5 pieces. Place the rabbit pieces, kidneys and liver in a large bowl and add the wine, half the bay leaves and the whole garlic. Marinate in the refrigerator overnight, turning the meat a few times.

Strain off the marinade liquid and reserve. Discard the garlic and bay leaves.

Preheat the oven to 150°C (300°F/Gas 2). Heat the oil in a heavy-based ovenproof pot and gently brown the rabbit on all sides until well sealed and golden.

Season with salt and pepper. Remove from the pot.

Add the onion and chopped garlic to the pot and fry until beginning to soften. Add the tomato paste and marinade liquid and cook for a minute. Add the tomato puree and water and mix well. Return the rabbit to the pot and add the potatoes and remaining bay leaves. Bring to a simmer then remove from the heat, cover with a lid and bake for 2½–3 hours.

SERVES 6

1 rabbit (1.5-2 kg/	salt and pepper
3 lb 4 oz-4 lb 6 oz)	1 onion, finely diced
350 ml (12 fl oz) red wine	3 tablespoons tomato paste
6 bay leaves	(concentrated puree)
6 garlic cloves, 4 peeled	1.5 litres (51 fl oz/6 cups)
and left whole, 2 finely	tomato puree
chopped	250 ml (8½ fl oz/1 cup) water
80 ml (2½ fl oz/⅓ cup)	3-4 potatoes, peeled and
extra-virgin olive oil	cut into chunks

With ingenuity the Maltese have adapted this dish from the English (Malta was once a British colony) and added an Arabic twist. Day-old bread is soaked in water then mixed with generous quantities of dried fruit, almonds and cocoa. *Puddina* is served in slices with black tea as an afternoon pick-me-up.

PUDDINA

Bread and Butter Pudding
from Rita O'Dwyer

Tear the bread into small pieces and soak in cold water for 15 minutes until soft.

Preheat the oven to 200°C (400°F/Gas 6). Tip the bread into a colander and squeeze out the excess water using a potato masher. Place the bread in a mixing bowl and stir in the sugar, custard powder, cornflour and cocoa. Add the eggs and mix well. Add the dried fruit, half the almonds and half the glacé cherries. Add vanilla to taste and the whisky, brandy or sherry. Pour into a baking dish and decorate the top with the remaining almonds and cherries. Bake for 45–60 minutes, or until a skewer comes out clean. Serve in slices, warm or at room temperature.

SERVES 10

1 day-old loaf of bread
370 g (1⅔ cup) sugar
2 tablespoons custard powder
2 tablespoons cornflour (cornstarch)
35 g (1¼ oz/⅓ cup) cocoa
2 eggs, beaten
500 g (1 lb 2 oz) mixed dried fruit such as sultanas (golden raisins), raisins, currants and chopped peel

250 g (9 oz) almonds
250 g (9 oz) glacé cherries, halved
vanilla extract
80 ml (2½ fl oz/⅓ cup) whisky, brandy or sherry

'Only the cook knows exactly what went into the pot'

If you had to invent a cuisine and could choose your favourite influences from around the world, you'd probably come up with something like the food of Mauritius. This combines techniques and ingredients from some of the most diverse nations on earth and blends them harmoniously and deliciously into a unique national cuisine. Indian and Sri Lankan curries, breads and pickles are cooked alongside slow-braised European daubes and Chinese stir-fried noodles – all given an African twist with local ingredients.

Take the sauce used every day by most Mauritians called *rougaille*. It's a clever mix of common ingredients such as tomatoes, onions, garlic and chillies, which are cooked with a couple of spices into a delicious fresh-tasting sauce. Vegetables, meats and seafood can then be cooked in the *rougaille* and eaten with *achards* (pickled vegetables) and dhal or rice. One of the things I was struck by is that most Mauritian dishes are cooked quickly – if you live in the tropics, you've got better things to do than stand over a hot stove!

Another quick dish to assemble is *vindaye* (pickled fish) - beautiful fresh fish (or octopus) is fried quickly then coated in a mixture of turmeric, mustard seeds, chilli, garlic, ginger, oil and vinegar. *Vindaye* was created to preserve fish before the days of refrigeration but it is still made in the traditional way and is one of the dishes that Mauritians hold close to their hearts.

Spices are also adored and used abundantly – turmeric, cinnamon, cardamom and cloves are found in many dishes, including the distinctive curries of the island. These curries rarely contain coconut milk and, interestingly, often feature more typically European herbs like thyme.

It's worth crossing the ocean for *gateaux piments* – these are incredibly more-ish, spiced split-pea cakes, a bit like falafel, which are available on every street corner – and *dholl puri*, a flatbread filled with a thin layer of mashed yellow split peas topped with all sorts of crunchy, yummy pickled vegetables and chutneys. It is always served as 'a pair of *dholl puri*', which doesn't mean two wraps but a double-layered one.

Mauritians love their sweets and have invented some beautiful tarts and biscuits that combine French techniques with local ingredients. The classic *tarte banane* is one indulgent example and I adore the impossibly cute pink-iced shortbreads sandwiched with raspberry jam called *napolitaines*. And as you would expect of a tropical island, fruit is abundant and enjoyed in cooking or as refreshing snacks. Green mango is finely shredded in salads or pickled in the sun with chilli and salt, and sliced pineapple with chilli salt is one of the most commonly sold snacks. The perfect food for lazing on the beach!

ESSENTIAL FLAVOURS

BANANA
Used green in curries, or ripe and cooked with sugar to fill lattice-topped tarts fried to perfection to make *beignets* (fritters).

CHILLI
Chillies are always used to complement a meal and most Mauritian families will have chilli paste in jars in their fridge. The most popular chillies are *petit piment* (little chilli), also known as *piment petard* (firecracker chilli) because it is so hot. *Piment rodrigues* is another type of small, hot chilli. Chillies are also eaten in snacks from a young age - one common way is crushed with salt and sprinkled over slivered, crunchy green mango or pineapple.

COCONUT
Finely grated fresh coconut is traditionally combined with mint, chilli and garlic for a refreshing chutney.

MURUNGA LEAVES
Rarely seen in Australia but well known in Sri Lanka as drumstick leaves, these are commonly grown in Mauritian backyards. Their slippery texture and tangy flavour is loved across the island and they are stir-fried with onion and garlic or made into protein-rich soups.

MUSTARD SEEDS
Dark brown or black seeds are most commonly used in Mauritian cooking, cooked in oil at the start of a curry or pickle to add a mildly nutty flavour.

SHALLOTS
Small, golden, papery-skinned bulbs with a more delicate and sweet flavour than their onion relation.

THYME
Thyme is often used in Mauritian curries and in the many French-derived braised meat dishes.

TURMERIC
A popular spice, used both fresh and powdered. Fresh turmeric is used in *achards*, pickles and curry pastes and dried turmeric is used in curry powders.

YELLOW SPLIT PEAS
A common staple in Mauritian cooking. They are made into curries and soups, provide the filling for *dholl puri* and are the key ingredient in *gateaux piment*.

These flatbreads have a filling of cooked yellow split peas. They're served warm wrapped around curries, *achards* (pickled vegetables) and chutneys to make a yummy snack. Try with the two *achards* on page 234 and the coriander chutney on this page.

A fresh-tasting chutney that works its magic in *dholl puris* and alongside any grills or barbecues. Best eaten on the day it's made.

DHOLL PURI

from Kavi Hurrydoss

Toast the cumin seeds in a dry frying pan. Grind in a mortar.

Drain and rinse the peas and boil in fresh water until just tender. Drain well and blend with the cumin in a food processor (the mixture should be like a powder). Add salt to taste.

Place the flour, turmeric and 2 pinches of salt in a large bowl and mix well. Add the water, mix to a smooth dough and knead for about 5 minutes. Cover the dough with a damp cloth and leave for 20–30 minutes.

Form the dough into balls weighing about 60 g (2 oz). Make an indent in the centre of each ball and stuff with the pea mixture. Seal the dough around the filling. Roll the balls out on a floured surface to very thin rounds.

Brush a frying pan (non-stick is ideal) with oil and cook each *dholl puri* over high heat for 2 minutes on each side. Before flipping, brush the top with a little oil.

MAKES 20-30 FLATBREADS

½ tablespoon cumin seeds
250 g (9 oz) yellow split peas, soaked overnight
salt
1 kg (2 lb 3 oz) plain (all-purpose) flour
½ teaspoon turmeric
400 ml (13½ fl oz) warm water
vegetable oil

CORIANDER CHUTNEY

from Kavi Hurrydoss

Blend the garlic, chilli, coriander and salt to taste until the ingredients form a paste. You can do this using a mortar and pestle or food processor.

Check the seasoning, adding more salt if desired.

MAKES 1 GENEROUS CUP

2 garlic cloves
4 small red chillies
2 bunches coriander (cilantro), chopped
salt

'Dholl puri must be eaten hot (both in terms of temperature and chillies).'

A delicious, simple, falling-from-the-bone duck curry in a rich, thick sauce. It is full of flavour but less tricky to make than other curries as it relies on curry powder rather than a complex spice blend (you will find the best curry powder at an Indian grocery store). It is lovely served with shallot *achard* (see page 234).

DUCK CURRY

from Jocelyn Riviere

Place the ginger, garlic, chilli and a pinch of salt in a mortar and pound to a paste.

Trim the duck of excess skin and fat. Chop the duck into medium-sized pieces, leaving the drumsticks whole. Place the pieces in a bowl and season well with salt and white pepper, tossing to coat.

Heat a large, heavy-based saucepan over medium–high heat. When hot, add a little oil and brown the duck pieces in batches. When all the pieces are browned, remove them from the pan and turn the heat down to medium. There should be a little melted duck fat left in the pan.

Add the onion and sauté until light brown.

Add the ginger, garlic and chilli paste. Fry for about 2 minutes, then turn the heat down to medium–low and add the curry leaves and curry powder. Cook, stirring, for another 2 minutes.

Add a little water, the duck pieces and any juices. Mix well and add extra water to come halfway up the contents of the pan. Season to taste. Bring to the boil then cover with a lid and simmer for 45–60 minutes, stirring occasionally until the meat is tender and almost falling off the bone.

Remove the lid and add the tomato. Turn the heat up a little to allow the tomato to break down and the sauce to reduce. Check the seasoning and add the coriander just before serving.

SERVES 6

8 cm (3¼ inch) piece of ginger, chopped
6–8 large garlic cloves, chopped
1–2 small red chillies
salt
1 duck (1.5–1.8 kg/3 lb 4 oz–4 lb)
freshly ground white pepper
vegetable oil
2 medium onions, finely chopped
small handful of curry leaves

4 tablespoons good-quality Indian curry powder, mixed with water to make a wet paste
4 medium-sized ripe tomatoes, seeds removed, roughly chopped
½ bunch coriander (cilantro), roughly chopped

'The best curries are cooked in old pots.'

It is said Mauritius is so beautiful and the pace of life so relaxed that no one wants to slave getting meals organised. *Achards* are a favourite and very easy to prepare – made with julienned vegetables or segmented shallots – they're the perfect accompaniment to curries or even simply eaten with rice. The pickled vegetables, with a hint of chilli, have a real flavour punch.

ACHARDS

Pickled Vegetables

from Kavi Hurrydoss

To make the shallot *achard,* toss the shallots in some salt and leave for 5 minutes. Rinse in cold water and pat dry with a clean tea towel.

Place the garlic, ginger, turmeric and mustard seeds in a mortar and pound to a paste.

Heat the oil in a frying pan over low heat.

Once hot but not bubbling, add the garlic mixture and stir briefly (don't let it fry). Add the shallots and chilli and cook gently for about 10 minutes – the shallots should still be a little crunchy. Add the vinegar and season to taste.

Fill sterilised jars and store in the refrigerator.

Leave for at least 2 days before serving.

To make the vegetable *achard,* heat the oil in a large frying pan and sweat the onion, garlic, chilli and mustard seeds. Add the remaining vegetables and mix well. Remove from the heat. Add the vinegar and season to taste.

Fill sterilised jars and store in the refrigerator. Leave for at least 2 days before serving.

Both *achards* will keep for 1 week.

SHALLOT *ACHARD*

500 g (1 lb 2 oz) shallots, quartered (leave enough base to hold the quarters together)

salt

10 garlic cloves

50 g (1¾ oz) ginger, chopped

25 g (1 oz) fresh turmeric, chopped

1 tablespoon black mustard seeds

1 tablespoon yellow mustard seeds

250 ml (8½ fl oz/1 cup) vegetable oil

2 long green chillies, sliced into strips

3 tablespoons white vinegar

VEGETABLE *ACHARD*

180 ml (2½ fl oz/⅓ cup) vegetable oil

2 large onions, finely sliced

10 garlic cloves, finely sliced

4 long red or green chillies, sliced into strips

2 tablespoons black mustard seeds

250 g (9 oz) cabbage, finely sliced

250 g (9 oz) carrots, julienned

250 g (9 oz) green beans, sliced into strips

250 g (9 oz) cauliflower, finely sliced

2 tablespoons white vinegar

salt

'Poor people never go hungry – there's always tasty and cheap *bouillon mooroome* (soup made from a backyard plant with a small green leaf).'

Pickled fish in a jar sounds unappetising until you try this beautiful, easy recipe for white fish fillets infused with ginger, garlic and spices - it's filled with flavour, low in fat (which always helps!) and high in protein and omega 3. I add *vindaye* to steamed rice for lunch or an easy dinner ... and I imagine that if I lived in tropical Mauritius, I'd want to eat this all the time to maximise the time spent under a palm tree rather than in the kitchen!

With abundant seafood, its no wonder Mauritius has a fast, easy prawn recipe. The delicious spicy tomato *rougaille* is cooked separately and the prawns sautéed in oil and garlic and quickly tossed through. The addition of wine and thyme adds a European touch, though many use curry leaves instead and skip the wine. However it is made, this is a winner.

FISH VINDAYE

from Robyn Touchard

Heat the oil for shallow-frying in a pan over medium heat. Fry the fish fillets until pale gold on both sides. Remove from the pan.

In the same oil, briefly stir-fry the onion, ginger and garlic cloves. Stir the turmeric into the vinegar and add to the pan, mixing well.

Return the fish to the pan and sprinkle over the mustard seeds and chilli. Mix gently to coat the fish in onion and spices. Put the fish into a large sterilised jar and top with the onions (which should still be crunchy) and liquid. Store in the refrigerator for a few days before using (it will keep for up to 2 weeks).

SERVES 4-6

vegetable oil	2 teaspoons turmeric
1 kg (2 lb 3 oz) firm, thick, white fish fillets or cutlets	200 ml (7 fl oz) white vinegar
2 medium onions, thickly sliced	1 teaspoon black mustard seeds, lightly ground
1 tablespoon grated ginger	2 small red chillies, finely sliced
5 garlic cloves	

PRAWN ROUGAILLE

from Vijay Baboo

Heat 2 tablespoons of olive oil in a saucepan over medium heat. Add the onion and half the garlic and fry until golden. Pour in half the wine to soften the onion, then add the tomatoes and cook for a few minutes over high heat to reduce. Stir in the cumin, paprika, salt and pepper and an extra drizzle of olive oil. Add the chilli, parsley and thyme and remove from the heat.

Heat a little more oil in a frying pan and fry the remaining garlic until fragrant. Add the prawns, season with pepper and cook for 2 minutes. Pour in the remaining wine to deglaze the pan.

Tip the prawns into the *rougaille* (tomato sauce) and stir through the coriander.

SERVES 4

olive oil	1 teaspoon white pepper
1 red onion, chopped	2 small red or green chillies, finely chopped
1 tablespoon finely chopped garlic	½ bunch flat-leaf (Italian) parsley, finely chopped
125 ml (4 fl oz/½ cup) white wine	2 thyme sprigs, leaves picked
500 g (1 lb 2 oz) tomatoes, peeled and chopped	1 kg (2 lb 3 oz) green king prawns (shrimp), shelled, heads and tails intact
1 tablespoon ground cumin	½ bunch coriander (cilantro), chopped
1 teaspoon sweet paprika	
1 teaspoon salt	

'Never cook a curry without salt.'

Mauritian sweets are very sweet and very delicious. As bananas grow in abundance, the sweet banana tart is a great favourite and popular as a dessert. Another classic is *gateaux napolitaine* – two melt-in-the-mouth shortbread biscuits with a thin layer of raspberry jam between and a coating of pink icing. No get together would be complete without these to serve with coffee or tea.

TARTE BANANE

from Jean-Marc Gooroovadoo

To make the pastry, rub the butter into the flour until the mixture resembles fine breadcrumbs, then add the whole egg and a little water if necessary to form a dough. (This pastry can be made in a food processor if desired.) Cover in plastic wrap and refrigerate for 1 hour.

To make the filling, mash the bananas and sugar together in a saucepan. Cook the mixture over low heat for 15 minutes, stirring regularly, until thickened but not too dry. Stir in the Parisian essence at the end, for colour.

Preheat the oven to 200°C (400°F/Gas 6) and butter small individual tart tins. Roll the pastry out on a floured surface. Cut out circles of pastry slightly larger than the tins, then gently press into the tins. Roll out the leftover pastry and cut into thin strips.

Spoon the filling into the pastry cases, smoothing the tops. Place strips of pastry in a lattice pattern over the filling, sticking the strips down at the edges. Brush with the beaten egg and bake for 15 minutes, or until the pastry is golden brown.

MAKES ABOUT 12 SMALL TARTS

....

175 g (6 ¼ oz) chilled butter, diced	10 ripe bananas
250 g (9 oz/1⅔ cups) plain flour	75 g (2¾ oz/⅓ cup) sugar
2 eggs, 1 beaten	a few drops of Parisian browning essence

MEXICO

Those who know and love true Mexican food rate it as one of the great cuisines on the planet – ancient yet highly developed. Expatriate home kitchens are a little slice of Mexico, full of cooking aromas that make you hungry – the tang of freshly squeezed lime, the warm smell of just-pressed corn tortillas cooking on the griddle and the toasty, rich waft of tomatoes and chillies roasting over a flame. It's tantalising and there's also an atmosphere of fun – shaping tamales then wrapping them in corn husks is done so quickly when done with friends.

Mexican foods such as tortillas, cactus, corn, chilli and tomatoes go back to pre-Hispanic times when the great Mayan and Aztec cultures held sway. The arrival of the Spanish in the sixteenth century saw new ingredients and produce introduced: sheep, pigs and cows as well as dairy products, garlic, wheat and many different herbs and spices. Spanish culinary traditions were also fostered by the missionaries that scattered across the country.

In Mexico each region has its specialities. Some are incredibly complex dishes, others are simple and quick. All of them have a fabulous depth of flavour and combine savoury and earthy ingredients with fresh herbs and at least two types of chilli at any one time (fresh or dried).

Many Mexican ingredients are readily available anywhere, while others can be grown at home - *tomatillos* or *epazote* (a native herb) - or ordered through specialist food importers. Useful implements I saw in Mexican kitchens are the lime squeezer; the Mexican mortar and pestle; the *comal* (a griddle for cooking tortillas, toasting chillies and garlic); and the earthenware *cazuelas*, although a heavy pot or Dutch oven will work as well.

There is much to learn about Mexican cuisine - for example, true guacamole doesn't include sour cream, mayonnaise or cream; and a taco is made with a soft corn tortilla not a crunchy one. There are many wonderful variations on the tortilla theme, all delicious - tacos are filled with cooked beans, salsa and grilled meat; burritos are made with a flour tortilla and filled with cheese, rice, beans, meat, onions and salsa; quesadillas are also made with a flour tortilla and filled with cheese and any number of additions and then returned to the hotplate to melt together. Tortillas are fundamental to each meal and work as cutlery, plate and napkin.

Moles, or sauces, are an essential part of Mexican cuisine and the basis of many of their delicious dishes. Some ancient *moles* combine up to 200 ingredients that are pounded or blended together, then meat or vegetables are added and cooked in the sauces. I tasted one of the top ten dishes of my life (so far!) in Mexico - a turkey *mole poblano* served wrapped in a leaf. It was a rich, black sauce full of incredible flavour including mellow, raisin-like chilli and a hint of chocolate. What a beautiful cuisine!

ESSENTIAL FLAVOURS

ACHIOTE
Known as 'annatto' in English, this is a red seed with a mild, earthy flavour. It is used in cooking for both its bright colour and subtle flavour and can also be used to dye fabric – in fact it is one of several ancient ingredients that were used as body paint. It is sold as a pressed block or in a common spice blend including salt, pepper and garlic.

AVOCADO
The avocado, which is native to South America, is thought to have originated in southern Mexico. It was cultivated well before the arrival of Europeans. Avocado is used in salsas and to make guacamole.

CHOCOLATE
The first people known to make chocolate were the ancient cultures of Mexico and central America. Mexican chocolate is dark and bitter and flavoured with cinnamon, almond and cloves. In Mexico chocolate is used as a flavouring in many *moles* (sauces) and commonly used to make hot chocolate drinks.

CORN
In its various guises corn is an indispensable part of Mexican cuisine. *Masa*, or corn flour, is ground from white, yellow or blue corn and is used to make tortilla. These soft, pancake-like flatbreads are steamed then eaten with most meals. Hominy is a dried white corn that is used to make a much-loved stew called *pozole*. It is so popular that some small restaurants in Mexico serve only this dish.

LIME
A key flavouring in many Mexican dishes, as in much of Latin America. Lime is widely used in salsas, marinades and margaritas.

MEXICAN CORIANDER
Native to Mexico and South America, this herb is from the same family as coriander, but has long leaves and a stronger taste. It is the most commonly used fresh herb in Mexican cooking. Its often sold in Asian stores as sawtooth coriander, coriander can be used in its place.

TOMATILLOS
Tomatillos look like a small green tomato but are actually a member of the gooseberry family. They have a very tart flavour and are used in many dishes, including salsas and stews. Canned *tomatillos* can be bought at Spanish and South American grocery stores.

This perfect, simple guacamole uses the best avocados mixed with fresh chilli, coriander, onion, tomato and lime. To help keep the vibrant green colour of the avocados, sit the avocado stones in the prepared guacamole and remove just before serving.

Its simplicity makes this a great all-purpose tomato salsa. It should be made on the day using the freshest ingredients – fresh is always best. You can add diced avocado for extra colour and flavour.

GUACAMOLE

from Luipta Feint

Halve the avocados, remove the seeds and use a spoon to scoop the flesh into a bowl. Add the chilli, coriander and onion. Mash together with a fork. Gently fold in the tomato, lime juice and salt. Taste for seasoning.

MAKES 4 CUPS

3 ripe avocados
½ fresh jalapeño chilli
  (optional), finely chopped
½ tablespoon chopped
  coriander (cilantro)

a little chopped red onion
1 tomato, diced
juice of ½ lime
1 teaspoon salt

PICO DI GALLO

Tomato Salsa

from Lupita Feint

Combine the ingredients, tasting for seasoning.

MAKES 2½ CUPS

3 tomatoes, diced
½-1 fresh jalapeño chilli,
  finely chopped
3 tablespoons chopped
  coriander (cilantro)

½ red onion, diced
1 teaspoon salt

'When chopping chillies if you happen to rub your hand in your eyes, quickly rub your eyes on somebody else's hair and that will get rid of the pain.'

There's a nice depth of flavour in this soup, which comes from the roasted tomatoes and onion and from the raisin-like dried chillies called *pasilla*. Strips of crunchy, fried tortillas are added to the soup just before serving. Fetta is not traditional but it makes a good substitute for Mexican cheese.

Tender pork cooked in a beautiful, fresh green *mole*, ingeniously coloured by the pumpkin seeds, vegetables, green chillies and herbs. Serve with Mexican rice and corn tortillas.

SOPA DE TORTILLA

Tortilla Soup

from Gina Castaneda

MOLE VERDE (GREEN SAUCE) WITH PORK

from Kimberley Chiswell

Roast the tomatoes, onion and garlic in a cast-iron pan until charred. Toast the chillies by holding them with tongs over a gas flame (they may catch fire). This heightens their flavour. Soak the chillies in hot water until soft, then remove the seeds.

Puree the tomatoes, onion, garlic and 2 of the chillies in a blender with a bit of the stock until smooth. Heat a little oil in a frying pan and sauté the tomato puree for a few minutes, then remove from the heat.

Bring the remaining stock to the boil in a saucepan and stir in the tomato puree. Season with salt and pepper and cook, covered, over medium heat for 15 minutes.

Wipe out the frying pan and add a little more oil. Fry the tortilla strips in batches until golden brown. Remove and drain on paper towel.

Arrange the red onion, fetta, avocado and lime on a plate. Slice the remaining chilli and add to the plate. Put the cream in a bowl or jug.

Add some of the fried tortilla to the soup. Ladle the soup into bowls and garnish with more tortilla. Each person can add red onion, fetta, avocado, lime, chilli and cream to taste.

SERVES 6

3 ripe tomatoes, halved	8-10 corn tortillas, cut in half,
½ onion	then in strips
2 garlic cloves	½ red onion, diced
3 dried *pasilla* chillies	150 g (5½ oz) fetta, diced
1.5 litres (51 fl oz/6 cups)	2 avocados, diced
chicken stock	3 limes, halved
oil	125 ml (4 fl oz/½ cup) thick
salt and pepper	cream

Place the pork in a saucepan with the bay leaf, onion and salt. Cover with water and bring to the boil, then simmer until tender (approximately 1 hour).

Toast the sesame seeds in a dry frying pan until golden. Remove from the pan and repeat with the almonds and then the pumpkin seeds.

Puree the seeds and nuts in a blender with a little water from the pork. Set aside.

Put the spring onions, garlic, tomatillos, capsicum, chilli and coriander in the blender with cumin, salt and pepper to taste. Add 2 cups of water from the pork and puree to a bright green sauce.

Heat a little oil in a saucepan and fry the seed and nut mixture for a few minutes. Add the green sauce and simmer for 5 minutes. Add the cooked pork and simmer for a few more minutes.

SERVES 6

1 kg (2 lb 3 oz) pork leg meat,	1 large green capsicum
cut into 2 cm (¾ in) cubes	(bell pepper), seeded and
1 bay leaf	roughly chopped
½ small onion	2 hot green chillies
salt	1 bunch coriander (cilantro),
3 tablespoons sesame seeds	roughly chopped
50 g (1¾ oz) almonds	ground cumin
100 g (3½ oz) pumpkin seeds	pepper
15 spring onions (scallions),	olive oil
roughly chopped	
1 garlic clove	
400 g (14 oz) tin tomatillos	

Chilli

This is the main flavouring ingredient in Mexican food with both fresh and dried forms used. To use most dried chillies, discard the stem and seeds, gently fry the chilli in oil until the chilli changes colour, then simmer in hot water for ten minutes. Common chilli varieties include:

Ancho: A mild, sweet dried chilli. When fresh it is known as poblano and looks similar to a large, pointed green capsicum. Its beautiful flavour is a traditional base for moles.

Guajillo (pronounced 'gwah-hee-yoh'): A large mild chilli. When dried it has a very tough leathery skin so may require long soaking. Its sweet heat is used in salsas, chilli sauces, soups and stews.

Habanero: A super hot variety of chilli that is available fresh and dried. It has a tropical fruitiness as well as a fiery heat that is useful in sauces.

Jalapeño ('hah-luh-paneyo'): The most common chilli in Mexican cooking. It is usually sold green and adds a warm spiciness to many dishes. When smoked and dried it is known as *chipotle* ('chee-poht-leh').

Pasilla ('pah-see-ya'): A mild to medium-hot dried chilli. Literally 'little raisin', it is also traditionally used as a base for moles.

The lovely orange colour and mellow flavour of this barbecued chicken comes from *achiote*, a spice paste made with annatto popular in the Yucatán region. Serve this chicken and salsa inside corn tortillas. The marinade can also be used for prawns - simply marinate green prawns in the same way as the chicken, thread them onto bamboo skewers and cook on a bar becue with a little olive oil for just a few minutes.

We all love this thick, frothy chocolate with its hint of cinnamon. A *molinillo* (chocolate whisk) and a block of Mexican drinking chocolate are the perfect present for the cook with everything!

POLLO PIBIL

Yucatán Barbecued Chicken

from Mary Carmen Dias

MEXICAN HOT CHOCOLATE

from Yvonne de Keizer

Prick the chicken thighs all over with a fork to allow the marinade to be absorbed. Using your hands, crumble the *achiote* paste into a wide bowl and add the orange juice and salt to make a smooth sauce. Thoroughly rub the mixture into the chicken.

Tear off 4 large squares of foil. Wrap each chicken thigh in foil. Refrigerate the parcels for at least 2 hours or ideally overnight. Combine the salsa ingredients in a bowl and refrigerate for at least 1 hour so the onion softens a little.

Preheat the barbecue.

Heat the vegetable oil in a frying pan and sauté the onion until translucent. Add the tomato slices and fry them gently on both sides until just soft. Unwrap the chicken parcels and add some onion and tomato to each one, then rewrap.

Cook the parcels on the barbecue for about 20 minutes, being careful not to overcook the chicken. Turn the parcels over halfway through cooking. Unwrap the cooked parcels and serve the chicken in corn tortillas topped with the red onion salsa.

Place about a litre of milk and 90 g (3 oz) Mexican chocolate in a saucepan. Slowly bring to the boil, then reduce the heat to a slow simmer. Whisk the mixture using a molinillo: hold the molinillo between both hands and rub your hands together until the chocolate is dissolved and the milk is velvety and frothy. Pour into cups.

SERVES 4

4 chicken thigh fillets
20 g (¾ oz) 'El Yucateco'
  ***achiote* paste**
juice of ½ orange
½ teaspoon salt
80 ml (2½ fl oz/⅓ cup)
  vegetable oil
1 red onion, finely sliced
2 tomatoes, sliced

RED ONION SALSA

1 red onion, finely sliced
1 tablespoon olive oil
½ tablespoon vinegar
splash of fresh orange juice
1 tablespoon dried oregano
salt

'Never arrive early or on time if you are invited to a Mexican home - thirty minutes after the stipulated time is perfect.'

MOROCCO

One of the most seductive cuisines, Moroccan food casts its spell as soon as you inhale – your nose fills with wonderful wafts of cinnamon, cumin, paprika and saffron and the fresh, green scent of coriander and parsley. Moroccan expatriate kitchens hint at the smells that would hit you walking through the souks in Morocco, where brilliantly coloured spices are piled in pyramid shapes – a far cry from our neat little spice racks in gleaming Western supermarkets!

My discovery of the food of this part of Africa took place many years ago when, after a visit to Tunisia (one of the three countries of the Maghreb – the others are Algeria and Morocco), I found my longing for exotic places, food and customs very well sated. I later visited Morocco and found the same delicious food and the same generous opening up of one's home, which comes from the Islamic teaching that all guests should be welcomed and fed (how generous they are!). I was lucky enough to spend time with a family in a small village and to prepare meals with the women of the family. It's fair to say that my life's course was set from that moment.

On this trip ensued some of the most memorable meals of my life. Beside a campfire in the northern Sahara I shared a communal dish of fragrant, spicy couscous cooked with vegetables and a lamb sacrificed in our honour; on a Mediterranean beach I shared freshly caught fish cooked with spices over charcoal with local fishermen; and in a village in the High Atlas Mountains I enjoyed a luscious carrot salad made with cinnamon and orange juice. The simple wonder of the street food is also enough to make you swoon. *Brik al oeuf* has stayed in my memory as one of the best food combinations of all time – this flaky golden delight is made by cracking an egg onto a square of pastry, adding generous spoonfuls of harissa, tuna and capers, then folding it all up and frying in oil. It is eaten hot with the yolk still runny. Marvellous!

The same warmth and generosity I experienced in Morocco is shown in expatriate homes. Your hands are cleaned and perfumed with orange-blossom water at the front door, then fresh dates stuffed with almonds are offered as the first of numerous traditional dishes prepared for you with love and care. Shut your eyes and you can almost imagine the desert at the back door.

ESSENTIAL FLAVOURS

CINNAMON

A fragrant bark harvested from the cinnamon tree. It is used to flavour many dishes, from lamb tajines to carrot salad. It is similar to cassia bark, which is also used as a spice, but cinnamon is much finer and has a more delicate flavour. To tell them apart when purchasing, cinnamon is rolled into small cylinders whereas cassia bark is thicker and flatter.

CUMIN

Used both as whole seeds and ground. Cumin has a slight liquorice flavour and is an essential addition to many spice blends. It is also used in marinades and salads.

HARISSA

A bright-red paste made from chillies, garlic and oil and often flavoured with ground coriander and cumin. It is served as an accompaniment to many meals. To extend the life of harissa paste, cover it with a layer of olive oil – it will keep for a few months.

ORANGE-BLOSSOM WATER

A distilled water made from the essential oil found in orange blossom. It has a wonderfully heady scent and flavour and is used in sweet and savoury dishes. It is also splashed onto the palms of guests in greeting.

PRESERVED LEMON

Whole lemons that have been preserved in brine. They are kept away from the light for at least forty days, during which time their flavour changes from acidic to mellow and sweet. To serve, the salty flesh is scooped out and discarded and the skin is finely chopped for marinades and as a garnish.

SAFFRON

The stigma of the crocus flower and also the world's most expensive spice. It is used both for its distinct flavour and colour - but in moderation as too much can be overpowering.

SWEET PAPRIKA

Made from sweeter, milder varieties of capsicum (bell pepper). It has a good depth of flavour and also adds a vibrant colour to many dishes.

Essential Etiquette

With overwhelming hospitality and an abundance of beautifully prepared food come a few rules of etiquette:

At a Moroccan feast never serve couscous before other courses. It fills up the guests so they won't be able to eat more of the other lovely dishes to come.

Never say no to food offered at a dinner party even if you don't like the dish on offer. You must try at least one or two mouthfuls, otherwise you will be regarded as snobbish and rude.

Most sensible Moroccans never eat meals consisting of chickpeas or fava beans before an important date for the sake of the other participants!

In Morocco it is traditional to eat with your hands. This requires some rules and great skill. The idea is to form a couscous ball with the three fingers and thumb of the right hand, then to pop the couscous ball into your mouth without your fingers coming into contact with your lips. Never use the left hand.

Refrain from eating garlic during the month of Ramadan – this will prevent 'garlic breath' throughout the fasting days when you do not drink water or eat between sun-up and sun-down.

Always say '*B'smilah*' ('In the name of Allah') before the start of a meal.

The secret to making the best instant couscous is in the steaming method. The couscous absorbs the fragrant steam from the ingredients being cooked below to become light and fluffy. (Moroccans say that couscous that has been made only by absorbing boiling water is 'uncooked' and they marvel that many people have yet to discover the magic of true couscous.) As well as improving the flavour of the couscous, the vegetables in this dish look colourful and delicious together and the whole dish can be on the table in well under an hour. The other secret of great couscous is in the finishing touch – in Morocco this is *smen* (preserved butter), but Saana uses light blue-vein cheese to add the same little kick.

CHEAT'S COUSCOUS WITH SEVEN VEGETABLES

from Saana Zaki

Put the vegetables (including the whole tomatoes and broad beans) in the bottom of a large pot that has a steam basket attachment. Add the spices, herbs and stock. Bring to the boil, cover with a lid and reduce the heat to a simmer.

Meanwhile, put the couscous in a bowl and add the vegetable oil. Stir with your hands to coat the grains. Add the salt and just enough water to moisten the grains but not drown them.

Stir well so the grains absorb the water evenly. Transfer to the steam basket and place over the vegetables. Cover with a lid.

Once the couscous begins to steam, remove the basket and tip the couscous into a bowl.

Crumble the cheese over the couscous and stir so it melts through. Sprinkle on a little more water and stir again. Return the couscous to the basket.

Place back over the pot of vegetables, cover with a lid and wait until the couscous begins to steam again. Tip the couscous onto a large platter and spoon over the vegetables and a little stock.

SERVES 6

1 swede, cut into large chunks
1-2 parsnips, cut into large chunks
1-2 carrots, cut into large chunks
1-2 zucchini (courgettes), cut into large chunks
small piece of pumpkin, skin left on, cut into large chunks
4 roma tomatoes
1 cup podded broad beans (fresh or frozen)
1 tablespoon ground coriander
1 tablespoon ground ginger
1 tablespoon ground cumin
1 tablespoon sweet paprika
handful of coriander (cilantro) sprigs
handful of flat-leaf parsley sprigs
1 litre (34 fl oz/4 cups) stock (ideally homemade)
500 g (1 lb 2 oz) instant couscous
2-3 tablespoons vegetable oil
1 teaspoon salt
150 g (5½ oz) light blue-vein cheese (such as Blue Castello)

'Without fingers the hand would be a spoon.'

Here is a dead-easy marinade for lamb that is full of incredible flavour. The cool taste of mint and the tang of yoghurt team beautifully with the barbecued meat. As well as backstraps or fillets, you can try this with chops.

MECHOUI (BARBECUED LAMB) WITH MINTED YOGHURT

from Aziz Bakalla

Put the lamb in a bowl and add the remaining ingredients. Use your hands to thoroughly coat the lamb. Cover and refrigerate for 1 hour.

Combine the ingredients for the minted yoghurt in a blender and keep cold in the refrigerator until ready to serve.

Barbecue (grill) the lamb to medium-rare and serve with the yoghurt.

SERVES 4

1 kg (2 lb 3 oz) lamb backstraps
   or fillets, cut into long strips
   about 2 cm (¾ in) wide
1 tablespoon ground cumin
1 tablespoon sweet paprika
2 tablespoons chopped garlic
1 tablespoon chopped
   coriander (cilantro)
1 tablespoon chopped
   flat-leaf (Italian) parsley
1 tablespoon lemon juice
generous drizzle of olive oil
salt

MINTED YOGHURT

1 cup natural yoghurt
¼ teaspoon sugar
3 teaspoons chopped mint

'Among walnuts only empty ones speak.'

This dish is wonderful. Although it takes a little while to prepare, all that fades when you bring the tajine to the table, lift off the conical lid and watch as your family and friends take a deep, satisfied breath. Serve with couscous and harissa. Like curries, it is even better on the second day.

CHICKEN TAJINE WITH PRESERVED LEMON AND OLIVES

from Hassan M'souli

Combine the marinade ingredients in a food processor and blend until finely chopped and thoroughly combined. Leave for 30 minutes before using (or you can make this up to 7 days in advance and store it in the refrigerator).

Wash and dry the chicken. Cut out the backbone and trim off the wing tips and any excess fat. Chop into pieces. Place in a bowl and rub with half of the marinade. Refrigerate for at least 2 hours or ideally overnight.

Combine the chopped tomato and onion with a little more marinade and spread over the base of a tajine (this will prevent the chicken from burning on the bottom). Arrange the chicken pieces in the centre of the tajine. Coat the potato wedges in a little more marinade and arrange around the chicken. Top with the sliced onion, then the sliced tomato, and push the olives into the gaps. Combine the remaining marinade with the coriander and water and pour over the top. Decorate with preserved lemon wedges.

Cover the tajine with the lid and cook over a very low heat on the stove for 45 minutes. Don't stir or lift the lid during cooking. Take the tajine to the table and serve with couscous and harissa.

SERVES 6

CHERMOULA MARINADE

- 2 garlic cloves, chopped
- ½ preserved lemon, rind only, rinsed and finely sliced
- 2 onions, chopped
- ½ small red chilli
- 1 tablespoon sweet paprika
- 1 tablespoon ground cumin
- 2 tablespoons chopped coriander (cilantro)
- 2 tablespoons chopped flat-leaf (Italian) parsley
- 2 bay leaves, torn in half
- ½ teaspoon saffron threads, soaked in a little water
- 125 ml (4 fl oz/½ cup) olive oil
- salt

CHICKEN TAJINE

- 1 small chicken weighing 1–1.2 kg (2 lb 3 oz–2 lb 10 oz)
- 2 tomatoes, 1 chopped, 1 sliced
- 2 onions, 1 chopped, 1 sliced
- 2 large potatoes, cut into wedges
- 150 g (5½ oz) pitted green olives
- 1 bunch coriander (cilantro), chopped
- 250 ml (8½ fl oz/1 cup) water
- 1 preserved lemon, rind only, rinsed and cut into 6 or 8 wedges

'What you have put into your pot comes out on your apron.'

Served warm as part of a mezze selection, *bissara* is a delicious and mellow dip. With its simple but effective spicing it is a low-cost, high-protein comfort food – and it's easy to make too. The recipe uses dried, split fava beans (broad beans), which are yellow; dried whole fava beans still have their skins on and are browny-green.

Put any ideas out of your head of a delicate salad lightly tossed in a little dressing - this version is a lot more liquid! In fact it is so full of juice that it's served in tea glasses or bowls with small spoons. The combination of fresh flavours wakes up the tastebuds and it is great as an appetiser or between courses in a Moroccan banquet. Make sure you get carrots that are snap-fresh.

BISSARA

Fava-bean Dip

from Aziz Bakalla

Drain the beans and pick out any discoloured ones.

Heat 2 tablespoons of oil in a saucepan and fry the garlic until fragrant. Stir in 3 teaspoons of cumin then add the beans and water. Cover and bring to the boil then reduce the heat to a simmer. Cook until the beans have absorbed all the water and have broken down to a smooth, velvety puree, like thick soup. Season with salt and pepper and pour into a serving bowl.

Garnish with paprika and extra cumin. Place an olive in the centre and drizzle with more olive oil. Serve with flatbread.

MAKES 3-4 CUPS

2 cups dried split fava beans (broad beans), soaked overnight	ground cumin
	1.5 litres (51 fl oz/6 cups) water
olive oil	salt and pepper
1 tablespoon chopped garlic	sweet paprika
	1 black olive

CARROT AND ORANGE SALAD

from Sara Ennaim

Grate or finely chop the carrots in a food processor.

Place the carrot in a bowl and squeeze the oranges over the top. Add the sugar, orange-blossom water and cinnamon and mix together.

SERVES 6

500 g (1 lb 2 oz) carrots, peeled	1 tablespoon orange-blossom water
4 oranges	
75 g (2¾ oz/⅓ cup) sugar	1 teaspoon cinnamon

This is the perfect end to a banquet – sweet, refreshing and warm with the spice of cassia. Use colourful seasonal fruit such as grapes, rockmelon, apple, pear, mandarin and banana and make the dressing in advance if you like as it keeps for at least a week in the refrigerator.

FRUIT SALAD WITH MOROCCAN DRESSING

from Omar Majdi

Place the dressing ingredients in a saucepan and bring to the boil, then reduce the heat and simmer for 5 minutes. Leave to cool then refrigerate for 1 hour. Mix the fruit and mint with the dressing.

DRESSING

250 ml (8½ fl oz/1 cup) water
3 tablespoons sugar
small piece of cassia bark
2 tablespoons lemon juice

½ tablespoon orange-blossom water

mixed seasonal fruit, cut into chunks
10 mint leaves, torn

'A peacock has too little in its head and too much in its tail.'

PAKISTAN

One of the things I enjoy most about finding out about different cuisines is the opportunity to spend time in other people's kitchens. In Pakistani homes I've learned many new and intriguing things, one of which is that women mix up chapattis (thin, round disks of unleavened whole-wheat bread) every morning then cook them on a heavy griddle to have hot for breakfast. To them it is as easy as pouring cereal into a bowl – and much more delicious.

In Pakistani food, spices are treasured, used cleverly and replenished every couple of weeks. Spicing is a measure of the esteem in which one holds a guest – I've learned that when presenting dishes such as the classic biryani (a spectacular combination of spiced rice cooked with meat), Pakistani people love to see the whole threads of saffron strewn among the toasted nuts and fresh herbs that characteristically garnish this masterpiece.

When it comes to sweets, especially the beautiful reduced-milk sweets and *burfis*, edible gold and silver leaf are used to signify importance and these precious materials are widely used for wedding feasts.

Although the country of Pakistan is relatively new (it was partitioned from India in 1947), the cuisine of the region has developed over centuries and incorporates elements from neighbouring India, Afghanistan and Iran. It is also heavily influenced by the predominantly Muslim population. Its blend of Indian, Far Eastern and Middle Eastern cooking techniques creates a simply beautiful cuisine.

Some of the key dishes are slow cooked – the famous *haleem* (a mix of grains, pulses, lamb and spices) is cooked for up to seven hours. I love the way Pakistanis use the phrase '*Haleem* – king of curries' as a mark of the respect they have for this rich comfort food. It is lovely and viscous, garnished with the fresh tastes of lemon, coriander and ginger and scooped up with Pakistan's favourite accompaniment – bread. This is either leavened naan that has been cooked in a tandoor oven, or unleavened chapattis or roti that have been cooked on the stove top.

As well as great bread, Pakistanis also produce some of the best rice in the world – their long-grain basmati rice is especially prized and is used to make biryani.

Sweets are as generous as the chefs in Pakistan and are rich with ghee, sugar and nuts such as pistachios and almonds. *Halwa* (meaning 'sweet') is one of the most popular sweets and can be made with flour or semolina, or even carrot or pumpkin. Many sweets are infused with fragrant essences like rosewater or crushed cardamom pods – delicate, exotic and a beautiful finish to a Pakistani feast.

ESSENTIAL FLAVOURS

CARDAMOM
A dried seed pod from a herb belonging to the ginger family, cardamom comes in both green and brown varieties. Green cardamom pods are crushed to release the black seeds inside and are used extensively in Pakistani cuisine. Stronger in flavour, the larger brown variety is reserved for meat and vegetable dishes.

CHAAT MASALA
A sour blend of spices typically including *amchur* (dried green mango powder), dried ginger, cumin, coriander (cilantro) and black pepper. This is used for the favourite fried dough snacks called *chaat*.

CUMIN
Regular brown cumin or the more exotic black cumin are used in many dishes including curries, rice dishes, breads and chutney. The seeds can be ground or used whole. They are usually toasted before use to release their flavour.

DAL
Dried beans, peas and lentils (whether whole or split) are known as 'dal'. They are a staple in Pakistani cuisine and are high in both protein and fibre. There are many varieties including *urid*, *chana*, *mung*, *toor* and *masoor* dal. Once cooked as a dish they are referred to as 'dhal'.

DRIED PLUMS
These impart a rich, tart flavour and are often used in dishes like biryani.

DRIED POMEGRANATE SEEDS
These seeds have a lovely sweet and sour flavour and are used both whole and ground.

GARAM MASALA
A toasted and ground mixture of spices that includes cumin, coriander (cilantro) seed, chilli and cardamom. Try to buy the freshest spices and make just the amount you need – the fragrance and flavour of the masala will deteriorate over time.

GHEE
Clarified butter with a higher burning point than unclarified butter and most oils. It is adored in curries, slathered on hot naan and used in sweets.

SAFFRON
The hand-picked red stigma of the crocus flower. Saffron is the most expensive spice in the world and is believed to have been first cultivated in Kashmir in the third century. Loved for its unique flavour and colouring ability, it is used extensively in curries, biryani and Pakistani sweets.

Beautiful little dumplings that are perfect starters or great party food – they're easy to make and fun for children too. Basil grew up with these in Pakistan and devised his recipe using the readily available wonton wrappers. They are served with yoghurt and parsley, although you can also add a dollop of dhal.

MANTU

from Basil Daniell

Heat the oil or ghee in a wok or frying pan and add the lamb. Fry over low heat until lightly browned, stirring to separate the meat. Add the onion and stir-fry until it is translucent. Add the garlic, spices and salt and stir-fry for another 3 minutes or until fragrant. Transfer to a bowl to cool.

Place a heaped teaspoon of lamb filling in the middle of a wonton wrapper. Brush the edges with a little water and draw two opposite corners together to meet in the middle. Draw in the other two corners and seal the edges. You should have a square pouch. Repeat with the remaining wrappers and filling.

Place the *mantu* in a steamer, making sure they don't touch, and steam for 10 minutes. Top each *mantu* with a spoonful of yoghurt and a sprinkling of parsley.

MAKES 40

3 tablespoons vegetable oil or clarified butter (ghee)
500 g (1 lb 2 oz) lean minced (ground) lamb
4 onions, finely chopped
2 teaspoons finely chopped garlic
½ teaspoon ground coriander
1 teaspoon ground cumin
¼ teaspoon chilli powder
½ teaspoon salt
40 Shanghai (square white) wonton wrappers
natural yoghurt
chopped flat-leaf (Italian) parsley

'Always brown the onions in whatever dish you are making – this is fundamental to getting the right taste.'

This recipe is from a beautiful Pakistani woman called Nighat who makes her own bread every morning and thinks nothing of catering for fifty people! The chicken with its incredible fresh mint sauce is simple and very, very delicious. Serve with roti, tomato and lettuce.

The all-purpose dhal is something made in every Pakistani home daily. It's healthy and easy to prepare. With its beautiful texture and flavour dhal compliments any curry. It is also a delicious accompaniment to mantu dumplings.

TANDOORI CHICKEN

from Nighat Hussan

To prepare the chicken, combine the ingredients except for the chicken in a bowl, stirring until well combined. Add the chicken and coat well (the best way is to rub the mixture in with your hands). Marinate in the refrigerator for at least 2 hours.

To make the mint sauce, combine the ingredients in a blender, adding chilli powder and salt to taste. Blend until smooth.

Preheat the oven to its highest temperature. Bake the chicken for 20 minutes, then reduce the temperature to 120°C (250°F/Gas 1–2) and cook until tender. Serve with the mint sauce.

SERVES 4-6

200 g (7 oz) natural yoghurt
1 tablespoon finely grated ginger
1 tablespoon crushed garlic
1 tablespoon tandoori paste
½ teaspoon tandoori food colouring (optional)
2 teaspoons ground cumin
2 teaspoons ground coriander
1 teaspoon garam masala
½ teaspoon chilli powder
½ teaspoon turmeric
salt
1 kg (2 lb 3 oz) chicken breast or thigh fillets

MINT SAUCE

200 g (7 oz) natural yoghurt
1 bunch mint, roughly chopped
1 bunch coriander (cilantro), roughly chopped
½ small onion, roughly chopped
1 tomato, roughly chopped
2 tablespoons dried pomegranate seeds, ground
1 teaspoon turmeric
chilli powder
salt

DHAL

from Basil Daniell

Place the lentils and water in a large saucepan and bring to the boil. Reduce the heat to a simmer and skim off any scum that rises to the surface. Cover and simmer for 40–50 minutes, or until the lentils are soft and the water has been absorbed. Stir in the chilli powder, ground coriander and salt.

Heat the ghee or oil in a small frying pan until very hot. Add the garlic and dried chillies and fry until the garlic is golden, stirring constantly so it doesn't burn. Stir the garlic, chilli and oil into the lentils. Cover the dhal to retain the aromas until serving.

SERVES 4

200 g (7 oz) red lentils
1 litre (34 fl oz/4 cups) water
¼–1 teaspoon chilli powder
1 teaspoon ground coriander

1 teaspoon salt
2 tablespoons clarified butter (ghee) or vegetable oil
2 garlic cloves, bruised
1–2 dried chillies

A marvellous creation of layers of perfectly cooked goat curry, beautiful rice and a fresh mix of tomato, herbs and chilli, all decorated with nuts and onion rings. This is a feast in its own right, but Sonya likes to serve it with a chopped salad called a *cachumbar* containing tomato, red onion, lettuce and vinegar, and with a yoghurt raita containing mint and cumin.

SINDHI BIRYANI

from Sonya Kayani

Heat a little vegetable oil in a large saucepan and fry the onion until golden brown. Add the goat and fry for a few minutes. Stir in the ginger and garlic, then add the yoghurt, ground spices, whole spices (reserve 8 green cardamom pods for the rice), bay leaves, dried plums, salt and pepper. Add the whole chillies and 250 ml (8½ fl oz/1 cup) of water. Cover and simmer for 45 minutes.

Meanwhile, boil the potatoes whole until tender, then drain and cut in half. Keep warm. Drain the rice and boil with the reserved cardamom. When cooked, drain and put half into a bowl. Add the saffron milk and stir until the rice is evenly yellow. Keep the plain and saffron rice warm.

Combine the tomato, coriander, mint and sliced green chilli. Add one-third of the tomato mixture to the goat curry. Cover and cook for a further 5-10 minutes.

Spoon half of the plain rice onto a large serving platter. Top with the goat curry. Spoon over half of the saffron rice and scatter with half of the remaining tomato mixture. Scatter with the boiled potatoes, then add final layers of plain rice and saffron rice. Scatter with the fried onion.

Top with the remaining tomato mixture then sprinkle over the sultanas and nuts. Serve immediately.

SERVES 6

vegetable oil
3 medium onions, finely sliced
1 kg (2 lb 3 oz) boneless goat meat, cut into large cubes
3 tablespoons grated ginger
1 tablespoon crushed garlic
100 g (3½ oz) natural yoghurt
1 tablespoon chilli powder
2 teaspoons turmeric
2 teaspoons sweet paprika
1 tablespoon ground coriander
2 heaped teaspoons ground cumin
2 teaspoons cumin seeds
10 cloves
4 cinnamon sticks
14 green cardamom pods
3 brown cardamom pods
5 bay leaves
10 dried plums
1 tablespoon salt
8 peppercorns, ground
4 long green chillies, 3 left whole, 1 finely sliced
3 medium potatoes
500 g (1 lb 2 oz) basmati rice, soaked for 30 minutes
1 tablespoon saffron threads, soaked briefly in milk
3 medium tomatoes, cut into thin wedges
1 bunch coriander (cilantro), chopped
1 bunch mint, chopped
onion rings, fried until dark brown and caramelised
25 g (1 oz) sultanas (golden raisins)
25 g (1 oz) slivered almonds
25 g (1 oz) walnuts
25 g (1 oz) cashews

This is the ultimate slow-cooked wonder, full of gentle spices and warm comfort, and a Pakistani favourite. *Haleem* gets its lovely sticky consistency from constant stirring, so give yourself up to the hypnotic cooking and enjoy the aromas as you do.

HALEEM – 'KING OF CURRIES'

from Javed Chaudry

Soak the dal and barley together overnight. Partly crush the wheat berries in a mortar and pestle and soak for 1½ hours.

Put the lentils and grains, meat and bones, garlic, ginger and water in a large, heavy-based pot and bring to the boil. Simmer for around 2 hours, stirring occasionally.

Remove the bones and continue to cook until the meat starts to fall apart (about another hour).

Add the ghee, saffron colour, fenugreek, coriander, cumin, *chaat masala*, chilli powder, turmeric and salt and cook for another hour, stirring regularly to help the ingredients break down and blend into each other. The stew will start to look very thick and sticky.

Heat the vegetable oil in a frying pan and fry the onion until brown and caramelised. Add the onion (reserving ¼ cup) and garam masala to the stew. Cook for a further 15 minutes.

Scoop onto plates and garnish with the remaining fried onions, *chaat masala*, chilli, ginger, coriander and lemon. Serve with roti, naan or chapattis.

SERVES 8

½ cup each of *chana* dal, *urid* dal, *mung* dal and barley
½ cup wheat berries
1 kg (2 lb 3 oz) beef or lamb on the bone, meat cut into chunks
2 tablespoons crushed garlic
2 tablespoons grated ginger
2.5 litres (85 fl oz/10 cups) water
2 tablespoons clarified butter (ghee)
pinch of saffron colour (optional)
¼ teaspoon ground fenugreek
1 tablespoon ground coriander
1 tablespoon ground cumin

1 tablespoon *chaat masala* spice mix
1 tablespoon chilli powder
1 teaspoon turmeric
salt
125 ml (4 fl oz/½ cup) vegetable oil
2 onions, sliced
1 tablespoon garam masala

TO SERVE

chaat masala spice mix
finely sliced green chilli
julienned ginger
coriander (cilantro) leaves
sliced lemon

Who ever would have thought carrots could make such a delicious, exotic and colourful dessert? This is fragrant with freshly ground cardamom seeds and luscious with a quick cheat's version of the famous reduced milk used in so many Indian sweets (which takes a long time to make!).

CARROT HALWA

from Sumaira Cheema

Steam the grated carrot for 10 minutes until fairly soft. A no-mess way to do this is to use a steam lock bag and cook it in the microwave. Alternatively wrap the grated carrot in some muslin (cheesecloth) and place it in a colander over boiling water.

Melt 100 g (3½ oz) of ghee in a non-stick frying pan over high heat. Add the crushed cardamom and the carrot and fry for 2 minutes. Add most of the almonds and pistachios and keep frying, stirring occasionally, until the ghee starts to separate from the carrot. Add the sugar and mix well. Turn the heat back to medium and cook for another 5 minutes.

Soften the extra ghee in a small saucepan and add the milk powder and cream, stirring until well combined. Add to the carrots and stir over high heat for another 2 minutes. Serve hot or warm garnished with the remaining nuts and a scoop of vanilla ice cream.

SERVES 4

1 kg (2 lb 3 oz) carrots, grated	15 almonds, cut into thin slivers
100 g (3½ oz) clarified butter (ghee), plus 1 tablespoon extra	15 pistachios, cut into thin slivers
7 cardamom pods, dry toasted in a pan, peeled and seeds crushed in a mortar and pestle	200 g (7 oz) sugar
	⅓ cup milk powder
	2 tablespoons cream

PERSIAN

Of all the cuisines I've explored, Persian would have to be the one I found most surprising – its wide range of ingredients are used to create some very unusual dishes. Persia was one of the ancient empires of the earth and its people have produced beautiful food for thousands of years. Highlights include exquisite rice dishes flavoured with saffron and studded with green pistachios, stews prepared with dried limes and handfuls of fragrant herbs, kebabs fit for a sultan, sweets that melt in your mouth ... and some really 'out there' dishes as well.

One treasured Persian tradition is *dizi*. Named after the small metal pot it's cooked in, this is a slow-cooked dish of meat, dried beans, a few spices, a little fat and water. Once cooked the liquid is poured out and eaten like a soup with bread. Then a metal masher that looks like a tall mushroom is used to squash the soft meat and beans that remain in the *dizi* and the result, which some devotees have called 'Persian pâté', is served with bread, fresh mint and slivers of red onion. This was customarily a meal adored by labourers as it sustained them through a long working day – I loved seeing some of the glossy young members of the Persian community tucking into hearty *dizi* too.

Also typical of Persia – and unusual – is a sweet called *falooda*, said to be the only thing capable of cooling you down on a 40-degree Tehran day. It's like an exotic slushie made with crushed ice and vermicelli noodles, which freeze in the icy mix. When you start eating the noodles they soften in your mouth.

At the pinnacle of all these great food experiences are the excellent kebabs, which are adored, and top kebab makers are in great demand – to skewer the fine lean meat for *barg* or lamb fillet kebab, to mould the minced meat on a sword-like skewer for *koobideh kebab*, to marinate the meat and to cook up to forty kebabs at a time, making sure they cook evenly and perfectly over charcoal or gas.

There is so much in Persian cuisine that is delightful – even the rice. Called 'pearls of Persian cuisine', rice is the centre of the meal rather than a side dish and it is exceptional – fragrant and fluffy, with each grain long and perfect. This is the result of using aged rice, which is at least two to three years old. Saffron is also prized and is used cleverly – I love seeing my friend Nadia grind a few precious strands with a little sugar and then soak it in some water; the saffron-flavoured liquid is then used for cooking rice, or it's added to chicken dishes or mixed through butter. In fact, Persian people seem to be surrounded by the scent of saffron, as well as rosewater ... Divine.

ESSENTIAL FLAVOURS

DRIED BARBERRIES

A dried fruit that looks like a cranberry grown mainly in the South Khorasan province of Iran. Its sour taste may be mellowed by adding sugar when cooking.

DRIED LIME

These limes are a low-acid variety that are salted then dried, before being sold whole or powdered. Buy whole limes, which are light as a feather, and crack them open before adding to stews to release maximum flavour. They soften and add a deep, musky and slightly sweet note after slow cooking.

PISTACHIOS

Due to its perfect hot, dry climate, these nuts have been grown and highly prized in Iran since ancient times. The principal producing area is Kerman, which is located in the arid southeast. Iranian pistachios are greener and more flavoursome than those grown elsewhere and they're widely used to garnish food or in many biscuit and dessert recipes. In any Iranian household, pistachios are always offered to guests.

ROSEWATER

Prized for many centuries, rosewater and rose petals are used to scent, flavour and decorate many foods, particularly sweet desserts and biscuits. Rosewater syrup is the basis of many refreshing drinks.

SAFFRON

With its exotic aroma and flavour, Persian food, from starters and entrees through to desserts, relies on this beautiful spice. Iran is the largest producer of saffron in the world and Persian saffron is said to be the strongest in flavour and colour.

Known as 'celebration rice' or 'jewelled rice', this is often cooked for weddings. It is made with wild, red barberries (*zereshk*), which give the dish its jewel-like appearance and an exotic, slightly tart taste.

ZERESHK POLOW

Barberry Rice
from Nadia Sajadi

Rinse the rice and put in a bowl with the salt.

Cover with water. Soak for 1–2 hours.

Meanwhile, place the saffron and a small pinch of sugar in a mortar and grind to a fine powder. Place in a cup and fill one-third full with hot water. Set aside.

Combine the spices, pepper and salt in a small bowl. Add the garlic, lemon juice, 250 ml (8½ fl oz/1 cup) of hot water and a tablespoon of the saffron water. Stir well.

Preheat the oven to 160°C (320°F/Gas 2–3). Wash the chicken, pat dry and place in a deep baking tray. Scatter with the onion and pour over the spice and garlic mixture. Cover with foil and bake for 1 hour.

Three-quarters fill a large saucepan with water and bring to the boil. Drain the rice and add to the water with 2–3 tablespoons of olive oil if desired to stop the grains sticking to each other. Boil the rice for 10–15 minutes, stiring gently a few times, or until al dente. Drain in a colander.

Put the pot back on the stove and add 3–4 tablespoons of oil. Lay the sliced potato in the base (to protect the rice, but also to create a delicious edible crust of rice and potato). Top with the drained rice and cover with a lid. Cook until the rice begins to steam (about 3–5 minutes), then turn the heat to low and wrap the lid in a tea towel (covering the underside) and place back on the pot. The tea towel catches the condensation, stopping it from dripping back onto the rice. Leave to steam for 45–60 minutes. By the end you should have perfect, fluffy, separated rice.

Meanwhile heat half the butter in a frying pan and add the barberries. Sauté for a few minutes then add 2 tablespoons of sugar and 2 tablespoons of the saffron water. Stir briefly then remove from the heat.

Place a layer of rice on a serving platter, followed by a sprinkling of barberries, nuts and a little saffron water. Keep layering, mounding up into the shape of a cone. Leave some barberries and nuts for the top. Melt the remaining butter and mix together in a bowl with the remaining saffron water. Mix in a large dollop of rice.

Arrange the chicken quarters around the platter then spoon the saffron rice on top of the mound. Add a final sprinkling of barberries and nuts.

SERVES 4-6

4 cups long-grain rice, rinsed	1 chicken, quartered
4 tablespoons salt	1 onion, finely sliced
3 pinches saffron threads	olive oil
sugar	1 large potato, sliced
½ teaspoon turmeric	4 tablespoons butter
¼ teaspoon sweet paprika	1 cup dried barberries, rinsed
½ teaspoon *baharat*	2 tablespoons almonds, cut into slivers
¼ teaspoon black pepper	
1 teaspoon salt	2 tablespoons pistachios, cut into slivers
2 garlic cloves, crushed	
1 tablespoon lemon juice	

In Persian households this is made every morning ready for lunch - the sound of the chopping of walnuts and parsley for the topping echoes throughout Persian neighbourhoods. The salty *kashk* cheese is a fermented byproduct from cheese making and is available from Middle Eastern grocery stores. With its strong flavour it resembles a liquid fetta cheese and is lovely mixed with the golden eggplant and dried mint.

KASHK-E BADEMJAN

Grilled Eggplant and Cheese Dip

from Afsaneh Charani

Heat 2 tablespoons of oil in a non-stick frying pan until really hot, then fry the eggplant until soft and golden. Drain on paper towel. Add the onion with a little more oil to the pan and fry until translucent, then stir in the turmeric. Push the onion to one side and add the garlic. Fry until fragrant then push to another side of the pan.

Remove the pan from the heat, add the mint and fry briefly in the remaining heat.

Put the eggplant in a bowl and mash.

Heat a little more oil in a saucepan and add the eggplant, *kashk*, most of the onion, garlic and mint (reserve some of each for garnish), and salt and pepper. Warm the ingredients through and combine. Spoon into a serving bowl and top with the remaining onion, garlic and mint. Sprinkle with walnuts and parsley and serve warm.

MAKES 3-4 CUPS

olive oil	2 tablespoons dried mint
4 eggplants (aubergines), peeled and finely sliced	2 tablespoons *kashk*
1 onion, finely chopped	salt and pepper
1 heaped teaspoon turmeric	chopped walnuts
3 garlic cloves, finely chopped	chopped flat-leaf (Italian) parsley

Qormeh sabzi is a delicious Persian *khoresh*, or stew. *Sabzi* is the herb mix integral to the dish and includes parsley, coriander, garlic chives and fresh or dried fenugreek leaves. The herbs are added in mountains and it's no wonder the dish turns a marvellously dark green - and the aroma of fenugreek fills the house (be warned!). This recipe is cooked with duck, but it can also be cooked with chicken or lamb - or you could even do a vegetarian version.

QORMEH SABZI

from Jason Aghamri

Heat the ghee or oil in a large, heavy-based saucepan over medium heat. Add the onion and stir for a few minutes until it softens. Add the duck pieces and turmeric and fry until the duck is golden brown. Remove the duck from the pan.

Add the fresh herbs and dried fenugreek to the pan and fry, stirring, until the herbs darken. Return the duck to the pot and add stock or water to just cover the meat. Add the dried lime and kidney beans and bring to the boil. Season with salt and pepper. Simmer for 1½ hours. Serve with rice.

SERVES 6

2½ tablespoons clarified butter (ghee) or vegetable oil	50 g (1¾ oz) coriander (cilantro), chopped
1 large onion, chopped	50 g (1¾ oz) dried fenugreek leaves
1 duck, chopped into large pieces	chicken stock or water
pinch of turmeric	6 dried limes, cracked
100 g (3½ oz) flat-leaf (Italian) parsley, chopped	200 g (7 oz) cooked kidney beans
100 g (3½ oz) garlic chives, chopped	salt and pepper

'There is a loving thing people say at the end of the meal which is loosely translated as "May your hand be relieved of the pain of preparing all this," to which the cook replies "Salute to your soul and body."'

Falooda is Iran's take on the slushie and it is perfect on hot days. Ice made from frozen sugar syrup is crushed and mixed with rice noodles and rosewater, and topped with lime juice or with strawberry, sour cherry or pomegranate syrup (available from Middle Eastern stores). It is deliciously refreshing!

FALOODA

from Jalal Dastyari

Heat the water and sugar, stirring until the sugar dissolves. Leave to cool, then freeze in a block for 24 hours.

Once frozen solid, place the ice in a large metal bowl and crush it with a hard implement such as a large pestle (you might need to let the ice thaw a little). Then put gloves on and use your hands to crush further, until the ice is smooth. Add the rice vermicelli and mix through – the noodles will become hard. Add the rosewater. Scoop into glasses and drizzle each with a tablespoon of lime juice or a little fruit syrup and serve immediately.

SERVES 6-8

1 litre (34 fl oz/4 cups) water
250 g (9 oz) sugar (or more to taste)
180 g (6 oz) rice vermicelli, cooked and drained

2 teaspoons rosewater
fresh lime juice or strawberry, sour cherry or pomegranate syrup

From the ancient world of the Incas to a country now boasting some of the world's top restaurants, Peruvian food is unique, offering an array of interesting and delicious tastes sourced from the country's diverse climates and growing areas.

Located on the mid-west coast of South America, Peru has 2000 kilometres of coastline and some abundant fishing grounds due to the cold Humboldt Current that brings waters rich in plankton. Running through the country like a spine is the towering Andes mountain range, where quinoa and amaranth come from – the protein-rich 'super grains' now in vogue in the West. The Peruvian Andes are also home to a staggering 2500 varieties of potato. Beyond is the Amazon jungle with its many ingredients and cooking styles.

Like Australia, immigration has really shaped Peruvian cuisine with settlers from Spain, China and Japan creating food that you don't find anywhere else.

The Spanish had the biggest impact, bringing cheese-making techniques, rice and wheat, and beef, chicken and pork. They also brought vines to start a wine industry, which quickly led to a new drink being created – pisco, the beloved clean clear spirit of Peru. 'I can't think of anything Peruvians get more passionate about than pisco,' explains Peruvian Australian pisco lover and home cook Luis Almenara. 'It's amazing how much Peruvians feel in their hearts about pisco!'

Luis' wife, Carmen, loves having her girlfriends over for afternoons of sipping pisco sour (a cocktail made with lime juice, sugar and egg whites) as they make *humitas* together. These are known as the bread of the Incas – a lovely mix of ground fresh corn made into a dough with corn masa flour, cheese, chilli and coriander, formed into parcels wrapped in corn husks and steamed.

The Chinese arrived with the gold rush in the nineteenth century and stayed on to create a unique fusion cuisine called Chifa, from the Cantonese word meaning 'eat rice'. Because many Chinese ingredients were difficult to access in Peru, their food began to blend in native Peruvian, Spanish and African styles. One example is the popular *lomo saltado* – stir-fried beef cooked in a smoking wok with tomatoes and french fries added, along with Peruvian chilli and soy sauce.

Peruvian food was also influenced by Japanese immigrants who arrived en masse in the early twentieth century in a government-sponsored resettlement program to relieve overcrowding at home. The raw fish dish *tiradito* served with a chilli and lime dressing can trace its roots back to Japanese sashimi.

A sweet finish to a meal was unknown until the arrival of the Spanish. Many desserts centre on milk, eggs and sugar – from Peru's version of crème caramel to *tres leches,* which is a luscious creamy cake made with three milks. One sweet that is universally loved is *manjar blanco,* a milk caramel that can be used to fill a swiss roll in *pionono;* piped into pastry horns; slathered between sweet biscuits called *alfajores;* or eaten just as it is.

ESSENTIAL FLAVOURS

CHILLI

Aji amarillo is the favourite chilli of Peru – citrusy yellow with medium heat. It is starting to be grown in Australia. If you can't find it fresh, it can be bought in jars as a paste (and can also be bought dried, when it is called *aji mirasol*, which means 'looking at the sun'). *Aji panca* is another popular chilli, commonly used in its dried form. It is dark red with mild heat and fruity flavours.

CORN

There are many varieties of corn, with one of the most popular Peruvian varieties being white corn. Ground fresh kernels are used to make *humitas*, and roasted dried kernels called *cancha* are eaten as snacks and to accompany ceviche. There's also a refreshing drink made with purple corn called *chicha morada*.

LIME

Lime was brought to South America by the Spanish and is essential for adding a citrus zing to everything from pisco sours to *tiradito*, salsas and many other dishes.

POTATOES

Over 4000 varieties of potatoes are native to the Andes, with around 2500 found in Peru alone. They are almost all the colours of the rainbow, from the white *papa blanca* through to the yellow waxy *papa amarilla*, and on to red, purple, black and green. There's even a dried variety called *chuño* that is naturally freeze-dried at high altitudes and looks like little stones.

Surely the crunchiest, sexiest chips in the world come from cassava - extra creamy inside and crunchy outside due to their low moisture content. While cassava can be bought frozen and cook up beautifully, look out for them fresh at Asian and Pacific island grocers. They look like a slightly more slender version of a sweet potato with dark brown skin. *Salsa huancaina* is a smooth and creamy sauce with a hint of chilli. It uses long yellow Peruvian chillies called *aji amarillo*, but if these aren't to be found you can use yellow banana chillies and small red chillies to boost the heat, or some bought *aji amarillo* paste. Mild *queso fresco* cheese is the other main ingredient (fetta can be used as a substitute), and traditionally a few dry biscuits give the sauce extra body. The sauce is also a great companion for potatoes or corn.

CASSAVA CHIPS AND SALSA HUANCAINA

from Jorge Chacon

Cook the whole cassava in lightly salted boiling water for 20 minutes or until soft. Drain, then when cool enough to handle cut it into thick chips and refrigerate until ready to fry. To make the salsa, heat the oil in a small frying pan over low-medium heat and add the garlic, onion and chillies (but not the chilli paste if using). Cook, stirring, for 3-4 minutes. Transfer to a blender and add the chilli paste if using, fetta, biscuits and half the milk and blend until smooth. Taste for seasoning, adjusting if needed, and add more milk if the mixture is too thick. Scrape into a bowl.

Heat the oil in a large saucepan or wok until very hot and fry the cassava chips in batches until golden and crisp. Drain on paper towel, then sprinkle with salt. Serve with the salsa for dipping.

SERVES 6-8

1 kg (2 lb 3 oz) fresh cassava, peeled, or frozen whole cassava, thawed
vegetable oil for deep-frying
sea salt

SALSA HUANCAINA

1 tablespoon olive oil
1 garlic clove, finely chopped
½ red onion, chopped
2 small red chillies, seeded and chopped

4 *aji amarillo* chillies, seeded and chopped (or a mixture of yellow banana chillies and extra small red chillies, or 3-4 tablespoons *aji amarillo* chilli paste)
400 g (14 oz) creamy fetta, crumbled
4 Sao or Salada biscuits, roughly broken
100-150 ml (3½-5 fl oz) evaporated milk

'We have 15 or 20 varieties of potatoes here ... Peru has over 2000!'

Get a couple of friends together to help you wrap these exotic steamed corn cakes that are closely related to Mexico's tamales. This version is savoury with chilli, onion, coriander and cheese, but there can be sweet versions too, such as with raisins and cinnamon. The mixture is tied up in corn-husk jackets. *Humitas* have been made virtually the same way for thousands of years.

HUMITAS

Steamed Corn Cakes

from Carmen Almenara

Peel the husks from the corn cobs and reserve. Remove and discard the silks.

Boil the husks for 5 minutes or until soft, then drain and set aside.

Cut the kernels from the cobs and measure out 500 g (1 lb 2 oz). Place in a food processor or blender with the garlic and evaporated milk and process until smooth. Transfer to a large bowl and stir in the *masa harina*, baking powder and coriander.

Heat the lard in a wok or large frying pan over medium heat and cook the onion until soft. Add the cumin and chilli and cook for another 2–3 minutes.

Add the corn mixture to the wok or pan along with the salt and pepper, and cook, stirring, for another 3–4 minutes. Remove from the heat, then return to the bowl to cool slightly before stirring in the fetta.

To wrap the *humitas*, lay 2 pieces of corn husk on a work surface, slightly overlapping and with the wider edges together at the bottom. Place 2–3 tablespoons of corn mixture in the middle. Fold in the wide bottom edge, then fold in the sides, and roll up into a rectangular parcel. Secure the parcel with thin strips of husk tied around the parcel like a ribbon. Continue with the remaining mixture.

Place the *humitas* in a steamer and steam for 25–30 minutes. Allow to cool for a few minutes before serving.

MAKES 12-15 PARCELS

- 4-5 corn cobs in their husks, to yield 500 g (1 lb 2 oz) kernels
- 2-3 garlic cloves
- 125 ml (4 fl oz/½ cup) evaporated milk
- 250 g (9 oz) *masa harina* (instant corn masa flour)
- 2 teaspoons baking powder
- 1 bunch coriander (cilantro), chopped
- 200 g (7 oz) lard
- 2 medium-large red onions, finely chopped
- 2 teaspoons ground cumin
- 3-4 *aji amarillo* chillies, seeded and chopped (or a mixture of yellow banana chillies and small red chillies, or 3 tablespoons *aji amarillo* chilli paste)
- 1 teaspoon salt
- ¼ teaspoon freshly ground black pepper
- 230 g (8 oz) creamy fetta, crumbled

'We have so many varieties of corn and it's so versatile – you can live on corn for years and you won't get tired of it!'

What a spectacular way to eat fresh seafood! *Tiradito* means 'to throw', giving the impression that this dish is rather easy to put together, and it is. In Danny's version prawns are boiled then blended with lime juice, oil and *aji amarillo* chilli to make a bright yellow sauce for just-out-of-the water-fresh kingfish and scallops, which are thinly sliced and laid out across a platter. Unlike the other famous South American dish of raw fish - ceviche (see page 339) - the fish is not stirred through the dressing, making the dish more like carpaccio.

SCALLOP AND KINGFISH TIRADITO

from Danny Parreno

Boil the prawns in their shells in a large saucepan of salted water for 5 minutes. Drain and refresh in a bowl of iced water.

Peel and de-vein the prawns, then place in a blender. Add the lime juice and blend until smooth. With the motor running slowly add the olive oil until the mixture has a smooth pouring consistency (you may not need all the oil). Blend in half the chilli, then taste the mixture and keep adding chilli until you reach your desired heat and flavour. Add salt to taste. Refrigerate until ready to use.

Slice the kingfish very thinly and lay out in the middle of a large platter (the slices can overlap each other). Cut the scallops in half horizontally without cutting all the way through, then butterfly them open and place them around the kingfish. Pour the dressing over the seafood, covering it evenly. Drizzle with a little sesame oil and scatter with coriander.

SERVES 8 AS AN ENTREE

500 g (1 lb 2 oz) green prawns (shrimp)	salt
200 ml (7 fl oz) lime juice	1 kg (2 lb 3 oz) kingfish fillet
200 ml (7 fl oz) olive oil	300 g (10½ oz) scallops
2-3 *aji amarillo* chillies, seeded and chopped (or a mixture of yellow banana chillies and small red chillies, or about 2½ tablespoons *aji amarillo* chilli paste)	sesame oil
	baby coriander (cilantro) sprigs or picked coriander (cilantro) leaves

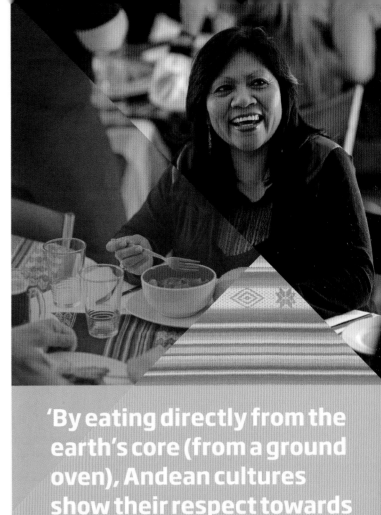

'By eating directly from the earth's core (from a ground oven), Andean cultures show their respect towards Pachamama, the source of fertility and life.'

Translating as the 'sigh of a woman (from Lima)', this is one of the best-loved desserts of Peru. The combination of rich caramel custard topped with voluptuous Italian-style meringue flavoured with a touch of port dates back to the 1800s and was created by Amparo Ayarez. She was married to a poet and when he first tasted her dessert, he loved it and named it, explaining: 'it is as soft and sweet as the sigh of a woman.'

SUSPIRO DE LIMEÑA

Caramel Custard with Meringue

from Rosanna Spiers Cordova

To make the custard, combine the condensed milk and evaporated milk in a saucepan and place over medium heat. Cook, stirring almost continuously for 15 minutes, or until the mixture has lightly thickened like custard. Remove from the heat.

Put the egg yolks in a bowl and whisk. Slowly pour half a cup of the hot milk over the egg yolks, whisking well. Strain the egg mixture back into the saucepan and add the vanilla, stirring well. Set over low heat. Cook, stirring constantly, for another 2 minutes, then remove from the heat and pour into serving glasses. Set aside to cool.

To make the meringue, combine the sugar and port in a small saucepan and stir over low heat until the sugar dissolves. Increase the heat to medium and bring to the boil. Cook without stirring until the syrup reaches a temperature of 120°C (250°F/Gas 1–2), or forms a firm sticky ball when a little mixture is dropped into a glass of cold water.

Just before the syrup is ready, beat the egg whites and salt to soft peaks. When the syrup is ready, gradually pour it into the egg whites with the beaters running. Continue to beat until the meringue is cool. It should be very thick and shiny. Spoon or pipe the meringue over the top of the *manjar blanco*, sprinkle with cinnamon, and chill in the refrigerator until ready to serve.

SERVES 8

MANJAR BLANCO (CARAMEL CUSTARD)	MERINGUE
395 g (14 oz) tin sweetened condensed milk	**220 g (8 oz/1 cup) sugar**
375 ml (12½ fl oz) tin evaporated milk	**3 tablespoons port**
4 egg yolks	**4 egg whites**
1½ teaspoons vanilla essence	**small pinch of salt**
	cinnamon to sprinkle

'We eat caramel every day. It takes us back to our childhood.'

Here is one of the most wildly colourful, full-on cuisines of this book. Filipino people have an energy and sense of fun that is very much a part of their cooking. Across 7000 tropical islands, there are endless regional variations of the food that take elements from Spanish, Chinese, Malaysian and even American styles of food. 'We're like a melting pot of different cultures and flavours that we've adapted and made better,' explains Filipino Australian chef Dennis Leslie.

There's a confident take-no-prisoners approach to flavour in the Philippines; sweet, salty and sour are all here in abundance. The sweetness comes from sugar – whether cane or palm sugar. The salty comes from soy sauce, fish sauce and the Filipino shrimp paste called *bagoong*. The sourness – in large doses – comes from vinegar and the adored citrus fruit calamansi. In fact, sour flavours are so pervasive that there are said to be more descriptive words for sour in the main Filipino language of Tagalog than in any other language on earth.

This is not food for the faint-hearted or the weight conscious! *Chicharon* – crackers made from deep-fried pork skin – are a popular snack, as is 'crispy *pata*', twice-cooked pork hocks. These are first poached with star anise, garlic and onion, then rubbed with fish sauce and deep-fried, giving meltingly tender meat and crunchy crackling.

Pork is part of every big family get-together – a whole pig or *lechon* is stuffed with lemongrass, pepper, garlic, star anise, pandan leaves and spring onion and turned slowly for many hours while basted with soy sauce. By the time it's served, the aroma has made sure everyone is ready for a feast.

At feasts everyone brings a dish so the table is covered with a wide range of favourites, including noodles or *pancit* cooked and served so many ways, and stews such as *pinakbet*, which stars lesser-known vegetables like okra, bitter melon and snake beans. And there is always rice, the accompaniment to just about every meal.

Baked goods are popular and the cherished bread of the Philippines is *pan de sal*, which translates as salted bread but is often sweet. These soft white rolls are eaten hot from the oven with a slice of cheese, cheese *pimiento* (cheese, grilled capsicum and mayonnaise spread), Cheez Whiz (yes, really!), liver spread or coconut jam. Then there's the snail-like buns called *ensaymada* that have been described by one devotee as 'like brioche on overdrive – stuffed with melted butter, sprinkled with sugar, and then topped with grated cheese.'

Desserts are a mardi gras of colour with purple yam or *ube*, which tastes like sweet potato, used in many cakes and sweets. Other desserts are green with pandan, and coconut is another big flavour. Look out for *macapuno* or coconut sport, which is a sweet preserve of thick coconut slices in a jar. And if you ever get the chance to try the Philippines' own version of crème caramel, the famous *leche* flan – don't say no!

ESSENTIAL FLAVOURS

BAGOONG
Pronounced 'bago-ong', this is the Philippines' version of shrimp or fish paste. It's strong and fermented in flavour and has more texture than other Asian shrimp pastes. One common version of it is fried with garlic and other ingredients and can be used straight from the jar as a dipping sauce. *Bagoong* adds a deep base note of flavour in dishes like *kare-kare* and *pinakbet*.

CALAMANSI
This small citrus fruit is somewhere between a lime, a cumquat and a mandarin. It's squeezed over seafood and noodle dishes and is also popular in drinks.

GARLIC
Garlic is used liberally in the Philippines, flavouring everything other than sweets!

SOY SAUCE
Filipino soy sauce is salty and dark and a key flavour in *adobo* and many other dishes.

VEGETABLES
Filipino vegetables are truly exotic. Moringa leaves are small round leaves with a grassy flavour used in classic dishes like *munggo guisado*, a stew with mung beans; and *tinola*, a chicken soup. The leaves are a great source of vitamins A and C, calcium and iron. Other common vegetables include *labanos* (daikon radish), okra and bitter melon.

VINEGAR
The vinegar used in the Philippines is predominantly cane or coconut vinegar, which both have a mellow flavour. Vinegar is used to make dipping sauces with garlic and soy sauce, and is essential in the national dish *adobo*.

Adobo is a deliciously simple dish that reminds you of what home is all about, according to Ricky Ocampo. Commonly made with pork, but here using chicken in a recipe from Ricky's grandmother, *adobo* is considered to be the national dish of the Philippines. It is flavoured very simply with garlic, bay leaves, black pepper, soy sauce and a generous amount of vinegar (cane vinegar is authentic, but apple-cider or white balsamic vinegar can be used instead). The result is tender chicken with a sauce that's beautifully syrupy. Serve with steamed rice.

CHICKEN ADOBO

from Ricky Ocampo

Heat the oil in a large saucepan over medium-high heat. Add the chicken pieces and cook, turning, until lightly browned all over, which should take about 5 minutes. Add the garlic and cook, stirring, for 1–2 minutes, until the garlic is starting to colour. Season with a little salt and plenty of black pepper. Stir in the bay leaves and soy sauce and simmer for another 2 minutes.

Add the vinegar and bring to the boil, then reduce the heat to low, cover with a lid and cook for 30 minutes, or until the chicken is cooked through and tender. Remove the lid halfway through cooking to allow the liquid to reduce by half.

SERVES 4

3 tablespoons oil
1 small chicken
   (around 1.2 kg/2 lb 11 oz),
   cut into 8 pieces
8 garlic cloves, roughly
   chopped

salt and pepper
3 bay leaves
3 tablespoons soy sauce
250 ml (8½ fl oz/1 cup) cane
   vinegar, apple-cider vinegar
   or white balsamic vinegar

'*Adobo* is our
national treasure.'

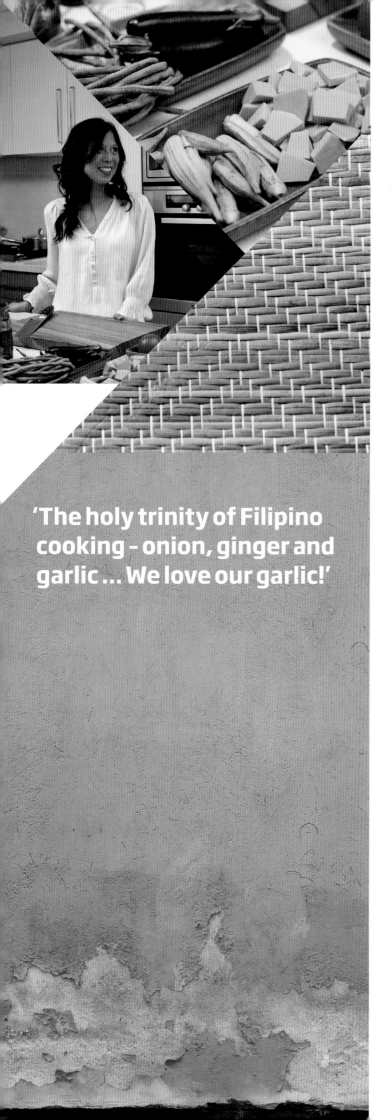

This classic Filipino stew features meltingly tender oxtail and other meat too (tripe can be added to this recipe), as well as a mixture of vegetables and a unique flavour combination of fried shrimp paste, annatto and peanut butter. Serve *kare-kare* with steamed rice for a complete meal.

KARE-KARE

Oxtail and Vegetable Stew

from Raquel San Juan

Put the oxtail in a large saucepan and cover with water. Bring to the boil, then reduce the heat to a simmer and cook for 3–4 hours. Halfway through cooking, add the tripe if using. By the end the oxtail should be very tender and just about falling from the bone. Add more water during cooking if needed.

Use a slotted spoon to transfer the oxtail and tripe to a plate, and reserve the stock.

Heat the oil in a pot over medium heat. Add the onion and garlic and sauté for 1 minute. Add the oxtail and tripe and stir briefly. Add the eggplant, pumpkin, snake beans, shrimp paste and annatto water and cover with stock. Stir well. Bring to the boil, then reduce the heat to a simmer and cook for 15–20 minutes, or until the vegetables are just tender.

Stir in the peanut butter. Continue cooking for another 5–7 minutes until the sauce is thick.

Stir in the bok choy, simmer for another minute or so, then remove from the heat. Serve with additional shrimp paste on the side.

SERVES 4

1 kg (2 lb 3 oz) oxtail, cut into 5 cm (2 in) pieces	handful of snake beans, cut into 10 cm (4 in) lengths
300 g (10½ oz) parboiled honeycomb ox tripe, cut into 5 cm (2 in) pieces (optional)	2 teaspoons fried shrimp paste (*bagoong*), plus extra for serving
3 tablespoons vegetable oil	1 teaspoon annatto powder, mixed with 2 tablespoons water
1 large onion, finely chopped	
4 garlic cloves, finely chopped	
1 medium eggplant, cut into chunks	2 heaped tablespoons peanut butter (or more if a thicker sauce is desired)
600 g (1 lb 5 oz) pumpkin, peeled and cut into chunks	1 bunch baby bok choy, leaves separated

The more you eat this the more you love it, says Trissa. The colourful combination of vegetables includes bitter melon, eggplant, okra, snake beans and pumpkin, which are studded with chunks of *bagnet* – crispy pork belly. It is spiked with fried shrimp paste for a beautiful depth of flavour. Serve with steamed rice.

PINAKBET

Vegetable Stew with Pork Belly

from Trissa Lopez

Put the pork belly, onion, garlic, bay leaves and salt in a saucepan. Cover with water and bring to the boil. Reduce the heat to a simmer and cook for 1 hour, or until the pork is tender.

Preheat the oven to 200°C (400°F/Gas 6). Drain the pork and place skin-side up on a tray. Roast in the oven for 30 minutes. (To further crisp the pork if desired, you can also deep-fry it after it comes out of the oven.) Set the pork aside to cool.

While the pork is cooking, cut the bitter melon in half lengthways and scrape out the seeds and pith. Sprinkle the inside of the melon generously with salt and leave for 30 minutes. This extracts some of the bitterness. Rinse off the salt and cut the melon into 1 cm (½ in) slices.

Chop the pork into bite-sized pieces.

Heat the oil in a large saucepan over medium heat. Add the onion, ginger and garlic and sauté for 5 minutes, until the onion has softened.

Now add the vegetables in layers. Start with the tomatoes, scattering them over the onion mixture. Next add the eggplant, then the whole okra, bitter melon, snake beans and pumpkin. Dollop the shrimp paste on top, spreading it out a little, then pour on about 100 ml (3½ fl oz) of water. Scatter with the pieces of pork belly and cover with a lid. Don't worry if the mixture comes to the top of the saucepan as it will cook down.

Simmer for 12–15 minutes, until the vegetables are tender but not mushy. Don't stir the vegetables as they cook, allowing them to hold their shape. Instead, shake the pan once or twice during the cooking to distribute the shrimp paste evenly. Serve with steamed rice.

SERVES 4

PORK BELLY

500 g (1 lb 2 oz) pork belly
1 onion, quartered
3 garlic cloves, bruised
2 bay leaves
30 g (1 oz) salt
oil for deep-frying (optional)

1 bitter melon
salt
2½ tablespoons vegetable oil
1 red onion, sliced
3 cm (1 in) piece of ginger, julienned

4 garlic cloves, finely chopped
3 tomatoes, cut into wedges
4 Japanese eggplants (aubergines), cut diagonally into 3 cm (1 in) lengths
10 okra
5 snake beans, cut into 5 cm (2 in) lengths
500 g (1 lb 2 oz) pumpkin, peeled and cut into chunks
2-3 tablespoons fried shrimp paste (bagoong), or to taste

'Without rice, there is no Filipino food – in every house the rice cooker is always switched on.'

This is like the most exotic spaghetti marinara you've ever eaten. 'Palabok' means garnishes or toppings, and the noodles are topped with boiled eggs and crumbs made from chicharon (deep-fried pork skin) and smoked fish, which add lovely salty shards of flavour. (Dried smoked fish is available from Asian grocers.) The sauce made with prawn heads and shells is rich and satisfying.

PANCIT PALABOK

Seafood Noodles

from Dennis Leslie

Preheat the oven to 220°C (420°F/Gas 7). Place the prawn heads and shells on a tray and roast for 10 minutes.

Meanwhile, soak the cornstarch noodles in cold water for 5 minutes. Bring a large saucepan of water to the boil and add the noodles, cooking for 5 minutes or until tender. (If using rice vermicelli, cook according to the packet instructions.) Drain the noodles, rinse well and set aside.

Heat half the oil in a large saucepan over medium-high heat. Add the onion, garlic, celery and carrot and sauté for 5 minutes. Add the roasted prawn heads and shells, lightly crushing them with the spoon to help release their flavour, then add the water and bring to the boil. Simmer for 20 minutes. Add the annatto seeds and simmer for another 10 minutes.

Strain the stock into a clean saucepan and discard the solids. Return to the boil over medium heat. Whisk in the cornflour mixture and simmer for 1 minute, or until the stock is slightly thickened. Remove from the heat.

While the stock is simmering, make the chicharon and fish crumbs. Put the chicharon in a food processor and process to coarse crumbs. Transfer to a bowl. Repeat with the smoked fish.

Heat the oil in a wok over medium-high heat. Fry the onion and garlic for 5 minutes, then add the chicharon and fish crumbs. Reduce the heat to medium and cook, tossing, for 5 minutes. Scoop into a bowl and set aside to cool.

Heat the wok over high heat and add the remaining 1 tablespoon of oil. When very hot, add the squid and prawn meat and toss until just opaque. Add the mussel meat and toss for another 30 seconds. Transfer to a bowl and set aside.

Add the noodles and 3 tablespoons of the stock to the hot wok and toss until well combined and heated through. Stir in half the chicharon and fish crumb mixture, then transfer to a platter and sprinkle over the remaining crumb mixture. Top with the seafood and dot with the quartered eggs. Scatter with spring onions. Spoon over a little more stock and serve with calamansi or lemon to squeeze on top.

SERVES 8

500 g (1 lb 2 oz) green prawns (shrimp), shelled (heads and shells reserved)
500 g (1 lb 2 oz) cornstarch noodles (*lug lug*) or rice vermicelli that is not too thin
2 tablespoons vegetable oil
1 onion, finely chopped
3 garlic cloves, finely chopped
1 celery stalk, cut into 1 cm (½ in) dice
1 small carrot, cut into 1 cm (½ in) dice
2 litres (68 fl oz/8 cups) water
2 teaspoons annatto seeds
60 ml (2 oz) cornflour (cornstarch), mixed with 3 tablespoons water
300 g (10½ oz) whole baby squid, cleaned, bodies cut into rings and tentacles cut into bite-sized pieces

600 g (1 lb 5 oz) mussels, steamed open and meat picked from the shells
8 eggs, boiled for 5 minutes, refreshed in iced water, peeled and quartered
5 spring onions (scallions), finely sliced
8 calamansi, halved, or 2 lemons, quartered

CHICHARON AND FISH CRUMBS

300 g (10½ oz) *chicharon* (deep-fried pork skin)
200 g (7 oz) dried smoked mullet or other fish, skin and bones removed, broken into pieces
1 tablespoon vegetable oil
1 onion, finely chopped
2 garlic cloves, finely chopped

This iced dessert in a tall glass is full of different textures and tastes, and is just the thing to end a Filipino feast. It is also a popular pick-me-up during the heat of the day in the Philippines. The name literally translates as 'mix-mix' and it can include many fruits, vegetables and sweets. Yasmin's version features banana and *macapuno*, or coconut sport, which is a sweet preserve made from the soft and fleshy macapuno coconut. She tops her *halo-halo* with slices of *leche* flan, the Filipino version of crème caramel. For the best light and fluffy shaved ice, you might like to invest in an ice crusher.

HALO-HALO

from Yasmin Newman

Preheat the oven to 160°C (320°F/Gas 3). To make the flan, put the sugar in a saucepan and place over medium heat. Cook without stirring, just swirling occasionally, until melted and turned to a deep amber caramel. Pour into the base of a small non-stick loaf tin (around 22 × 11 cm/8½ × 4½ in).

Combine the eggs, evaporated milk and condensed milk in a bowl and whisk until well combined. Strain through a fine sieve into the tin. Cover the tin tightly with foil and place in a baking dish. Pour boiling water into the dish to come halfway up the tin. Bake for 50-60 minutes, or until just firm. Remove from the oven and leave to cool, then chill in the refrigerator.

To make the sweetened bananas, combine the sugar and water in a saucepan and cook, stirring, over medium heat until the sugar dissolves. Add the banana and bring to the boil, then reduce the heat and simmer for 5-8 minutes. Transfer to a bowl to cool, then chill in the refrigerator.

To make the caramel syrup, combine the sugar and water in a small saucepan and place over medium-high heat, stirring until the sugar dissolves. Cook for 8 minutes or until slightly thickened. Remove from the heat and leave to cool.

Run a knife around the flan and invert it onto a plate. Cut into 1 cm (½ in) slices, then cut each slice into 3 or 4 small pieces.

Finely crush the ice in an ice crusher or blender.

To assemble the halo-halo, place 2 tablespoons of coconut sport in the bottom of each serving glass. Drizzle with 2 teaspoons of caramel syrup, then add 2 tablespoons of sweetened bananas. Fill the glasses with shaved ice, then fill with evaporated milk. Top each glass with a few slices of the flan. Serve immediately.

SERVES 6

LECHE FLAN

110 g (4 oz/½ cup) white sugar
6 eggs
375 ml tin evaporated milk
395 g (14 oz) tin sweetened condensed milk

SWEETENED BANANAS

220 g (8 oz/1 cup) white sugar
250 ml (8½ fl oz/1 cup) water
4 lady finger bananas, cut into 1 cm (½ in) cubes

CARAMEL SYRUP

100 g (3½ oz/½ cup) brown sugar
125 ml (4 fl oz/½ cup) water

TO SERVE

10 cups ice cubes
340 g (12 oz) coconut sport (*macapuno*)
2 × 375 ml tins evaporated milk

'We eat non-stop - we eat six times a day ... The culture revolves around food!'

Polish food is always on a generous scale, whether it's a big platter of cured meats and sausages, the slow-cooked wonder of pork, sausage and sauerkraut that is the national dish *bigos*, or a luscious cheesecake. This is hearty fare to enjoy with others and help keep out the cold. The beloved Polish vodka comes in handy, too.

Polish cuisine has its roots in survival food to sustain people through long winters, like that of many of its surrounding countries. Traditions such as smoking, pickling and preserving are still loved and used today to give people a supply of meat, vegetables and fruit throughout the year. When Polish friends talk about gherkins, for example, they're more than just a food – there's comfort in the fact they are always on hand, with their delicious crunch and lovely sourness. 'It's all about the tang and the tart,' says Judyta Slupnicki.

The many different sausages are another essential part of life. 'Polish people can't live without smallgoods – from generation to generation, we eat for breakfast, lunch and dinner,' says smallgoods-maker Roman Narel. They are stored in the pantry so there's a smoky, garlicky welcome every time you open the door, and were traditionally made in farmhouses when the weather turned cold, using the family pig, garlic, juniper, marjoram and other favourite spices. Sausages and hams, together called cold cuts, are laid out on platters with accompanying mustard or horseradish to fire up the taste buds, as well as gherkins and rye bread.

Baking started in the farmhouses and then developed into small village businesses, and was always based on good ingredients – local rye flour and a treasured 'sour' or starter that gives a unique flavour and takes the place of yeast. Some sours are at least a hundred years old, providing their own magic. Rye bread is made to last a week and is served with most meals. It has a crunchy crust when it's first baked, and an open crumb perfect with lashings of butter.

The main meal in Poland is eaten in the afternoon, and certainly ticks the comfort-food box, usually based on meat and carbohydrates. That can mean *golabki* – cabbage rolls served with a tomato sauce and mashed potato; or *pierogi*, the fabulous dumplings that might be filled with potatoes and cheese, mushrooms and sauerkraut, or meat, and are always served with a sauce of some kind such as simple butter and breadcrumbs or sour cream and chives. Other popular dishes are roast pork, chicken or duck, crumbed pork cutlets, and *roladki* – beef roll-ups sometimes served with mushroom sauce.

Sweets are marvellous and range from baked cheesecakes to jam-filled donuts, fruit *pierogi*, yeast cakes called *babka*, poppy seed rolls, and *szarlotka* – Polish apple pie.

The last word on Polish food goes to the very charming home cook Ela Chylewska. 'We love our food … to cook, eat and entertain. Whether a guest is a family member, old friend or total stranger, in a Polish home he or she will be greeted with warm hospitality. It's no joke when the Polish say "*Jedzcie, pijcie i popuszczajcie pasa*! (Eat, drink and loosen your belt!)" Polish cuisine is very rich and one needs quite a long belt to really enjoy it!'

ESSENTIAL FLAVOURS

GHERKINS

In Poland these small cucumbers are traditionally pickled in brine and may be flavoured with mustard seeds, stalks of flowering dill, garlic, horseradish root or leaves, and oak or cherry tree leaves. They can also be pickled in vinegar for a slightly crunchier result. They are a favourite snack and an accompaniment to cold cuts.

HORSERADISH

Grated fresh in soup, or in jars ready to dip a sausage into, this is the sharp, nostril-clearing bite that adds sparkle to so many Polish dishes. It's one of the main ingredients in the beetroot relish called *cwikla*.

SAUERKRAUT

Like Polish gherkins, the main ingredient when pickling cabbage to make sauerkraut is salt. The cabbage gets its sour taste from the natural process of lacto-fermentation. Sauerkraut is very nutritious and is used in the national dish *bigos*, in *pierogi*, and as an accompaniment to many meals.

SOUR CREAM

The beloved sour cream is dolloped over soups, pancakes or steaming *pierogi*, used in salad dressings, and stirred into sauces.

A good waxy potato is a delight and just what you need in this clever celebration of carbohydrates. Ela serves the simple pancakes with a creamy mushroom sauce, with sour cream on the side - all of a sudden the dish feels decadent. It's great for winter, especially if you've spent the day in the pine forests gathering the mushrooms!

POTATO PANCAKES WITH MUSHROOM SAUCE

from Ela Chylewska

To make the mushroom sauce, heat the butter and oil in a large saucepan over medium heat. Add the onion and sauté for 4-5 minutes, or until soft and lightly golden. Add the mushrooms and sauté for 2-3 minutes. Sprinkle over the flour and stir it into the mushrooms for a few seconds before adding the stock. Simmer for 2 minutes. Stir in the cream and allow to heat through, then season to taste and remove from the heat. Set the pan aside.

Peel the potatoes and onion and grate them into a bowl on the medium holes of a grater. The potato and onion should be quite fine and a little pulpy. Add the egg and flour and some salt and pepper and stir to combine.

Heat a little oil and butter in a large frying pan over medium heat. When the butter is foaming, add a large spoonful of potato mixture into a corner of the pan and spread it out slightly to form a pancake. Keep adding mixture to the pan in spoonfuls - you should be able to fit about 3 medium pancakes in the pan at a time. Cook for 2-3 minutes on each side, or until golden and crisp. Drain on paper towel and keep warm in a low oven while you continue making pancakes with the rest of the mixture, adding more oil and butter to the pan with each batch.

Reheat the mushroom sauce. Serve the hot pancakes topped with the mushroom sauce, a good sprinkle of parsley and a dollop of sour cream.

SERVES 4

MUSHROOM SAUCE

- 25 g (1 oz) butter
- 1 tablespoon olive oil
- 1 small onion, finely chopped
- 500 g (1 lb 2 oz) slippery jack or pine mushrooms, or other mushrooms, sliced
- 1-2 teaspoons plain (all-purpose) flour
- 125 ml (4 fl oz/½ cup) chicken or vegetable stock (homemade if possible)
- 125 ml (4 fl oz/½ cup) cream
- salt and pepper

POTATO PANCAKES

- 500 g (1 lb 2 oz) kipfler or other waxy potatoes
- 1 small onion
- 1 egg
- 1 tablespoon plain (all-purpose) flour
- salt and pepper
- olive oil
- butter
- chopped parsley
- sour cream

'"Na zdrowie i smacznego!" (Here's to good health and good taste!)'

'We've been picking mushrooms since we came to Australia … The house is filled with the smell of mushrooms.'

What a great combination roast duck, apples and fragrant marjoram is. Bohdan's recipe involves stuffing the duck with sliced apple and seasoning it with the marjoram, salt and pepper, then standing it in the refrigerator overnight (ideally) for the crispiest skin. Before roasting, the duck is brushed with a mix of oil and honey for a beautifully golden finish. Alongside is a simple dish of apples, cranberries and *krupnik*, which is a Polish honey liqueur.

DUCK WITH APPLES, MARJORAM AND CRANBERRIES

from Bohdan Szymczak

Rinse the duck and pat it dry. Lay it on a board with the drumsticks pointing up. Cut a small slit through the skin at the base of each breast and push the ends of the drumsticks into the slits. This gives a neat presentation when the duck is roasted.

Lightly prick the duck through the skin all over to help release some of the fat during cooking. Cut off the parson's nose (the pointed tail tip), as it contains oil glands that can alter the taste of the dish. Season the duck inside and out with salt, pepper and 1 teaspoon of the dried marjoram.

Quarter, core and slice 1 apple and combine it in a bowl with the orange zest and 1 teaspoon of the dried marjoram. Mix well, then stuff inside the duck. Place the duck on a tray or plate and refrigerate uncovered for at least 2 hours, or overnight.

Remove the duck from the refrigerator 30 minutes before roasting.

Preheat the oven to 220°C (420°F/Gas 7). Place the duck on a rack set above a roasting tray. Combine the olive oil and honey in a small bowl and brush it all over the duck. Roast the duck for 20-25 minutes, or until the skin is starting to brown, then reduce the temperature to 180°C (350°F/Gas 4) and roast for another 1½ hours. Every 20-30 minutes, baste the duck with the juices that have dripped into the tray.

Remove the duck from the oven and rest in a warm place for 10-15 minutes.

While the duck is resting, peel, quarter and core the remaining apples and cut them into wedges. Heat a large frying pan over medium-high heat. Add the apples and toss for 1-2 minutes, then add the sugar and season with salt and pepper to taste. Continue tossing for 5 minutes or until golden and caramelised. Add the remaining 1 teaspoon of dried marjoram and the butter and toss well, then add the cranberries, apricots, walnuts, *krupnik* (if using) and fresh marjoram (if using). Toss to combine, then remove from the heat.

Cut the duck into pieces and serve with the caramelised apples.

SERVES 4

1 duck weighing 1.8-2 kg	100 g (3½ oz) frozen
salt and freshly ground	cranberries, or 50 g (1¾ oz)
black pepper	dried cranberries soaked
3 teaspoons dried marjoram	for a few hours
3 granny smith apples	1 tablespoon finely chopped
(or a mixture of red and	dried apricots
green apples)	1 tablespoon chopped toasted
grated zest of 1 small orange	walnuts, briefly soaked
2 tablespoons light olive oil	in ½ tablespoon *krupnik*
1 tablespoon honey	if using
1 tablespoon sugar	1 tablespoon *krupnik* (optional)
3 teaspoons butter	2 teaspoons fresh marjoram
	leaves (optional)

The smell of *bigos* cooking is enough to make any homesick Pole weep with delight. The stew of pork, sausage, sauerkraut, fresh cabbage, mushrooms and prunes is traditionally served with rye bread, and can also be served with mashed or steamed potatoes. This is Judyta's mother's recipe and, like many stews, Judyta says it tastes even better when reheated the next day.

BIGOS

Hunter's Stew

from Judyta Slupnicki

Put the sauerkraut in a large saucepan, cover with a little water and place over medium heat. Simmer for 20 minutes, then drain and set aside.

Heat 1 tablespoon of the fat or oil in a pot over high heat. Add the pork neck and onion and cook, stirring, until browned. Add the bay leaves, sausage, bacon or speck, fresh mushrooms, allspice and a good dose of pepper. Cook, stirring, for 1–2 minutes. Reduce the heat to medium, add the sauerkraut and cook for 30 minutes, stirring regularly to make sure the mixture isn't sticking to the bottom of the pot.

Heat the remaining fat or oil in a small saucepan and add the tomato paste. Cook, stirring, for 1 minute, then add the flour and cook for another 1–2 minutes. Gradually pour in the stock, stirring until smooth and thick. Strain into the stew and add the wine. Stir well and simmer for another 30 minutes.

Meanwhile, drain the porcini mushrooms, reserving their water. Combine the savoy cabbage, garlic, porcini and 250 ml (8½ fl oz/1 cup) of the mushroom water (top up with fresh water if needed) in the saucepan used for the sauerkraut. Place over medium heat and cook for 15 minutes, or until the cabbage is wilted.

Stir the cabbage and prunes into the stew. Put the lid on slightly ajar, then reduce the heat to as low as possible and cook for 2 hours, stirring occasionally.

Taste the stew for seasoning and adjust if needed. Serve sprinkled with parsley.

SERVES 6

4 cups roughly chopped sauerkraut

3 tablespoons pork or duck fat, or oil

250 g (9 oz) pork neck, cut into 2 cm (¾ in) cubes

1 onion, finely chopped

4 bay leaves

200 g (7 oz) mixed Polish sausage (or sausage ends), chopped

60 ml (2 oz) smoked bacon or speck, chopped

100 g (3½ oz) mushrooms, halved and sliced

1 teaspoon ground allspice

black pepper

5 tablespoons tomato paste (concentrated puree)

2 tablespoons plain (all-purpose) flour

500 ml (17 fl oz/2 cups) beef stock

3 tablespoons red wine

10 g (¼ oz) dried porcini mushrooms, soaked in water for 30 minutes

½ medium savoy cabbage, shredded

2 garlic cloves, finely chopped

8 prunes, pitted and chopped

chopped parsley to serve

'It's hard to say what Polish food is ... I'd say it's that warm bear hug you want at the end of the day.'

'In Poland you have a shot of vodka with a slice of rye bread on hand – you smell the bread to help ease the pain.'

A gorgeous easy dish for warm weather. Bella remembers 'pink soup' as she was growing up, with its clean tastes of beetroot, cucumber, yoghurt and lemon, finished with sour cream, chives and the sharp lift of freshly grated horseradish. If you can't find fresh horseradish, seek out a good-quality jarred horseradish from a European deli and add a little to taste when blending the soup.

CHLODNIK

Chilled Beetroot Soup

from Bella Jakubiak

Combine the beetroot, potato and stock in a saucepan and place over medium heat. Cook until the vegetables are tender. Pour into a bowl and refrigerate until chilled.

Tip the chilled beetroot mixture into a blender and add the shallots, cucumber and yoghurt. Blend until smooth, then add lemon juice, salt and pepper to taste. If desired you can thin the soup with a little water.

Pour into bowls and add a dollop of crème fraîche or sour cream. Sprinkle with chives and finely grate horseradish over the top.

SERVES 4

300 g (10½ oz) beetroot, peeled and cut into 1 cm (½ in) slices	1 small Lebanese cucumber, chopped
100 g (3½ oz) potato, peeled and cut into 2 cm (¾ in) slices	250 ml (8½ fl oz/1 cup) natural yoghurt
500 ml (17 fl oz/2 cups) vegetable stock	juice of ½–1 lemon
2 small shallots, roughly chopped	salt and white pepper
	crème fraîche or sour cream
	1½ tablespoons finely snipped chives
	1–2 cm (½–¾ in) piece of horseradish

The secret to this luscious cake is the special continental-style cottage cheese, which has a slightly grainy texture and a light tang. Together with orange zest and sultanas, the cake is bright, sweet and creamy at the same time, and the lattice top is so pretty. The whole effect is quite show-stopping.

SERNIK KRAKOWSKI

Krakow-style Cheesecake

from Ryszard Janczewski

Butter the base of a 24 cm (9½ in) springform cake tin and line it with baking paper. To make the pastry, combine the butter and sugar in a bowl and cream together with a wooden spoon or with electric beaters. Sift in the flour and use your hands to mix to a dough. Lightly flour a work surface and roll out two-thirds of the dough to a circle the size of the base of your tin. Lay it inside the tin, leaving the sides free of pastry, and chill in the refrigerator for 30 minutes.

Meanwhile, for the lattice top, mix the egg into the remaining dough to make a richer pastry. Mix well and shape into a ball. Cover in plastic wrap and refrigerate until needed.

Preheat the oven to 180°C (350°F/Gas 4). Prick the pastry base with a fork and bake for 12–15 minutes, or until lightly golden. Set aside to cool while you make the filling.

Mix the cheese with half the sugar in a bowl. Add the sour cream, orange zest and sultanas and stir well. Beat the whole eggs, egg yolks and remaining sugar in a separate bowl, then fold into the cheese mixture. Fold in the flour.

Roll out the reserved pastry to about 5 mm thick. Cut into thin strips.

Spoon the cheese mixture on top of the pastry base and smooth out the top. Arrange parallel strips of pastry across the surface, then more strips crosswise to make a lattice pattern. Lightly beat an egg and brush it over the lattice. Bake the cheesecake for 30–40 minutes, or until the lattice is golden and the filling is set.

SERVES 10-12

PASTRY

200 g (7 oz) unsalted butter, softened
100 g (3½ oz) caster sugar (or you can use half vanilla sugar)
300 g (10½ oz/2 cups) plain (all-purpose) flour
1 egg, plus 1 egg for brushing

FILLING

750 g (1 lb 11 oz) continental-style cottage cheese or quark (or substitute ricotta, well drained)
150 g (5½ oz) caster sugar
75 g (2¾ oz) sour cream
grated zest of ½ orange
75 g (2¾ oz) sultanas (golden raisins)
3 eggs plus 2 egg yolks
50 g (1¾ oz/⅓ cup) plain (all-purpose) flour

'I love the Polish Easter and Christmas – lots of vodka and a loud family!'

One of the things I find endlessly fascinating about food is that each cuisine is an edible snapshot of history. In Portugal the country's fortunes changed with two simple ingredients – cod, caught in the cold waters off Scandinavia, and salt. When combined these allowed cod to be preserved, which in turn fuelled a great nation of explorers who set off for new lands, opening trade routes and discovering new foods as they went. The Portuguese diaspora soon stretched into colonies in Angola and Mozambique in Africa, the Canary Islands off the African coast, the trading port of Goa in India, and Brazil in South America. And it all started with the beloved salted cod or *bacalhau,* which resembles a thick, smelly, salt-crusted parchment.

My friend Fatima has been entranced by this fish all her life – after it's been chopped into large chunks and soaked for twenty-four hours, you can start to see its magic too. Here is a perfectly white fish that flakes beautifully and can be used in a vast range of recipes. Fatima also adores the large, plump Portuguese sardines with their thick skins and decent layer of fat. She buries her sardines (bought frozen from Portuguese grocery stores) under rock salt in a baking dish and bakes them in the oven; once cooked she slides their skins off like a wetsuit and dresses the fillets with slivers of roasted capsicum, parsley and the lovely thick, green olive oil of Portugal. What a great Portuguese combination.

Actually the smell of sardines cooking over charcoal is my lasting memory of the country. In every small town terracotta braziers were smoking as this favourite fish was being simply grilled to accompany pale green Portuguese wine (*vinho verde*).

While the coastline bordering the Atlantic and Mediterranean is famous for great seafood dishes, inland the pig rules. People raise chickens and sheep as well but the pig is fundamental to much of the food and to village life. Villages spend time during winter slaughtering pigs and making numerous smallgoods, including the garlic- and paprika-laced *chouriço* sausage and the blood sausage *morcilla.*

Another edible slice of history is the now-familiar Portuguese chicken. It is hard not to love this flattened, marinated chicken, which is served with the chilli-spiked *piri piri* sauce – a recipe developed in Angola when it was a Portuguese colony. The dish became a big hit in Portugal and South Africa and is now making its way around the world like those early explorers.

Another familiar food from Portugal is the *pasteis de nata,* or custard tart. Like many popular desserts it is made largely from eggs and sugar, which create a creamy and luscious filling for crisp golden pastry. What a great gift to the world!

ESSENTIAL FLAVOURS

BACALHAU

Cod that has been dried then preserved in salt. It is said that in Portuguese cooking there is a different dish using *bacalhau* for every day of the year. It needs to be soaked for 24 hours in several changes of water before using – this reconstitutes the fish and removes excess salt.

BAY LEAVES

They can be bought as whole dried leaves or ground. Bay leaves are one of the few herbs that don't lose their flavour when dried, rather the flavour becomes more intense.

CHOURIÇO

A smoked pork sausage that is flavoured with garlic and paprika, which gives it a rich, red colour. *Chouriço* can be bought fresh or dried. One traditional way of heating and serving it is in an *asador* (a terracotta cooking dish). The *chouriço* sits in the *asador* on a rack and a type of Portuguese grappa is poured beneath it and set alight. This gives a wonderful smoky flavour to the sausage.

PAPRIKA

Known as *colorau* in Portuguese, this is without doubt the most widely used spice in Portuguese cooking. A sweet, smoked paprika is commonly used rather than a hot version.

QUINCE PASTE

A staple in every home and often served with a mild cheese. Children eat it on sandwiches and it is regarded by some as the Portuguese equivalent to Vegemite.

ROCK SALT

This salt is a larger crystal than regular salt and is widely used – chicken and beef are coated with rock salt before hitting the barbie and sardines are covered in it and baked.

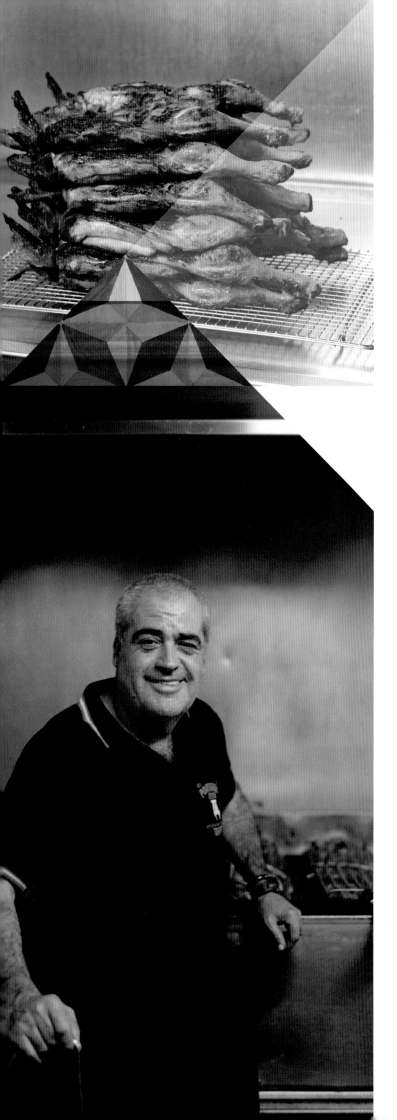

A gorgeous peasant recipe for lamb, which becomes incredibly tender after its bath in wine and paprika followed by slow cooking. Find the right pot and the work is done – it marinates, it cooks and you eat. What could be simpler? Serve with new potatoes boiled in their skins.

CHANFANA

from Cidalia Rendeiro

Scatter some of the onion in the base of a large casserole pot, followed by some garlic and a layer of lamb chunks. Sprinkle with rock salt, white pepper, a torn bay leaf and 1 teaspoon of paprika. Repeat the layers until all the lamb is used. Pour in red wine to cover the lamb. Cover the pot and leave to marinate for at least 4 hours, unrefrigerated.

Preheat the oven to 200°C (400°F/Gas 6). Check the wine level – you may need to top it up as the meat soaks some up while marinating. Pour over the olive oil and place the stems of parsley on top. Cover with a tight-fitting lid or foil, making sure the pot is well sealed around the edges. Cook for about 45 minutes (or until you can smell the wonderful aroma), then reduce the heat to 180°C (350°F/Gas 4) and cook for another 2¼ hours.

SERVES 6-8

1 large onion, finely chopped	white pepper
1 large head of garlic, cloves separated, peeled and bruised	dried bay leaves
	sweet paprika
	2 bottles red wine (or enough to cover the meat)
3 kg (6 lb 10 oz) lamb shoulder, trimmed of excess fat, cut into large chunks	80 ml (2½ fl oz/⅓ cup) olive oil
rock salt	1 bunch flat-leaf (Italian) parsley

This recipe is a derivation of the famous one from Angola, where Luis' grandmother devised a marinade and sauce that would later travel the world. Angola was of course a colony of Portugal and many Portuguese families were encouraged to settle there. The Fernandez family was one.

'As you read a recipe, learn to visualise how it will look and taste. Don't be afraid to change the ingredients according to your taste.'

CHARCOAL CHICKEN WITH PIRI PIRI SAUCE

from Luis Fernandez

Trim the chicken of excess fat. Use a sharp knife or kitchen scissors to cut the chicken through the breastbone. Open the chicken out, turn over and flatten it by pressing down on the backbone. Make a small cut under each wing to help the chicken flatten further. Make several slashes in the flesh with a sharp knife to allow the flavours of the marinade to get in and the fat to drain out. Prick the chicken all over with a fork.

Combine the garlic, lemon juice, bay leaf powder, paprika, whisky and butter, mixing well. Brush the chicken on both sides with the mixture and sprinkle with rock salt. Cover and marinate in the refrigerator for 30–45 minutes.

Mix the *piri piri* ingredients into a thickish sauce.

Cook the chicken on a hot charcoal barbecue (grill), turning frequently and basting continuously with the leftover marinade, for 30 minutes or until golden brown. Cut the chicken into pieces and brush with the *piri piri* sauce.

SERVES 6

1 large chicken
8 garlic cloves, crushed
juice of 2 lemons
1 teaspoon bay leaf powder
2 teaspoons sweet paprika
80 ml (2½ fl oz / ⅓ cup) scotch whisky
2 tablespoons butter, softened
rock salt

PIRI PIRI SAUCE

10-12 small red chillies, finely chopped (or less to taste)
pinch of salt
juice of ½ lemon
100 ml (3½ fl oz) olive oil
2 tablespoons garlic powder (fresh garlic makes the sauce too runny)

A beautiful combination of thick white fish, little potatoes and a crunchy topping of cornbread (*broa*) crumbs. (This dense bread is available from Portuguese bakeries.) Perfect with a glass of mellow Portuguese red wine! Begin soaking the *bacalhau* the day before.

BACALHAU COM BROA

from Fatima Barroso

Cover the *bacalhau* with water and soak for 24 hours, changing the water 3 times.

Drain the fish, place it in a saucepan and cover with milk. Add the red onion, bay leaves, whole garlic and peppercorns. Simmer gently for 20 minutes.

Meanwhile, roast the potatoes with olive oil and salt in a hot oven until golden brown. At the same time roast the strips of capsicum.

Heat more olive oil in a heavy-based saucepan and fry the sliced onion over high heat until browned. Reduce the heat and cook gently until soft and nearly caramelised.

Finely crumble the cornbread into a bowl and mix with the chopped garlic, parsley and egg yolks. Remove the fish from the milk (the milk can be used on another occasion to make a béchamel sauce). Remove the skin and bones and break the fish into chunks.

Preheat the oven to 180°C (350°F/Gas 4). Place the roasted potatoes on a board and smash each one with your fist to flatten them. Lay them in a baking dish and cover with the fish chunks, followed by the soft onions and the breadcrumb mixture. Drizzle with olive oil and season with black pepper. Stud with olives and scatter with strips of roasted capsicum. Bake for 20-30 minutes. Drizzle with more olive oil before serving.

SERVES 6

600 g (1 lb 5 oz) thick *bacalhau* fillet	salt
milk	1 red capsicum (bell pepper), cut into thin strips
½ red onion, cut into chunks	4 brown onions, finely sliced
3 dried bay leaves	4 thick slices of cornbread
3 garlic cloves, 2 left whole, 1 chopped	4 flat-leaf (Italian) parsley stalks, leaves picked and chopped
1 teaspoon peppercorns	3 egg yolks
1 kg (2 lb 3 oz) small new potatoes	¾ cup pitted black olives (Portuguese if possible)
olive oil	

'Olive oil, bread and wine are essential on any table.'

This is a wonderful salad with its finely sliced dark green leaves, crunchy breadcrumbs, pine nuts, and beans for colour and texture. Great on its own or with grilled meat – and Andrea says it's terrific with a classic Aussie barbecue!

A luscious dessert - as you'd imagine with 12 eggs and the fragrances of cinnamon, lemon and vanilla. The lovely thing about these flans is that they are velvety, but firm. They look so wonderful when you turn them out of the little ramekins and their caramel topping runs down the sides. Make ahead of time for dinner parties. These are impressive but so easy.

MIGAS

from Andrea de Souza

CARAMEL FLAN

from John De Almeida

Wash the kale and pat dry. Place the leaves on top of each other and roll up into a tight cylinder. Use a sharp knife to shred the leaves very, very finely.

Heat the oil in a frying pan. Throw in the garlic and fry briefly to flavour the oil, then remove. Add the breadcrumbs and fry until golden brown. Add the kale, pine nuts and black-eyed beans and toss until heated through. Season with salt and pepper.

SERVES 6

1 bunch kale (Chinese broccoli is a good substitute), leaves only	Portuguese cornbread or a good sourdough)
3 tablespoons olive oil	½ cup pine nuts
1 garlic clove, cut in half	¾ cup cooked black-eyed beans
½ cup fresh breadcrumbs (preferably from	salt and pepper

To make the caramel, pour the water into a heavy-based saucepan and add the sugar, pouring it into the centre of the water so it doesn't touch the sides of the pan. Cook over medium heat for 10 minutes without stirring. The caramel will slowly colour from blonde to a rich, dark brunette. Pour into ramekins to set.

To make the custard, put the sugar in a bowl and whisk in the eggs one at a time until the mixture is slightly frothy.

Put the milk, cinnamon, lemon and vanilla in a saucepan and bring to the boil, then remove from the heat and stir into the egg mixture, being careful not to over-stir.

Preheat the oven to 150°C (300°F/Gas 2). Strain the mixture into a jug, then pour into each ramekin, swirling as you do so the toffee doesn't crack in one spot. Place the ramekins in an ovenproof dish and fill the dish with water to halfway up the ramekins.

Bake for 30 minutes, turning the dish around after 15 minutes so the flans cook evenly. Rest for 30 minutes before running a knife around the edges of the ramekins and turning the flans onto serving plates.

MAKES 6-8 FLANS

CARAMEL	CUSTARD
50-75 ml (2-2½ fl oz) water	200 g (7 oz) sugar
200 g (7 oz) sugar	12 eggs
	1 litre (34 fl oz/4 cups) milk
	1 cinnamon stick
	1 strip of lemon rind
	1 teaspoon vanilla extract

'Cook what you feel like eating – it will turn out to be delicious.'

When I think of Singapore, I think of spicy food being cooked and eaten in warm tropical air – wafts of *rempah* (spice paste) cooking; fish grilling; noodles being stir-fried; satay sticks being fanned over charcoal ... This to me is heaven. Even now that air conditioning has moved a lot of the hawker centres (groups of small food stalls) inside, food and the quest for delicious specialities remain a national obsession.

Every taxi driver is a culinary expert – you can't say that about most countries but Singapore is unique. It started as a fishing village and morphed into one of Asia's most dynamic cities, a centre for some of the best food in Southeast Asia. Settlers and traders from China, India and Malaysia all brought their own cuisines to Singapore, which have flourished. A distinctly new cuisine has developed as well called Peranakan or Nyonya. This was the result of local Malay women marrying Chinese merchants and labourers – the fusion of Chinese Hokkien ingredients and Malay flavourings has resulted in hot and spicy dishes that often start with a *rempah* made from chilli, shallots, lemongrass, candlenuts, turmeric and *belachan* (shrimp paste).

My friend Helina remembers the days when the laksa man would either cycle or walk the streets, ready to assemble noodles, stock, coconut milk and more into a tasty dish served right at her door. She also recalls evenings watching Chinese operas while munching on the classic Singaporean salad called *rojak* (crunchy fruit and vegetables in a salty–sweet dressing sprinkled with peanuts); family celebrations with chicken rice (delicate poached chicken served with rice cooked in stock) as the centrepiece; and, in the days before blenders, mounds of aromatic herbs and spices being pounded before each meal.

As well as *rojak*, Singapore has many other distinctive dishes, including *otak-otak*, which is fish cooked with coconut milk, chilli paste, galangal and herbs then wrapped in a banana leaf; *poh pia*, which are soft spring rolls; fish-head curry, which is often eaten from a banana leaf; and the renowned Singapore chilli crab, which is stir-fried with tomato sauce, soy sauce, sugar and, of course, plenty of chilli.

Tropical fruit is a great way to finish a Singaporean banquet but this food-obsessed country has many of its own dessert recipes as well, including *bubur cha-cha*, a colourful mix of sago, sweet potato, sometimes black-eyed beans, tropical fruit and coconut milk.

ESSENTIAL FLAVOURS

CHILLI
Large or small but usually red, chillies are an integral ingredient of most dishes including Singapore chilli crab.

PANDAN LEAF
Pandan leaves are used in both savoury and sweet dishes. They are often put into the pot when rice is cooked, to perfume it.

SHRIMP PASTE
Known as *belachan*, this has an awful smell but once roasted the odour fades and the paste adds a beautiful depth of flavour to many dishes. It is sold as a pressed block.

To use, cut a small amount from the block, wrap it in foil and place in a hot oven or hold over a flame for a minute or two using tongs. Then remove from the heat and once it is cool, crumble and add to your dish.

TOMATO SAUCE
Somewhat surprisingly, this is used for richness and sweetness in sauces when no further chilli is desired. It's an integral part of the sauce used to make Singapore chilli crab.

This is a classic Singaporean dish of delicately poached chicken infused with ginger, which is accompanied by rice cooked in chicken stock, a bowl of the hot stock itself, and various sauces. Tiffany makes quick chilli and ginger sauces and also serves this with *kecap manis* and cucumber.

HAINANESE CHICKEN RICE

from Tiffany Wong

Rub the inside of the chicken with the rice wine and half the soy sauce. Pound the garlic, half the ginger and half the spring onion to a paste in a mortar (or blend in a food processor). Rub the paste inside the chicken.

Bring a large pot of water to the boil, then turn off the heat and add the chicken, remaining ginger and spring onion. Cover with a lid and leave to stand in the water for 1 hour. After the first 5 minutes, lift the chicken out and drain the water from its cavity, then return to the water. Repeat 2 or 3 times during the hour (this ensures that there's enough hot water inside the chicken to cook it through). After 30 minutes, bring the water back to almost boiling then turn the heat off again. Cooking the chicken without boiling it ensures it is tender and juicy. Remove the chicken from the water. Combine the remaining soy sauce with the sesame oil and salt and rub into the chicken. Leave to cool. To make the stock, add the chicken carcasses, ginger and spring onions to the pot of water and boil for 1-2 hours, until the stock has a strong chicken flavour. Strain the stock through muslin (cheesecloth).

Meanwhile, make the chilli sauce. Pound the chilli, garlic and ginger to a paste in a mortar (or blend in a food processor). Add ½ tablespoon of chicken stock and lime juice and salt to taste.

To make the ginger sauce, pound the ginger and garlic to a paste in a mortar (or blend in a food processor) and add the lime juice, salt and 2 tablespoons of chicken stock.

To make the chicken rice, heat the chicken fat in a wok until it releases oil, then add the ginger and garlic and fry until golden. Discard any solid pieces of fat. Add the rice and salt and stir-fry briskly for 1-2 minutes. Transfer the rice to a saucepan or rice cooker and add 3½ cups (875 ml/41 fl oz) of

chicken stock and the pandan leaves if using. Cover with a lid and cook until the stock is absorbed (you may need to add a little more stock towards the end if the rice seems dry).

To serve, slice the chicken into bite-sized pieces. Reheat the remaining chicken stock and ladle into small serving bowls, garnishing with sliced spring onion or blanched shredded cabbage. Serve the stock alongside the chicken, rice, chilli sauce, ginger sauce, *kecap manis* and cucumber.

SERVES 6

CHICKEN

- 1 very fresh chicken (preferably free-range), fat trimmed and reserved for the rice
- 1 tablespoon Chinese rice wine
- 2 tablespoons light soy sauce
- 1 garlic clove, roughly chopped
- 6 slices of ginger
- 2 spring onions (scallions), roughly chopped
- 1 teaspoon sesame oil
- ½ teaspoon salt

STOCK

- 1 kg (2 lb 3 oz) chicken carcasses (or legs or wings)
- 3 slices of ginger
- 2 spring onions (scallions)

CHILLI SAUCE

- 10 long red chillies, seeded and roughly chopped
- 1-2 garlic cloves, roughly chopped
- 5 cm (2 in) piece of ginger, roughly chopped
- lime juice
- salt

GINGER SAUCE

- 75 g (2¾ oz) ginger, roughly chopped
- 6 garlic cloves, roughly chopped
- ½ tablespoon lime juice
- ½ teaspoon salt

RICE

- fat from the chicken (or peanut oil as a healthier alternative)
- 2-3 cm (¾-1¼ in) piece of ginger, grated
- 3-4 garlic cloves, finely chopped
- 3 cups long-grain rice, rinsed and well drained
- 1-2 teaspoons salt
- 2 pandan leaves, each tied in a knot (optional)

TO SERVE

- sliced spring onion or blanched shredded cabbage
- *kecap manis*
- sliced cucumber

Sweetened with many shallots, this tangy tamarind-based sauce is a perfect match for thick cutlets of oily fish such as mackerel. The fish is dusted in turmeric-laced flour then fried and added to the sauce. A wonderful dish that is perfect as a main dish or shared as part of a banquet.

ASSAM FISH

Tamarind Fish

from Chui Lee Luk

Pound the *rempah* ingredients to a fine paste in a mortar, or blend in a food processor.

Combine the tamarind pulp and water and leave to soften, then strain.

Coat the fish pieces in flour mixed with a little turmeric. Heat some oil in a frying pan and fry the fish pieces until lightly coloured. Set aside.

Heat a little more oil in a heavy-based saucepan and fry the *rempah* paste over high heat until fragrant. Add the lemongrass, tomato, chillies and tamarind water and bring to the boil. Season to taste with sugar and salt – the flavour should be a mix of hot, sweet, sour and salty. Add the fried fish and simmer over low heat for 5 minutes.

SERVES 2

REMPAH (SPICE PASTE)

10 shallots
2 long red chillies
½ head of garlic, peeled
1.5 cm (½ in) piece of young ginger
½ teaspoon shrimp paste, roasted

TAMARIND FISH

1½ tablespoons tamarind pulp
500 ml (17 fl oz/2 cups) water
400–500 g (1 lb 2 oz) thick Spanish mackerel cutlets (or other strong-flavoured oily fish)

plain (all-purpose) flour
turmeric
oil
1 lemongrass stalk, bruised
2 tomatoes, peeled, seeded and quartered
2 long red chillies, halved lengthwise, seeded
2 long green chillies, halved lengthwise, seeded
sugar
salt

This is the freshest tasting salad - crunchy fruit and vegetables with fried tofu in a sweetly sticky, slightly sour dressing, sprinkled with roasted peanuts. It includes some unusual ingredients, but they can be found at Asian grocers. Yam bean (also called *jicama*) is a pale brown tuber with crisp white, slightly sweet flesh. Water spinach (called *kang kong* in Malay but common throughout Asia) is a crunchy, hollow-stemmed green with long pointed leaves. Fried dough sticks are deep-fried strips of unsweetened dough and are also known as Chinese doughnuts or crispy crullers. Serve this salad with bamboo skewers, as done in Singapore.

'Singaporeans greet each other with: "Have you eaten rice today?"'

ROJAK

from Helina Lee

To make the dressing, soak the tamarind pulp in a little water until soft. Strain it into a large bowl - it should be a thick puree. Add the remaining dressing ingredients and mix well to a thick sauce consistency. Taste to see if you have added enough chilli and palm sugar.

Blanch the bean sprouts for 10 seconds in boiling water. Remove with a slotted spoon and leave to drain. Repeat with the water spinach. Drain and roughly cut.

Place the tofu puffs and dough stick under a griller or in a hot oven for a few minutes to crisp up. Leave to cool, then cut into bite-sized pieces.

Add the sliced fruit and vegetables to the dressing along with the bean sprouts, water spinach, tofu and dough stick. Mix well, coating everything in the dressing. Spoon into serving bowls and scatter with the peanuts.

SERVES 4

DRESSING

2 tablespoons tamarind pulp
1-2 teaspoons crushed red chilli (small or long chillies depending on desired heat)
1 tablespoon shrimp paste from a block (*belachan*), roasted
2 tablespoons shrimp paste from a jar
2-3 tablespoons grated palm sugar (jaggery)
juice of ½ lemon

SALAD

handful of bean sprouts
handful of water spinach, ends trimmed
2 large fried tofu puffs
1 fried dough stick
handful of peeled, sliced green mango
handful of peeled, sliced pineapple
handful of peeled, sliced yam bean (*jicama*)
handful of sliced cucumber
½ cup roughly crushed roasted peanuts

A whole crab, preferably a mud crab, is served in a thick, sweetish tomato sauce warmed by chilli. Traditionally it's served with triangles of dry white toast but, whatever the accompaniment, eating it with your hands is a must!

SINGAPORE CHILLI CRAB

from Alex Lee

Put the crab to sleep by freezing for 1–2 hours. Remove the crab's top shell (retain for garnish if you like) then chop the crab into quarters. Crack the claws to allow the flavours to get in. Wash the pieces well.

Blend the onion and chilli to a puree in a food processor.

Heat the oil in a wok and add the onion and chilli puree and the shrimp paste and fry until most of the liquid evaporates. Add the vinegar, tomato paste, purée and sauce, soy sauce, sugar and salt and mix through. Add the crab and cook over high heat until the shells turn red. Add the cornflour or potato starch followed by the egg and gently stir through to thicken the sauce. Garnish with coriander.

SERVES 2

1 large mud crab	2 tablespoons tomato sauce
2 onions, roughly chopped	80 ml (2½ fl oz/⅓ cup)
8 small red chillies	light soy sauce
125 ml (4 fl oz/½ cup) oil	75 g (2¾ oz/⅓ cup) sugar
thumb-sized piece of	½ teaspoon salt
shrimp paste	¼ teaspoon cornflour
½ tablespoon white vinegar	(cornstarch) or potato
1 tablespoon tomato paste	starch, mixed with 125 ml
(concentrated puree)	(4 fl oz/½ cup) water
400 ml (13½ fl oz) tomato puree	1 egg
	coriander (cilantro) leaves

'To eat well means to have lots of wealth.'

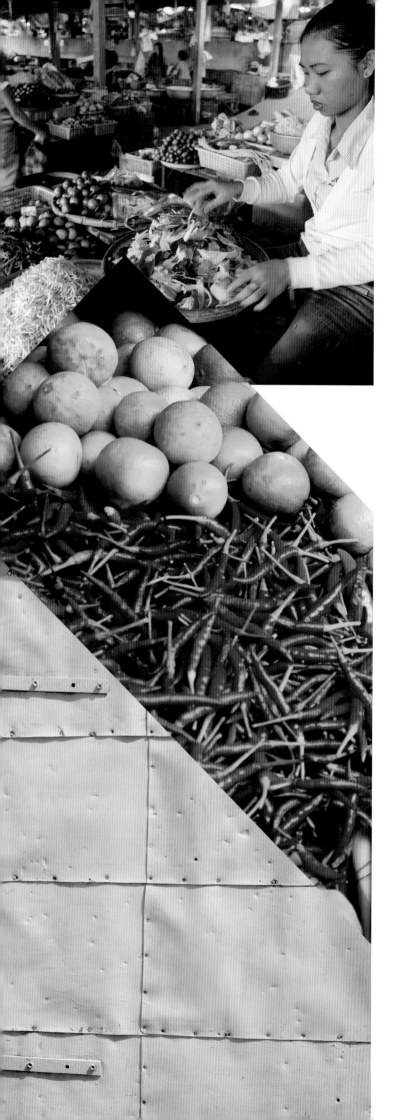

Ikan bilis, or dried anchovies, are a popular snack. This dish of *ikan bilis* with peanuts and chilli paste is just the thing to have with a cold Tiger beer (Singapore's local brew) and the salty flavours make a great prelude to a meal. It can also be served with the famous *nasi lemak* (see page 221).

FRIED IKAN BILIS AND PEANUTS

from Helina Lee

Dry-fry 300 g (10½ oz) of *ikan bilis* and the peanuts in a large, heavy-based frying pan over low heat for 30 minutes. Remove from the pan and leave to cool.

Pound the extra *ikan bilis* to a powder in a mortar. Add the remaining ingredients other than the oil and pound to a paste (or you can use a food processor).

Heat a little oil in the frying pan and fry the paste until fragrant, then mix in the *ikan bilis* and peanuts, stirring well to coat. Cool and store in an airtight container.

MAKES 2 CUPS

300 g (10½ oz) *ikan bilis*,
 plus 2 tablespoons extra
200 g (7 oz) raw peanuts
 with skins on
1 onion, chopped

2–3 garlic cloves
small red chillies to taste
8 candlenuts
1 tablespoon chilli powder
oil

This dessert is the most colourful mix of tastes and textures - a perfect finish to a flavoursome meal. There are many versions and this recipe includes sago, sweet potato and taro. Taro are brown-skinned tubers covered in rough ridges - their flesh comes in various colours but is often white flecked with purple. You can find them at Asian grocery stores.

BUBUR CHA-CHA

from Chee Ong

Put the palm sugar, water and pandan leaf in a saucepan and bring to the boil, stirring until the sugar dissolves. Add the taro and sweet potato and simmer until just soft. Leave to cool then chill in the refrigerator.

Boil the sago in plenty of water until soft, then drain and rinse in cold water. Tip into a bowl, fill with cold water and set aside.

To make the coconut soup, place the palm sugar, half of the coconut water and the pandan leaf in a saucepan and boil until lightly caramelised. Remove from the heat while you pour in the remaining coconut water. Return to the heat and simmer for 1 minute. Turn off the heat and stir in the coconut cream and salt. Leave to cool, then chill.

To make the coconut crisps, preheat the oven to 150°C (300°F/Gas 2). Shave thin slices of coconut with a knife. Place the coconut on an oven tray and bake for around 1 hour, until light golden and dry. Leave to cool.

To serve, put pieces of taro and sweet potato into bowls. Scatter with sago and spoon over a little coconut soup. Garnish with coconut chips.

SERVES 4-6

½ cup grated light palm sugar (jaggery)
750 ml (25½ fl oz/3 cups) water
1 pandan leaf, tied in a knot
200 g (7 oz) taro, peeled and cubed
200 g (7 oz) sweet potato, peeled and cubed
75 g (2¾ oz) large coloured sago

COCONUT SOUP

½ cup grated light palm sugar (jaggery)
125 ml (4 fl oz/½ cup) water from the coconut (below)
1 pandan leaf, tied in a knot
750 ml (25½ fl oz/3 cups) coconut cream
pinch of salt

COCONUT CRISPS

1 coconut, cracked and peeled

'Street food in Singapore – It's cheap! It's hot! It's *shiok* (delicious)!'

It's as if the whole history of South Africa – the 'rainbow nation' – is written in its food. The marvellous cuisine brings together the food of the Afrikaners, whose roots are with the Dutch who arrived in the seventeenth century; the richly spiced food of the Cape Malay community; the unique food of the largest Indian population outside the subcontinent; and of course the original food of the African inhabitants.

Indigenous South Africans love their *mielie pap* – made from ground dried white corn cooked with water to a firm porridge, very much like white polenta. It is often served with *umngqusho*, a stew of beans and *samp* (broken dried corn kernels) cooked with chilli and vegetables. 'This is a huge staple for so many people in South Africa,' explains chef Graeme Shapiro. 'It's a mix of protein and starch and makes sense as corn and beans grow together.'

The Portuguese, Dutch, English, French and Germans all brought different influences to South Africa, still evident today. In backyards you'll find the same type of round three-legged cast-iron cooking pots called *potjie* used by the Voortrekkers, the Dutch settlers who ventured into the wild expanse of South Africa's interior in the nineteenth century. The slow-cooked meat and vegetable stew called *potjiekos* is still made by many families, in pots that have been passed down through generations.

Another favourite from settler days is biltong, South Africa's adored dried meat. It has a special place in South African hearts – activities such as watching the rugby or travelling any distance in a car are unthinkable without it. A dried sausage called *droëwors* is also popular.

Cape Malay people originated from Indonesia and India, as well as Malaysia as their name suggests. One Cape Malay woman, Hazel McBride, has her own take on how her ancestors helped to enliven South African cuisine. 'They came in as slaves and servants and worked for the Dutch and the British, and they used spices to boost the meals because the cuisine was so boring!' The stews of Europe met the curries of Asia and dishes like *bobotie* were born, with its spiced meat base and creamy custardy topping; along with other hybrids such as the famous donut-like *koeksisters*, which are fragrant with sweet spices, drenched in syrup and rolled in coconut – a European recipe with flavours of Asia.

The majority of South Africa's Indian population arrived from the 1860s as indentured labourers to work on the sugar plantations of Natal. They brought with them the hot curries of Gujarat and Tamil Nadu, where many of them came from. The street food of Durban on the east coast of South Africa developed from these roots, with unique dishes such as 'bunny chow' – a curry served in a hollowed-out quarter- or half-loaf of white bread. The word 'bunny' is thought to derive from the word '*bannia*', the name of an Indian caste that traded in Durban.

South African desserts are comfort food – plus lovely warm baked puddings with sauce – and their names give you an idea of their Dutch provenance: *armmanspoeding* (poor man's pudding with suet and raisins); *damespoeding* (ladies pudding with currants, jam and brandy); and *jongmans poeding* (young men pudding with candied peel and sultanas). Then there is malva pudding with its marshmallow consistency, and the simple but delicious baked custard in a pastry shell called milk tart. Like much of South African food, these desserts manage to be both familiar and exotic at the same time.

ESSENTIAL FLAVOURS

CURRY POWDER AND GARAM MASALA
While Durban curries are known for being fiery and intense, Cape Malay curries tend to be milder with the use of sweet spices such as cinnamon, nutmeg and cloves. There are a few brands of Cape Malay curry powder available and it is worth tracking one down. Garam masala is also common in South African cooking.

DRIED FRUIT
On the old Afrikaner farms where supplies came in slowly from Europe, dried fruit was a staple, and is still a big feature of South African cooking. Dried apricots are used in the delicious *sosatie* lamb skewers, and raisins and sultanas are used in curries and *bobotie* and to adorn rice dishes. Dried fruit also appears in baked goods from cakes to puddings.

MRS BALL'S CHUTNEY
Mrs Ball's products now travel the world, and are considered an essential accompaniment to virtually all South African curries alongside bananas, coconut and salads called sambals. The chutney comes in a tall jar and is also used in marinades, *bobotie* and the Afrikaner dish *potjiekos*.

TURMERIC
Ground turmeric is found in most South African pantries, being essential in curries and to colour and flavour yellow rice.

This classic dish is like an exotic shepherd's pie with its base of cooked minced meat, but it gets a whole lot more interesting with flavours of ginger, turmeric, garlic, chilli and dried spices. The topping is not potato but a beautifully creamy bechamel layer. *Bobotie* is always served with plenty of accompaniments such as Mrs Ball's Chutney, sliced banana, fresh grated coconut mixed with lime juice, and yellow rice (page 331). Ross also includes recipes for two salads.

BOBOTIE

from Ross Lusted

Put the coriander seeds, cumin seeds and allspice in a mortar and grind to a powder. Add the curry powder, salt, ginger, turmeric, garlic and chillies and pound to a paste.

Break the bread into pieces and pour over 125 ml (4 fl oz/½ cup) of the milk. Leave to soak for about 10 minutes, then strain off the excess milk (you can use the milk in the topping later). Fluff the bread up with a fork.

Heat the oil in a frying pan over medium heat. Add the shallots or onion and sauté for 4–5 minutes until soft. Add the spice paste and fry for another 2 minutes, then add the beef and lamb and stir to break up the lumps. Continue to cook for 7–8 minutes or until browned.

While the meat is cooking, preheat the oven to 160°C (320°F/Gas 3).

Stir the apple, chutney, raisins, lemon juice and bread into the meat. Season with salt and pepper to taste, then remove from the heat. Spoon the mixture into a baking dish.

To make the topping, whisk the eggs with the remaining 200 ml (7 fl oz) of milk, then pour it over the meat. Decorate the top with the bay leaves and bake for 20–25 minutes, or until the topping is golden. Leave the *bobotie* to rest for 10 minutes before serving.

You can make the salads while the *bobotie* is in the oven. To make the tomato and cucumber salad, combine the oil, lime juice, salt and sugar in a small bowl, stirring until the sugar dissolves. Combine the remaining ingredients in a serving bowl, pour over the dressing and toss to combine.

To make the carrot salad, combine the oil, orange juice, salt and sugar in a small bowl, stirring until the sugar dissolves. Combine the remaining ingredients other than the coriander in a serving bowl, pour over the dressing and toss to combine. Scatter with the coriander.

Serve the *bobotie* with the salads, banana and chutney.

SERVES 6

2 teaspoons coriander seeds, toasted
1 teaspoon cumin seeds, toasted
½ teaspoon whole allspice
1 teaspoon curry powder
pinch of salt
2–3 cm (3/¾–1 in) piece of ginger, roughly chopped
3 cm (1 in) piece of fresh turmeric, roughly chopped (or 1 teaspoon ground turmeric)
3 garlic cloves
2 small red or green chillies, sliced
½ long green chilli, seeded and sliced
2 slices of sourdough bread
325 ml milk
2½ tablespoons vegetable oil
6 shallots, sliced, or 2 medium onions, finely chopped
500 g (1 lb 2 oz) minced (ground) beef
500 g (1 lb 2 oz) minced (ground) lamb
1 green apple, peeled, cored and finely chopped
1 tablespoon Mrs Ball's Original Chutney, plus extra for serving
75 g (2¾ oz) raisins, soaked in warm water for 20 minutes, drained
1 tablespoon lemon juice
pepper

2 large eggs
4 bay leaves
lady finger bananas, sliced, to serve

TOMATO AND CUCUMBER SALAD

2 tablespoons vegetable oil
juice of 1 lime
½ teaspoon salt
½ teaspoon brown sugar or grated palm sugar (jaggery)
10 small-medium tomatoes, chopped, or 2 punnets cherry tomatoes, halved
3 shallots, finely chopped
1 Lebanese cucumber, peeled and chopped
1 bunch coriander (cilantro), finely chopped
1 long green chilli, seeded and finely chopped

CARROT, RAISIN AND ORANGE SALAD

3 tablespoons vegetable oil
juice of 1 orange
½ teaspoon salt
½ teaspoon caster sugar
4 carrots, grated
½ cup raisins, soaked in warm water for 20 minutes, drained
4 small red chillies, finely chopped
coriander (cilantro) leaves

This dhal-like stew of beans and broken dried corn kernels (*samp*) is a staple in South Africa, called *umngqusho* by the Xhosa people. (This word is roughly pronounced 'oom-noo-sho' - but the 'q' makes a clicking sound so it is rather difficult to say!) Philile uses a mix of three colours of capsicum in her recipe, and says the dish tastes even better the next day. She serves it with chicken or oxtail and with *mielie pap,* which is South Africa's version of polenta.

These spiced lamb skewers have plump dried apricots and bay leaves tucked in between the meat. Once they hit the barbecue the aroma is heaven! Lance says that if you don't have time to marinate the meat overnight (or even for a few nights), you can heat the vinegar mixture that forms the basis of the marinade and pour it over the meat while hot. The hot marinade penetrates the meat faster and you only need around 6-8 hours marinating. (While he uses lamb leg or shoulder here, he also says that the recipe works well for lean backstraps, which only need marinating for 30 minutes-4 hours with a hot marinade.)

UMNGQUSHO

from Philile Zwane

SOSATIE

Lamb and Apricot Skewers

from Lance Rosen

Drain and rinse the corn and beans, then combine in a large saucepan and cover with water. Bring to the boil and simmer for 1 hour, or until soft, adding more water if necessary. Drain through a colander set above a bowl or saucepan to catch the liquid.

Heat the oil in a large saucepan over medium heat. Add the onion and sauté for 3-4 minutes or until soft. Add the capsicum and cook for another 2-3 minutes. Add the spices, curry leaves and chilli and cook, stirring, for 2-3 minutes until fragrant.

Add the drained corn and beans along with 250 ml (8½ fl oz/1 cup) of the cooking liquid and the stock powder (if using) and mix well. Season with salt. Cover and simmer for 10-15 minutes, stirring occasionally to prevent sticking. Add more liquid if necessary. The stew should have the consistency of dahl.

Combine the lamb, coriander seeds, ginger, chilli flakes, salt and pepper in a large bowl and use your hands to rub the spices into the meat.

Heat the oil in a medium saucepan over medium heat. Add the brown sugar and curry powder and stir into the oil. Turn off the heat and stir in the vinegars. Pour the mixture over the meat. Add the apricots and bay leaves to the bowl. Marinate in the refrigerator overnight, or for 2 nights.

Soak 18 bamboo skewers in water for 30 minutes. Thread the lamb onto the skewers with 2 apricots and 2 folded bay leaves tucked in between the meat on each one. Reserve the remaining marinade.

Heat the grill of a barbecue to medium-hot. Put the skewers on the grill and cook for 2 minutes on each of the 4 sides, basting with the reserved marinade as they cook. Briefly rest the meat before serving.

SERVES 6 AS A SIDE DISH

1 cup *samp* (broken dried corn), soaked overnight	2 star anise
1 cup dried borlotti beans, soaked overnight	5 cloves
	1 teaspoon ground coriander
2 tablespoons olive oil	2 teaspoons medium curry powder
1 onion, finely chopped	3 fresh or dried curry leaves
½ yellow capsicum (bell peppers), finely chopped	1 long red chilli, seeded and finely chopped
½ red capsicum (bell peppers), finely chopped	1 long green chilli, seeded and finely chopped
½ green capsicum (bell peppers), finely chopped	1 tablespoon chicken stock powder (optional)
piece of cassia bark or a cinnamon stick	salt

MAKES 18 SKEWERS

2.5 kg (5 lb 8 oz) boneless lamb leg or shoulder, cut into 3-4 cm (1-1½ in) cubes	3 tablespoons olive oil
	1 tablespoon brown sugar
	1 tablespoon curry powder
¼ cup coriander seeds, toasted	750 ml (25½ fl oz/3 cups) white vinegar
2 teaspoons ground ginger	500 ml (17 fl oz/2 cups) malt vinegar
½ teaspoon chilli flakes	
1½ tablespoons salt	36 whole dried apricots
2 teaspoons freshly ground black pepper	36 bay leaves

With chunks of fresh fish in a delicious curry sauce, this is a wonderful dish that can be whipped up in under 30 minutes. The spices all 'marry together', says Hazel – 'a lovely balance of sweet and sour.' Serve with yellow rice (page 331).

CAPE MALAY FISH CURRY

from Hazel McBride

Season the fish with salt and pepper. Heat the oil in a wok over medium-high heat. Add the fennel and cumin seeds and fry for 30 seconds or until fragrant. Add the onion and fry for 5 minutes or until golden brown. Add the garlic and chilli and toss for another minute, then add the remaining spices and cook, stirring, for 1–2 minutes, adding a little water as necessary to prevent the spices sticking and burning.

Add the tomato, tamarind water and sugar and reduce the heat to low. Scrunch the curry leaves in your hands to help release their flavour then add to the wok. Simmer for 10 minutes.

Add salt to taste and extra sugar if desired. The sauce should not be too watery; if it is, you can simmer it a little longer to allow more water to evaporate. The sauce should also not be too thick; if it is, add a splash of water.

Add the fish and stir in very gently, spooning the sauce on top of the pieces. Cover with a lid and simmer for 7–8 minutes or until the fish is just cooked. Scatter with the coriander and serve.

SERVES 4

- 700 g (1 lb 9 oz) firm white fish fillets such as rockling, skin and bones removed, cut into chunks
- salt and pepper
- 3 tablespoons vegetable oil
- ¼ teaspoon fennel seeds
- ¼ teaspoon cumin seeds
- 1 onion, finely chopped
- 1 teaspoon crushed garlic
- 1 small red chilli, split in half
- 1 teaspoon ground coriander
- 1 teaspoon ground cumin
- 1 teaspoon ground fennel
- ½ teaspoon garam masala
- ½ teaspoon turmeric
- 1 tablespoon hot Malay-style curry powder or other hot curry powder, or to taste
- 1 teaspoon medium curry powder
- 3 tomatoes, peeled and finely chopped
- 1 teaspoon tamarind pulp, soaked in 3 tablespoons boiling water, strained
- 1 tablespoon raw sugar
- 10 curry leaves
- ½ cup chopped coriander (cilantro)

'"Melting pot" in South Africa means everybody is cooking everybody else's recipes. It's all "fusion food" from a "rainbow nation".'

This delicately spiced rice with raisins, almonds and lemon is the perfect accompaniment to many South African dishes, including *bobotie* (page 324).

This delicious bouncy pudding flavoured with apricot jam and vanilla is doused in a luscious sauce when it comes out of the oven. The pudding soaks up the sauce so each bite is moist and makes your heart flutter. Graeme suggests serving it with lightly whipped cream or crème anglaise. Custard or vanilla ice-cream are other options.

YELLOW RICE

from Hazel McBride

Heat the oil and butter in a large saucepan over medium-high heat. Add the onion, garlic, ginger, turmeric and spices and cook, stirring, for 3–4 minutes, or until the onion is lightly coloured. Add the rice and stir for another 30 seconds.

Pour in enough water to come 1 cm (½ in) above the rice and add the lemon zest. Bring to the boil, then reduce the heat to low and cover with a lid. Cook for 20 minutes, or until all the water is absorbed. Remove the lemon zest and add the raisins, almonds and lemon juice. Stir gently, season to taste and rest for 5–10 minutes before serving.

SERVES 4-6

2½ tablespoons vegetable oil
40 g (1½ oz) butter
1 medium onion, finely chopped
2 garlic cloves, crushed
1 teaspoon grated ginger
1 teaspoon grated fresh
   turmeric (or 1 teaspoon
   ground turmeric)
1 teaspoon coriander seeds,
   toasted and ground
1 teaspoon cumin seeds,
   toasted and ground

piece of cassia bark
3 cardamom pods, cracked
4 cloves
2 cups basmati rice
1 lemon, zest removed in strips,
   juiced
½ cup raisins, soaked in warm
   water for 20 minutes,
   drained
½ cup almonds, roasted

MALVA PUDDING

from Graeme Shapiro

Preheat the oven to 180°C (350°F/Gas 4) and butter a medium baking dish (about 2 litres [68 fl oz/8 cups] in capacity). Combine the sugar, butter, jam and egg in a mixing bowl and beat with electric beaters until pale and fluffy.

Combine the milk, vinegar and vanilla in a small bowl, stirring the vanilla into the milk.

Sift the flour, bicarbonate of soda and salt into a third bowl.

Fold the flour and the milk mixtures into the batter alternately, ensuring the mixture is well combined. Pour into the dish. Cover with lightly oiled foil and bake for 40–45 minutes or until just firm.

Make the sauce just before the pudding is ready. Combine the hot water, cream or milk, sugar and butter in a saucepan and stir over medium heat until the butter melts and the sugar dissolves. Bring to a gentle simmer then remove from the heat.

Pour the hot sauce over the hot pudding. Allow the sauce to soak in before serving the pudding warm.

SERVES 6

220 g (8 oz/1 cup) caster sugar
15 g (½ oz) unsalted butter,
   softened
3 tablespoons smooth
   apricot jam
1 egg
250 ml (8½ fl oz/1 cup) milk
2 teaspoons vinegar
1 teaspoon vanilla-bean paste
150 g (5½ oz/1 cup) plain
   (all-purpose) flour

1 teaspoon bicarbonate
   of soda
pinch of salt

SAUCE

3 tablespoons hot water
250 ml (8½ fl oz/1 cup) cream
   or evaporated milk
110 g (4 oz/½ cup) sugar
100 g (3½ oz) unsalted butter

It's amazing to think that much of the world's favourite food originally came from this vast and beautiful place – cacao beans from the north and from Central America, potatoes from the Andes, an amazing array of chillies from across the continent, plus tomatoes, peanuts and corn of many varieties. Imagine kimchi without chilli, spaghetti bolognaise without tomato, fish without the chips, and all of us without chocolate! The world as we know it would be much less vibrant.

In many South American countries the cuisine is a blend of native foods, strong layers of Spanish or Portuguese from the colonial era, and more recent influences from around the world. These are vibrant cuisines full of texture and flavour. In some places gastronomy has developed to a high art, such as in Lima, Peru. In others the simple flavours speak for themselves and are treasured across the world – look at the reach of the Brazilian *churrasco* barbecue, or the 'meat pie of South America', the empanada.

Special mention needs to go to the extraordinary influence the church had on South American cuisines – in particular the convents that were established from the sixteenth century. The nuns became renowned for their exceptional biscuits and cakes, pasties and pies. In Chile there's a famous saying when giving praise to someone who is a great baker: 'Tiene mano de monja' ('She/he has the hands of a nun').

The foods and dishes of South America vary with the terrain and climate. The famous flat pampas land of Argentina is perfect for beef cattle so it's no wonder the national staple is meat and lots of it – barbecues are truly show-stopping and use every part of the animal. In Patagonia, which is the southern tip of the continent and part of Argentina and Chile, lamb and venison are best suited to the climate; while Brazilians love pork; and in the Andes meat gets even more interesting with the use of alpaca, llama and guinea pig. Of course, the long coastline and the cold Humboldt Current that sweeps up the west coast also mean abundant fish and seafood.

Corn is a recurring feature as it is such a staple – some yellow, some white, some purple, some giant – and so versatile. It's used by Colombians and Venezuelans to make *arepas* (corn cakes like thick tortillas that are filled or topped with meat or cheese for snacks). Argentines use white corn to make *mazamorra*, a sweet, milky pudding, while roasted dried corn kernels called *cancha* are a popular accompaniment to the famous marinated seafood dish *ceviche*.

Among all the dishes I've tried over the years, I have to say one of the most challenging was served as part of an Argentine asado. I had been really looking forward to learning the secrets of this legendary meat feast – the cuts of grilled meat, the chimichurri sauce, and the *chinchulines*, which sounded at first like a great name for a cocktail. In fact it's the intestines of a cow. These are a local delicacy and often served with *mollejas* (sweetbreads), chorizos and *morcillas* (blood sausages). After a tentative mouthful of *chinchulines* – a bit rubbery and a bit fatty – I decided this was not for me. However, the perfectly cooked and tender beef was delicious with the vibrant *chimichurri* sauce.

There is so much to learn from South America and we hope you enjoy these starter recipes, along with those in the Brazil and Peru chapters.

ESSENTIAL FLAVOURS

ADOBO SPICE MIX
This mix of oregano, paprika, chilli and thyme is the base of the famous *chimichurri* sauce for barbecued meat. It is also used as a marinade.

AJI CHILLI
Also known as the 'Peruvian chilli', these long yellow/orange chillies have a fruity rather than spicy flavour, being more like a capsicum (bell pepper) than a chilli. They are sold as dried whole chillies or ground into powder.

BEEF
South America, particularly Argentina, is a meat lover's paradise. Meat, mostly beef, is usually barbecued. The most popular cuts are the *vacio* (flank steak) and *asado de tira* (spare ribs). Other favourites include *chinchulines* (chitterlings or intestines) and *mollejas* (sweetbreads).

CASSAVA
A root vegetable closely related to potato, the cassava makes flour and great chips.

CHORIZO
The chorizo sausage is an essential part of South American cuisine. Made from pork, flavoured with paprika and garlic, it is used in stews, grilled on the barbie or enjoyed on its own as a snack.

CORIANDER (CILANTRO)
Known in Spanish as *cilantro*, coriander features prominently in South American cuisine and is an essential ingredient in the versatile *pebre* salsa.

QUINOA
A seed that has been cultivated in the Andean highlands since 3000 BC. It has a light, fluffy texture when cooked. Its mild and slightly nutty flavour makes it a perfect alternative to rice or couscous and it also makes great salads.

Asado and Chimichurri

Asado is a technique for cooking cuts of meat (usually beef) as well as sausages and offal on a barbecue (grill). It is a traditional dish of Argentina, Chile, Uruguay and Paraguay and generally goes hand in hand with *chimichurri*, a spicy, garlicky parsley sauce. The meat is cooked without any embellishments, just very slowly over coals, until it melts in your mouth and cuts like butter. *Chimichurri,* which is poured over the cooked meat is made with finely chopped parsley, garlic, olive oil, balsamic vinegar and brown vinegar and flavoured with both chilli and *adobo* spice mix.

In Chile this all-purpose salsa is a big favourite, often served with pumpkin fritters and some good local wine. It's also an excellent accompaniment to barbecued meat and fish. *Pebre* includes a large quantity of onion, but soaking the onion in sugar, then salt, softens the raw flavour. (Instead of onion you could use a bunch of finely chopped chives.)

This Colombian snack food consists of a cornmeal patty cooked in a frying pan and served simply with butter and salt or with any number of fillings. Split the *arepas* open and fill with avocado, cheese, tomato, meat, fried chicken, beans or salsa. Or try the '*arepa* pizza' where chorizo, cheese and spicy chicken or beef strips are used as a topping rather than a filling. In northern Colombia, fried egg *arepas* are a favourite – the egg is fried into the patty. *Arepas* are also a good accompaniment to main meals.

PEBRE

from Gema Badiola

Put the onion in a colander and sprinkle with the sugar and some hot water (not boiling). Mix with your hands and leave to stand for 10 minutes. Rinse the onion and mix in a handful of salt. Transfer to a bowl, fill with cold water and leave to stand for a further 10 minutes, then tip the onion back into the colander, rinse again and drain well.

Combine the tomato, capsicum, garlic, chilli and coriander in a bowl. Add the onion, lemon juice, vinegar and oil and mix well. Sprinkle with a little oregano and add salt and pepper to taste.

MAKES 4 CUPS

4 medium onions, diced	2-3 bunches coriander
2 tablespoons raw	(cilantro), finely chopped
(demerara) sugar	(including stems)
salt	juice of ½ lemon
3 tomatoes, diced	2 tablespoons white vinegar
½ green capsicum (bell pepper)	3 tablespoons grape-seed oil
(or red or yellow for a more	dried oregano
colourful salsa), diced	pepper
3-4 garlic cloves, finely	
chopped	
2 green Chilean chillies, seeded	
and finely chopped (or use	
Chilean chilli paste)	

AREPAS

from Juan Gomez

Drain the corn and cook in boiling water for 1 hour or until al dente. Drain and place in a food processor with the butter and salt. Grind as finely as possible. Transfer to a work surface and knead for a few minutes until the dough is smooth without any lumps.

Take balls of dough weighing around 120 g (4½ oz) each and flatten with a rolling pin to patties 5 mm-1 cm (¼-½ in) thick. Heat a non-stick frying pan or barbecue (grill) without any oil or butter and cook the *arepas* for 5 minutes on one side, then 3 minutes on the other (the *arepas* are ready to be turned when you can slide them around).

MAKES 10-12 *AREPAS*

1 kg (2 lb 3 oz) dried snow	1 tablespoon butter
corn (white corn),	1 tablespoon salt
soaked overnight	

'To praise a good cook say "*De tus manos veneno!*" (From your hands, even poison!), meaning that no matter what she cooks, she has the gift of turning it into a magical meal.'

Debate rages over which country invented the empanada and many varieties using different sorts of pastry abound. Empanadas are the ultimate snack food. They can be filled with any combination of cheese, chilli, meat, tuna, prawns, vegetables, egg and olives. Some are baked whereas others are deep-fried.

EMPANADAS

from Yvonne Cutro

Heat the oil and butter in a large, heavy-based saucepan over medium heat and add the onion and spring onion. Fry until the onion is translucent. Add the *aji* powder, then the beef. Cook until the meat is brown, then add the hot stock and simmer until the beef is cooked through. Add the sugar and season with salt, then add the paprika, cinnamon, ground cloves if using and a little water. Cook over low heat until the liquid has evaporated. Leave to cool.

Preheat the oven to 200°C (400°F/Gas 6). Take pieces of pastry about the size of golf balls and roll out to circles 10–15 cm (4–6 in) in diameter. Dust lightly with flour. Put a generous spoonful of meat filling in the centre of each round and add a few pieces of olive, some sultanas and egg. Sprinkle with cumin. Fold the pastry into a half-moon, then fold in the edges, crimping them with your fingers as you go. Place the empanadas on a greased tray and brush the tops with melted butter. Bake for 25 minutes or until golden.

MAKES 12-15 EMPANADAS

3 tablespoons vegetable oil
130 g (4 ½ oz) butter
200 g (7 oz) onions, chopped
200 g (7 oz) spring onions (scallions), chopped
½ teaspoon *aji* chilli powder
1 kg (2 lb 3 oz) minced (ground) beef (not too lean)
250 ml (8½ fl oz/1 cup) hot beef stock
3 tablespoons sugar
salt
1 teaspoon sweet paprika
½ teaspoon cinnamon
½ teaspoon ground cloves (optional)
1 kg (2 lb 3 oz) shortcrust pastry
plain (all-purpose) flour
handful of green olives, chopped
130 g (4 ½ oz) sultanas (golden raisins)
3 hard-boiled eggs, peeled and roughly chopped
ground cumin
extra butter, melted

Most South American countries now have their own version of *ceviche* but it's thought to be Peruvian in origin. Essentially it is marinated raw fish or crustacean that is 'cooked' by the acidity of citrus juice (you can try prawns in this recipe instead of fish if you like). Passionfruit and tamarillo have been added to the marinade for extra flavour. It is a delightful, refreshing hot-weather meal and reported by some South Americans to be a cure for a hangover! It can be served with cinnamon scented sweet potato, but it is often served with *cancha serrana* (dried corn kernels that are roasted and salted).

Manjar blanco is a caramel of milk, vanilla and sugar that is simmered until thick and rich. It is a traditional sweet enjoyed daily throughout South America – as a filling for pastries, the sweet centre of *alfajor* biscuits and *tejas* (filled chocolates) or simply enjoyed on its own – one devotee described it as 'pan-scrapingly good'!

CEVICHE

from Alejandro Saravia

Boil the sweet potato with the sugar and cinnamon until just soft. Leave to cool, then cut into 2 cm (¾ in) cubes.

Blanch the chilli then peel off the skin and remove the seeds. Place in a mortar with a little lime juice, salt and pepper and grind to a paste.

Combine the fish, remaining lime juice and a few ice cubes in a bowl. Add a pinch of salt, a little pepper and a little chilli paste to taste and mix together. Stir in the coriander, yellow chilli slices and red onion. Place in a serving bowl with the sweet potato on the side. Eat immediately: the fresher, the better.

SERVES 2

1 small sweet potato, peeled
1 tablespoon raw (demerara) sugar
1 cinnamon stick
1 long red chilli
juice of 2 limes
sea salt and freshly ground black pepper

2 skinless, boneless white fish fillets such as snapper (porgy), as fresh as possible, cut into 2 cm (¾ in) cubes
ice cubes
1 tablespoon finely chopped coriander (cilantro)
1 long yellow amarillo chilli, sliced thinly
½ red onion, finely sliced

MANJAR BLANCO

from Carmen Almenara

Heat the butter, a quarter of the milk, the white sugar, bicarbonate of soda and vanilla in a saucepan. Bring to the boil and cook, stirring constantly with a wooden spoon, until the mixture starts turning a caramel colour. Add another quarter of milk and the brown sugar. Continue stirring. When the mixture starts thickening, add another quarter of milk. As it thickens again, add the remaining milk and the glucose, turn down the heat and continue stirring until the mixture is thick enough for you to see the bottom of the saucepan when you move the spoon through it, or until a little bit put on a plate doesn't run. The mixture cooks for approximately 40 minutes in total. Remove from the heat and keep stirring for a few minutes before pouring into a bowl.

1 tablespoon butter
1 litre (34 fl oz/4 cups) full-cream milk
230 g (8 oz) white sugar
¼ teaspoon bicarbonate of soda

1 vanilla bean, split
50 g (1¾ oz) brown sugar
30 g (1 oz) liquid glucose

'My grandma told me to always get involved in the kitchen work because "The one in charge of serving up in the kitchen always gets the best portions!"'

In Australia we have fallen head over heels for the Spanish tapas tradition, fully embracing this array of delicious snacks that is traditionally served with a drink as a prelude to a meal. We love the sizzle of garlic prawns, will cross town for good Iberian *jamón,* have dived into sangria like it's water and have learned just how good Spanish olive oil, paprika and saffron can be. We're also learning that Spanish food is incredibly varied due to the influence and enrichment of the Moors, Arabs, Sephardic Jews, French and Italians who have all settled at various times in the country. The result is food with soul.

Each region in Spain has its own specialities, dictated by geography. Spain's long coastline, its rugged mountains, its baking plains and its rich farming land are all background to a vast range of dishes, which all have one thing in common - they're simple, unpretentious and use beautifully fresh, seasonal ingredients.

To the Spanish, eating is more than simply looking after hunger pangs - food is savoured and enjoyed communally and many culinary traditions have evolved over the years. I especially love the Spanish version of the fellas manning the barbecue - on a Sunday the women go to church and the men stay home to make paella for the army of family and friends that arrive sometime after midday. There's a lot of male pride bound up in getting the special *calasparra* or *bomba* rice cooked just right in olive oil and stock, and the added seafood, meat and vegetables also cooked to perfection. When they're finished the aroma of saffron hangs in the air and the whole paella pan looks like the best edible artwork on earth.

Most people are familiar with some of the main Spanish exports like paella and sangria and are still coming up to speed with the lesser-known ones, such as the fabulous *zarzuela* seafood stew and *fino,* a dry sherry that makes a great aperitif and goes well with the strong flavours of many tapas dishes. It's always worth seeking out the best and most authentic ingredients - good Spanish paprika, saffron and olive oil - and being generous with garlic and wine also help!

ESSENTIAL FLAVOURS

CHEESE
Spain produces some beautiful cheeses such as the hard sheep's milk *manchego* (look for '*queso puro de oveja*' on the label) and the piquant cow's milk *mahón*. From Andalucia to the Basque country – each region of Spain has its own specialty cheeses just as France has.

GARLIC
What would Spanish food be without garlic? Known as *ajo* in Spanish, garlic is used extensively in Spanish cooking.

JAMÓN
The most common variety, which is found all over Spain, is *jamón serrano* (mountain ham). This is a young salt-cured ham that is deep red in colour and served in thin raw slices. It dries out a little with age but when fresh it will melt in your mouth. *Jamón de pata negra* is made from free-range black Iberian pigs, which have grazed on acorns. This *jamón* is aged for 18 months and because of the care taken to produce it, it's very expensive. It has a nutty, slightly sweet flavour and a melting texture.

OLIVE OIL
Known as *aceite de oliva*, Spanish olive oil is 'fruitier' than Italian versions and is used for cooking, salad dressings and also drizzled over dishes to finish.

PAPRIKA
A spice made of dried, ground capsicums (bell peppers). There are many different varieties - smoked (*ahumado*), sweet (*dulce*), spicy (*picante*) or the intense, sun-dried *pimentón de Murcia*. For an authentic Spanish flavour it is important you use the right type specified in a recipe.

SAFFRON
The stigma from the crocus flower and the most expensive spice in the world. Fortunately a small amount is enough to impart its distinctive flavour, enticing aroma and rich colour. It is essential for making paella.

SHERRY VINEGAR
Both sherry and vinegar have been produced in southern Spain for centuries. Like balsamic vinegar, sherry vinegars are aged for up to 75 years and are used to enhance the flavours of soups, stews, sauces and dressings.

Thank God the Spanish came up with gazpacho to sparkle up our hot summers. Master this and you will change your summer entertaining. A good tip is to pop all the ingredients in a big bowl to chill in the fridge the night before, so the bread can soften and the ingredients are super-cold when you puree it, just before your guests arrive. Delicioso!

Buy a terracotta *cazuela* dish to cook this in and make this recipe your own - you'll look great and friends will never come down with colds! Cooking anything in a *cazuela* will give it that special Spanish 'something' - the smaller clay dishes can be used on the stove to make dishes such as this, the larger ones to bake meat on the bone until it is really tender or to gently cook vegetable dishes.

GAZPACHO ANDALUZ

from Penelope Lopez

Combine the water, vinegar and olive oil in a large bowl. Add the bread, garlic and vegetables. Mix well with your hands and add the salt. Cover and chill in the refrigerator. Puree the mixture in a blender and strain before serving.

SERVES 8

2 litres (68 fl oz/8 cups) water
250 ml (8½ fl oz/1 cup) white vinegar
125 ml (4 fl oz/½ cup) extra-virgin olive oil
1 day-old vienna or *pane di casa* loaf, crusts removed, roughly cut
2 garlic cloves, sliced
1 onion, chopped
5-6 medium-sized soft red tomatoes peeled, roughly chopped

1 red capsicum (bell pepper), seeded, roughly chopped
1 green capsicum (bell pepper), seeded, roughly chopped
1 large cucumber, half peeled (a little skin left on adds flavour), roughly chopped
3 tablespoons salt

GAMBAS AL PIL-PIL

from Penelope Lopez

Pour oil into a small frying pan or *cazuela* dish to about 1.5 cm (½ in) deep. Heat over medium-high heat. Add the garlic, chilli and prawns - they should start sizzling immediately. Cook for 15 seconds then turn the prawns over. Add the salt, white wine and parsley, then serve straight away.

SERVES 2-3

olive oil
4 garlic cloves, sliced
small red chilli, chopped
12 green prawns (shrimp), shelled, tails intact

pinch of salt
2 tablespoons white wine
½ tablespoon chopped flat-leaf (Italian) parsley

This lovely pork dish is meltingly wonderful, with molten cheese inside and a crisp breadcrumb coating. Serve it on top of *asadillo de pimientos* (see the recipe following) – a great combination!

A simple summer salad of roasted capsicum, onion and garlic with tomato and cumin. Use the best extra-virgin olive oil you can find.

PORK SAN JACOB

from Frank Camorra

Lay each medallion out flat and slice through the middle horizontally without cutting all the way to the end. Open the medallions out like little books and flatten them slightly with a meat mallet. Season with a little salt and add some thyme leaves. Top each medallion with a slice of *jamón* and cheese. Close over and seal by lightly tapping with the mallet. Dust lightly in flour, dip into the beaten egg and coat with breadcrumbs.

Preheat the oven to 180°C (350°F/Gas 4). Heat a frying pan with olive oil and gently pan-fry the pork on both sides. Transfer to the oven for about 10 minutes, until cooked through. Drain on paper towel and serve on top of *asadillo de pimientos*.

SERVES 4

4 pork loin medallions (150 g [5½ oz] each)	4 slices of *mahón* cheese
salt	plain (all-purpose) flour
thyme leaves	2 eggs, lightly beaten
4 slices of *jamón*	fresh breadcrumbs
	olive oil

ASADILLO DE PIMIENTOS

from Frank Camorra

Preheat the oven to 180°C (350°F/Gas 4). Place the whole capsicums, onions and heads of garlic in a baking dish. Drizzle with some of the olive oil and sprinkle with sea salt. Roast for 30 minutes or until the onion is soft. Transfer to a bowl, cover with plastic wrap (the steam will help loosen the skins) and set aside until cool enough to handle.

Put the tomato and parsley in a separate bowl. Squeeze the onions from their skins, roughly chop them and add to the tomato. Cut the tops off the heads of garlic and squeeze the cloves into the bowl. Peel the capsicums and discard the seeds. Tear the flesh into strips and add to the bowl. Pour over the remaining oil and the sherry vinegar. Sprinkle with the cumin and add salt to taste. Toss well with your hands.

SERVES 4

6 red capsicums (bell peppers)	½ bunch flat-leaf (Italian) parsley, roughly chopped
2 onions	125 ml (4 fl oz/½ cup) sherry vinegar
2 heads of garlic	1 tablespoon cumin seeds, toasted and crushed
250 ml (8½ fl oz/1 cup) extra-virgin olive oil (arbequina if possible)	
sea salt	
500 g (1 lb 2 oz) tomatoes, peeled, seeded and roughly chopped	

This is simplicity itself - as well as being creamy and delicious. It is great to add to your tapas repertoire, to take to a picnic or to add to a Mediterranean spread. The clever way of turning over the tortilla is using a plate to make that lovely golden circle of flavour look neat and perfect. Eat at room temperature.

TORTILLA DE PATATAS

Potato Omelette

from Paola Horta

Heat the oil in a large frying pan and gently cook the potatoes, stirring from time to time so they don't burn on the bottom. Once the potatoes are almost soft, drain them in a colander set over a bowl to remove the excess oil (keep it for another use). Leave 2 tablespoons of oil in the pan.

Beat the eggs in a bowl and season with salt. Add the potatoes, mix well and check the seasoning.

Reheat the frying pan over medium heat and pour in the potato and egg mixture. As the omelette begins to cook, shake the pan from time to time so the omelette doesn't stick to the bottom. Once the bottom of the omelette has set, turn it by placing a plate on the pan and quickly turning the pan and plate over. Gently slide the omelette back into the pan and continue cooking, shaking the pan from time to time, until the omelette is set through.

SERVES 6-8

250 ml (8½ fl oz/1 cup) olive oil

4 medium potatoes, peeled, quartered and thinly sliced

6 eggs

salt

'"Vamos con el arroz" (We are going with the rice) means dinner will be ready when the rice is cooked so everyone better be ready too!'

Traditionally paella is made on a Sunday and because women need a day off from cooking it is usually made by the men. I have bought a paella pan and gas ring so my family are always enjoying this lovely dish. *Calasparra* is a low-starch, short-grain rice and when cooked it is fluffy with separate grains. It is the best rice to use for paella – it can absorb heaps of liquid so it bursts with flavour. To increase the quantities and serve more people (although you will need a giant paella dish), allow about 80 g (2¾ oz) of rice per person.

I'm sure my family have clocked their one-hundredth round on this recipe – we love it and make it all the time. Although using the condensed milk might be cheating a little bit, it makes a creamy, luscious and very indulgent dessert – thank you Rosalia! (In case you're wondering, Rosalia says this definitely can't be made with skim milk – 'You use full-cream then go for a run!')

PAELLA

from Carlos Lopez

Roast the whole capsicum in a moderate oven until blistered, then peel it, discard the seeds and tear the flesh into thin strips. Set aside.

Grind the saffron with some salt in a mortar.

Heat the oil in a large paella pan (or frying pan) over medium heat. Add the onion, garlic, tomato, fresh capsicum, chicken, squid and rice and stir for 1 minute. Add the stock, paprika and crushed saffron, stir for the last time and bring to the boil. When the stock boils and the grains begin to swell, lay the prawns and crab on top. Cook over medium heat for about 10 minutes until the stock has reduced enough that you can see the rice underneath. Push the mussels and pippies into the rice and cook until their shells open. Scatter with the peas, strips of roasted capsicum and parsley and cook for another 5 minutes over low heat.

SERVES 4

2 red capsicums (bell peppers), 1 left whole, 1 finely chopped	200 g (7 oz) squid, diced
10 saffron threads	300 g (10½ oz) *calasparra* rice
salt	750 ml (25½ fl oz/3 cups) fish stock
3 tablespoons olive oil	3 teaspoons Spanish smoked paprika
1 onion, finely chopped	4 large green prawns (shrimp)
2 garlic cloves, crushed	1 blue swimmer crab, halved
1 large tomato, peeled and finely chopped	8 mussels
300 g (10½ oz) chicken breast or thigh fillets, diced	12 pippies
	200 g (7 oz) peas
	¾ cup chopped flat-leaf (Italian) parsley

ARROZ CON LECHE

Rice Pudding

from Rosalia Ugarte

Place the rice in a saucepan and cover with water. Bring to the boil and cook for 5 minutes. Drain. Heat the milk in the saucepan with the cinnamon sticks and lemon rind. When it comes to the boil, add the rice and turn the heat down to low. Cook, stirring constantly, until the rice is half cooked. Add the condensed milk and continue cooking and stirring until the rice is cooked through (test by squashing a rice grain in your fingers). Spoon into bowls and dust with ground cinnamon.

SERVES 8

250 g (9 oz) medium-grain rice	395 g (14 oz) tin sweetened condensed milk
1.25 litres (42 fl oz/5 cups) full-cream milk	ground cinnamon
1-2 cinnamon sticks	
1 strip of lemon rind	

If Sri Lankan cuisine has a signature smell and sound it would have to be the intense fresh aroma and firecracker sound of fresh curry leaves and mustard seeds popping in hot oil. This is the prelude to many incredible dishes and with a start like this even a simple plate of greens is transformed into something with sexiness and soul.

It's hard not to fall in love with this food, which is a combination of Muslim, Tamil and Sinhalese recipes. It also seems that every nationality that has visited and traded over the centuries has left a mark on the cuisine – the Dutch, Portuguese, English, Arabs, Malays, Moors and Indians have all added some of their magic to the fresh fruit, vegetables and spices that are grown locally in abundance.

Some ingredients are virtually unknown outside Sri Lanka such as drumsticks, which are a long, bitter pod used in curries and accompaniments – their leaves are a popular addition to the favourite crab curry. It's rare to find a Sri Lankan family that hasn't planted their own curry leaf tree in the backyard, although the drumstick tree needs the intense heat of the tropics to flourish.

The tropical climate in Sri Lanka is also perfect for coconuts, which are used fresh and can be grated into *sambols*, wonderful accompaniments to rice and curry. I love that Sri Lankans refer to 'rice and curry' always in that order, denoting the importance of rice. A simple meal might be rice and *sambol*, pickles or chutney to liven up the flavour with at least one vegetable curry or dhal. Depending on the occasion, there may be even more dishes – meat curries, seafood curries, endless *sambols* and accompaniments, and even spicy scrambled eggs, which our local goddess of Asian food, Charmaine Solomon, made for me when she shared her tried-and-true chicken curry recipe. After this I can never eat plain scrambled eggs again – hers were creamy and full of fresh herbs and mellow spices.

At many special banquets you'll be served lovely little pancakes that have the sweet name of hoppers (*appam*). They're made in a deep, circular pan and the rice-flour mixture is rolled around the pan so it comes right up the sides. Crispy on the bottom, these pancakes are broken into pieces to scoop up curries – similar to how you'd use Lebanese bread. If you're even luckier you'll also discover their unusual cousin the stringhopper (*idiyappam*), which are made from fine rice-flour strings that have been squeezed through a sieve onto a little circular mat and steamed – they are a little nest of noodle-like strands and a feature of banquets for special occasions. Trying to eat these fiddly but delicious things with curry sauces running up your arm is quite an art – but very yummy!

ESSENTIAL FLAVOURS

CHUTNEYS, PICKLES AND *SAMBOLS*

It would be unthinkable to have a meal in Sri Lanka without these accompaniments. They serve to enhance the flavours of curries and awaken the tastebuds. There are many different types, ranging from savoury eggplant and tomato pickles, tangy lime and date chutneys, to fiery *sambols* based on salt, lime, maldive fish, chilli and shallots.

COCONUT AND COCONUT OIL

The coconut palm is referred to in Sinhalese as a gift of the gods. Every part of the tree is used - in building, for utensils, right down to the milk, the oil and of course the flesh. Finely grated in *sambols* and *mallungs*, added to curries and baked into sweet delights, it is the quintessential Sri Lankan ingredient. Coconut oil is traditionally used for cooking and is beautifully fragrant, but use it sparingly due to its high saturated-fat content.

CURRY LEAVES

Picked from a tree related to the citrus family, curry leaves are often fried in oil before being used in curries and chutneys. Although also available in dried or powdered form, they are at their aromatic best when fresh. You can use fresh leaves still attached to the stem for extra flavour.

CURRY POWDERS

Sri Lankan curry powders get their dark colour, aroma and distinctive flavour from roasting the spices - which might include coriander (cilantro), cumin, fennel, fenugreek and cardamom. As well as the classic dark roasted powder, special blends such as fish curry powder and meat powders are commonly used.

FENUGREEK

No Sri Lankan curry is complete without these small, brown, square-shaped seeds which add a slight bitterness and have a thickening effect on sauces. They must be heated slowly to prevent them from becoming too bitter.

GORAKA

A souring and thickening agent unique to Sri Lanka is this fluted orange fruit whose segments are dried, turning black. It can be soaked in hot water and ground to a paste or added whole and removed after cooking.

MALDIVE FISH

Dried, smoked and finely shaved, maldive fish is the shrimp paste or fish sauce equivalent for Sri Lankan cuisine. It is a key ingredient in *sambols* and is also sparingly used as a thickening agent in curries. Store in a screw-top glass jar as it's quite pungent!

PANDAN LEAF

Most Sri Lankan households grow the pandan plant, whose long green leaves are used to perfume curries and rice. Pandan is often referred to as the vanilla of Asia, such is its beautiful aroma.

Sambols are fresh or cooked relishes that enliven Sri Lankan meals of rice and curry. This version, made from chilli, maldive fish and fresh coconut, will give your tastebuds a warm but mellow tingle.

The word *mallung* means literally 'to mix up' and this delightful dish can feature any number of different vegetables. In this recipe it is a combination of shredded leafy greens, maldive fish, green chilli and coconut. For the greens, Paul says you could use almost anything: spinach, silverbeet, chicory, chrysanthemum leaves, beetroot or turnip leaves or mustard greens. Mix a few kinds together if you like - say, mild spinach with peppery turnip leaves.

POL SAMBOL

Coconut *Sambol*

from Paul Van Reyk

Finely grate the coconut flesh with a hand grater or in a food processor. Grind the maldive fish to a powder in a mortar. Mix the coconut, maldive fish and chilli powder until the coconut turns orange. Add the shallots, lime juice and a small sprinkle of salt. Mix well and taste, adding more lime or salt if desired.

LEAFY VEGETABLE MALLUNG

from Paul Van Reyk

Heat a little oil in a wok or large frying pan and add the mustard seeds. Fry until they begin to pop, then add the curry leaves, turmeric, salt and maldive fish if using, stirring constantly to prevent the curry leaves burning. Immediately add the shredded leaves and stir rapidly. When the leaves have darkened and become limp, add the green chilli and coconut and stir for another 1–2 minutes. Remove from the heat and serve.

MAKES 3 CUPS

1 coconut, cracked and peeled	2 shallots, finely chopped
1 tablespoon maldive fish	juice of ½ lime
2 teaspoons chilli powder	salt

SERVES 6

oil	1 tablespoon maldive fish, finely ground (optional)
1 teaspoon black mustard seeds	1 bunch leafy vegetables, shredded
handful of curry leaves	1 green chilli, finely chopped
1 teaspoon turmeric	1 cup grated fresh coconut
pinch of salt	

'Nothing tastes as good as when it's cooked over a wood-fired stove.'

A creamy, velvety dish with delicious depth of flavour. This is achieved by including prawn pieces in the curry sauce (to be strained out with the aromatics later) and pureeing and straining a few heads just like in a French bisque. The recipe includes Peter's impressive serving suggestion of nestling pairs of prawns into each other to create a seafood version of the yin-yang symbol, all stacked up and served in a moat of sauce. It's a perfect dinner party dish as you can make the sauce in advance then cook the prawns in it very quickly just before serving. Serve with rice and pickles.

PRAWN CURRY

from Peter Kuravita

Remove the heads from the prawns, reserving half of them. Cut the bodies into pieces through the shells.

Heat the oil or ghee in a saucepan and add the curry leaves, shallots, garlic and ginger. Fry until the shallots are translucent. Add the prawn pieces, spices, green chilli, *goraka* and pandan leaf. Stir briefly to coat the prawns, then add half the coconut milk and salt to taste. Simmer for 8–10 minutes.

Meanwhile, puree the reserved prawn heads in a food processor. Strain through a fine sieve, discarding the solids. Mix the strained puree with the remaining coconut milk. Add to the curry and bring back to a simmer without boiling. Remove from the heat.

To serve, fit pairs of shelled prawns into each other by laying them flat, facing them towards each other and sliding them together to form circle shapes. Arrange the pairs in the base of a frying pan (as they cook, they stick together a little). Strain the curry sauce over the prawns until just covered. Cover the pan with a lid and bring to a simmer, cooking until the prawns turn opaque. Add the lemon juice.

Stack the prawn circles up on serving plates, spoon over the sauce and garnish with coriander.

SERVES 4

CURRY SAUCE

10 green prawns (shrimp)
2 tablespoons coconut oil or clarified butter (ghee)
30 curry leaves
10 shallots, sliced
12 garlic cloves, sliced
3 cm (1¼ in) piece of ginger, finely chopped
1 tablespoon fenugreek seeds
5 cardamom pods
2 cinnamon sticks
5 cloves
2 tablespoons ground cumin
4 tablespoons ground coriander
¾ tablespoon chilli powder

1 tablespoon turmeric
2 tablespoons sweet paprika
½ tablespoon fish curry powder
2 long green chillies, sliced
1 piece of *goraka*
1 pandan leaf, cut in a few pieces
1 litre (34 fl oz/4 cups) coconut milk
salt

TO SERVE

24 large shelled green prawns (shrimp)
juice of ½ lemon
coriander (cilantro) leaves

A classic chicken curry that's full of flavour and best made with chicken on the bone. Charmaine has made this dish for decades – it's always a marvellous meal. Serve with stringhoppers if you can (or otherwise rice) and with coconut *sambol* (see page 352).

CHICKEN CURRY

from Charmaine Solomon

Heat the ghee or oil and fry the fenugreek seeds and curry leaves until the leaves start to brown. Add the onion, garlic and ginger and fry gently until the onion is soft and translucent. Add the ground spices, salt and vinegar and stir well. Add the tomato, whole spices, lemongrass and pandan leaf, then add the chicken.

Stir to coat the chicken pieces in the spices, then cover and cook over low heat for 40–50 minutes. The curry will look dry at first but liquid will be released from the chicken. Stir in the coconut milk and taste for salt. Add a squeeze of lemon juice if desired.

SERVES 6

2 tablespoons clarified butter (ghee) or vegetable oil (or a combination)
¼ teaspoon fenugreek seeds
10 curry leaves on the stem
2 large onions, finely chopped
4–5 garlic cloves, finely chopped
2 teaspoons grated ginger
1 teaspoon turmeric
1 teaspoon chilli powder
1 tablespoon ground coriander
½ teaspoon ground fennel
1 teaspoon ground cumin

2 teaspoons sweet paprika
2 teaspoons salt
2 tablespoons vinegar
2 tomatoes, peeled and chopped
6 cardamom pods, cracked
1 cinnamon stick
1 lemongrass stalk, bruised
1 pandan leaf, folded
1.5 kg (3 lb 4 oz) chicken thighs on the bone
250 ml (8½ fl oz/1 cup) thick coconut milk
lemon juice (optional)

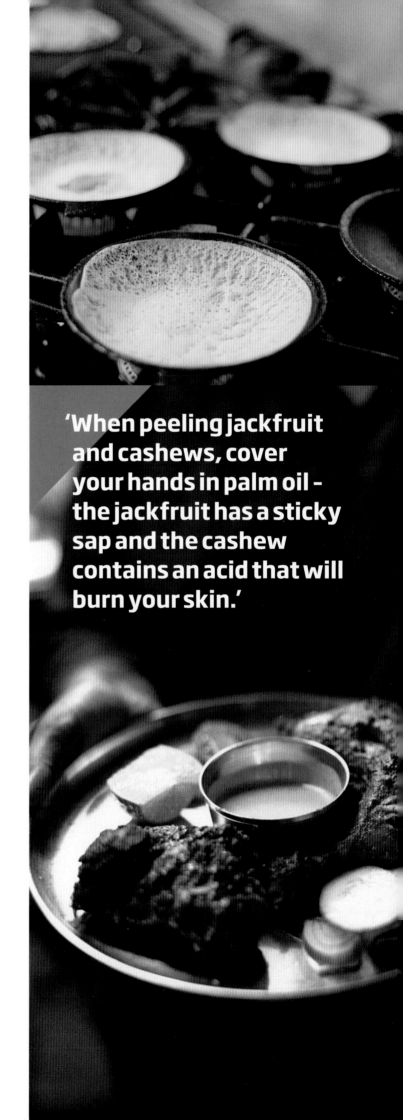

'When peeling jackfruit and cashews, cover your hands in palm oil – the jackfruit has a sticky sap and the cashew contains an acid that will burn your skin.'

A simple but delicious vegetable curry that uses Sri Lanka's dark roasted curry powder and is thickened and flavoured with toasted rice and desiccated coconut. A glorious dish.

A beautiful, dense, spiced custard that makes a perfect finish to a meal. It can be served warm or chilled, in which case you can make it a day in advance. Make a little extra syrup to spoon on top if desired.

WATTAKA KALU POL

Pumpkin Curry

from Sunil Ranasinghe

Heat the oil in a large saucepan and add the onion, curry leaves, garlic and green chilli. Fry briefly then add the mustard and fenugreek seeds and continue frying.

Quickly toss the pumpkin in a bowl with the seeded mustard, ground spices and salt and add to the pan along with the coconut milk. Bring to the boil and cook over high heat until the pumpkin is tender.

Meanwhile, heat a small frying pan and dry-fry the rice and coconut until brown and fragrant. Grind to a powder in a mortar or blender.

Add the rice and coconut powder to the curry and cook for a few more minutes.

SERVES 6

2 tablespoons vegetable oil
2 medium red onions, finely sliced
2 sprigs of curry leaves
4 garlic cloves, finely sliced
3 long green chillies, sliced
½ teaspoon black mustard seeds, ground
½ teaspoon fenugreek seeds
1 kg (2 lb 3 oz) pumpkin, cut into cubes, skin left on

1 teaspoon seeded mustard
2 tablespoons dark roasted curry powder
1 teaspoon chilli powder
1 teaspoon turmeric
1–2 teaspoons salt
500 ml (17 fl oz/2 cups) coconut milk
2 tablespoons short-grain rice
¾ cup desiccated coconut

WATTALAPPAM

from Deborah Solomon

Put the palm sugar (jaggery) and water in a saucepan and heat, stirring, until the sugar dissolves. Leave to cool.

Preheat the oven to 140°C (280°F/Gas 1). Whisk the coconut milk with the spices and rosewater. Strain in the syrup, whisking to combine, then add the cream followed by the eggs. Pour into 8 small ramekins and place in a baking dish. Pour hot water to come halfway up the ramekins and bake in the oven for 50–60 minutes, or until the custards are just set.

MAKES 8 CUSTARDS

175 g dark palm sugar (jaggery), roughly chopped
100 ml (3½ fl oz) water
375 ml (12½ fl oz/1½ cups coconut milk (homemade, or use a good-quality brand like Kara)

½ teaspoon ground cardamom
¼ teaspoon ground mace
pinch of ground cloves
1 tablespoon rosewater
200 ml (7 fl oz) cream
4 large eggs, lightly beaten

SYRIA

Syrian cuisine is full of delights – you'll find the freshest, most delicious salads and inventive dips, as well as main courses that sing with exotic spices and desserts and sweets that are legendary throughout the Middle East. While many dishes are similar to food from neighbouring Lebanon, a couple stand apart as distinctly Syrian and they are simply wonderful.

One of my favourites is the national dish *kibbeh*. It is made from very fresh, finely minced lamb or beef that's seasoned, spiced and mixed with burghul (cracked wheat), and it comes in many varieties – raw, baked or fried. The taste and texture are superb whichever way you have it. Other popular dishes are based on Mediterranean vegetables such as zucchini and eggplant, which are often hollowed out and stuffed with meat and rice. *Ma a'loube* is a delicious Syrian meal of eggplant that is stacked and layered with rice and lamb.

The Syrian palate adores salty, tangy and sour flavours. Along with a generous use of salt in cooking, cheeses like *labneh, shankleesh* and *jibne baida* satisfy some of their salt cravings. Lemon juice is used liberally for its sour tang, as are generous pinches of sumac, a deep-red spice that adds a lemony taste to salads and meats. Another slightly tangy flavour comes from the fresh herb *baqli* (or purslane, as it's called in English).

One ingredient found commonly in Syria and its neighbours is freekeh, a young wheat that is harvested then roasted to give it a smoky flavour. Freekeh has a chewy texture like brown rice and is delicious served with meat or poultry. Syria also boasts truffles, which are found in the desert and have a wonderful earthy flavour and aroma – although they are nowhere near as strong as those found in France. The combination of freekeh, truffles and perfectly poached chicken is simply lovely.

One of the highlights of Syrian food is *mezza*, the tapas of the Middle East. *Mezza* is a generous spread of small dishes, mostly eaten without cutlery, using flatbread, lettuce or vine leaves instead to scoop up dips or wrap up morsels and colourful salads. Many who are new to the concept of *mezza* mistake the endless array of dishes as the meal itself rather than the prelude to even more food! Amid the social bustle and conversations of family and friends, Syrian meals are to be enjoyed for more than an hour or two. This reflects their culture of hospitality and generosity, where everything to do with food is presented on a large scale.

Smoky baba ghanouj and creamy hoummus, both well known in the West, are key elements of a traditional *mezza* feast. Another favourite in Syria is *muhammara*, a spicy capsicum and walnut dip made with pomegranate molasses. Popular salads include tabbouleh, the well-known parsley and burghul salad that is often served with baby cos (romaine) lettuce leaves to eat it with; and *fattoush*, which includes toasted or fried pieces of bread in a crunchy mixture of fresh cucumber, radish, tomato and herbs. *Fateh* is a favourite comfort food – a warm bowl of chickpeas, yoghurt, tahini and garlic. Tasty finger foods include *sambusic,* golden pastries filled with minced meat and spices; and *sfeeha,* baked lamb pies. And those are just for starters!

The sweet makers of Damascus are famous, as are their creations. They use wonderful seasonal fruit such as sour cherries and dried fruit such as apricots to make *qamar al-deen* (thin sheets of sweetened 'apricot leather'); use delicious nutty tahini to make *halwa* (halva, a sweet based on tahini, sugar and often pistachios); and have perfected a luscious clotted cream called *ashta*. Being a lover of sweets, one of my Syrian favourites is Damascus rose, which features baked rounds of filo pastry that are sandwiched with *ashta* then drizzled with syrup and crushed nuts. Exquisite!

ESSENTIAL FLAVOURS

BAHARAT
This is a spice mix that blends allspice, white and black pepper, lots of cinnamon, cloves, nutmeg, coriander (cilantro) and caraway. Syrian *baharat* is sometimes known as seven-spice mix and it's often used in meat dishes like baked *kibbeh* and freekeh with chicken.

FREEKEH
A roasted wheat grain very popular in Syria, which is cooked in a similar way to risotto rice. Freekeh is harvested from wheat while the seeds are still young and green – the wheat is set alight, which burns the dry straw and bran but not the seeds. These are then left to dry in the sun. The resulting grain has a nutty, smoky flavour.

NUTS
Syrians love to cook with almonds, walnuts and pine nuts. These nuts are often toasted in butter and used as garnish to add flavour and crunch to rice dishes. Pistachios are also much loved. The pistachio trees of Aleppo are famous, providing bountiful produce that is used particularly in sweet dishes like *baklawa*, *halwa* and *ma'moul* (date pastries).

POMEGRANATE MOLASSES
Made from pomegranate juice, lemon juice and sugar that are reduced over a low heat for a couple of hours to create a thick caramelised syrup with a tangy, piquant taste. It is a condiment readily found in Middle Eastern grocery stores and increasingly in major supermarkets as well. It is used in cooking to give a tart flavour to dishes and is a good tenderiser for meat.

PURSLANE
Generally considered a weed by those unfamiliar with its use as a leaf vegetable, purslane has long been valued by Lebanese and Syrians for its slightly sour and salty taste.

SHANKLEESH
A sharp-tasting cheese made from *labneh* that is formed into balls and rolled in oregano. It is often served broken up in to a rough crumble with chopped tomato and onion and drizzled with extra-virgin olive oil.

SUMAC
Made from dried, powdered berries that grow around the Mediterranean, sumac gives a nice sour tang to dishes. It is sprinkled on kebabs and *pilav* and used in the spice mixture *za'atar*.

TAHINI
A creamy paste made from sesame seeds that have been soaked, crushed, soaked again in highly salted water to remove their husk, toasted and then ground. It is used as the basis of many dips, sauces and in some sweets like *halwa*.

After tabbouleh, *fattoush* is the most well-known salad of Syria and for many it's the favourite too. The sharp flavour of sumac in the dressing, the chunky tomato pieces, the crisp cucumber and radish, and the thin, baked pieces of bread that soak up the dressing are all delicious. Syrians often eat *fattoush* by spooning a manageable amount into a lettuce or vine leaf, wrapping it up into a little parcel and eating it with their fingers.

FATTOUSH

from Sharon Salloum

Mix the dressing ingredients in a small bowl. If desired you can add more sumac or lemon juice.

Crisp the pita bread in a moderate oven or under a grill.

Place all the vegetables and herbs in a large bowl. Break the bread into small, rough pieces into the bowl. Add the dressing and toss well with your hands.

SERVES 4

DRESSING
- 3 garlic cloves, crushed
- 1 teaspoon salt
- 2 teaspoons sweet paprika
- 2 teaspoons sumac
- 2 tablespoons olive oil
- 2 tablespoons lemon juice

SALAD
- 1 pita bread
- 2 Lebanese cucumbers, halved lengthwise, cut into 1 cm (½ in) slices
- 2 medium tomatoes, cut into chunky pieces
- 4-5 radishes, halved and thinly sliced
- ½ red capsicum (bell pepper), cut into 2 cm (¾ in) cubes
- ½ green capsicum (bell pepper), cut into 2 cm (¾ in) cubes
- 4 iceberg lettuce leaves, torn
- handful of purslane leaves
- ½ cup chopped mint
- ½ cup chopped flat-leaf (Italian) parsley
- 3 spring onions (scallions), sliced

'Never lift a boiling saucepan without saying "Isem Allah" (In God's name) – this will protect you from dropping the pot and burning yourself.'

Similar to the popular dish *riz a'djaj* (poached chicken served on rice), this recipe uses toasted freekeh wheat with its distinctive nutty taste. The wheat is cooked slowly like a risotto with chicken stock, minced meat, spices and onion until it is soft and flavoursome. The dish is then piled high onto a serving platter and served with poached chicken pieces, Syrian truffle (if available), pine nuts and almonds.

FREEKEH WITH CHICKEN

from Ayman Abbassi

Wash the freekeh and remove any burnt grains or stones.

Put the chicken in a pot and cover with water. Add the brown onion, cinnamon sticks, bay leaves, cardamom and 1 teaspoon of salt. Cover with a lid and bring to the boil. Simmer for 30 minutes or until cooked through. Remove the chicken from the pot (leaving a light stock) and set aside until cool enough to handle. Remove the skin and break the meat into large pieces, removing the bones.

Bring the chicken stock back to a slow simmer. Heat the ghee or olive oil in a large saucepan and add the red onion. Fry until beginning to soften, then add the lamb or beef, if using, and cook until browned. Stir in the freekeh. Add the *baharat* and 1 heaped teaspoon of salt and stir through.

Add 1 litre (34 fl oz/4 cups) of hot chicken stock and bring to the boil. Lower the heat, cover and simmer for 40 minutes.

Melt a little butter in a large frying pan over medium heat. Add the almonds and cook until lightly toasted. Remove from the pan and repeat with the pine nuts. Remove from the pan and add another knob of butter. When it melts, add the truffles, if using, and coat with butter. Add the chicken pieces, ground cinnamon and 500 ml (17 fl oz/2 cups) of hot stock. Bring to the boil, reheating the chicken.

Spoon the freekeh onto a large serving plate. Place the chicken and truffles on top and scatter with the nuts.

SERVES 6

2 cups freekeh	1 red onion, finely chopped
1 medium free-range chicken (about 1.5 kg/3 lb 4 oz)	300 g (10½ oz) minced (ground) lamb or beef (optional)
½ brown onion, quartered	1 teaspoon *baharat*
3 cinnamon sticks	butter
4 bay leaves	½ cup almonds
6 cardamom pods	½ cup pine nuts
salt	4-6 small Syrian truffles, peeled and sliced (optional)
2 tablespoons clarified butter (ghee) or olive oil	1 teaspoon ground cinnamon

'When baking bread, always mark the sign of the cross on the top of the bread dough before you let it rest.'

The sound of the hot syrup as it's poured onto the hot pastry is one of the best things, only surpassed by the sound of your first crunchy bite into this golden delicacy. Yum!

BAKLAWA

from Amal Malouf

Lightly crush the nuts in a food processor. Tip into a bowl and mix with the sugar, orange-blossom water and rosewater.

Preheat the oven to 180°C (350°F/Gas 4). Brush a baking tray measuring 20 × 30 cm with melted ghee or butter. Add a layer of filo in the base of the tray and brush with more butter. Keep layering with buttered filo until you have used half the filo. Spread the nuts in an even layer on top. Continue layering with the remaining filo.

Carefully cut the *baklawa* into diamond shapes. Pour a little melted butter over the top and bake for about 55 minutes, or until golden brown.

Meanwhile, prepare the syrup. Combine the sugar and water in a saucepan and bring to the boil. Simmer for 15 minutes, until slightly thickened, then remove from the heat and add the orange-blossom water, rosewater and lemon juice. Pour the hot syrup over the hot pastry. Cool before serving.

MAKES 20 PIECES APPROX

2-3 cups walnuts or pistachios
2 tablespoons sugar
2 teaspoons orange-blossom
    water
1 teaspoon rosewater
350 g (12½ oz) clarified butter
    (ghee) or unsalted butter,
    melted
375 g (13 oz) filo pastry

SYRUP

440 g (15½ oz/2 cups) sugar
250 ml (8½ fl oz/1 cup) water
½ teaspoon orange-blossom
    water
½ teaspoon rosewater
squeeze of lemon juice

'"*Sallem hal eid*" is the phrase spoken to protect the hand that prepared the food (the hand is symbolic of the person).'

Syria's national dish of minced meat and burghul is so deeply loved that over the years its fans have found many different ways to prepare it. The secret is using fresh, very finely minced meat. This is carefully spiced then served raw, baked or fried in endlessly varying shapes, often with delicious fillings (that often include more minced meat). This recipe is for a kind of *kibbeh* sandwich: a layer of cooked, spiced meat and pine nuts is pressed between two layers of fine *kibbeh*, then baked and served in wedges like pieces of cake. Serve with salad and drained yoghurt (natural yoghurt that has been drained in muslin [cheesecloth] until thick).

KIBBEH BIL SANIEH

from Najla Atmaja

To make the filling, heat the oil in a frying pan over low heat and add the meat. Cook, stirring constantly to break up the grains of meat. When the meat is browned and separated and the moisture is starting to evaporate, stir in the onion, spices, salt and pepper and keep cooking until the onion is soft.

Meanwhile, melt the butter in a small frying pan and add the pine nuts. Fry until they start to brown, then stir into the meat mixture. Remove from the heat and set aside to cool.

To make the *kibbeh*, combine the burghul, meat, onion, *baharat*, salt and pepper in a bowl and mix well by hand until it forms a paste. You may need a little water to keep the mixture soft. Cover and leave to rest for 30 minutes.

Preheat the oven to 180°C (350°F/Gas 4) and oil a round baking tray with deep sides (around 2 cm [¾ in]). Dampen your hands and layer the tray with half of the *kibbeh* by forming small balls of the mixture then flattening them over the tray. Smooth the surface and make sure there are no gaps. Spread the cooled meat filling on top, pressing it down a little to keep the layers tight. Top with the rest of the *kibbeh* using the same technique. When the surface is smooth, push a small hole through the centre of the *kibbeh* with your finger. Slice into wedges fanning around the hole. Brush with the olive oil and bake in the oven for 25 minutes.

SERVES 6

FILLING

3 tablespoons olive oil
800 g (1 lb 12 oz) minced (ground) lamb or beef
4 large onions, finely chopped
1 teaspoon *baharat*
½ teaspoon cinnamon (optional)
1 teaspoon salt
1½ teaspoons freshly ground black pepper
1 tablespoon butter
3 tablespoons pine nuts

KIBBEH

1½ cups fine burghul, soaked overnight in 250 ml (8½ fl oz/1 cup) water, drained well
800 g (1 lb 12 oz) lean, finely minced (ground) lamb or beef (ask your butcher to mince it twice)
2 large onions, finely grated
1 teaspoon *baharat*
2 teaspoons salt
3 teaspoons freshly ground black pepper
1 tablespoon olive oil

The world's love affair with Thai food has been long and satisfying, and the number of Thai restaurants now in big cities and small towns is a tribute to our desire for these fresh flavours. We can all recognise great tom yum soup, green chicken curry and pad thai noodles - at their best, Thai dishes perfectly balance sweet, sour, salty, spicy and bitter flavours to make your tastebuds tingle.

One thing I have discovered is the distinction Thai people make between foods they cook at home and ones they eat in restaurants. The famous chicken and holy basil stir-fry (*gai pad graprow*) is a great example. When the many pounded chillies hit the hot oil, the fumes must be like a good dose of capsicum spray - intense and choking. The stir-fry is delicious but it's no wonder Thai people prefer to eat this dish in restaurants - it is so pungent that 'all the neighbours know what you're having for dinner!'

There are usually a couple of different types of chilli used in every recipe, both fresh and dried, and roasted chilli powder is sometimes added as well. This is one of the world's really hot cuisines! One useful piece of kitchen equipment that will help you get the best out of chillies (and other ingredients) is a deep mortar and pestle, which is in constant use in Thai kitchens. Some cooks also use a blender to mix up curry pastes or to chop fresh coconut with a little warm water ready for squeezing through a fine sieve to make really fresh coconut milk.

Eating Thai-style is to be served all the dishes at the same time in the centre of the table - there is no separation into entree/main course. It's a great way to eat as the cook gets to sit down and not be ferrying food backwards and forwards. Rice is an integral part of every meal, along with soup, a couple of curries and side dishes. Thai people generally eat with a spoon and fork and use the fork to push the food onto the spoon - the fork is never actually eaten from.

In the northeast, the way of eating is different - the Isaan style of cooking prefers sticky rice that is served in bamboo baskets and eaten by rolling the rice into a ball to scoop up the fiery curries and salads.

I've always been interested in how people from different cultures serve their food and I love the way Thai people use banana leaves as a backdrop to whatever they serve - sometimes the leaf is carefully cut to fit the serving plate exactly. It all adds to the sense that food is a form of art and it's all beautiful, aromatic and delicious - a totally sensual feast. Even some of the desserts are created like artworks. One popular dessert is called *luk chup*, which are moulded fruit shapes made from mung bean paste that are coloured and dipped in agar agar jelly to glaze. Some find these sweets too gorgeous to eat!

ESSENTIAL FLAVOURS

BASIL
Thai basil, with dark green leaves and purple stems, has a mild aniseed smell and sweet flavour. Holy (or hot) basil has a minty, peppery flavour. Both are freshly torn into salads or cooked dishes.

CHILLI
Many different types of chillies are used in Thai cooking, both fresh and dried. Fresh chillies include long chillies and small, fiery birdseyes (also known as 'scuds'). Dried chillies (long or small) are usually softened in water before using – dried long chillies aren't too spicy but add warmth and colour to dishes such as red curries. Many recipes also call for roasted chilli powder.

FISH SAUCE
Known as 'nam pla', this fishy-smelling fermented sauce is clear, pale and salty. The most popular is the Squid brand.

GALANGAL
This root has a distinctive flavour that is similar to ginger but sharper – it gives tom yum soup its special taste. Galangal has a woody texture and is harder to cut than ginger.

KAFFIR LIME
Similar in size to a normal lime but with a bumpy skin. Both the leaves and grated skin are used to flavour stir-fries and curries. When grating the skin, make sure that you only use the coloured surface. The flesh of the fruit is not used at all and the fruit yields very little juice (instead the juice from regular limes is used to add tang to salad dressings). The leaves, which are easily recognised by their unique double leaf, are often shredded very finely and added to salads.

LEMONGRASS
A woody, aromatic herb that is used to flavour many Thai dishes. The tough outer layers need to be removed to expose the more tender, white and purple-edged centre.

THAI EGGPLANTS (AUBERGINES)
'Apple eggplants' (aubergines), are about the size of a golf ball and can be either white or green – the white type is used in curries and the green, which is more crunchy, is used in salads. Also commonly used is a very small pea eggplant, which is eaten whole and bursts in your mouth.

THAI SEASONING SAUCE
A Thai-style soybean sauce that has a different flavour to Chinese soy sauce. Popular brands include Golden Mountain or Maggi.

This is a wonderful dish that combines the deliciously rich and creamy texture of banana flower with crunchy cashews and chicken and prawns spiked with roasted chilli and lime juice. Banana flowers resemble large bell-shaped buds and they're not difficult to find fresh, although they're also available preserved from Asian grocery stores – soak preserved buds in cold water for 10 minutes and rinse before use.

BANANA FLOWER SALAD

from Rachda Mahamontchir

Bring 500 ml (17 fl oz/2 cups) of water to the boil. Add the chicken, reduce the heat to a simmer and poach for 5 minutes. Add the prawns and continue poaching for 3 minutes, until cooked through. Drain and set aside.

Pour the lime juice and 500 ml (17 fl oz/2 cups) of water into a bowl. Cut the banana flower in half and remove the soft, pale heart from each half, discarding the outer leaves. Finely slice on the diagonal and add to the bowl. Soak for 5 minutes; the lime will prevent discolouration.

Combine the dressing ingredients in a large bowl, stirring until the palm sugar dissolves. Drain the banana flower, gently squeeze out the excess water, and add to the dressing along with the poached chicken and prawns, dried shrimp, sliced shallots and cashews. Mix well.

Serve sprinkled with fresh chilli, fried shallots and coriander.

SERVES 4

100 g (3½ oz) chicken breast fillet, sliced
200 g (7 oz) green king prawns (shrimp), shelled and de-veined
2 tablespoons lime juice
1 banana flower (about 200 g/7 oz)
50 g (1¾ oz) dried shrimp, finely chopped
1 tablespoon sliced shallots
2 tablespoons cashews, roasted and crushed
finely sliced long red chilli
fried shallots
handful of coriander (cilantro) leaves

DRESSING

2 tablespoons fish sauce
3 tablespoons lime juice
1 tablespoon grated palm sugar (jaggery)
1 tablespoon roasted chilli paste
2 teaspoons Thai roasted chilli powder
3 tablespoons coconut milk

'To tell a cook their food is delicious you must screw up your face with intense emotion and say "*Aroi mahk*" with great determination!'

Once you've seen this popular dish made in a Thai kitchen, you realise how easy it is if you know how! It is a wonderful combination of noodles, prawns, crunchy fresh vegies and that distinctive sweet and tangy sauce. A little dried shrimp and preserved radish, with its soft but chewy texture and unique flavour, are two of the essential ingredients. You can adjust the amount of sauce you add to the noodles according to how strong a flavour you like. This quantity of sauce is about right for four people but you can keep any unused sauce in a jar in the refrigerator for next time.

PAD THAI

from Jay Phao-Chinda

Combine the tamarind and warm water in a bowl. Break up the pulp with your fingers until it is dissolving into the water. Strain the water into a saucepan, squeezing all the liquid from the pulp. Add the palm sugar, caster sugar and seasoning sauce. Bring to the boil, then simmer until reduced and slightly syrupy.

Heat a little oil in a wok and when hot, add the prawns. Fry until they curl and change colour then add the dried shrimp, onion, tofu and radish. Stir-fry briefly then push the ingredients to one side and crack in the eggs, breaking them up just a little. Without letting them cook completely, add the noodles, 2 tablespoons of water, a few scoops of tamarind sauce (or to taste) and some chopped garlic chives, bean sprouts, fried shallots, peanuts and chilli powder to taste. Stir briefly then serve garnished with whole garlic chives, more bean sprouts, fried shallots, peanuts and wedges of lime.

SERVES 2

SAUCE
100 g (3½ oz) tamarind pulp
300 ml (10 fl oz) warm water
200 g (7 oz) palm sugar (jaggery)
50 g (1¾ oz) caster sugar
150 ml (5 fl oz) Thai seasoning sauce

oil
6 large shelled green prawns (shrimp)
10 g (¼ oz/⅓ cup) dried shrimp
¼ red onion, sliced
40 g (1½ oz) firm tofu, sliced

40 g (1½ oz) shredded preserved radish
2 eggs
200 g (7 oz) flat rice noodles, soaked in warm water for 30 minutes, drained
garlic chives (some chopped and some left whole to garnish)
bean sprouts
fried shallots
chopped roasted peanuts
roasted chilli powder
lime wedges

'Always leave a little food on your plate after you have eaten to show you are satisfied, but never leave rice on your plate as it is considered wasteful.'

My friend Air swears by making fresh coconut milk every day! If this sounds a bit extreme, you can always do what Sujet does before he starts this recipe, which is to boil tinned coconut milk for 5 minutes to rid it of the 'tinned taste'. The curry is finished with Thai basil, which you should always add after you've turned off the heat to stop the leaves turning black.

KAENG PED PETT YANG

Red Duck Curry
from Sujet Saengkham

Put the curry paste ingredients other than the oil in a blender and process to a smooth paste. Heat a little oil in a small frying pan and fry the paste for 10 minutes to remove the raw taste. Spoon into a jar.

Heat half of the coconut milk in a saucepan over medium heat. Add 3 tablespoons of curry paste (store the rest in the refrigerator) and stir well to combine. Cook for about 5 minutes, until the oil starts to come to the surface. Add the duck, fish sauce, lychees, lychee juice, pineapple and remaining coconut milk. Bring to the boil and add the eggplants and chilli. Cook for a few minutes, until the eggplants are just tender. Stir in the lime leaves, then remove from the heat and stir in the basil. Serve with steamed rice.

SERVES 4

RED CURRY PASTE

- **10 dried long chillies, softened in warm water for 10 minutes, drained**
- **2-3 fresh small red chillies**
- **1 lemongrass stalk, white part only, sliced**
- **2 cm (¾ in) piece of galangal, sliced**
- **1 cm (½ in) piece of fresh turmeric, sliced**
- **7 garlic cloves**
- **1 shallot, sliced**
- **rind of 1 kaffir lime**
- **1 tablespoon shrimp paste**
- **125 ml (4 fl oz/½ cup) water vegetable oil**

RED DUCK CURRY

- **400 ml (13½ fl oz) coconut milk**
- **300 g (10½ oz) roasted duck meat, skin removed, broken into large bite-sized pieces**
- **1 tablespoon fish sauce**
- **4 tinned lychees and 1 tablespoon juice from the tin**
- **4 bite-sized chunks of fresh pineapple**
- **100 g (3½ oz) apple eggplants (aubergines), cut into wedges**
- **100 g (3½ oz) pea eggplants (aubergines)**
- **1 long red chilli, diagonally sliced**
- **6 kaffir lime leaves, torn**
- **50 g (1¾ oz) Thai basil leaves, torn**

'We only appreciate the worth of salt when the soup is tasteless.'

One of the favourite dishes among Thai people,
often ordered for breakfast with a deep-fried egg,
sunny-side up, on top.

A lovely dessert and an impressive one to make at
home. Try to grate your own fresh coconut for the true
Thai flavour!

GAI PAD GRAPROW

Chicken and Holy Basil Stir-fry

from Rachda Mahamontchir

Put the garlic and chillies in a mortar and pound to a rough
paste. Heat a wok until smoking hot then add the oil and swirl
to coat the surface. Add the pounded chilli and garlic and
stir-fry for 15–20 seconds. Add the chicken and stir-fry for
1–2 minutes, or until most of the chicken has changed colour.
Stir in the oyster, soy and fish sauces and add the pepper,
onion, spring onion and extra chilli. Keep stir-frying and
when the chicken is just cooked, add the chicken stock.
Turn off the heat and toss through the basil leaves. Transfer
to a serving plate.

To fry the eggs, wipe out the wok and add the oil. When
hot, gently pour in the eggs. Be careful as they crackle and
pop. Fry the eggs until golden (they should stick together),
then lift out with a slotted spoon and place on top of the
chicken stir-fry.

SERVES 4

10-12 garlic cloves, sliced
10 long red chillies, sliced
2-3 tablespoons vegetable oil
500 g (1 lb 2 oz) chicken thigh
   fillets, finely sliced
1 tablespoon oyster sauce
1 teaspoon soy sauce
1 teaspoon fish sauce
pinch of white pepper
1 small onion, sliced
2 spring onions (scallions), cut
   into 3 cm (1¼ in) lengths

extra 1-2 long red chillies,
   finely sliced
2-3 tablespoons chicken stock
½ bunch holy basil, leaves
   picked

FRIED EGGS

125 ml (4 fl oz/½ cup) vegetable
   oil
4 eggs, cracked into a bowl

BLACK STICKY RICE PUDDING

from Pacharin Jantrakool

Rinse the rice and place in a saucepan with the water. Bring to
the boil over medium heat and cook until the grains are soft
and split and most of the water has been absorbed. Add the
sugar and continue cooking until dissolved.

Meanwhile, make the sweet coconut cream. Combine
the ingredients in a saucepan and gently bring to the boil,
then remove from the heat. The rice flour should thicken
the cream.

To make the caramelised coconut, put the grated coconut
and sugar in a saucepan with a little water and stir constantly
over medium heat until thick.

Spoon the black sticky rice into serving bowls and top
with the coconut cream and caramelised coconut.

SERVES 4-6

2 cups black glutinous (sticky)
   rice, soaked overnight
1.25 litres (42 fl oz/5 cups)
   water
440 g (15½ oz/2 cups) sugar

SWEET COCONUT CREAM

250 ml (8½ fl oz/1 cup)
   coconut cream
2 teaspoons rice flour

½ teaspoon salt
pinch of sugar

CARAMELISED COCONUT

2 cups freshly grated coconut
   (or dried shredded coconut)
200 g (7 oz/1 cup)
   brown sugar

For lovers of food, there's nothing like that first taste of something that fires up all your senses and makes your heart beat faster. With Turkish food my magical moment was from a single spoonful of thick, creamy yoghurt topped with sour cherries in syrup, which I tasted in a little village on the Turkish coast. That was it – from that first picturesque breakfast under grape vines at a table full of delights, I've sought out Turkish food and learned as much as I can about it.

Because Turkey stretches from the Mediterranean to the Middle East there's a huge range of ingredients and culinary styles throughout the country. Some food is beautifully rustic while other is highly developed, having been fostered by the Ottoman Empire, which capitalised on Turkey's place at the centre of spice routes. These highly travelled routes brought exotic ingredients to Turkey from all around the world.

There would have been no better place to be than in the Ottoman Empire at the apex of this golden age of food – provided you were part of the upper classes. It's said that Turkish delight (*lokum*) was created by order of Sultan Abdul Hamid who wanted to please his legions of mistresses who revelled in new, delicious flavours and textures.

Turkish food in Australia has gradually evolved beyond kebabs and dips. More bakeries are turning out basic pide – the paddle-shaped bread that is a central part of many meals and essential fare at Ramadan – as well as alluring versions stuffed with white cheese and spinach, or spicy lamb or beef with an egg cracked on top. More butchers are making *sucuk* (a spicy sausage) and *bastourma* (spice-coated, air-dried beef), and there are now many Turkish sweets palaces, restaurants and cafes.

You shouldn't discount the kebabs however – Turkish know-how is a wonderful thing. Whether beef, lamb or chicken kebabs or spiced minced lamb on skewers with long chillies and tomatoes, this is some of the best simply cooked food you can find.

If you're lucky enough to spend time in a Turkish home, you'll be overwhelmed with offers of food and drink. These might start with freshly roasted nuts and move on to endless dishes, including a range of vegetable dips that are all colours of the rainbow. The feast might finish with sweet flaky pastries and rich Turkish coffee served in little cups.

Turkish coffee is renowned the world over – and deservedly so. It is made in a long-handled pot (*jezve*) with the special pulverised coffee beloved by Turks. The coffee is sweetened and stirred then allowed to gently boil up the sides of the pot a couple of times so a thick, dark crema appears on top. The art is then to carefully pour the coffee into cups, making sure each cup has a layer of smooth crema. Hot, strong and wickedly sweet!

ESSENTIAL FLAVOURS

CHILLI
Biber dövme are hot red chilli flakes made from semi-dried chillies. Look for one that is slightly oily. *Biber salçasi* is a chilli paste that can be hot or mild.

NIGELLA SEEDS
Small black seeds also known (incorrectly) as black cumin. These are commonly sprinkled over bread such as pide before it's baked.

SUCUK
A paprika and garlic sausage sometimes used to fill pide bread, very similar to chorizo sausage.

SUMAC
A dark red spice made from the sumac berry, which has a tangy, lemony flavour. Used in marinades and salads.

YOGHURT
Used in dips and desserts as well as served with grilled meats and vegetable dishes. It is also used to make the cold drink *ayran*, which is often thinned with either milk or water and flavoured with salt - it is traditionally served with kebabs.

POMEGRANATE MOLASSES
Turkey's delicious sweet and sour flavour is made from squeezing the juice from pomegranates and slowly cooking it to a lovely syrup. Pomegranate molasses is used as a salad dressing, in marinades and beyond the Turkish world it is a lovely glaze for roast chicken or duck. A salad dressing from Ulku Gani: blend together 25 ml (1 fl oz) olive oil, 1 tablespoon pomegranate molasses, 1 tablespoon vinegar (or use lemon juice), ½ tablespoon honey, and a sprinkle of salt.

Turkish food is all about beautiful presentation as well as taste and these two dips look fabulous. They're delicious as well as colourful, and healthy too: lots of vegetables, only a little oil and yoghurt in abundance. Most Turkish families eat a great deal of yoghurt every week. Buy the freshest carrots for this recipe and take time to decorate your serving bowl or plate with a pattern of black olives.

The Turks were using beetroot long before its renaissance as a vegetable. Parboiling saves time and softens the beetroot before baking brings out their lovely natural sugars. As you'd imagine, this dip looks beautiful and is just the thing to go with Turkish pide.

YOĞURTLU HAVUC

Carrot Dip

from Esma Koroglu

Cook the carrots in a frying pan with ½ tablespoon of olive oil until just softened. Remove from the pan and leave to cool. Combine the yoghurt, garlic and salt and mix well. Stir in the cooled carrot. Scoop into a serving bowl, decorate with olives and drizzle with a little olive oil.

MAKES 2 CUPS

6-7 carrots, grated	1 garlic clove, crushed
olive oil	pinch of salt
200 g (7 oz) Greek-style yoghurt	black olives

KIZ GÜZELI

Beetroot Dip

from Esma Koroglu

Parboil the beetroots, then bake them until soft. Peel and cut into quarters. Finely chop in a food processor or blender.

Combine the yoghurt, garlic and salt and mix well. Stir in the beetroot. Scoop into a serving bowl and drizzle with olive oil.

MAKES 3 CUPS

3 beetroots	1 garlic clove, crushed
200 g (7 oz) Greek-style yoghurt	pinch of salt
	olive oil

'At the start of a meal say to the cook, "*Eline sag˘lik!*" (Health to your hands!)'

This *pilav* is described as a 'no-stir risotto', with the red of the tomato and chilli paste adding colour and flavour.

Kofte is perfect for the barbecue, the pan or the oven, says Serif. I couldn't agree more - this recipe is simple and delicious. All it needs is a salad.

BURGHUL PILAV

from Ishil Itiyar

LAMB KOFTE

from Serif Kaya

Heat the oil in a saucepan and add the onion, chilli paste and tomatoes and season with salt and pepper. Cook for a few minutes until the onion and tomato are starting to soften. Stir in the burghul, add the stock and bring to the boil. Reduce the heat to a simmer, cover and cook for 15–20 minutes, or until the stock has been absorbed.

Mix the ingredients together with your hands, kneading until smooth. Wet your hands and roll walnut-sized pieces of mixture into balls. Flatten them slightly. Fry the *kofte* on a lightly oiled barbecue grill, or in a chargrill pan, for about 1 minute on each side.

SERVES 6-8

- 3 tablespoons olive oil
- 2 small onions, chopped
- 1 teaspoon Turkish chilli paste (*biber salçasi*)
- 3 tomatoes, diced
- salt and pepper
- 2 cups coarse burghul, rinsed
- 1 litre (34 fl oz/4 cups) chicken stock

SERVES 6

- 500 g (1 lb 2 oz) minced (ground) lamb
- 1 medium onion, grated
- 2 garlic cloves, crushed
- pinch of allspice
- pinch of freshly ground black pepper
- pinch of chilli flakes
- pinch of sweet paprika
- pinch of ground cumin
- 1 teaspoon salt
- 1 egg

'You shouldn't put water in a meal already cooked.' (Don't meddle.)

A colourful, fresh and clever dish. Try to use a range of vegetables with this rice and pine nut stuffing as they'll look so pretty together on a serving platter.

DOLMA

Stuffed Vegetables
from Bulent Pektuzun

Heat all but 2 tablespoons of the olive oil in a large saucepan. Add the onions, pine nuts and some salt and fry over medium heat for 5 minutes, stirring frequently, until the onion softens. Add the rice and continue to stir for a few minutes. Add the diced tomato, currants, chilli and extra salt and pepper and cook for a few more minutes. Add enough boiling water to cover the rice, then stir in the herbs. Reduce the heat to a simmer, cover and cook for about 10 minutes, until the water has been absorbed. The rice should be al dente. Leave to cool a little.

Cut the stems from the eggplants and hollow out the flesh using a small melon baller or teaspoon, leaving a shell about 5 mm thick. Slice through the zucchini one-third to halfway down from the stem (so the opening is not too narrow) and scoop out the flesh as for the eggplants. Slice the tops off the capsicums without cutting all the way through, so the tops stay attached like lids. Remove the seeds. Slice the tops off the tomatoes as for the capsicums and scoop out the flesh.

Fill the vegetables with the rice and arrange in the base of a wide saucepan or frying pan. Fit them in snugly so they stay upright. Decorate the tops of the eggplants and zucchini with slices of tomato. Drizzle over the remaining olive oil and enough warm water to come 2–3 cm (¾–1¼ in) up the sides of the vegetables. Cover with a lid and simmer on medium heat for around 20 minutes.

SERVES 6-8

185 ml (6 fl oz) olive oil
4 medium onions, finely chopped
100 g (3½ oz) pine nuts
salt
500 g (1 lb 2 oz) medium-grain rice, rinsed
400 g (14 oz) tin diced tomatoes
100 g (3½ oz) currants
1 teaspoon chilli flakes (or to taste)
pepper
½ bunch dill, finely chopped
¼ bunch mint, leaves picked and finely chopped
½ bunch flat-leaf (Italian) parsley, finely chopped
2 small tomatoes, sliced

TO STUFF

6 small eggplants (aubergines)
6 Lebanese zucchini (courgettes)
6 small red capsicums (bell peppers)
6 medium tomatoes

'Problems will arise if one eats and the other watches.'

With the Turkish diaspora spread throughout Greece, Cyprus, Syria, Iraq and the Balkans, it's no wonder many countries in the region also lay claim to this lovely light cake.

RAVANI

Semolina Orange Cakes
from Gulbahar Kaya

Preheat the oven to 180°C (350°F/Gas 4). Butter a muffin tray that has 6 large moulds.

In a large bowl beat the egg whites with a pinch of sugar until stiff. In a separate bowl, beat the egg yolks with 1 tablespoon of sugar and the orange zest until pale. Add the semolina, flour and pistachios to the egg whites and partly mix through. Add the egg yolks and fold through until combined. Spoon into the muffin tray and bake for 30 minutes.

Meanwhile, make the syrup. Put the orange juice, zest and sugar in a saucepan and bring to the boil over medium heat, stirring until the sugar dissolves. Simmer for 10 minutes or until syrupy and reduced by half. Leave to cool.

Whip the cream until thick and stir in the yoghurt.

Segment the oranges by cutting off the peel with a small sharp knife, making sure you remove all the white pith. Cut on either side of each segment, removing wedges of flesh but leaving the membranes.

When the cakes are cooked, ladle over some of the cooled syrup and leave to soak for at least 10 minutes (or longer if you prefer the cakes softer). Serve the cakes with the whipped cream and yoghurt, orange segments and a little extra syrup.

MAKES 6 CAKES

5 medium eggs, separated
1 tablespoon sugar, plus 1 pinch extra
grated zest of 1 orange
50 g (1¾ oz) fine semolina
50 g (1¾ oz) plain (all-purpose) flour
100 g (3½ oz) ground pistachios

SYRUP

600 ml (20½ fl oz) fresh orange juice
grated zest of 1 orange
500 g (1 lb 2 oz) sugar

TO SERVE

300 ml (10 fl oz) cream
300 ml (10 fl oz) Greek-style yoghurt
2 oranges

Ask any American expatriate about food from home and they'll start listing numerous dishes that quickly show you that what's on offer is a far cry from hot dogs, burgers and fries. Among other things, they'll speak lovingly of Thanksgiving feasts and special foods from different regions. From the wonderfully fresh foods grown in sunny California to the plentiful seafood of Maryland's Chesapeake Bay, this is a country rich in produce and know-how. Given this abundance and variety, food from the United States is complex, from delicate crab cakes to the more hearty fare of the Deep South. American-Indian cooking traditions have fused with those brought by early settlers and waves of immigrants and a sophisticated cuisine has developed that is distinctly 'American'.

The Mississippi Delta captures this blending of cultures perfectly. New Orleans is the heart of Creole and Cajun food, which were influenced by the French, Spanish, Irish and Italians and the huge population of African-Americans in the South. This city has given us many culinary delights such as jambalaya, gumbo, fried chicken, collard greens and grits.

The African black-eyed pea is an important ingredient in southern 'soul food'. As well as introducing this staple, African slaves were resourceful - chickens were easy to keep, catching a fish was free and collard greens grew like weeds. Further north, the food couldn't be more different and the New England region is renowned for its maple syrup, baked beans, brown bread, clam chowder and clambakes.

Almost every kind of cooking can be found in New York City while in the other parts of the mid-Atlantic, Dutch influences are prominent - particularly among the Amish community of Pennsylvania.

Two feasts are always mentioned in discussions of American food. The first is Thanksgiving, which is a reminder of the first harvest feast the new settlers celebrated with the local Indians. Americans still celebrate this holiday with some of the same food - cranberries, pecans and turkey.

The other feast is the all-American 'cookout'. In these extravagant barbecues, cooks use many different types of wood to achieve a wonderful smoky flavour, enhanced by combinations of dry spices used to make rubs and marinades.

As a sweets lover, I have to also mention those lovely high wedges of all-American pies. Each region uses local produce to make wonders such as key lime pie, shoofly pie (made with molasses), lemon meringue pie and pecan pie. Oh yeah!

ESSENTIAL FLAVOURS

BARBECUE SAUCE
The preferred flavours of this accompaniment to barbecued meat varies around the country, but most draw on a tomato base that is sometimes mixed with vinegar, capsicum, chilli or sugar. Tastes range from sweet to smoky or spicy.

BEEF
The New York steak and the ubiquitous hamburger made from minced (ground) beef are America's most popular exports and have colonised tastebuds around the world. The name 'hamburger' comes from the German city of Hamburg, where this pounded style of meat is common - not from the word 'ham'.

CLAMS
Clam chowder is a very popular dish and there are a number of different versions, for example with the clams cooked in milk or cooked in a stock broth with tomato.

CORN
A staple vegetable that is native to the Americas. It's thought that the American-Indians taught early settlers how to grow and eat corn, thereby saving their lives. Whether eaten straight off the cob or processed into cornmeal it can be used in endless ways. Cornbread and grits, made from ground corn, are southern favourites.

CRAB
Beloved up and down the American seaboard, blue crabs and king crabs are the most common varieties. On the West Coast dungeness crab is also popular, while in Alaska it's the red king crab. On the East Coast, the crab season in Chesapeake Bay marks the start of summer.

GRITS
Similar to polenta, grits are made from hominy, which is corn that has been soaked in lye water to remove the outside shell of the corn kernel. The hominy is then dried and ground to a slightly coarser texture than polenta.

It is commonly cooked like porridge and eaten for breakfast with butter and sugar, or with cheese for a savoury version, but it can be flavoured with anything - garlic, chilli, meat, vegetables and so on.

PECANS
Native to the United States, the pecan tree is a type of hickory that produces the edible pecan nut. Pecans hold a special place in the American heart, the most famous recipe being the much-celebrated pecan pie.

PUMPKIN
The orange pumpkin that is famously used as a jack-o-lantern at Halloween is the only member of the pumpkin family that is called a 'pumpkin' in the United States. Other varieties with golden or green outer skins are generally referred to as squashes.

TABASCO SAUCE
The brand Tabasco has become synonymous with this hot chilli sauce made from tabasco peppers, vinegar and salt. It can be used to spice up many sauces and dishes.

TOMATOES
Native to South America, tomatoes are a popular accompaniment to grilled or barbecued meat. Fried green tomatoes or other green tomato recipes put unripe late-season tomatoes to good use and tomato-based salsas employ tomatoes in a way inspired by neighbouring Latin America.

'When making jambalaya let it simmer like a man's heart so that it develops full flavour and always wants more!'

A classic Creole dish from New Orleans and a true one-pot wonder blending French, African, Spanish and American influences. Make sure you use parboiled or 'converted' rice. Serve with cornbread muffins (see page 386).

JAMBALAYA

from Victor Kimble

Mix the spices with the dried herbs. Heat some olive oil in a pot and add the onion, celery and capsicum. Fry for a few minutes then add the garlic and 2 teaspoons of the spices and herbs. Stir well. Add the sausage, chicken, tomatoes, tomato paste, rice, stock, salt and the remaining spices and herbs. Mix well and bring to the boil. Boil for 3-5 minutes then reduce the heat and simmer for 20-25 minutes. Keep stirring to prevent the rice from sticking to the bottom of the pot. Add a little water if needed.

SERVES 6-8

½ tablespoon sweet paprika
1 teaspoon cayenne pepper
½ tablespoon dried oregano
½ tablespoon dried thyme
olive oil
1 red onion, diced
4 celery stalks, diced
1 red capsicum (bell pepper), diced
2 teaspoons crushed garlic (or garlic powder)

500 g (1 lb 2 oz) *andouille* or chorizo sausage, diced
1 kg (2 lb 3 oz) chicken breast fillets, diced
6-8 large tomatoes, diced
2 tablespoons tomato paste (concentrated puree)
1 kg (2 lb 3 oz) parboiled rice
750 ml (25½ fl oz/3 cups) chicken stock
1 teaspoon salt

This dish is traditionally made from blue crab in the Chesapeake Bay region of Maryland, but crab cakes are also popular along all of America's coasts. They are sometimes served with a sauce such as this remoulade, or with tartare sauce, mustard or ketchup. The recipe uses

Old Bay Seasoning, a traditional spice blend for crab cakes, 'crab boils' and other favourite American shellfish dishes, but if you can't find it add a large pinch of ground celery seeds, smaller pinches of pepper and ground cardamom, and extra paprika and cayenne pepper.

CHESAPEAKE BAY CRAB CAKES WITH CAJUN REMOULADE

from George Francisco

Combine the crab cake ingredients except the flour and oil and mix well. Form into 6 cakes. Refrigerate for 15 minutes to help the cakes bind.

To make the remoulade, beat the egg yolks in a bowl and add the liquid from the cornichons, then the lemon juice. Gradually beat in the vegetable oil; the mixture should thicken like mayonnaise. Stir in the cornichons, capers and herbs and add paprika and cayenne to taste (it is supposed to be spicy). Season with salt.

Dust the crab cakes in flour and fry in generous oil over medium heat until golden. Serve with the remoulade.

SERVES 6

CRAB CAKES
500 g (1 lb 2 oz) crab meat (blue swimmer crab if possible)
40 g (1½ oz/½ cup) breadcrumbs
2 tablespoons Old Bay Seasoning
2 tablespoons dijon mustard
pinch of sweet paprika
pinch of cayenne pepper
salt
1 egg plus 1 egg yolk
2 tablespoons chopped tarragon
2 tablespoons chopped flat-leaf (Italian) parsley
plain (all-purpose) flour
vegetable oil

REMOULADE
2 egg yolks
50 g (1¾ oz) cornichons (or gherkins), finely chopped, plus ½ tablespoon liquid from the jar
juice of 1 lemon
250 ml (8½ fl oz/1 cup) vegetable oil
1½ teaspoons salted capers, rinsed and chopped
¼ bunch chives, finely chopped
¼ bunch chervil, finely chopped
¼ bunch flat-leaf (Italian) parsley, finely chopped
¼ bunch tarragon, finely chopped
pinch of Spanish smoked paprika
cayenne pepper
salt

'The ultimate compliment to an African-American is, "That gumbo was screamin!".'

Oh, yum! Cornbread muffins are made every day in the South. Victor's grandmother would have pounded the corn kernels by hand but he says tinned creamed corn is really handy and much easier! These muffins are lovely by themselves or served with collard greens, gumbo or jambalaya.

Fried chicken is the traditional Sunday lunch of the southern states. Thought to have evolved during slavery as most slaves were permitted to keep poultry, the dish has become mainstream and travelled the world. This lovely recipe is from Ashley's beloved black nanny, Blanchie, and contains her clever tip to tenderise the chicken in buttermilk. Serve with grits (see page 390) and southern greens (see page 390).

CORNBREAD MUFFINS

from Victor Kimble

Preheat the oven to 180°C (350°F/Gas 4) and butter a muffin tray. Mix the polenta, flour, sugar, salt, butter and eggs until well combined. Stir in the creamed corn and milk. Spoon the mixture into the muffin tray and bake for 15–20 minutes or until golden brown.

MAKES 12 MUFFINS

---

90 g (3 oz/½ cup) polenta	150 g (5½ oz) butter, melted
225 g (1½ cups) self-raising flour	3 eggs
	1 cup creamed corn
110 g (4 oz/½ cup) caster sugar	250 ml (8½ fl oz/1 cup)
pinch of salt	full-cream milk

SOUTHERN FRIED CHICKEN

from Ashley Sheridan

Marinate the chicken pieces in buttermilk in the refrigerator overnight.

The next day, combine the dry ingredients in a wide bowl. Drain the chicken pieces of excess buttermilk and dip them into the beaten egg, then coat them evenly in the flour mixture. Place the pieces on a sheet of baking paper to rest for about 15 minutes.

Add enough oil or lard to a large frying pan to come halfway up the chicken pieces. Heat over high heat until almost smoking. Add the chicken and cook for 10–12 minutes or until golden brown on the first side. Turn and cook the other side for 8–10 minutes. Drain on a wire rack.

SERVES 6

---

1 medium chicken (about 1.5 kg/3 lb 4 oz), chopped into pieces	½ tablespoon Old Bay Seasoning (or use ½ teaspoon cayenne pepper and 1½ teaspoons sweet paprika)
600 ml (20½ fl oz) buttermilk, to cover the chicken	
225 g (8 oz/1½ cups) plain (all-purpose) flour	1 tablespoon dried tarragon
1 tablespoon Creole seasoning	1 tablespoon dried dill
1 tablespoon onion powder	salt and pepper
½ tablespoon garlic powder	1 large egg, beaten
	vegetable oil or lard

A finger-lickin' good recipe with layers of flavour from the spice rub, the homemade *chipotle* barbecue sauce and the final sizzle on the barbecue. Delicious! The sauce can be made a day in advance and stored in the refrigerator.

BARBECUED RIBS

from Victor Pisapia

To make the sauce, heat the butter in a saucepan and sauté the onion and jalapeño chilli. Put in a blender with the tomato puree, *chipotle* chilli, molasses, sugar and garlic and blend to a puree. Return to the saucepan, add the remaining ingredients and bring to the boil over medium heat. Simmer until reduced to a thick sauce consistency.

Combine the dry ingredients for the ribs. Rub 2-3 tablespoons of the spice mixture into the ribs, coating them on both sides. (Store the remaining spices in a jar for next time.) Place the ribs in a large dish and pour over the beer. Marinate in the refrigerator for 1-2 hours.

Bring the ribs to room temperature. Preheat the oven to 160°C (320°F/Gas 2-3). Place a large piece of foil over a large baking sheet and put the ribs on top, removing them from the beer. Wrap tightly in the foil and bake for 2 hours.

Preheat a barbecue grill to medium heat. Take the ribs out of the foil and place on the grill. Brush with barbecue sauce and cook for 6-8 minutes on each side. The sauce should caramelise a little on the surface.

Break the ribs into pieces and serve with extra barbecue sauce.

SERVES 6-8

CHIPOTLE BARBECUE SAUCE

- **25 g (1 oz) butter**
- **1 large onion, chopped**
- **1 fresh or pickled jalapeño chilli, chopped**
- **400 ml (13½ fl oz) tomato puree**
- **1 dried *chipotle* chilli**
- **1 tablespoon molasses**
- **1 tablespoon dark brown sugar**
- **2 garlic cloves, chopped**
- **3 tablespoons white-wine vinegar**
- **80 ml (2½ fl oz/⅓ cup) Worcestershire sauce**
- **80 ml (2½ fl oz/⅓ cup) Tabasco sauce**
- **½ tablespoon tomato paste (concentrated puree)**

RIBS

- **2 tablespoons sweet paprika**
- **2 tablespoons salt**
- **2 tablespoons garlic powder**
- **1 tablespoon onion powder**
- **1 tablespoon pepper**
- **1 tablespoon cayenne pepper**
- **1 tablespoon dried thyme**
- **1 tablespoon dried oregano**
- **4 racks of baby pork back ribs (about 3-4 kg)**
- **1-2 bottles dark beer**

'Never buy dandelion greens when you can pick them in the front yard.'

This dish is typically made from collard, which has leaves that look a bit like pale silverbeet and have a slightly bitter taste. Turnip leaves, mustard greens, kale, dandelion or Australia's native spinach (otherwise known as warrigal greens) also work well.

This is a very popular dish in the South, traditionally cheap and readily available. It is delicious served with fried chicken or other Southern dishes. Everyone has their favourite recipe, savoury or sweet, and it can be boiled, baked or fried. This recipe is a tasty, savoury porridge that is flavoured with cheese, but a mixture of goat's cheese and semi-dried tomatoes would also work wonders.

SOUTHERN GREENS

from Ashley Sheridan

Put the water, onion and ham hocks in a pot and bring to the boil. Add the greens, reduce the heat, cover and simmer for 2 hours.

Remove the ham hocks from the pot and take the meat off the bone. Cut or break into bite-sized pieces and return to the pot. Add dashes of Tabasco and malt vinegar to your liking.

SERVES 4

1 litre (34 fl oz/4 cups) water	1 kg (2 lb 3 oz) greens,
1 cup chopped onion	leaves picked
2 small-medium smoked ham	Tabasco sauce (optional)
hocks	malt vinegar (optional)

GRITS

from Ashley Sheridan

Heat the water in a saucepan until almost boiling then add the grits, butter and salt and pepper to taste. Bring to the boil then reduce the heat and cook for about 30 minutes or until the grits are the consistency of mashed potatoes. Stir in the buttermilk, cheese and paprika (if using).

SERVES 6-8

500-750 ml (25½ fl oz/3 cups)	salt and pepper
water	dash of buttermilk
2 cups grits (or instant	3 tablespoons grated
polenta if you can't find	extra-tasty cheese
the real thing)	dash of sweet paprika
2 tablespoons butter	(optional)

My friend Norma whips up this easy and delicious pie in just over 10 minutes. It makes wonderful use of America's native nut, which is ground and used in the pie crust as well as the filling.

PECAN PIE

from Norma Barne

To make the crust, grind the pecans in a food processor. Add the flour, butter and salt and blend until combined. Slowly add the water while the machine is running until the mixture comes together in a ball. Remove from the food processor, cover in plastic wrap and refrigerate for 30 minutes.

Preheat the oven to 200°C (400°F/Gas 6) and butter a medium pie tin. Roll the pastry out on a lightly floured surface and line the tin, trimming off the excess pastry. Prick the pastry to stop it puffing up and bake for 15 minutes.

Reduce the oven temperature to 180°C (350°F/Gas 4). Whisk the eggs with the sugar, butter and corn syrup. Stir in the pecans and cornflour. Pour into the pie crust and bake for about 1 hour. Leave to cool before serving with scoops of ice cream.

SERVES 10-12

CRUST

10 pecans, roasted
225 g (8 oz/1½ cups) plain (all-purpose) flour
½ tablespoon butter
pinch of salt
3 tablespoons water

FILLING

3 eggs
110 g (4 oz/½ cup) caster sugar
3 tablespoons butter, melted
250 ml (8½ fl oz/1 cup) dark corn syrup
2 cups pecans, roasted
130 g (4½ oz/1 cup) cornflour (cornstarch)

VIETNAM

Vietnamese food is dangerously seductive ... its lightness and freshness make it very healthy and its depth of flavour and variety of textures will always have you coming back for more. The magic starts working from your very first fragrant bowl of pho, with its clear star anise-scented broth, thin slices of beef, noodles and many aromatic herbs. I've been lucky enough to have spent a lot of time in Vietnam and I have to say that after ten days of Vietnamese food, I feel like a new person. My chef friend Angie calls pho the Vietnamese equivalent of Jewish chicken soup – it's good for both the body and soul.

While a bowl of pho will soothe you back to health with its gentle fresh flavours, a few mouthfuls of green papaya salad is instant zing and terrific when you and your palate are feeling jaded! It's crunchy, fresh and chilli hot.

More than any other cuisine, Vietnamese food centres on herbs and uses an amazing array in many dishes, along with plenty of salad greens. These herbs are eaten for their healing properties as well as for their taste. And the way they're used makes the token garnish of curly parsley in Anglo cooking look positively pathetic – in Vietnam they're used by the bunchful for salads and accompaniments, and piled on as a garnish. Each herby mouthful is different, fresh and exciting and may include purple-stemmed basil and coriander, fresh cumin leaves, lemon verbena and Vietnamese mint.

Vietnamese cuisine is such an interesting and delicious blend of age-old flavours and techniques with the food of colonial visitors. One such example is the combination of crisp golden baguette (a legacy of French colonial times) that is brushed with the classic Vietnamese *nuoc cham* (a mixture of fish sauce, garlic and chilli) then topped with shredded chicken or pork meatballs, lots of crisp salad and herbs. This taste sensation now has people lining up at the many Vietnamese sandwich shops of our big cities!

The best news is that most Vietnamese dishes are very easy and quick to cook. Most Vietnamese homes I've visited in Vietnam only cook using one or two gas burners and never for less than eight people at a time, so dishes have to be simple to prepare. Other than the stock for pho, which simmers for a long time, most dishes are quickly whipped together and served with easy salads or shredded vegetables. With such beautiful flavours so readily prepared, it's no surprise this food does such good things for people!

ESSENTIAL FLAVOURS

ANCHOVY SAUCE
Widely used as a condiment in central and southern Vietnamese food, this sauce is made from fermented, salted anchovies and is sold in a bottle. It is very strong in taste and smell and is normally diluted when used.

CASSIA
This spice is the bark of the cassia tree and it also comes in powdered form. It is used in marinades for roasted chicken or duck, beef braises and pho.

FISH SAUCE
The essence of Vietnamese food and a source of flavour as well as protein. *Nuoc mam nhi* is the first pressing - the equivalent of extra-virgin olive oil. Use this clear, clean sauce for dipping sauces and salads. The second pressing is less expensive and is used for cooking. The famous sauce made from fish sauce is called *nuoc cham*.

SESAME SEEDS
Used every day in Vietnamese cooking. Toasted and crushed sesame seeds are used to flavour dipping sauces and marinades or to coat sweets and other foods. After toasting they lose flavour rapidly, so be sure to toast them as close to serving as possible.

SHRIMP SAUCE
This mash of marinated shrimp is widely used as a dipping sauce in the north. It has a very strong smell but is an excellent marinade for fish and meat. Many people also like to use it as a condiment on its own.

STAR ANISE
A six-to-eight pointed star, this spice is as beautiful as it is fragrant. Its flavour resembles cinnamon and cloves and it's used in soups and stews as well as marinades. It is one of the vital ingredients in pho.

Herbs

Herbs (*rau*) are essential to Vietnamese cuisine where they are used not only for flavour and aroma but also for their medicinal qualities. When purchasing herbs, choose the freshest bunch you can find, handle them delicately and wash them only when you are ready to use them. These are the most widely used Vietnamese herbs:

BETEL LEAF
This glossy, dark-green, heart-shaped leaf has a slightly bitter taste and is mostly used as a wrapper for grilled meats.

CORIANDER (CILANTRO)
A very popular widely used herb - the leaves, stems and roots of the plant are all used. They enhance the flavour of sour fish soup and crab soup and are fabulous in salads and for garnishing.

DILL
These very fine leaves are often used in fish soups or with shellfish in northern Vietnamese cuisine. Dill can also be mixed with shrimp paste or fried fish.

FISH HERB
Considered by some as an acquired taste, this herb has a definite fishy smell and flavour. Often used in soups.

GARLIC CHIVES
Dark-green, flat chives with a garlic flavour and aroma.

MINT
Both spearmint and peppermint are used in salads and served with the famous pho soup. Vietnamese mint has long, pointed leaves that are green or crimson-brown in colour. It has a hot and spicy flavour, which combines well in salads and some shellfish dishes. Also called laksa leaf, it is said to help lower cholesterol and increase the libido.

PERILLA
Large leaves that are purple on one side and dark green on the other. The leaves are shredded and used in eggplant dishes and rice-paper rolls. Also known as shiso in Japanese cookery.

SAWTOOTH HERB
A long, dark-green leaf with serrated edges and a fragrance similar to coriander (cilantro) but stronger. It enhances the flavour of fresh bamboo shoots and can be added to soups and salads.

THAI BASIL
This fragrant, purple-stemmed herb is used in salads, especially with marinated grilled meats wrapped in lettuce leaves. It is also an essential accompaniment to pho, arriving in sprigs to be torn into the soup.

For Nhut and his seven brothers and sisters, this dish was looked forward to all year – his beloved mother used to prepare it for Vietnamese New Year. He says, 'In the years when we were farmers and very poor in the Vietnamese countryside, meat was hard to get so this dish was so good … And now I love watching the silence as people discover the rich flavours of this great regional Vietnamese dish in my restaurant.' Coconut juice - the clear water from the centre of the coconut rather than the milk or cream that is extracted from the flesh - imparts a sweet, mellow coconut flavour to the dish and is available frozen from Asian supermarkets.

PORK BRAISED IN COCONUT JUICE WITH EGGS

from Nhut Huynh

Combine the pork, garlic, shallots, spring onion, fish sauce, soy sauces, pepper, sugar and star anise in a bowl, stirring to coat the pork. Marinate in the refrigerator for at least 3 hours or ideally overnight.

Heat the oil in a large, heavy-based saucepan and add the onion. Fry until golden then remove the pork from the marinade and add to the pan. Seal over high heat. Add the marinade, coconut juice and water. Bring to the boil and skim off any scum that rises to the surface. Gently simmer for 1 hour, skimming occasionally. Add the eggs and simmer for a further hour. Garnish with coriander and serve with jasmine rice.

SERVES 6-8

1 kg (2 lb 3 oz) pork belly (not too fatty), cut into 5 cm (2 in) cubes	2 tablespoons grated palm sugar (jaggery) or dark brown sugar
2 garlic cloves, finely chopped	4 star anise
4 shallots, finely chopped	1 tablespoon vegetable oil
2 spring onions (scallions), bruised and finely chopped (roots included)	½ onion, finely chopped
	750 ml (25½ fl oz/3 cups) young coconut juice
3 tablespoons fish sauce	375 ml (12½ fl oz/1½ cups water
3 tablespoons light soy sauce	
1½ tablespoons dark soy sauce	8 eggs, hard-boiled and peeled
½ teaspoon freshly ground black pepper	coriander (cilantro)

Nuoc cham is Vietnam's key dipping sauce and accompanies salads and many other dishes. It's said that a prospective mother-in-law can tell a lot from the *nuoc cham* served when they visit a girl's family - for one thing it's important that the garlic and chillies float on the surface. *Nuoc cham* will keep in the fridge for up to a week.

NUOC CHAM

from Hanh Nguyen

Pound the garlic and chillies to a paste in a mortar. Combine the fish sauce, sugar, water and lemon juice in a bowl. Stir thoroughly until the sugar has dissolved. Stir in the garlic and chilli paste; the chilli should float on the surface.

MAKES 1½ CUPS

1 garlic clove	130 g (4½ oz) sugar
3 small red chillies	2 tablespoons water
140 ml first-grade fish sauce (*nuoc mam nhi*)	juice of 1 lemon

'Never waste a grain of rice or in the next life that grain will become a maggot you have to eat in hell!'

A delicious, crunchy, fresh-tasting salad that is easy to make. The texture is fantastic when the papaya and carrot are grated as finely as possible - a mandolin with a grater attachment is ideal. I love Hanh's suggestion of serving the salad on Vietnamese rice crackers - traditionally they're cooked over a flame but Hanh's brother Peter found it works incredibly well in the microwave.

GREEN PAPAYA SALAD

from Hanh Nguyen

To make the dressing, combine the fish sauce, vinegar, soy sauce, water and sugar in a bowl, stirring until the sugar dissolves. Combine the papaya, carrot, prawns, pork, mint and fried shallots in a separate bowl. Pour a liberal amount of dressing over the salad and toss well.

Cook the rice crackers on high in the microwave for 1 minute, or until puffed. Use them as plates, spooning the green papaya salad on top. Garnish with chilli, beef jerky and crushed nuts. To eat, break off pieces of rice cracker and use them to scoop up mouthfuls of salad.

SERVES 4

3 tablespoons fish sauce
3 tablespoons white vinegar
3 tablespoons light soy sauce
3 tablespoons water
110 g (4 oz/½ cup) sugar
1 green papaya, peeled, halved, seeded and finely grated
2 carrots, finely grated
8 cooked prawns (shrimp), sliced in half crosswise
16 thin slices of cooked pork belly
⅓ cup shredded Vietnamese mint
3 tablespoons fried shallots

TO SERVE

4 large sesame rice crackers
finely sliced red chilli
beef jerky, broken into small pieces
crushed roasted peanuts or cashews

'The rite of passage for young Vietnamese girls is to learn how to mix the *nuoc cham* dipping sauce - if the chilli doesn't float on the surface, their chances of impressing a future mother-in-law are very slim.'

Luke grew up on this very authentic southern dish, which makes a perfect light lunch. 'Bun' is the vermicelli noodles, 'bo' is the beef and 'xao' means to stir-fry – the beef is quickly marinated and charred in a hot wok and served on top of cold noodles, cucumber, bean sprouts and herbs. You simply add *nuoc cham* (see page 395) and garnish to taste.

Fish cooked in caramel sauce may not sound appetising and yet it's one of the yummiest things. Take your time to get the caramel right and it will be a sure success.

BUN BO XAO

from Luke Nguyen

CARAMELISED FISH IN A CLAY POT

from Lanna Tran

Combine the beef with 2 tablespoons of fish sauce, half the garlic and a little of the lemongrass. Marinate for 10 minutes.

Put the noodles into bowls and top with the bean sprouts, cucumber and most of the herbs.

Heat the oil in a wok over high heat and add the onion and remaining lemongrass. Stir briefly then throw in the beef, allowing it to char and develop a smoky flavour. Add the extra fish sauce and remove from the heat. Add the beef to the bowls and sprinkle with the remaining herbs. Garnish with pickled vegetables, peanuts and fried shallots and dress with *nuoc cham*.

To make the caramel, put the sugar in a small saucepan and melt over medium heat. Cook until it turns dark brown. Add the water, reduce the heat to low and cook until the sugar blends into the water and the mixture becomes syrupy. Remove from the heat.

Heat the oil in a clay pot (or saucepan) and add the garlic. Fry until golden then add the fish. Stir in the caramel and cook for about 5 minutes until the fish changes colour.

Add the fish sauce, water, spring onion and salt. Bring to the boil then reduce the heat and simmer for 5 minutes. Add the potato starch and cook until the sauce has thickened. Remove from the heat and add the chives, coriander and pepper. Serve with steamed rice.

SERVES 4

500 g (1 lb 2 oz) rump steak, finely sliced	10 perilla leaves, finely shredded
2 tablespoons fish sauce, plus 1 teaspoon extra	10 mint leaves, finely shredded
½ tablespoon crushed garlic	10 Vietnamese mint leaves, finely shredded
1 lemongrass stalk, white part only, finely sliced	2 tablespoons vegetable oil
500 g (1 lb 2 oz) rice vermicelli, cooked and cooled	1 small onion, sliced
handful of bean sprouts	pickled vegetables (from Asian food stores)
1 cucumber, halved lengthwise and sliced	crushed roasted peanuts
	fried shallots
	nuoc cham (see page 395)

SERVES 4

CARAMEL	3 spring onions (scallions), white part only, sliced
1 tablespoon sugar	1 teaspoon salt
3 tablespoons water	½ tablespoon potato starch, mixed to a smooth paste with a little water
3 tablespoons vegetable oil	3 tablespoons chopped garlic chives
1 garlic clove, crushed	3 tablespoons chopped coriander (cilantro)
500 g (1 lb 2 oz) firm white fish cutlets such as blue eye, cut into large pieces	¼ teaspoon pepper
1 tablespoon first-grade fish sauce (*nuoc mam nhi*)	
3 tablespoons water	

Pho (pronounced 'fahr') is a light, fragrant soup eaten for breakfast and all through the day. It is one of the Vietnamese's most loved dishes. The secret lies in the quality of the stock - along with the beautiful spices. Delicious!

'How Vietnamese women don't get fat: food is shared communally and everyone has to wait for the eldest to start and to ask permission to finish the last morsel, so one tends to eat only as much as one needs.'

PHO

from Angie Hong

To prepare the stock, sear the onion and ginger over a naked flame or under a grill for about 15 minutes. Remove any charred skin and set aside.

Place the bones in a large pot and cover with cold water. Bring to the boil and cook vigorously for 3 minutes. Discard the water and rinse the bones in warm water. Wipe out the pot, return the bones to it and add 6 litres (202 fl oz/24 cups) of water. Bring to the boil then reduce the heat to a gentle simmer. Skim off any scum. Add the onion, ginger and remaining ingredients and cook for 1½ hours. When the meat is cooked (slightly chewy but not tough), remove it and set aside in a bowl of cold water for 10 minutes. Remove from the water and refrigerate. Leave the broth to cook for a further 1½ hours. Strain and refrigerate. Skim off the fat when cold.

To serve, reheat the stock. Thinly slice the cold meat. Soak dried noodles (if using) in hot water for 15-20 minutes, until soft. If using fresh noodles, briefly heat them in boiling water. Arrange the noodles in the bottom of deep serving bowls and add slices of cooked meat and raw sirloin on top. Garnish with onion, spring onion and coriander. Season with pepper. Ladle over the hot stock.

To eat pho, taste the broth first, then add lime juice and chilli to taste followed by generous amounts of basil or mint and bean sprouts.

SERVES 6

STOCK

2 onions
10 cm (4 in) piece of ginger
2½ kg (5½ lb) beef soup bones
5 star anise
6 garlic cloves
8 cm (3¼ in) piece cassia bark
450 g (1 lb) beef brisket or chuck steak
1½ tablespoons salt
80 ml (2½ fl oz/⅓ cup) fish sauce
1 tablespoon palm sugar (jaggery)

FOR BOWLS

1 kg (2 lb 3 oz) dried or fresh pho noodles (rice sticks)
225 g (8 oz) beef sirloin, finely sliced across the grain
1 onion, finely sliced
4 spring onions (scallions), green part only, finely sliced
⅓ cup chopped coriander (cilantro)
black pepper

GARNISHES

lime wedges
sliced chillies
Thai basil or Vietnamese mint sprigs
bean sprouts

Tropical Fruits

CARAMBOLA OR STAR FRUIT
Either yellow, orange or green, this fruit reveals its star shape when cut into cross sections. Eaten raw and finely sliced, the young star fruit has an acidic taste and is often served on a Vietnamese vegetable platter along with sliced unripe banana.

DRAGON FRUIT
There are two varietes of dragon fruit: one with bright red flesh and the other with white; both have tiny black seeds. Although it can be bland in flavour it is a striking addition to a fruit platter.

DURIAN
This has a very strong odour but the taste is lush and tropical. Thought by many to have aphrodisiac qualities.

JACKFRUIT
A large, green fruit with a tough, knobbly skin that reveals yellow segmented flesh when opened. It is naturally sweet when ripe but the young jackfruit is used like a vegetable in cooking or in salads.

LONGAN
A small, brown-skinned fruit that grows in the Mekong Delta and in the north. The inside is a juicy cream colour with seeds.

LYCHEE
Exquisite tropical fruit encased in red-brown skin that is peeled to reveal white, juicy flesh. The lychee tree is cultivated in the humid tropical regions for its fruit and wood.

MANGOSTEEN
A fruit with thick purple skin and creamy white segments inside. Discard the skin and enjoy the delicious flavour of the flesh.

RAMBUTAN
The fiery red, spiky skins give the rambutan the look of tiny suns. They have tender white flesh and a cool, sweet flavour.

ACKNOWLEDGEMENTS

This book is the result of the work of lots of people who have shared their recipes and culture. They are the soul of this book and Australia is a richer place for them being here. Their names appear with their recipes and many of their voices are heard in the wisdom that peppers each chapter – the sort of things you hear as you spend time in kitchens – after all, that's where the best lessons are learned – about food and life.

Other friends across many cuisines contributed gems – among them Mona Charabati, Aurora Charabati, Clare Horikawa, Eric Moschietto, Liz Kaydos, Sam Cosentino, David Kim, Russoul Sajadi, Jinan Ammourh, Jorge Chacon and Margie Burke. And to the conduits to some great thoughts – Aisha Cooper for tapping into the wisdom of Guillaume Brahimi; Rosie Adesua for getting the best from Kunle; Meera Joshi for some great words from Ajoy; Shinji Halim from Rohanna; Masako Fuukui from Kei and Edna Barzel for battling ancient technology to send emails from the wilds of Brazil. I must also mention the unquenchable force that is Stephen (Istvan) Oroszvari who gathered a cracking list that ran to pages of great Hungarian sayings about food and eating ... all of which were fabulous. Thanks as well to the delightful Ulku Gani who came to the studio to show off how to make bulgur kofte, and the charming Mauritian families – the Madeleine, Saupin and Burton families who came together to cook and be photographed.

We have tried so hard to make sure that nothing is lost in translation – from the measurement of spices to how a dish is served. That has meant a lot of painstaking explanations of how something comes together, often on top of a barrage of late night emails and phone calls – thank you so much.

The faces who smile from these pages are all largely from small family businesses who work so hard to make what they do so delicious. We visited Al-Jamil Market, Fairfield; Arzum Markets, Auburn; Azuma Japanese Restaurant, Sydney; Baalbek Bakery, Canterbury; Billu's Indian Eatery, Harris Park; Bluefire Churrascaria Grill, Docklands; Casa Iberica, Fitzroy; Chat Thai Restaurant, Haymarket; Churrasco Restaurant, Woolloomooloo; Dalmatino Restaurant, Port Melbourne; Dench Bakers, North Fitzroy; Eilat at Hadassa, Bondi; Frank's Fruit Market, Haberfield; Gato's Pastizzi, Carramar; Grand China Restaurant, Haymarket; Hellas Cake Shop, Richmond; Hellenic Bakery, Marrickville; Illawarra Meat Market, Marrickville; Janani Restaurant, Homebush; Jasmine One Lebanese Restaurant, Punchbowl; Kam Fook Restaurant, Chatswood; La Bergerie, Canterbury; La Patisserie, Petersham; Los Amatas Mexican Kitchen, Fitzroy; Madang Restaurant, Sydney; Mado Café, Auburn; Mamak Restaurant, Haymarket; Margarita's Cecinas Butchery, Fairfield; Mesnoy Injera Retail Shop, Footscray; MGM Spices, Surry Hills; Mykababyan Filipino Store, Fairfield; Paesanella, Haberfield; Pal-do Kim-Chi Pty Ltd, Canterbury; Portuguese Butchery, Petersham; Portuguese Style Chicken, Petersham; Springbok Delights, Lane Cove; Real Turkish Delight, Auburn; Rob's British & Irish Butchery, Dandenong; Souk in the City Restaurant, Surry Hills; Sulfaro Paticceria, Haberfield; Valley View Spices, Bankstown; Vatan Restaurant, Auburn; Yum Yum Pizza, Punchbowl.

Thanks also to Imtiaz Ahmed from Curry On Crown for posing with sacks of Basmati rice; Habib Afghan Baig, Afghan Bakery, Fairfield; Jesper Hansen, Blonde Catering, Marrickville; Shahid Sheikh, Bonfire Cafe, Springvale; Michael Klausen, Brasserie Bakery, Banksmeadow; Paulo and Merica La Silva, Casa Iberica, Fitzroy; Tona and Ketty Inthavong, Green Peppercorn, Fairfield; Ipermachou family, Earlwood Wines; Louise Nguyen and Tony Inthavong, Holy Basil, Canley Heights; Ivan Spehar, Ivan's Butchery, Chester Hill; Bow Lapthanaphanit, Khao Pla, Chatswood; Grace and Roberto Le Grange, La Torre, Fairfield; Shady Waseef, Pioik Bakery, Pyrmont; Andrew and Hannah Lipisko, Rye Crust Bakery, Dandenong; Max and Rudi Dietz, Stuyvesant House, Crows Nest; Milushka and Jesus Quinteros, Tierras Latinas, Fairfield; Efthymiou family, Trianon Cakes, Earlwood; Victor Pisapia, Victors Food; Melia Rumayar, Warung Gudeg Indonesian Restaurant, Clayton; the Brull family at Wellington Cake Shop, Bondi; and Edmar Martius Guilherme and Renata Hutrtado Stehling.

Without the photographs of food and faces from supremely talented photographers Alan Benson, Sharyn Cairns and Mark Roper, this book wouldn't be the joy it is. Their photos capture faces that may not be known to you but whose cooking and food skills have made Australia the culinary mecca it is today. And the food pictures make you want to cook and taste! Special thanks to stylists Trish Heagarty, Sarah O'Brien and Greg Proebstel; and chefs Samantha Joel, Kerry Ray and Georgie Young. Thanks also to supremely diligent, hardworking copy editor Rachel Pitts for checking and re-checking – making sure it is all correct; the designers, Hamish and Klarissa of Pfisterer+Freeman, who have patiently and stunningly brought it all together; and this book's godmother – Hardie Grant's hardworking publisher Pam Brewster – for helping to shape this beautiful book which we hope will guide you in recreating some wonderful food.

Our tiny but wonderfully talented crew from Kismet Productions deserve thanks – they helped breathe life into such a gorgeous looking TV show on which this book is based; and many thanks also to SBS where I've worked since 1990, a rich source of invaluable contacts and warm food-loving people. To Margaret Murphy for her wisdom and eternal support and to Matt Campbell and management for loving the whole food concept and going with it.

Sincere thanks to my Gourmet Safaris family – our wonderful energetic guides who open up their worlds to the public and who have been such an inspiration and support and source of knowledge; to the unflappable, supremely organised Suzy Brien, Georgie Neal, and of course to my partner-in-crime Toufic Charabati for his clear-headed direction and support.

INDEX

An SBS book

Published in 2014 by Hardie Grant Books

Hardie Grant Books (Australia)
Ground Floor, Building 1
658 Church Street
Richmond, Victoria 3121
www.hardiegrant.com.au

Hardie Grant Books (UK)
5th & 6th Floor
52–54 Southwark Street
London SE1 1RU
www.hardiegrant.co.uk

A Cataloguing-in-Publication entry is available from the catalogue of the National Library of Australia

Complete Food Safari
ISBN 978 1 74270 8973

Publisher: Pam Brewster
Editor: Rachel Pitts
Designers: Pfisterer+Freeman
Photographers: Sharyn Cairns, Alan Benson, Mark Roper, Gorta Yuuki, Omid photography
Stylists: Glen Proebstel, Sarah O'Brien, Trish Heagarty, Georgia Young
Production Manager: Todd Rechner
Colour reproduction by Splitting Image Colour Studio

Printed and bound in China by 1010 Printing International Limited